# FOUL PLAY

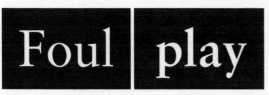

# Foul play

## The Inside Story of the Biggest Corruption
## Trial in British Sporting History

## DAVID THOMAS

## BANTAM PRESS

LONDON · NEW YORK · TORONTO · SYDNEY · AUCKLAND

TRANSWORLD PUBLISHERS
61–63 Uxbridge Road, London W5 5SA
a division of The Random House Group Ltd

RANDOM HOUSE AUSTRALIA (PTY) LTD
20 Alfred Street, Milsons Point, Sydney,
New South Wales 2061, Australia

RANDOM HOUSE NEW ZEALAND LTD
18 Poland Road, Glenfield, Auckland 10, New Zealand

RANDOM HOUSE SOUTH AFRICA (PTY) LTD
Endulini, 5a Jubilee Road, Parktown 2193, South Africa

Published 2003 by Bantam Press
a division of Transworld Publishers

A catalogue record for this book is available from the British Library
ISBN 0593 049659

Typeset in 11/14pt Sabon by
Falcon Oast Graphic Art Ltd.

Printed in Great Britain by
Mackays of Chatham plc, Chatham, Kent

1 3 5 7 9 10 8 6 4 2

**To Clare**

# Contents

# Acknowledgements

So many people helped me with this book over such a protracted period that there is no room to thank them all. And besides, much of it was so long ago that I've forgotten who they were.

So to all the regulars at Winchester Crown Court – all the reporters, coppers, lawyers, and even the accused – thanks. Thanks, too, to Daniel Taylor, at the *Sun*, for taking all my calls so patiently. Thanks to all the publishers who have had this book in their catalogues, without it ever reaching the bookshelves, over the past eight years. Thanks to Christopher Little and Patrick Walsh for taking it on, as agents, in the early summer of 1995. It all ended in tears, three years, two court cases and one publisher later. But since J. K. Rowling walked into Christopher's office just as I was walking out, I'm pretty sure he's recovered. Thanks to Julian Alexander for picking up the representative baton, and Doug Young for putting the book in his catalogue, too. Thanks to Nigel Parker . . . I think, though I've often had my doubts . . . for getting me started on it in the first place. Thanks to Chris Vincent and Bernice Bala'c for all those hours of interviews, though, in Chris's case at least, you got your payback in money, sweat and grief, over the next few years.

Above all, thanks to my wife Clare. She deserves my gratitude more than anyone. And she does not need to be told why.

David Thomas
West Sussex, 2003

# Prologue: Crook Cheat Liar Traitor

In Britain a man is innocent until proven guilty. And he is particularly innocent if proven not guilty. Even if he happens to be Bruce Grobbelaar.

In January 1997, the former Liverpool and Southampton goalkeeper was tried at Winchester Crown Court. He stood accused of conspiring with the former Wimbledon footballer and TV presenter John Fashanu and a Malaysian businessman called Heng Suan Lim (otherwise known as Richard Lim, or simply 'The Short Man') to fix the results of football matches. He was also accused of corruptly accepting a £2,000 bribe, with a view to fixing matches, from his former business partner Chris Vincent. The Wimbledon goalkeeper Hans Segers was also accused of corruption, in a separate count, alongside Fashanu and Lim.

The first trial ended with a deadlocked jury. But the bulk of its members were so sympathetic to the defendants, and so convinced of their innocence, that some of them even turned up on the first day of the second criminal trial, in the summer of 1997, to show their support for Grobbelaar and co. That second trial ended in acquittal for all four men on the main corruption charges. The jury was again unable to come to a verdict on Grobbelaar's bribery charge, and so the case was dismissed.

Bruce Grobbelaar was now, officially, an innocent man. So, in July 1999, he sued his principal accusers, the *Sun* newspaper, for libel. Again he stepped into the witness box, this time at the High Court in London, again he gave evidence and again the jury came down on his side. He was awarded £85,000 in damages, plus costs.

So three juries examined the case against Bruce Grobbelaar, and not one of them found him guilty. How much more innocent can a man get? Well, he could try not being corrupt.

Bruce Grobbelaar most certainly was involved in a conspiracy to fix football matches. I say this for three reasons. First, because I have always been convinced of his corruption, irrespective of the juries' verdicts. Secondly, because I have had access to information that either was never made available to the juries, or has come to light since the criminal trials. And thirdly, because some of the most senior judges in the British Isles agree with me.

This extraordinarily protracted case made legal history in January 2001, when three Appeal Court judges unanimously upheld an appeal by the *Sun* against the libel verdict, on the grounds – unique in British legal history – that the jury's verdict had been perverse. Grobbelaar, the three judges agreed, was so obviously guilty, and his evidence was so utterly implausible – 'quite literally incredible' in the words of Lord Justice Simon Brown – that no reasonable jury could possibly have found in his favour. The three judges agreed that the secretly filmed videotapes, recorded by the *Sun*, contained actual confessions by Grobbelaar of actual corruption, as well as genuine plans for future corruption. They dismissed out of hand his claims that he had been fabricating imaginary crimes, in order to entrap his old friend and colleague Chris Vincent, who was – though Grobbelaar did not know this at the time of their taped meetings – the *Sun*'s informant for their story.

The three judges further agreed that Grobbelaar's account of his relationship with Lim, which he had maintained went no further than providing football information for Lim to pass on to gamblers in the Far East, 'beggars belief at every turn'. And they found against Grobbelaar on one other crucial issue, too. In November 1993 he suddenly came into possession of tens of thousands of pounds. Both the *Sun* and the criminal prosecution claimed that Grobbelaar had collected £40,000, in cash, from a meeting with John Fashanu at the Hampstead home of Fashanu's then girlfriend. This, they said, was a payoff for a Liverpool defeat by Newcastle United. Grobbelaar had claimed that this money had, in fact, been accumulated in his sock drawer, the result of cash payments made to him for after-dinner speaking in South Africa, and football coaching in Norway. Lord Justice Brown was utterly dismissive: 'His explanation for having large sums of cash at around that time seems to me equally implausible.'

Talk about a game of two halves. If the trials had been a football match, Grobbelaar would have been three up and cruising. But suddenly the opposition had scored a golden goal. The *Sun* ran an exultant front-page headline: 'Crook Cheat Liar Traitor'. But the contest was not over. There was still one more twist to come.

Grobbelaar appealed against the Appeal Court verdict. He took his case to the House of Lords, there to be heard by five Law Lords. This was the fifth time the case had come to court and for the fourth time Grobbelaar won . . . up to a point.

Their Lordships upheld his appeal, but awarded only 'derisory damages' of £1, on the basis that Grobbelaar's reputation was worth no more than that. Their reasoning, boiled down to its essence, was that the *Sun* had claimed (which the prosecution specifically did not, in either of the criminal trials) that Grobbelaar had not just conspired to let in goals, but had actually done so. There was no evidence to support this contention. The former Arsenal goalkeeper Bob Wilson had stated in court, based on his analysis of videotapes of games Grobbelaar was alleged to have tried to throw, that he could see no examples at all of deliberately poor goalkeeping. So no jury could be deemed perverse if it had ruled against the *Sun* on that basis.

On the other hand, their Lordships had no doubt that Grobbelaar really had conspired to throw games, and really had taken bribes, even if he had not, in the end, kept his side of the bargain. He was thus guilty of the crimes of which he had been accused in court. In the words of Lord Bingham of Cornhill, 'He had in fact acted in a way in which no decent or honest footballer would act and in a way which could, if not exposed and stamped on, undermine the integrity of a game which earns the loyalty and support of millions.' Grobbelaar was, according to Lord Bingham, 'a man shown to have acted in . . . flagrant breach of his legal and moral obligations'.

I believe that the Law Lords' judgement exactly describes the facts of the case: Bruce Grobbelaar wanted to throw football matches, he conspired to throw football matches, he accepted money to throw football matches. He just wasn't any good at actually throwing football matches, for reasons he himself described, on tape, to Chris Vincent. That, however, leads us to a question which neither the Law Lords nor the Court of Appeal were asked to consider: if Grobbelaar committed the crime of which he was accused, and if his taped confessions were genuine, where does that leave the men who were accused of conspiring with him, and whom he named on those tapes?

The only co-conspirators who have ever been linked with Bruce Grobbelaar – aside from Chris Vincent and his *Sun* sting – are John Fashanu and Heng Suan Lim. It was no part of their defence that the cops had got the wrong men, or that Grobbelaar had conspired with anyone else. It was commonly agreed that he did meet with Fashanu and Lim; that the three men did discuss football and gambling; that Grobbelaar did provide information, and that he did receive small sums of money for his services. It was also agreed that Lim had a close relationship with known gamblers in the Far East, and that both he and Fashanu received huge sums of money from these men. The defence argued that neither these contacts nor the payments had anything to do with football corruption. In the case of Bruce Grobbelaar, at least, eight senior judges appear to have disagreed.

And there is more. In his evidence against Grobbelaar, Chris Vincent claimed that the subject of throwing matches first arose at a meeting between Grobbelaar and Lim, at the Manchester Airport Hilton, on 30 September 1993. Vincent had accompanied Grobbelaar to the hotel, but had not gone into the actual meeting with Lim. Vincent's explanation for his exclusion was that Grobbelaar and Lim did not want him to be present when they discussed match-fixing. Grobbelaar, he alleged, had told him in advance that this was the meeting's purpose, and had confirmed as much afterwards.

Grobbelaar disagreed. He claimed he had gone to talk to Lim about a safari-camp business he was hoping to start with Vincent in their home country, Zimbabwe. The reason Vincent had not attended the meeting was that he had failed to provide a business plan, dealing with the safari camp's financial prospects, that he had promised to have ready for the meeting. Grobbelaar, embarrassed by his friend's failure, had then taken the meeting by himself. Indeed, he said, while giving evidence under oath, there had never been any business plan for the safari camp.

That was untrue. There was a business plan and I know this for a fact because I have a copy of it in my possession. I also have good reason to suppose that it had been prepared months before the meeting with Lim. So, if Grobbelaar was not apologizing, in private, to Lim for the failings of his friend, what was he talking about? Only one alternative has ever been suggested: throwing football matches.

And what of Lim himself? At his two criminal trials, he was presented to the court as a young man from a humble background, who had come to England to study accountancy and pursue a business career. In April 1987, a few months after his arrival in England, Lim went to dinner with a fellow-Malaysian, Ong Chee Kew. A letter from Ong Chee Kew was found in Lim's possession, after his arrest. Ong wrote, 'You must try your best to tackle Wimbledon and some other club [sic]. Make use of your time, for you can do it.' He also mentioned that he and Lim could make money on the Kuala

Lumpur gambling markets if Lim supplied him with football information that would not be available in the Far East.

To the two juries, this might have seemed like evidence that Lim was interested in both football and gambling, but they knew that already. They also knew – because the prosecution told them – that Ong had been prosecuted for gambling offences in Malaysia, where gambling is illegal. What they did not know, because nobody at that stage knew, was that Ong Chee Kew was still a gangster. And his crime was football corruption.

On 10 February 1999 Ong Chee Kew was caught red-handed while trying to sabotage the floodlights at a Premiership match between Charlton Athletic and Liverpool. Police found Ong with Eng Hwa Lim, a fellow-Malaysian, and Wai Yuen Liu – a Hong Kong-born businessman and convicted fraudster, with suspected links to Triad gangs – as they attempted to use a circuit-breaker to make the lights go out, thereby causing the game to be abandoned. They had used the same means to cut the lights at an Upton Park match between West Ham and Crystal Palace and a Wimbledon match against Arsenal at Selhurst Park.

The trio wanted to black out British football matches because any game that had to be abandoned was treated by Far Eastern gamblers as a finished match. The score at that point was considered the final score, for the purposes of paying or collecting on bets. If the conspirators could kill a match at a point where the score was beneficial to them, they could make huge sums of money.

The three men were found guilty at Middlesex Guildhall Crown Court, and Ong Chee Kew was sentenced to four years in jail. One of Heng Suan Lim's earliest contacts in England, with whom he discussed football betting, is now, therefore, a convicted football match-fixer. That does not, of course, make Lim a guilty man. Nor does any of the evidence relating to Bruce Grobbelaar incriminate Hans Segers. At no time, prior to their arrests, did Grobbelaar have any knowledge of any involvement by Segers in any alleged or actual conspiracy to fix football matches, nor did he ever say anything to Vincent, on or off tape, that implicated Segers.

It would be a brave author who suggested that a man such as Heng Suan Lim, who has been found not guilty by twelve of his peers, was in fact – like Bruce Grobbelaar – guilty of at least one of the crimes of which he was accused. So I'll let the Law Lords suggest it instead.

Lord Bingham accepted that the case against Lim was not as clear-cut as that against Grobbelaar. But, he observed, 'There can be no doubt but that the appellant's statements recorded on the tapes, if accepted as wholly true, were very clear evidence of a corrupt agreement between him and Mr Lim, [and] of the corrupt receipt of money by him from Mr Lim.'

In a dissenting judgement finding in favour of the *Sun* on all counts, Lord Steyn went further. Discussing both Grobbelaar's relationship with Heng Suan Lim and his acceptance of the £2,000 bribe from Chris Vincent (provided, as a sting, by the *Sun*), Steyn ruled that, 'I am satisfied that both conspiracies were established. The roles of Mr Grobbelaar, Mr Lim and Mr Vincent were interwoven. The conspiracy with Mr Vincent was established beyond rational argument. The conspiracy with Mr Lim did not solely depend on Mr Grobbelaar's admissions. As counsel for the *Sun* demonstrated there was ample corroboration and confirmation of this conspiracy. The jigsaw is complete: both conspiracies were proved with compelling clarity and certainty.'

In other words, according to Lord Steyn Bruce Grobbelaar was guilty. Heng Suan Lim was guilty. And there really was a conspiracy, backed by Far Eastern gamblers, to try to fix the results of Premier League football matches.

When this case first came to light, almost nine years ago, that seemed an implausible, even absurd proposition – one of the reasons, perhaps, why three juries found it so hard to believe. Yet the years since then have made the concept of corruption more credible, not less. The South African cricket captain Hansie Cronje was revealed to have accepted bribes from Indian bookmakers, in exchange for throwing matches. And the entire regulatory structure of horse-racing is being changed in response to repeated allegations of fixed races and inadequate protection for race-goers and punters.

In every case, the initial allegations of corruption have been greeted with dismissive contempt by the authorities of the sports concerned, the protagonists involved in them (players, jockeys, managers, trainers and so on), and many of the media pundits who cover them. There are enormous vested interests at stake, and strong biases in favour of the status quo: no one likes to step out of line.

The fact is, however, that football has been corrupted, and could be corrupted again. The danger is particularly acute as the game, having enjoyed an astonishing commercial boom, is entering harder times. Bruce Grobbelaar was open to corruption because he was not rich enough to say, 'No.' He earned around £150,000 a year. The offer of £125,000, to throw a single game against Manchester United, was very seductive indeed.

Today, a top goalkeeper can earn that much in a month. But tomorrow may be different. As the game's TV income diminishes, clubs are tightening their belts. Wages are declining rather than rising. More and more players are facing unemployment. So the temptation to make a quick killing is bound to increase. It would be naïve to assume that everyone will be able to resist.

What follows, then, is the story of one conspiracy that found willing accomplices, and a warning of others that may follow. It is a story that I have had to write and rewrite several times over the years, as a string of legal rulings made it more or less open to the risk of a libel action. The first draft, written before the very first criminal case at Winchester Crown Court, was a partisan, highly coloured account of the relationship between Chris Vincent and Bruce Grobbelaar. It took Grobbelaar's guilt for granted and accepted Vincent's account as accurate, including allegations he made about private conversations that were not supported by any outside evidence.

As the case began, however, it was Vincent, not Grobbelaar,

who was in jail. By the time it ended, Grobbelaar was, officially, an innocent man. I had to delete all Vincent's unsupported allegations and rely only on facts that had been either established by objective sources (phone records, bank statements, etc.), or agreed by all sides to be true, or given in evidence in court. The book became a very different story, in which events were presented in a neutral light, often without immediate explanations, for reasons that only later became clear.

Now that Grobbelaar's credibility has been demolished, and the cost of libelling him established as £1, it's very tempting to go back to my starting point and take his guilt as self-evident from the beginning. I have, however, decided not to do that, and for one very simple reason. It's not enough to believe that Grobbelaar was guilty. You have to know, too, why three successive juries might have thought that he was not guilty.

So I will let the evidence build up bit by bit, fact by fact, allegation by allegation, and incident by increasingly bizarre incident. At the end, I hope, the picture will be complete. Then you can decide for yourself exactly who did what, and why, and how.

One final thought. One of the pleasures that kept me going through the long months in which my entire existence seemed to be bound up with proceedings in Winchester Crown Court was the rich absurdity involved in observing what happens when a bunch of dim-witted sleaze-bags try to get rich at other people's expense. It's tempting to adopt a high moral tone, preaching the sanctity of sport and fulminating about the evils of those who would corrupt our national game. But as the story unfolds, and the full might of Fleet Street and the legal system bear down upon the Grobbelaar case, the temptation to laugh at the rampant greed and foul-mouthed idiocy of the people involved may prove just as strong. Please feel free to give in.

# 1

## 'He Was the Man Who Mixed the Stuff That Made the Bomb Go Boom!'

Walking out of Courtroom No. 3 at Winchester Crown Court one morning in February 1997, I fell into conversation with another member of the press pack covering the case of the Crown vs Lim and Others. We had just heard the former Liverpool goalkeeper Bruce Grobbelaar describe meeting a Zimbabwean businessman called Christopher Vincent at the Old Harkers Arms, a Chester wine bar known to regulars as Harkers, in July 1992. The two men got on well and quickly discovered something in common: both had fought for the Rhodesian Army in the civil war that led to the end of white rule and the creation of Zimbabwe. After a while Vincent took out some maps and photographs, spread them on the table and told Grobbelaar about his plans for creating a safari camp – the best in southern Africa, he said – catering for wealthy tourists who wanted to photograph African wildlife. He was keen for Grobbelaar to invest in the scheme.

'When do you want a decision?' asked Grobbelaar, lifting his glass.

'By the time you've finished your beer,' replied Vincent.

Grobbelaar downed the drink and said yes. The next day, he gave Chris Vincent a cheque for £5,000. Over the following two years he handed over a further £50,000 or more, not a penny of which he ever saw again. Now he was standing trial, accused – alongside John Fashanu, Hans Segers and Heng Suan Lim – of taking part in a conspiracy to fix the results of football matches. Chris Vincent had been the chief witness for the prosecution.

He had also been the source for a *Sun* exclusive, published on 9 November 1994, which claimed to expose an amazing bribery scandal funded by mysterious Far Eastern gamblers, in which Grobbelaar had been a central player. Grobbelaar, the winner of thirteen championship and cup medals with Liverpool, had been publicly denounced as a cheat. His family had been put under terrible strain. His finances had been all but ruined. And all because of that drink at Harkers.

Which was why the reporter turned to me and sighed, 'Unbelievable. He meets a bloke he's never clapped eyes on in his life before, has a few drinks in some Chester boozer, and less that twenty-four hours later he's writing out a cheque for five grand. How fucking stupid is that?'

'Oh, I don't know,' I replied. 'I got a scholarship to Cambridge University. And I did exactly the same thing.'

But then, the man with whom I had decided to do business had not borne much resemblance to the one on display in Winchester Crown Court. On the morning of 22 January 1997, Christopher Vincent had sat in the witness box looking as miserable as a moulting ferret. The moment that should have been his greatest triumph, his vindication, and the justification of everything he had done over the past three years had turned instead into an orgy of humiliation and public contempt. He had hoped to be the man whose evidence proved the existence of what he claimed was the greatest scandal in British sporting history. Yet it was he, not the men he had accused, who had been locked up in jail since the previous October, and he who was being treated as the criminal.

The physical contrast between himself and the men in the dock could not have been more pronounced. Vincent was a small sandy-haired man, thin-faced, moustachioed and balding.

He had been brought to the courtroom direct from Her Majesty's Prison, Winchester. The months of incarceration had robbed him of his habitual tan – the result of a lifetime spent under the African sun – and given him an unaccustomed pallor. He looked like a snitch.

Not so John Fashanu or Bruce Grobbelaar. They strode into the court building every morning as free men, and left it the same way. Fashanu's demeanour exuded an absolute assurance that wherever he went he would be the most physically dominant presence in the room. He was also, as it later transpired, a man so paranoid that he insisted on sweeping guests with a device that detected bugs. He held crucial conversations in the dark, so as not to be observed. He played music to confuse any listening devices. But no one saw that private, secret Fashanu. All they were given was the fine façade of the ultimate self-made hero.

As a small boy, John Fashanu had been placed in a Barnardo's home. Yet as a man, he had achieved sporting success, media celebrity, considerable wealth and political status. Fashanu was an official Unicef ambassador and a confidant of many African heads of state. He was tall and powerfully built with a face composed of straight lines and unbroken circles – the utter absence of any sagging, any jowliness, any wavering about the eye suggesting a similarly clear-cut sense of purpose.

Invariably dressed in immaculate suits and impeccably polished shoes, Fashanu had treated the entire court process like an extended political campaign. In March 1996 I had watched him saunter through the lobby of Eastleigh Magistrates' Court, where he had come to attend his committal hearing. As befitted the lesser status of that court, his attire was marginally more informal than it would be during the main case itself – a beautifully cut tweed jacket, pale blue shirt, patterned tie and dark grey trousers.

Naturally, he attracted attention and supplication. An elderly lady stepped out from behind the small counter from which members of the Women's Royal Voluntary Service dispensed coffee and biscuits. She held a ring-bound notebook in front of Fashanu, who wrote a brief message while the woman basked in the warmth of his charm. A few minutes later, I happened to see the notebook. It was lying open at the page on which Fashanu had written the following words in capital letters: 'BE GOOD. WORK HARD. LOVE FASH.'

In Winchester, the same rules of engagement applied. On the first morning of the case he arrived, beaming his *Gladiators* grin, pumping the hands and slapping the backs of all the attendant journalists. A claque of middle-aged black supporters had come to lend him moral support. At the end of that first day's proceedings Fashanu emerged from the courthouse and stood at the top of the broad stone steps that swept down to a little square, where his car awaited. Behind him came his followers. Fash paused, turned and high-fived the twenty-odd people behind him. Then the two groups went their separate ways – he to his Mercedes, they to the coach or train that was taking them back to London.

He was, it must be said, an equal-opportunity schmoozer. A couple of days later I saw him leave the court in the company of two police officers, one male, one female, their fluorescent yellow jackets gleaming in the TV lights. Fashanu, dashing as ever in houndstooth tweed, was walking between them, chattering happily, his teeth almost as bright as the jackets in the glare of the arc-lights.

No one was too humble or too young to escape his attentions. Standing in the lunch queue for the court canteen one day, he happened to meet a journalist who had brought his teenage daughter along for the day. 'Are you following in your father's footsteps, then?' enquired the affable Fash. The girl, overwhelmed by his charisma, stammered a reply. Fashanu smiled indulgently and reached into his inside-left jacket pocket, pulling out a picture of himself posed against a lurid yellow and red background. 'Here,' he said, 'throw a dart at that.'

Grobbelaar could not quite match that sort of star-power. He was as tall as Fashanu and similarly athletic, but in January

1997 his appearance was undermined by the straggle of hair – more rat's tail than pony tail – that drooped over his collar from the back of his scalp. With his bald pate and black moustache it made him look like a pantomime oriental, half way between Wishee-Washee and Fu Manchu.

Nor could he compete sartorially: his habitual maroon over-coat and matching fedora were a considerable aesthetic mistake. But even so, in an area of Hampshire that still remembered him fondly from his days as Southampton's goalie, he was constantly beset by autograph hunters and his bearing in court was undeniably impressive. In the dock he sat bolt upright, his head held high, looking down his nose as events unfolded in front of him. In the witness box, he was similarly assertive and erect. The message to the jury was clear: look at me, remember Vincent – which of us, do you think, is the crook?

In this contest, Vincent was on a distinctly uneven playing-field. Even the prosecution, whose main witness he was, had made their distaste for him plain. In his opening to the case, Mr David Calvert-Smith, a small, bespectacled Old Etonian with the drooping gown, diffident manner and razor-sharp mind of one of his old school's Latin masters, had told the jury: 'Christopher Vincent is a fellow-countryman of Mr Grobbelaar – they both hail from Zimbabwe – and a former business associate. He will give evidence that, over a period of a year or so, Mr Grobbelaar admitted his involvement in a corrupt scheme, and that he was with Mr Grobbelaar when many of the acts in furtherance of that scheme were performed. Eventually, Mr Vincent approached the *Sun* newspaper, which assisted him in recording an admission by Mr Grobbelaar.

'Most, if not all of you, will have little sympathy for Mr Vincent. His decision to expose Mr Grobbelaar was the result of a business quarrel, not a desire to prevent corruption. His decision to expose Mr Grobbelaar through the *Sun*, rather than going to a police station, was the result of a desire to enrich himself. He has already been paid substantial sums and no doubt hopes to be paid more.

'Although Mr Vincent was not directly connected with the scheme, he certainly did nothing to stop it and was happy to benefit from its proceeds. There is every reason to scrutinize his evidence with great care. Finally, he has recently been charged with a serious offence himself. This is yet another reason to ask yourselves, "Before we accept what this witness says, we have to look at it very carefully."

'The Crown suggests, however, that what Mr Vincent has said, and will say, is directly or indirectly supported by evidence quite independent of Mr Vincent. We suggest that although he is a witness for whom you may have no sympathy, in fact, what he says is borne out by the evidence.'

That final clause was the crux of the matter. The case against the defendants depended in large part on the credibility of Vincent's evidence. It was therefore vital, from their point of view, to discredit him and his story alike. Mr Rodney Klevan QC, acting for Bruce Grobbelaar, led the assault on Vincent. Of medium height and somewhat portly, he had a jutting lower lip and heavy jowls that, when combined with his wig, gave him the air of a character from a Hogarth painting or Rowlandson cartoon. He spoke in a rich, fruity voice, overlaid with a light Manchester accent, the sort of voice that might at any moment inform the ladies and gentlemen of the jury that Mr Kipling did indeed make exceedingly good cakes.

Klevan's favourite crowd-pleasing tactic was the irrelevant but hugely entertaining question, often delivered with a masterful show of ignorance or even a plaintive sigh. On one occasion, for example, he stood to cross-examine a Crown witness called Glynn Mason, or 'Mace', who was an employee of John Fashanu. In his evidence, Mace had mentioned the business dealings that he and Fashanu had had with the former Chelsea manager Ian Porterfield, whose job as manager of the Zimbabwean national side had been arranged via their company, Blue Orchid.

Klevan – who affected a total ignorance of football – told Mace: 'I only have one question – a romantic dalliance . . .' He paused to ensure maximum effect and then continued, 'This man Ian Porterfield, was it he who scored the only goal for lowly Sunderland, when they defeated mighty Leeds in the Cup Final of 1973?'

'Yes,' said a smiling Mace, amidst much chuckling in the courtroom.

'Thank you,' sighed Klevan.

The judge, who had a soft spot for these moments of light relief, remarked: 'For a man who knows nothing about football, that was a very good question.'

'Thank you, m'lud,' bowed Klevan, and retired to his seat.

This actorly command of inflexion, pitch and timing could be used to destructive as well as humorous effect, as Chris Vincent was to find out. Klevan's purpose was to portray Vincent as a money-grabbing, treacherous, deceitful liar: to amplify the Crown's remarks about Vincent's character failings, while eliminating the suggestion that he might, nevertheless, be telling the truth.

On his first day of cross-examination, Klevan looked at the financial benefits that Vincent had derived from the story to date, and might reap from a conviction. 'Get the right result, you can make yourself a small fortune. The wrong one, and you are back in the gutter, aren't you?'

'Yes sir,' said Vincent.

'You have been hawking yourself and your wares in the market-place,' continued Klevan. 'You come as a witness to this trial having laid the groundwork in advance, as far as any man could, for his future financial success.'

'That's correct, sir.'

'It's in your interest by every word you utter to try to secure a conviction against one or all four of these defendants.'

'I think it's not for me to decide whether they get convicted or not, sir,' replied Vincent.

Klevan examined Vincent's record as a businessman. There had, he said, been four occasions, before he met Bruce Grobbelaar, in which Vincent had been involved in failed ventures: 'You've used other people's money, then the company collapses, is that fair?' he asked. Vincent admitted that it was.

'You go from one business to another, which collapses . . . You make sure when it's a business venture that you reap the rewards, if there are any, but none of the liabilities . . . are you proud of your commercial track record?'

'I have been subject to an incredible amount of bad luck,' said Vincent.

Klevan wound up his first day's interrogation on a theme to which he would return on the following morning. 'You turned like a viper on Bruce Grobbelaar when he had been the best of friends to you,' said the QC. 'You'll be glad at whatever happens to Mr Grobbelaar, so long as it is bad and destroys him.'

'Yes,' said Chris Vincent, and the trial was adjourned.

On the following day, his battering continued. Rodney Klevan portrayed Grobbelaar as an innocent man who had been the victim of a senseless act of vengeance. 'Bruce Grobbelaar could not have done more for you,' he observed. 'From 1992 to 1994, at no time did he behave as anything other than a great friend. He didn't do a single thing to hurt you . . . you were the apple of his eye.' Yet, continued Klevan, Vincent had turned on Grobbelaar after Mondoro, the safari company the two men had set up after that fateful drink at Harkers, fell apart in acrimonious circumstances. 'Unless someone is with you all the way, he's against you – the slightest doubt of you, and you fall out. How about your brother Keith? Was he close to you, was he a good friend? Keith . . .' another dramatic pause, '. . . the lion-hunter.'

Once again, the message was obvious: Keith Vincent, hero; Chris Vincent, worm. The jury were not to know – for nobody had told them – that Chris Vincent's one indisputable achievement was his record as a decorated war-hero, albeit in a war fought for the white regime in Rhodesia against black African rebels. All they knew was that Christopher Vincent was a man whom even his own family despised, as Klevan now pointed out.

'Have you bothered with [your brother] since the collapse of Mondoro?'

'No sir.'

'And your father . . . you haven't spoken to him since 1994. You are at war with your own father. He thinks you're a bit of a rogue.' A sigh, a beat, then the punchline: 'You *have* been unlucky in your life.'

Some time later, having been through the specific details of Vincent's case against Grobbelaar, and having disputed any suggestion of illegal activity, Klevan returned to the conflict between the two men. When Vincent had fallen out with Grobbelaar, he had denied his best mate the chance to put his side of the story, or to get a third party to intercede between the two of them.

'In our country, it would be normal to make peace face-to-face,' said Vincent.

'Like men,' commented Klevan.

'Yes, sir.'

'What kind of man are you?' asked Klevan.

'I would say normal,' replied Vincent.

Klevan let the remark sink in, then muttered, 'Heaven help us from the abnormal.'

The delivery of that remark was melodramatic, but the question was a reasonable one: what kind of a man was Chris Vincent? I'd been wondering that since the summer of 1995, when I received a telephone call from an old university friend, Nigel Parker, a partner at a firm of solicitors specializing in the entertainment business. He normally worked for rock stars like Mick Hucknall, or the Rolling Stones. But now, said Parker, he had a new client, Chris Vincent, in whom he thought I might be interested. For a moment, I could not place the name. Then it was explained: he was the man who had blown the whistle on Bruce Grobbelaar. He had, said my friend, an amazing story to tell. One that would make a great book.

I was sceptical: wasn't Vincent a bit dodgy?

Parker thought not. He had heard Vincent's story and been convinced. Vincent, he said, had chosen to expose Grobbelaar because he believed the latter had failed to live up to a series of undertakings he had given when their business broke down.

Now he had incredible stories to tell, not just about match-fixing, but about an entire hard-drinking, skirt-chasing, big game-hunting lifestyle in both Britain and Africa. Interested, I told Nigel I'd make a few phone calls and get back to him.

One call was all it took. When asked whether the police believed that Vincent's evidence was reliable, a spokesperson at Hampshire Police headquarters in Winchester pointed out that the force would hardly have spent almost nine months and several hundred thousand pounds pursuing the case as far as it had if that were not the case. 'Vincent was the catalyst,' said the cops' PR. 'He was the man who mixed the stuff that made the bomb go boom!'

A few days later, I met Chris Vincent. He was living in Windsor at the Hart and Garter Hotel, a run-down establishment (since refurbished) directly opposite the castle at the top of the High Street. It was a pleasant summer's evening and Vincent was waiting for me outside the hotel. I had not known quite what to expect. What I found was a small dapper man in khaki shorts and short-sleeved blue shirt, both neatly pressed, with a baseball cap pulled down low over his eyes. This, I would come to learn, was his uniform for any but the coldest weather: if at all possible, he always dressed as though still back home in Zimbabwe.

We walked down the hill towards the Thames and into a wine bar called – appropriately enough, since we were about to discuss an alleged betting scam – Punters. I bought a beer for myself, while Vincent asked the barmaid for a 'spook 'n' diesel'. He was obviously a regular, because she immediately reached for Bacardi and Coca-Cola, while Vincent explained to me that spook 'n' diesel was Zimbabwe's favourite cocktail, the 'spook' being cane spirit and the 'diesel' the Coke. He opened a packet of red Marlboros and lit up. When the waitress, an extremely attractive woman in her late twenties, came to take our order, she smiled and laughed as Vincent chatted her up with an easy familiarity.

One of the hardest things for the Winchester jury to understand must have been why a winner like Bruce Grobbelaar should ever have become friends with a loser like Chris Vincent.

The figure they saw in the witness box had been ground down by imprisonment. The man I met in Windsor – though he was, as it would soon emerge, completely penniless – was an ebullient, cheery, energetic fellow. He was a fine sportsman, he played the guitar, he could sketch with elegant fluency and he told outrageously funny anecdotes. Over the following couple of years, I never once walked through Windsor with Christopher Vincent without at least one pretty girl coming up to him in the street and bidding him hello – and never the same girl twice. Nor was he short of male friends: gregarious, middle-aged types who liked to while away their afternoons on golf courses or in bars, flirting with women who were certainly not their wives.

But back to that first evening . . . As one drink followed another, followed by steaks, more spooks and countless cigarettes, Chris spun me his yarn. He spoke in a broad Zimbabwean accent – as near to South African as makes no difference to the British ear – and his language was as dramatic as the events it described. Money was always 'greenbacks', preferably paid in 'grunters' or thousands. Black people were 'munts'. Events were described in a rich vein of homophobic metaphor. 'I bent him over and fed him a good one,' he might say, or 'He lined me up and gave me one, right up the nought.' Or 'He knows that if he tries to shaft me on this one, he'll really be seeing his arse.' There was a variation on that theme for when things got really bad, to wit: 'He'll be seeing his arse in technicolour.'

It all sounded like the basis for a great book. Here, I thought greedily, was a sure-fire winner that was bound to be good for a stonking advance, a six-figure newspaper serialization (it wasn't, not remotely), and a slew of film and TV rights. More than that, it was a great yarn whose ingredients were the stuff of best-selling fiction, let alone factual reportage. It had money, sex, tabloid scandal-mongering, Premier League football, Wilbur Smith-style African adventures, even an unproven, unsubstantiated allegation of triple homicide . . . what more could anyone want?

Ironically, I had been caught in the same web of enthusiasm and avarice that had ensnared Bruce Grobbelaar. Like him, I sealed my pact with Chris Vincent over a drink. Like him, too, I was soon reaching for my wallet: Vincent asked for a cash payment of £3,000, later raised to £4,000, to cover his hotel bill and his living expenses until such time as we would paid a publisher's advance. Though I did not know it, and would not find out for several months, he had been declared bankrupt on 21 March 1995, with debts of £98,820.97.

We would, we agreed, split any money we made fifty-fifty. My only, and absolute, condition was that I would have complete editorial control. This book would be written in the third person and would be honest about Vincent's own failings. After all, I insisted, how could he expect anyone to believe what he said about other people if he was not first honest about himself? To his credit, Vincent agreed.

For all its entertainment value, little of the story that Vincent had to tell, or of the events that followed its telling, could be said to have much in the way of heroism, nobility or moral virtue. So the significance, if any, of what follows resides in two aspects of the case. The first is what it says about human emotion. Right at the heart of the whole affair are impulses that have remained unchanged for thousands of years: friendship, lust, betrayal, greed and revenge, to name but five. The second aspect is less timeless.

Towards the end of the first Grobbelaar trial, while we were waiting for the verdicts, I was sitting in the canteen drinking one of the endless cups of coffee with which we all whiled away the time, with Neil Bennett, one of the BBC's correspondents at the trial. Neil is a slight, unobtrusive sort of man, with a manner that is characteristically wry, even gentle. But for once, he seemed genuinely angry. 'I blame it all on Thatcher,' he snarled.

Taken aback by his vehemence, I asked why. Surely even Maggie could not be held responsible for a bunch of alleged match-fixers?

Neil explained what he meant. The whole case, he said,

centred on the unjustified payments of huge sums of money. Whichever way you looked at it, the four accused had been paid countless thousands of pounds in cash, salted away in a variety of bank accounts, none of it apparently declared to the taxman. The chief witness had sold his story for one fortune and wanted to make another. It was all evidence of a society that had ceased to measure its values in anything but financial terms. We were obsessed by money. We would do anything to attain it. And that, he concluded, was Thatcher's fault.

I countered that money-lust had hardly been Margaret Thatcher's invention. Nor has there been any diminution in our materialism in the years since her departure. But I took, and take, Bennett's point. The Grobbelaar case is an emblem of our times: of our greed; of our obsession with celebrity (and the tabloid journalism that is celebrity's most intimate companion); above all it is a reflection of our mania for football.

Mrs Thatcher hated football and its hooligan supporters. In the mid-eighties the game had reached its hooliganized nadir – 'a slum game played in slum stadiums', as one broadsheet newspaper called it. Yet it was Mrs Thatcher who, however unintentionally, provided the means for football's revival. In the wake of the Hillsborough disaster of 1989, in which ninety-five Liverpool fans were killed, she commissioned the Taylor Report, which insisted on safe, all-seater stadiums. And it was Thatcher's great media ally, Rupert Murdoch (proprietor, of course, of the *Sun*), whose Sky satellite network provided the millions of pounds, in TV rights, that funded football's astonishing revival. By the nineties the sport had become chic, fashionable, a fit subject for literature and erudite conversation. But the game's new-found intellectual respectability could not entirely hide the signs of a culture that had long existed on nods, winks and bundles of cash stuffed into brown envelopes.

The Grobbelaar case came at the end of a long line of financial controversies in football. George Graham had been sacked as manager of Arsenal and banned from football for a year by a special FA committee of inquiry, after admitting receiving £425,000 from the Norwegian players' agent Rune

Hauge. Terry Venables had been the subject of constant investigation, rumours and even smears concerning his business and football affairs. During Venables' long battle with Alan Sugar, chairman of his former club Tottenham Hotspur, some 2,500 pages of sworn statements had been amassed. In one of them Sugar claimed that a large cash payment had been handed over to the Nottingham Forest manager Brian Clough at a motorway service station, as part of the transfer deal that saw Teddy Sheringham move from Forest to Spurs. This claim was vehemently denied by Clough. An FA inquiry had been set up to look at the whole question of financial corruption in football and both the VAT and income tax authorities had been rumoured to have set up special task forces to look into the affairs of well-known managers. In short, sleaze was at least as common on the road to Wembley as it was in Westminster.

Finally, there was the whole cultural context in which the Grobbelaar case was set. By the start of 1997, Britain was at the peak of the decade-long run of sensationalist, kiss 'n' tell intrusions into the lives of famous people that would reach its terrible crescendo with the death of Diana, Princess of Wales. The *Sun* investigation that led to the exposure of Bruce Grobbelaar was a legitimate inquiry into a matter of genuine public interest. But it had been prompted – as was this book – by the greed and vengefulness of a man who wanted to expose an old friend and make a great deal of money in the process.

Which takes us full circle, back to brutal human emotions and the story of the friendship between Bruce Grobbelaar and Chris Vincent. And that reached its high point in a helicopter, flashing about the overwhelming landscape of Africa, the continent where both men hoped to make their fortune.

# 2

## Jungleman Bruce Grobbelaar

The helicopter hovered for a second, fifty feet above the ground, as noisy, excitable and yet hesitant as an insect inspecting a wound, wondering whether to plunge in. Then without warning it made up its mind, darting a few yards to a point where the parched earth beneath seemed to vanish, falling into a sheer crevasse eight hundred feet deep. The pilot rammed the cyclic forward, sending the helicopter screaming into the gorge. Giant cliffs, just a few hundred yards apart, swallowed it whole, rising above and around it until there seemed to be no possibility of escape.

The chopper was dropping like a stone. Below it, rushing closer with every second, the waters of the River Zambezi raged through some of the fiercest rapids in the world, crashing and breaking against giant boulders, pounding downstream at more than sixty miles an hour. Any man who fell into the maelstrom would be dead within seconds, smashed to pieces long before he could drown.

Now they were just 200 feet above the torrent . . . 100 . . . 50 . . . Suddenly, when it seemed as though the spray was already exploding around them, the pilot pulled back, simultaneously switching the engines to maximum power. The helicopter pulled out of its dive and rocketed forward at 120 knots, skimming over the rapids no more than six or seven feet above the water, its windshield awash with foam.

As they powered upstream they faced a new threat – the implacable rock face. At every bend in the gorge the pilot aimed his craft and its passengers directly at the cliffs. At the very last moment he would climb almost vertically up the surface of the rock, slowing right down as he did so, before briefly stalling the rotors, twisting the helicopter and falling back into the turn.

Within a couple of minutes they were over the Number Nine Rapids, where the river was no more than forty feet wide, the entire force of the Zambezi – nearly 9 million gallons per second – concentrated into a tiny bottleneck. A couple of years earlier some businessmen, keen to make white-water rafting a local tourist attraction, had put an unmanned raft through the rapids to see what would happen. Seconds later it had disappeared from sight, sucked into the 200 foot deep waters. It reappeared almost a minute later half a mile downstream, torn to pieces. In future, it was decided, the rapids would just be walked around.

No one had considered the possibility that a man would be mad enough to fly through Number Nine. But that hadn't stopped an ex-Marine called Greg Andrews – Captain Click to his friends – from seeing what would happen if you did. Fanatically fit, short-haired, with a baseball cap pulled low over his eyes. Andrews had yet to find a place he would not take his yellow Jet Ranger. As the rapids disappeared behind him he shouted into the intercom, 'This is better than sex!'

One of his passengers, a tall, moustachioed man, whose dark hair was rapidly receding from his forehead, laughed out loud. '*Ja!*' he agreed, in a guttural southern African accent. 'The only thing better than this is doing it . . . and having sex at the same time!'

The passenger was Bruce Grobbelaar. He had only arrived in Zimbabwe at six o'clock on that morning in December 1992, flying in from London with his driver and would-be business manager, a retired Liverpool policeman called Tony Milligan (or Moany Tilligan, as his employer liked to call him). Chris

Vincent had met the two men at Harare international airport and, shortly after seven, they had all taken the fifty-minute flight to the town of Victoria Falls in the very north of the country, close to the Zambian border. Once there, Vincent left for a business meeting accompanied by his brother, Keith, who lived in Victoria Falls.

The brothers hired a car at the airport. Grobbelaar and Milligan borrowed Keith Vincent's truck and headed into town. En route they were stopped by a black Zimbabwean traffic cop, conducting random tests of passing cars. The brakes, indicators and so on were given a cursory examination. Grobbelaar, who was driving, was told to sound his horn. Nothing happened. Then the cop leaned in through the driving window. Suddenly he realised who was driving the car. 'Jungleman!' he yelled. 'Jungleman Bruce Grobbelaar!'

Here was a national hero – the only white man in the national soccer team, and a living symbol of racial unity. Behind them another driver, impatient at the hold-up, tooted his horn.

'Was that your hooter?' the policeman asked Grobbelaar.

'Yes,' came the reply.

The officer shrugged his shoulders and waved Grobbelaar on. 'Ah well,' he sighed, 'why do you need a ticket, eh?'

The two men reached their hotel – the luxurious Elephant Hills Country Club, where, as always, Grobbelaar had the best rooms. They showered, changed and played some holes of golf until the Vincent brothers arrived shortly before lunch. A few beers were swiftly despatched and then the quartet set off for a full round of the golf course.

Then the serious fun began. Chris Vincent and Bruce Grobbelaar liked to lead their lives at maximum speed and full volume. Keen to see the land on which their planned safari camp would sit, they had hired a helicopter at 4,000 Zimbabwean dollars per hour (then roughly £400). After Captain Click had plunged into the Zambezi gorge they found themselves roaring through the most exclusive and exciting roller-coaster ride in the world. Finally they turned a bend in the river and came upon the glorious sight of Victoria Falls. The helicopter rose above the mountainous cascade of water, bisecting the rainbow that hung in its spray. For a while they ventured along the calmer waters upstream, flying over hippos, crocodiles and herds of buffalo, spotting elephants in the distance and then, to cap their extraordinary journey, happening upon a pride of seven lions below them in the bush.

Now, their bodies flooded with adrenaline, Grobbelaar and Vincent were in the mood for a party. Sure enough, they found one that night at another local hotel, the Illala Lodge. As was their habit, they drank as if alcohol were about to be prohibited, downing ice-cold beers and spook 'n' diesels. As was also their habit, they chatted up any pretty girls that came within range. One of their targets was a beautiful blonde German encountered in the reception area. She was in a state of mild distress. On the way to the hotel, she and her boyfriend (who had temporarily disappeared) had almost hit a small crocodile sprawled across the middle of the road. Thinking that it must have escaped from a nearby crocodile farm, they had picked it up. Now it was in the boot of their car. Sure enough, when the boot was opened there was the croc, looking up at them with an irritated gleam in its eye.

Roaring with laughter, the two men headed off in search of more drinks and more 'fresh' – their name for available female flesh. When Victoria Falls' best bar, Explorers, finally closed for the night, they headed back to Elephant Hills, happily oblivious to any worries about drink-driving. There is, after all, little late-night traffic in rural Zimbabwe. Except, that is, for the occasional hippo, one of which was standing immobile in the middle of the road. Vincent's response was instant: he drove their hired Mazda off the road and made a brief detour into the bush. There the car's headlights picked out a 700-pound waterbuck. Whooping and hollering with delight, they chased the startled antelope across the grass. Suddenly there was a thud, then a splash, from the front of the car. Vincent had steered them straight into the Zambezi.

'I knew I was close,' he shouted across to Grobbelaar, 'but not that close!'

Luckily they were upstream from the Falls, where the banks are shallow and the waters run relatively calmly. They were able to reverse the car, make their way back to the road and drive back to Elephant Hills. Five hours later, they were back out on the golf course.

For Bruce Grobbelaar and Chris Vincent, in the final days of 1992, life was as good as it could possibly get. All the fun, all the money, all the girls in the world were poised within their reach. They had a business project, Mondoro, that interested everyone who looked at it. Zimbabwean landowners were queuing up to offer them sites for their camp. Investors were promising to support them. What could possibly go wrong?

Grobbelaar in particular seemed to lead a charmed life. His gifts as an athlete, and his determination to exploit those gifts, had taken him from a humble background in Africa to the heights of first world affluence. His older daughter, Tahli, had presented a bouquet to the Queen when she visited Liverpool. Even Clint Eastwood had been impressed.

Bruce had an anecdote he liked to tell about the day he met Dirty Harry. In the summer of 1989 Eastwood came to Zimbabwe to film *Black Hunter, White Heart*, a fictionalized account of the making of John Houston's classic *The African Queen*, based on a novel by Peter Viertel. By chance Bruce, his wife Debbie and their two small daughters, Tahli and Olivia, were on holiday near to the set. When word got out that the Jungleman was close by the locals all agreed that the two great men should meet. So the Grobbelaars were escorted to the hotel which was being used as the backdrop to the story. With his customary, laid-back good grace, Eastwood came over to say hello. As he did so, five-year-old Tahli, who had inherited both her mother's blonde colouring and her father's cheeky smile, piped up, 'Are you as famous as my daddy?'

Grobbelaar wished that the ground would open up and swallow him. But the actor just smiled and said, 'I don't know. What does your daddy do?'

'He plays football for Liverpool,' announced the proud little girl.

Eastwood whistled, as if deeply impressed. 'Well, now,' he said, 'I've heard of Liverpool. Your daddy must be pretty famous.'

He was a good daddy, too. As Tahli and Olivia grew up, Bruce would make their breakfast every morning and get them ready for school. 'He was fantastic with the kids,' remembers Bernice Bala'c, a colleague of Grobbelaar and Vincent in their safari business. 'He taught them all about Africa and the wildlife there. That's how I see Bruce – as a family man. At dinner, for example, if Olivia didn't want to eat something, Bruce would feed her and explain to her why she ought to eat it. The girls meant the world to him, and although he felt constrained because Debbie liked to have the last say, you could see his influence on them.'

A natural athlete, Grobbelaar had been a brilliant baseball player as well as a footballer. He had kept goal for Rhodesia's national side while still a schoolboy and, like all successful sportsmen, possessed a fierce competitive streak. Even at primary school, one fellow pupil recalled, 'He would sob his eyes out when he let in a single goal. Nothing mattered more to him than a clean sheet.'

The same principle applied when he became an adult and a professional. According to Mark Lawrenson, who played with Grobbelaar at Liverpool before becoming a TV soccer analyst, 'He's an intensely proud man. When he used to concede a goal, he'd blame everyone else but himself, in terms of, "You let somebody score past me." It was an insult to his intelligence that anyone could score against him.' Even a minor mistake was enough to infuriate him. In the 1986 FA Cup Final, in which Liverpool beat Everton 3–1, he punched his team-mate Jim Beglin after a defensive mix-up that had passed off without any serious danger to the Liverpool goal. Ten years later, Beglin told listeners to BBC Radio Five Live that he had thought of hitting Grobbelaar back, 'But then I remembered he was a jungle-fighter and thought I'd better not!'

For all that, however, Grobbelaar never seemed to take the game quite as seriously, or self-importantly, as many other football people. At any moment he was equally likely to pull off a save of astonishing agility or to make a mistake of implausible incompetence. His famous eccentricity, his clowning around and his jokey relationship with football crowds home and away suggested that he, at least, did not subscribe to the dictum first spouted by the legendary Liverpool manager Bill Shankly and since turned into the game's most fatuous cliché: 'Football isn't a matter of life and death. It's more important than that.'

Those words had come back to haunt Liverpool in 1985, when their fans went on the rampage during the European Cup final, played against Juventus in the Heysel Stadium, Brussels. Forty Italian fans had died, a slaughter that led to the banning of British clubs from European competition.

Heysel had seemed like the ultimate sporting nightmare. But four years later, on 15 April 1989, Grobbelaar was to witness an even more horrific occasion. In the FA Cup semi-final at Hillsborough, the home of Sheffield Wednesday, ninety-five Liverpool supporters were crushed to death against the fences penning them in at the Leppings Lane end of the ground.

Grobbelaar was keeping goal just in front of the Liverpool fans, who cried out to him in desperation, their faces contorted in agony. He tried to persuade a policewoman to open a gate in the fencing to let the fans spill out on to the pitch, but it was not until the third time he approached her that anything was done. The match was only six minutes old when it was stopped, but by then it was too late.

In the aftermath of the tragedy Grobbelaar, his team-mates and their wives became community workers, talking to bereaved parents, visiting the wounded in hospital and attending funeral services. It was an absolutely pivotal moment in the development of British football. On 29 January 1990, Lord Justice Taylor published his report on the Hillsborough disaster. Its 104 pages contained 76 specific recommendations for improving crowd safety at sporting events, of which by far the most important was a call for all-seater stadiums.

Over the next decade, hundreds of millions of pounds would be spent transforming British football grounds from antiquated sporting slums to modern, hi-tech arenas. At the same time enormous new sources of revenue would open up for the game via satellite television, commercial sponsorship and the merchandising of team strips and souvenirs. Within a decade football would be transformed from a national embarrassment to a national obsession.

But as the cash rolled in, so the traditional ties between communities and players were loosened. The Liverpool team of 1989 reacted as it did because it was the city's focal point, its greatest source of pride, its heartbeat.

Fans became increasingly middle-class: much as they loved football, it did not matter quite so much to them – they had other means of creating a sense of personal achievement, of self-worth. And players slowly adopted the mentality of the freelance rather than that of the employee. Paid sums that were unimaginable even five years ago, they now moved where the money was, or where their sponsors wanted them to go. Of course, they still tried their best – their value in the market-place depended upon their success. But how can one football club be a matter of life and death to a player when he may soon be somewhere else, in another country, on another continent?

The story of the friendship between Bruce Grobbelaar and Chris Vincent, and its tortured consequences, was played out against the background of a sport that was on the cusp of major change. In the years 1992–4, the Premier League was formed and Sky Sports began to become a dominant, perhaps *the* dominant player in the game. But the effects of the changes had yet to impact fully upon the players themselves. The most that Bruce Grobbelaar ever earned from Liverpool in a single season, for example, was £160,000. Nowadays, there are players who can make that in ten days.

All of this was a world away from the scene that confronted Bruce Grobbelaar when he first arrived at Anfield in the spring of 1981, aged twenty-three, having been transferred from the Vancouver Whitecaps of the North American Soccer League. At the time, Ray Clemence was the Liverpool goalkeeper. He was one of the all-time great English keepers, but Grobbelaar immediately proclaimed that his place in the first team was in jeopardy. Sure enough, Clemence was on his way to Tottenham Hotspur before the year was out, and Grobbelaar began a twelve-year run as Liverpool's first-choice keeper.

To some football-lovers outside Liverpool, Grobbelaar's flashy personality was more irritating than endearing. To others his style, in which he often acted as an extra defender, rushing from his penalty area to play the ball with his feet and clear it upfield, was a revelation. Athletic, forceful and brave, he did not let the game come to him but imposed himself upon it. The proof of his talent lies in his club record: during his time at Liverpool the club won six First Division Championships, three FA Cups, three League Cups and a European Cup. No wonder the Kop-ites adored him and the powers-that-be at Liverpool FC added his portrait to the select band of Reds whose faces line the corridors at Anfield. Bruce Grobbelaar was well on the way to becoming a legend. Then, in July 1992, he met Christopher Vincent.

# 3

## 'An Intelligent and Determined Individual'

In the days of white rule, there was little class snobbery in Rhodesia. Any distinctions between one European and another were swamped by the superiority they all felt over the majority population of black Africans – the term 'munts', by which they were known to all white Rhodesians, derived from the word 'amuntu', meaning 'people', from the language used by the Shona tribe, the most populous in the country.

Even so, Christopher James Edward Vincent came from a rather more elevated section of society than Bruce David Grobbelaar. Whereas the latter's father was a humble railway worker, Norman Vincent was a successful, highly paid executive in the sugar industry. He and his elder son, who was born on 6 January 1958, did not see eye to eye. Throughout his teens young Christopher was a competent scholar, but made up for any academic shortcomings with his excellence as an athlete. He was of no more than medium height, but he had a runner's barrel chest and natural lung-power. He could be relied upon to win his school's cross-country prize, usually with a record time for his age.

To his pals at school his most notable feature was his enormous, toothy grin. When Vincent smiled his mouth did not curve up, but widened in a great semi-circle that almost seemed to meet behind his head. It made him look like a crocodile, or a 'flattie' as the predator was called in Rhodesia. Flattie became his nickname and it stuck with him throughout his time in southern Africa. Some of his friends later claimed to have been suspicious about the ambitions that Vincent, like a crocodile, was hiding behind his smile. One of them, Terry McCormick, told British journalists that young Chris was 'a bullshitter', adding, 'He would brag about hunting this animal, dating that girl – stories that were very entertaining. He wanted glory and the spotlight. He craved it.'

Perhaps, but Vincent's final report from Fort Victoria High School in July 1976 describes a stalwart of the Drama Club, a school prefect and a hard worker. His headmaster concluded: 'Vincent intends to train for a career in engineering. He is well suited to this as he has a practical bent, he works quickly and effectively and is speedy in extracting basic outlines and patterns in science. I wish him every success for the future and have every confidence and pleasure in introducing him to all with whom he may have contact.'

It was a glowing testimonial, but not one with which Norman Vincent would have agreed. A tough, stubborn Ulsterman, Vincent had, in his son's eyes, been an unbending parent, seldom bothering to attend any of Chris's winning races, and insisting that he make do with borrowed or second-hand sports equipment. But just as Vincent was leaving school, his father had a change of heart. Apparently regretful of the cold shoulder he had turned towards his elder son, he showered his younger boy, Keith, with love, affection and money. He tried to mend his fences with Chris, too, but the breach between them never healed. From then on the two men might sometimes have good times together but their equally implacable natures ensured that conflict would always break out again sooner or later.

If Chris felt any resentment about the disparity in treatment it was aimed at his father rather than his brother, for despite their five-year age-gap the two boys were always partners in arms. Growing up together on a giant sugar estate, they led an existence that centred on the extraordinary wildlife that surrounded them. They went fishing, canoeing and camping. They learned to identify plants and trees, to track animals by their spoor, to shoot birds and hunt game. Keith would grow up to be one of the finest hunters and wildlife experts in Zimbabwe.

On his eighteenth birthday Chris Vincent joined the army, to begin his compulsory two years of National Service. He was one of 650 young men who applied for selection as an officer in the regular army. Of these, just eighteen were eventually commissioned. Vincent was one of them. He became a second lieutenant in the Rhodesian African Rifles, commanding a platoon of thirty black soldiers based at Fort Victoria, in the south-east of the country. For the next two years he and his troops would operate in four-man patrols, venturing deep into the bush to locate and intercept guerrillas entering the country from Zambia or Mozambique.

In the tall elephant-grass that covered much of the country, you might not see the enemy until they were no more than five feet away. Survival depended on total concentration and the ability to be quicker on the trigger than anyone you might meet. Junior officers in the Rhodesian Army had a life expectancy of twenty-five 'contacts', or encounters with the enemy. Beyond that, it was reckoned, you were living on borrowed time. Within four months of joining the Rhodesian African Rifles, Vincent had logged twenty contacts. By the time he left front-line service, a year later, his contact score stood at fifty-six. Adrian Reed, who fought alongside Chris Vincent and was later part of the Victoria Falls set with whom both Vincent brothers worked and socialized, remembers Chris as 'a very good soldier. He had good leadership qualities. I think his men trusted him and were prepared to follow him anywhere.' Vincent was awarded the Bronze Cross of Rhodesia, one of the country's highest decorations – equivalent to a British Military Cross – for 'gallantry and determination in action'. But when the day came for the medal to be awarded, Vincent's parents were absent from the ceremony. This was a slight which Chris would never forget nor forgive, and it would colour his relations with his family from that day on. Equally profound was the effect upon him of war itself.

Vincent was no stranger to slaughter. His citation referred to three separate actions during which he killed more than half a dozen of the enemy. During the war as a whole, he was – by his own reckoning – personally responsible for the deaths of more than one hundred people, some of them civilians. Soldiers under his command killed many more. In a conflict fought among farms and villages, you fired at anything that moved before it had a chance to fight back. There were many occasions when a man would catch sight of movement, or just a shadow behind a bush, empty a magazine at his target and then pull aside the vegetation to reveal the tattered body of a little child who had been cowering in fear at the soldiers' approach.

If you uproot a boy of eighteen from home and school, and transplant him into a world which forces him to choose between his own death and that of strangers, it is foolish to suppose that he will survive the experience unmarked. Physically, at least, Chris Vincent was astonishingly lucky. He suffered severe hearing loss when a grenade went off close to his face, but that aside, by far the most serious injury he received was self-inflicted.

The soldiers worked on a six-weeks-on, two-weeks-off cycle. After more than a month of combat duty, Vincent and his fellow officers would feel the need to let off steam in the manner beloved of fighting men down the ages: they would get mind-bendingly, liver-shockingly drunk. One night in December 1979 Vincent was given charge of a two-and-a-half ton Unimog truck, filled with sandbags. By the end of the evening, having consumed considerable quantities of beer and spirits, he found himself in Fort Victoria doing sixty miles an hour down the wrong side of the street. He drove straight over the first two roundabouts, but when he came to the third Vincent foolishly attempted to steer the hurtling truck around it. He was going far too fast to make the turn. The truck rolled through 180 degrees, spinning on to its top and smashing Vincent's face against the steering wheel. He was found by a passing policeman, half-buried under a pile of sandbags. He had lost four teeth, seriously twisted his knee and given himself facial injuries that required forty stitches.

Within a few weeks he met a young teacher called Helen Fowler. She was petite, blonde and extremely intelligent. To a man who had spent the past years getting shot at for a living, she seemed 'so straight, so pure and so naïve – the perfect antidote to me'. Here, he thought, was a woman with whom he could lead a normal, post-war life. He'd work nine-to-five and play golf on the weekends. They'd buy a house and raise a family. She'd be a teacher and he'd make a good living in the sugar industry. Their future seemed assured.

What no one – not even Helen – could see were the psychological scars left by the carnage Chris Vincent had witnessed and even caused. 'She thought she was on a good wicket,' he later recalled. 'She didn't realize I would get bored once I wasn't getting my daily dose of adrenaline. I'd spent four years in the Army and it had a hell of an effect. But you just don't realize it at the time.' The dogmatism of his Ulster Protestant ancestry, the constant criticism he received from his father and the distorting effect of war had combined to flatten Vincent's personality. An effervescent, energetic schoolboy who was equally happy on the running track or the concert stage became a man who could only see the world around him in absolute terms of black and white. It was almost as if the appreciation of subtlety, or the awareness that most human actions are a series of grey-shaded compromises, was crushed out of him.

'I can't imagine what I must have been like to live with,' Vincent confessed. 'Helen walked around like she was on hot coals, trying to be the perfect wife. It didn't matter how well she did anything, I'd always find fault. I had such a blinkered view of other people. They were either 100 per cent on my side, or they were the enemy. There was no room for discussion. All my mates were the same way. But none of us had anyone to talk to about it. I look back now and think, "Jesus, what a bunch of turkeys we were back then."'

Back in civilian life, Vincent established a business career. And there, what may have been a more subtle effect of the war began to show itself. Chris Vincent had always been an ambitious boy who dreamed of glory. As a soldier, he had achieved it. He had been a genuine hero – a star. And thereafter, it was as though he could never be satisfied with the mundane achievements of everyday folk. He would always be reaching for the biggest, juiciest fruits on the tree. More often than not, he would over-reach himself and come tumbling down, where-upon he would dust himself down, clear his head and start climbing all over again. That in itself was not a problem. But as he fell from his latest tree, he had an unfortunate habit of pulling other people down with him.

After two years at the Triangle Sugar Corporation, he moved via a year in a transport company to a job in South Africa, working for a company called Interboard which used the waste products of sugar refining to manufacture chipboard for the furniture industry. When sugar is made, the cane residue left behind is known as 'bagasse'. It has two main constituents: the pith from the centre of the cane, and the fibrous husk that covers it. Interboard shipped the bagasse to their factories, separated the husk and used that for their chipboard, then sent the pith back to the sugar mills to be used as fuel for the refinery boilers. Vincent pointed out that it would be simpler to find another use for the pith, rather than send it back where it came from. Mixed with molasses, salt, urea, vitamins and minerals, it would make a first-class cattle feed. Ed Dutton, the owner of Interboard, agreed. He set Vincent up in an inde-pendent subsidiary of Interboard called Interfeed. The latter company would be based in an Interboard plant and be 73 per cent owned by Dutton's offshore trust, which was called Dumae. The real point of Interfeed to Dutton, however, had as much to do with cash as with cattle feed.

In the final years of the apartheid regime, the South African government was desperate to encourage foreign investment. It set up a special exchange rate scheme known as the Financial Rand, which allowed foreign entrepreneurs to buy South African currency at highly favourable rates, provided that the money was then invested in South Africa. Dutton wanted to fund Interfeed with 3.5 million Financial Rand, brought into the country from his Dumae trust. Unfortunately, however, the South African authorities turned down Dumae's application. Without that cash, Vincent had no money for his new business. Dutton gave his employee ninety days to raise the money elsewhere or Interfeed would revert to him. Vincent was unable to meet the deadline.

This combination of a good idea and inadequate investment, leading inevitably to business failure, was one that would dog Chris Vincent over the following decade. His inability to raise adequate, secure finance, and his consequent dependence on individuals' personal money – much of which was then lost, as businesses collapsed – would repeatedly prove to be his Achilles heel. It would, in hindsight, account for almost all his subsequent difficulties and the ill feeling, controversy and unhappiness that flowed from them.

Still, he had no trouble in getting another job in South Africa, working as a general manager at African Projects – a consultancy firm that advised companies on factory start-ups. By 1988, when Vincent was thirty, he and Helen were living in a fine house in Johannesburg. He was making good money and driving a company BMW 325. She was enjoying her career as a teacher.

None of this, though, was getting Vincent any nearer his real ambition, treasured since his days in the Army. He wanted to set up the finest safari operation in the world. Everyone who knew him had got used to his speeches about the way he would stock his land with game; how he would insist on the presence of the Big Five animals – lion, elephant, rhino, leopard and buffalo – that are crucial to the success of any African tourist operation; how the accommodation and service in his camp would beat any in Africa. It was a project for which he was, in many ways, well qualified. He had grown up in the bush, fought there and hunted there. He had a proven record as a manager of men, and, crucially for an African project, he had led black troops in battle and worked with black staff in peace-time. In October 1988, he decided to gain some practical experience in the safari business by going back to Zimbabwe and working with his brother Keith and an old friend called Charles Davy, who was now a major landowner. For the next nine months he worked in Zimbabwe, learning the ropes in the safari business. As his experience grew, so his ideas began to crystallize. But if the business was going to work on the scale he envisaged he needed money, and lots of it. So, in July 1989, he left Africa behind and, taking Helen with him, went to seek his fortune in the UK.

For a while Vincent did temporary management jobs on short-term contracts. But in 1990 he took up a full-time post as a plant manager for Kronospan, the world's biggest chipboard manufacturers, who had a giant factory near Chirk in North Wales. The salary was £36,000, plus a company car, flat and bonuses that could almost double his basic pay. He set up home in a flat in Chirk, alone. 'We sat down one Sunday morning and said, "This isn't working, is it?" Helen just packed up and went back to South Africa. I don't think she has any animosity towards me, and I certainly don't have any towards her. We each hope that the other one can have as good a life as possible,' he said.

By Christmas the job at Kronospan was over, too, after Vincent fell out with one of the other managers at the plant. Undeterred, he set up his own chipboard operation, which he called Nationwide Boards. As with Interfeed, it was based on an innovative industrial process. In this case, Vincent had secured the UK rights to a method of edging chipboard with PVC in such a way that the laminate ran uninterrupted from the top to the bottom of the board, rather than it having to be applied in two main sheets, plus an edge trim. He secured back-ing from the Welsh Office, who were keen to encourage local employment. He was promised a grant of £60,000 to help develop his factory, which was provided by the Welsh

Development Agency and located on a Wrexham industrial estate. He then borrowed a further £100,000 from the National Westminster Bank.

This time, Chris Vincent felt sure he was on to a good thing. He spent Christmas 1990 with his brother Keith in Victoria Falls. On the night before he was due to return to Britain, he and Keith went out for a night's drinking at Explorers. Chris borrowed a couple of hundred Zimbabwe dollars – then worth roughly £20 – from Keith to cover the cost of his drinks. At the end of the evening, he took whatever change remained and threw it across the bar, shouting, 'You can keep this Mickey Mouse money! I'm going to make some real green-backs!' Keith was furious, but he contained his rage for long enough to accept Chris's offer to become an equal partner in the business. Borrowing £10,000 from his father, Keith came in for 50 per cent of the shares of Nationwide Boards. The entire NatWest bank loan, however, was guaranteed by Chris Vincent alone.

What happened next is a matter of some dispute. According to Chris Vincent, Nationwide Boards quickly acquired orders worth £2.5 million. But before the orders could be met, the plant had to be up and running. Vincent had been assured by the Welsh Office that they were operating on the principle of matching funds. Once he had secured and spent £60,000 from other sources, they would step in with their own £60,000. He says that he spent the money, applied to the Welsh Office – and was turned down. Their accountants claimed that the expenditure of £60,000 had to have taken place after the factory was set up and staff had been taken on. Vincent had spent £24,000 of that sum on start-up costs, so by their analysis he could not get his grant until he spent a further £24,000. He went to the bank and asked for an extension to his overdraft. If NatWest let him go £24,000 further into the red, he could pay them back £60,000 from the Welsh Office. If they did not, he would go bust, taking all their money with him. It seemed like a simple proposition, but this was 1991, in the very depth of the recession, and all over the country small businessmen were discovering that banks were calling in their debts, regardless of the consequences. The bank refused a further loan. The Welsh Office were therefore unable to award their grant, and a company which had millions of pounds' worth of orders went into receivership for want of £24,000.

Vincent left the ruins of his company with nothing to show for his efforts, and as a direct result of the bank guarantee he was eventually declared bankrupt in 1995. But even as the company was lurching towards its formal wind-up in April 1992, he was off and running on another project. He had had it with manufacturing. Finally, he was going to make his dream come true. The story of Chris Vincent's safari company, Savannah Management, or – as it later became – the Mondoro Wildlife Corporation, is absolutely central to the story of Bruce Grobbelaar's fall from grace. But before it is told there is another character who needs to be introduced. And he is John Fashanu.

# 4

## The Barnardo's Boy

If Chris Vincent's business career was littered with good ideas that somehow never quite worked out, John Fashanu's CV appeared to contain one triumph after another. Fashanu had overcome poverty, family break-up and racial disadvantage to become an international footballer, capped by England; a millionaire businessman; a Unicef representative, and then, almost as an afterthought, the host of one of the top-rating shows on British television. He was handsome, intelligent, charming – the absolute epitome of classless, multicultural achievement.

He was born on 18 September 1962, the son of Patrick Fashanu, a Nigerian barrister, and Pearl Gopal, a nurse from what was then British Guiana. The couple had been living together while Patrick was a law student in London, but when John was just eighteen months old his father went back to Nigeria. Patrick would later tell his son that he had had no choice: his own father had insisted he return to Nigeria as soon as he was qualified as a lawyer, and Pearl, whose mother and brother were living in England, had not wanted to go with him.

Pearl was left with five children to bring up – a daughter, Dawn, and four boys, Philip, Justin, John and Nicholas – and despite her efforts, the task proved too much. Justin and John were sent to the Barnardo's home at Wood Green in North London. Pearl visited her sons every weekend, but the shock of being parted from her affected John badly. He was backward in his speech, talking in a private body-language that only Justin could understand. Then, when John was three, a white, middle-aged, middle-class couple from Norwich visited the home.

What happened next became an essential part of Fashanu's personal mythology, irresistible to any Fleet Street profile-writer. 'I remember sitting at the top of a slide,' Fashanu told the *News of the World*'s Colin Wills, 'when this particular couple arrived. I was looking at them all the time and my eyes were saying, "Choose me . . . please choose me." They walked around for a bit, but they obviously liked me and Justin. They sat us on their laps. Their names were Betty and Alfred Jackson. My nose was running, and I remember Alfred wiping it with my handkerchief. Betty kept stroking my face. She obviously liked the feel of my skin, you know, the soft skin small black children have. I longed to go and live with them. They seemed so kind and loving. But I didn't have the words to tell them properly. Eventually they took us both. We went to Norwich to be with them.'

The Fashanu brothers moved to a flint-walled lodge at the end of a country lane. Their new father owned an engineering business, while Betty Jackson played the organ at the thirteenth-century local church and taught music. The Jacksons gave their foster-sons dinghies to sail, bikes to ride and guns to shoot. They never tried to cut the boys off from their real mother, who visited them on a monthly basis. Above all, they gave them a powerful work ethic and a determination to succeed. As soon as John was big enough to lift an axe, he was sent out to chop logs for the fire. His faith in the virtues of discipline and hard graft were soon established and never forgotten.

At the age of eleven, the Fashanus were sent to Attleborough High School, just outside Norwich. They were the only black pupils, but they experienced no racism and John's days at school 'were some of the happiest of my life'. One of the reasons that John and Justin were popular was that both were star athletes. Both played soccer for the county and John was a Norfolk schoolboy boxing champion. Somewhat to Betty Jackson's chagrin, they decided on careers in professional sport. Justin was signed by Norwich City as an apprentice, quickly making it into the first team. After brief spells as a junior at Peterborough and Cambridge, John followed him to Norwich as well.

Justin soon became one of Britain's first million-pound footballers when he was transferred to Nottingham Forest. In those days he was the one expected to go on to great things, and was already earning a six-figure annual salary – impressive stuff in the First Division of the early eighties – when John was getting by on £50 a week. And yet the turmoil of his early years had evidently scarred Justin in ways that were not evident on the surface. From his teenage years he had suffered terrible, violent nightmares, during which he had been known to lash out with his fists, punching through windows and even wooden doors. And, though this would not be made public until 1990 when he came out in the *Sun*, Justin Fashanu was also gay. Finally, his status as a footballer began to decline virtually from the moment he signed his deal with Forest in 1980.

When his football career went irreversibly on the slide, due to injuries and loss of form, Justin Fashanu's life went from bad to worse. He tried to make money selling stories of his involvement in celebrity sex scandals – stories which, for the most part, he had invented. By 1998 he had moved to the USA and was living in Howard County, Maryland, halfway between Washington DC and Baltimore, where, he said, he was going to be involved with a new local soccer team. On the night of 24 March he is alleged to have raped a seventeen-year-old boy, who reported the assault to the police the next day. Fashanu left the USA a wanted man. On 2 May he was found in a garage in East London. He had committed suicide by hanging himself.

John Fashanu attended his elder brother's funeral. His brother's life had been marked by dazzling promise, giving way to later disappointment. But John was made of sterner, more unyielding stuff. He had always been determined to succeed and from an early age showed signs of a natural head for business. At the age of seventeen he bought a second-hand Ford Escort and charged his fellow apprentices fifty pence a ride from the Norwich ground at Carrow Road to the club's training pitch. He could get six lads into the car. If they did not pay, they walked.

Norwich sent him on loan to Crystal Palace. From there he moved to Lincoln City and Millwall. Fashanu was never the most skilful of players. What he had to offer was his pace, his imposing six-foot-two, 190-pound physique and his unstoppable drive. And he found the perfect home for his talents at Wimbledon. This unknown club from the genteel suburbs of SW19 had risen from non-league obscurity to the heights of the First Division. The Dons' ground, Plough Lane, was a sorry sight compared to the footballing palaces of Highbury, Anfield or Old Trafford, and their crowds frequently struggled to reach five thousand. Wimbledon's players called themselves the Crazy Gang. To many of the grander clubs they were an unsightly embarrassment, made all the more irritating by their annoying habit of beating their supposed betters.

Wimbledon's tactics – in the early days at least – were simplicity itself. Having obtained the ball with tackles of unabashed ferocity, they would hoof it as high and long as possible into enemy territory. John Fashanu, who now sported a black headband and was nicknamed Fash the Bash, would leap for the ball in a flailing whirl of arms and legs, either nodding it on to a team-mate or bundling it into the back of the net. In public Fashanu downplayed his image as a hard man, but opponents who got in the way were apt to regret it. In 1988 John O'Neil of Norwich had to retire from the game after snapping knee ligaments in a tackle with Fashanu. Five years later, in 1993, the Spurs captain Gary Mabbutt suffered seven facial fractures in a clash with Fashanu's elbow. 'His ideal pitch would have a rope around it . . . like a boxing ring,' said one black-and-blue opponent.

Wimbledon's greatest moment came in 1988, when they beat

Liverpool 1–0 to win the FA Cup. After the match John Fashanu received his winner's medal from Princess Diana, the patron of Barnardo's. But for all its triumphs on the field of play, the club was only surviving from year to year by selling its most talented players to other, richer clubs. Fashanu, however, stayed on. He was rewarded for his 107 goals for the club with a contract that rose to £200,000 per annum by 1990. On top of that basic pay he was rumoured to be on a bonus of £3,000 per goal. Gossip about his riches became so pervasive at the club that their chairman, Sam Hammam, was forced to reveal that three other Wimbledon players earned even more. Alan Cork, the team's longest-serving member, was not convinced. He walked into the dressing room and told Fashanu, 'I've pledged £100 to Children in Need if you show me your wage-packet.'

Fash the Bash had now become Fash the Cash. Admiring profile-writers invariably focused on his affluence, and Fashanu was only too happy to encourage them. He promoted himself through his own company, Fash Enterprises; had the Admiral sportswear concession for Nigeria; ran a management company called Blue Orchid, dealing with African players who wanted to make a career in Europe; and was a director of the radio station Kiss FM. He had interests in hotels and rental properties and lived in a penthouse nestled between Lord's cricket ground and Regent's Park, where the furnishings were black and gold, the mirrors were tinted, the rugs were sheepskin, and financial magazines were neatly piled on the coffee-table.

Oddly enough, figures read out in court would later suggest that many of John Fashanu's public ventures were less successful than his PR efforts had suggested. The two Winchester juries were told that Fash Enterprises registered a small profit in 1993–4. Blue Orchid had not filed accounts since 1992, when it made a small loss. His third company, Hanler Construction, a property management and maintenance firm, had never filed any accounts. That Fashanu had access to substantial amounts of money was not in doubt; the question was where they came from. In court it was claimed that tens of thousands of pounds in cash were deposited in London bank accounts and despite years of investigation, the police were not able to find any routine explanation for them.

In between his business deals, Fashanu kept in contact with Barnardo's and did community work in inner-city schools. His growing status as a role model brought him to the attention of the Establishment. As his entry to Debrett's *People of Today* proudly testified, he had won a Lloyds Bank award for business and another award from the World Sports Corporation, honouring his role as a black man in the media. The government appointed him to the Physical Education Working Group advising on the role of sport in the National Curriculum for children of school age.

Sometimes his business activities approached the very margins of respectability. In 1994, he told *Business Age* magazine how he had been injured during a fight at the Wimbledon training ground. As he was being driven away in an ambulance one of the paramedics told him that the vehicle was just an old Bedford van, fitted with a couple of beds and a siren. 'I suddenly realized I could make a lot of money if I bought a load of old vans and beds, converted them to ambulances and flogged them to Africa. I was happy again.' Yet, for all the conspicuous achievement, there were indications of the wounds left behind by his childhood, of needs that could never be satisfied. His interviews of the late eighties and early nineties are filled with remarks that – either directly or by implication – suggest a man riven with insecurity. 'It's only in the last few years that I've stopped having to tuck myself up in bed very tightly to make myself feel secure,' he admitted in 1988, adding, 'I'm a workaholic. I can't just put my feet up and relax. I can only sleep well when I feel I've achieved something special.'

That same year, just before the FA Cup Final, he remembered how he had felt as a boy, being examined by his prospective parents at Barnardo's. 'I promised myself that neither I, nor anyone I cared for, should ever face such uncertainty again. Security is the goal, I'm not interested in the fripperies, the baths with gold taps. I want to earn enough to safeguard my family against suffering.'

'Deals, deals, deals,' complained his then girlfriend, Maria Sol. 'He never stops. He's always on the phone.'

'Maybe it's my insecurity,' he remarked in January 1991, 'but I like apartments that are high. Hence my penthouse off Regent's Park.'

Here was a man who could never have enough, never be far enough removed from the uncertainties and fears of life at street level. By 1991 John Fashanu seemed to have enough wealth to keep him comfortable for the rest of his life. Over the next three years he would be chosen as a representative by Unicef, while meeting Nelson Mandela, while being feted by senior politicians across Africa, and while becoming a hero to millions of British youngsters glued to *Gladiators* on a Saturday evening. So what possible need could he have to turn to crime?

That question, which would one day be put by Fashanu's own representatives to a jury in a court of law, would never have been raised were it not for the failure of a small safari business that spent two years trying to get started in Cheshire before a brief and inglorious existence in Zimbabwe. To be specific, John Fashanu would never have been arrested, charged or tried, never subjected to two years of investigation and suspicion, if only someone had paid for a single second-hand Toyota Landcruiser. The connection between that truck and Fashanu's future could be found at an office in Lower Bridge Street, Chester, where Chris Vincent was just starting work on his latest business venture.

# 5

## The Spirit of the Lion

Neither the failure of Nationwide Boards, nor the debts that it left behind, did anything to dent Chris Vincent's determination to set up a safari business. In fact, it merely convinced him that the time had come to stop talking about his plans or distracting himself with other ventures, and just get on with the job.

While working in North Wales, he had met two property developers who seemed interested in financing Vincent's plans and were, they said, well able to raise the necessary money. In July 1991 Vincent had formed a company, Savannah Management Ltd, and that December he went out to Zimbabwe with his brother Keith and began looking for a suitable site for his operations. It took no time at all for the brothers to find what they needed. Their friend Charles Davy, with whom Chris had worked in the months prior to his move to the UK in 1989, was keen to see two plots of land – one, of 27,000 acres, three miles south of Victoria Falls, and another, of 15,000 acres, a further 35 miles to the south. The first estate was handily located for the town and airport of Victoria Falls, not to mention the spectacular falls themselves, while the second ran alongside the Matetsi Safari Area, which boasted some of the best hunting, especially of sable antelope, in Africa.

As well as his land, Charles Davy was also proposing to

sell the Vincents a 109-foot, eight-bedroomed luxury tourist boat, the *Catalina*, which Chris Vincent had helped design for him and was now moored on Lake Kariba. All Davy wanted in return was £2 million. This was an excellent price and Vincent was confident he could meet it. His Welsh investors had told him they were willing to put £6.5 million into Savannah Management.

Throughout the spring and early summer of 1992 Vincent waited for the money to come through. Davy was phoning on an increasingly frequent basis, asking, 'What's going on, Flattie? When am I going to see some greenbacks?' But none were forthcoming.

Nervous, but not deterred by the delay, Vincent worked on his formal business proposal. He set out the capital cost of his operation, its likely running costs and the projected return on investment, given varying rates of room occupancy. He supported himself by working with Stephen Wundke. A former cricketer who had reached the fringes of the Australian national side, Wundke was now running Ace Golf and Leisure, a Chester company that owned a golf equipment shop, organized golf days at country clubs and sold golfing holidays. Vincent had rented some space at Ace Golf's offices in Lower Bridge Street, Chester. This was to be his working base for the next two years.

By July, Vincent had agreed to go out to Zimbabwe with one of his would-be backers to meet Charles Davy and confirm the purchase of his land and boat. In the meantime, Vincent was searching for further investors who could put in enough money to keep Savannah Management going until the land deal was made and the camps could be set up. He was proposing to sell 30 per cent of the company for £30,000. So whenever he made new business contacts he would ask them if they were interested, or knew anyone who might be.

There was, by now, a particular urgency to his enquiries. Chris Vincent was potless. He had no money other than that which he carried in his pocket. He owed rent for his flat in Chirk and he was behind with his water and electricity bills. For personal as well as corporate reasons, he needed money fast. Then one day in mid-July the perfect opportunity arose, thanks to one of Vincent's local contacts called Gwyn Thomas. 'Have you spoken to Bruce Grobbelaar?' asked Thomas when he heard about the money-raising plans. 'I know how to get hold of him. We play golf together.'

The two men had never met. It had, however, crossed Vincent's mind that the footballer might be keen to invest in his own home country, so he leaped at the chance of an introduction. Thomas gave him Grobbelaar's number and Vincent called him up, explaining that he was looking for backers for a top-class safari operation. Grobbelaar agreed to meet him at 5 p.m. that Friday at a wine bar known as Harkers on the canal in Chester. It was a homely-looking place, converted from an old church and popular with prosperous young professionals – local doctors, lawyers and accountants – wanting to relax after a hard week's work.

The first thing that struck Vincent about his compatriot was his size: he seemed much bigger than his image on television had ever suggested. Grobbelaar was dressed in black jeans and a black T-shirt, a look that set off his equally dark hair and moustache to the maximum dramatic effect. They met and shook hands by the bar, then retired to a private table tucked away beyond an arch and surrounded by bookshelves.

'What's that,' asked Grobbelaar when he saw Vincent's drink, 'a spook 'n' diesel?'

Chris Vincent laughed. The two men clearly had one thing in common right from the off.

Once Grobbelaar had ordered a drink of his own, Vincent pulled out his maps and began explaining what it was he proposed to buy. One of the Welsh property developers, who had joined the two Zimbabweans at Harkers, confirmed that his company was planning to invest £6.5 million. But until that money was in the bank, continued Vincent, he needed to finance his company.

Grobbelaar was told that if he wanted in, he needed to be aware of two things. In the first place, this was a long-term investment. If it went well, everyone could expect to make a great deal of money. But success would take time: it was not a case of get-rich-quick. Secondly, Vincent did not intend to use Grobbelaar, or his name, as a marketing tool. The business, he said, was good enough to sell itself. His investment was a matter for himself alone.

Grobbelaar said, 'I'm in. When do you want the first cheque?'

Vincent was due to fly to Zimbabwe on the following Monday, and did not want to waste any time. 'Tomorrow morning,' he replied.

Grobbelaar, too, was leaving the country. Liverpool were going to Italy, via Heathrow, in the morning, to start high-altitude pre-season training. He wanted to buy 10 per cent for £20,000. He would pay £5,000 that night, and the rest when he got back.

Delighted with their transaction, the men moved on to another pub, the Albany. A bite to eat was suggested, but Grobbelaar said that he would not be able to make it. His wife and children were away in Portugal and he was due to have dinner with an old friend who worked for British Airways. They agreed to meet up again afterwards at a night-club called the Copacobana. But by 1 a.m. Grobbelaar had not turned up, so Vincent called him on his mobile. When he answered, he sounded irritable and out of breath.

'Meet me at Manchester airport at nine in the morning,' he muttered. 'I'll be in the domestic departure area.'

That was where Vincent found Bruce Grobbelaar, as promised, the following morning. When he saw his new business partner, Grobbelaar wasted no time. He sat down, took out a Lloyd's Bank chequebook and wrote out a cheque for £5,000, made out to Chris Vincent and drawn against a joint account shared with his wife, Debbie. Then he got on his plane. Two days later Vincent too flew out of the country, taking one of his prospective investors on a reconnaissance trip to southern Africa, checking out luxury camps of the sort Vincent was intending to set up.

When he got back to Chester, Vincent finalized his deal with

Bruce Grobbelaar. Together they went to Rathbone's, the accountancy firm that looked after Grobbelaar's affairs. Grobbelaar had recently been granted a testimonial match against Everton, which had raised around £175,000. His personal accountant at Rathbone's, Ian Taylor, was taking care of the money. In the course of a thirty-minute meeting Vincent showed Taylor the Savannah Management prospectus, described his hoped-for £6.5 million finance package, and gave details of the company's accountants and solicitors. Taylor authorized a £15,000 cheque from the fund to Savannah, thereby completing the first £20,000 of Grobbelaar's investment, in exchange for which he would receive his agreed 10 per cent of the company.

Everything was ready to roll. But for the final four months of 1992, nothing happened. The £6.5 million had not arrived, and Charles Davy was still having to ring up his old pal Chris Vincent to find out what on earth was going on. Vincent, for his part, was becoming as irritated as Davy. Every time he went to see the property developers he was met with smiles and bland assurances, but no cash. The only decisive action he could take was to change his company's name. Savannah Management became the Mondoro Wildlife Corporation. The name was taken from the *mhondoro*, which in the Mkori-kori dialect of Shona means 'spirit of the lion'.

By now, Charles Davy was keen to see some return on the time and money he had invested in Vincent's scheme. When Vincent flew to Zimbabwe for Christmas, he met Davy to try and sort things out. His old friend's first words, when they met at Bulawayo airport, were enthusiastic enough – a cheery cry of 'Hello, Flat-fucker!' But within minutes Davy was making his point in the clearest possible language. 'Either these people put their money on the table, or fuck off.' Vincent explained that he had a written undertaking, drawn up by a solicitor, authorizing him to negotiate a purchase contract. He promised that the £6.5 million would be forthcoming. Davy was not impressed. So Vincent came up with another suggestion. Mondoro, as it now was, would pay Davy £10,000 per month, deductible from the final purchase price, to keep their option open until they were able to complete the deal.

That was more like it. Davy sat down with the Vincent brothers and a team of lawyers, and together they worked out the details of the land deal, which would amount to the biggest private purchase in Zimbabwe's history. Bruce Grobbelaar also signed the papers.

A month later, in January 1993, Keith and Chris Vincent began work on an alternative deal in case the first one fell through. This time the prospective seller was Neil Hewlett, a forty-four-year-old landowner and businessman. The son of a rich Rhodesian farmer, Hewlett had further increased the family fortunes by owning the Massey Ferguson tractor concession in Natal, South Africa. But despite his wealth and background, he had been the first white man to join Robert Mugabe's ZANU party, which led the opposition to the regime of Ian Smith. Hewlett had left Rhodesia rather than fight in the civil war. Now, with millions in the bank and a brother who was an MP in the Zimbabwe Parliament, he was spectacularly well connected.

In 1992 Hewlett had bought 14,000 acres of land from Charles Davy, adjacent to the southernmost of the two sites Vincent wanted to purchase. He had intended to use the land as a game farm and private reserve, but wildlife and its management were not subjects on which he was an expert and little progress had been made. Now he suggested that Chris and Keith Vincent might care to take it off him, and he invited them down to take a look for themselves. The brothers spent three days at Hewlett's farm and then signed an agreement to buy it. It seems scarcely credible that the Vincents were prepared to commit themselves to yet more purchases. But at least they had the comfort of knowing that Hewlett was prepared to structure the deal on a long-term basis. All he needed upfront was £20,000. That was not a lot to ask. But when Chris Vincent got back to Britain in February 1993, it became painfully obvious that it would be a struggle to raise any money at all.

The Welsh developers had been given twenty days to come up with the first £10,000 monthly payment to Charles Davy. They did not make the deadline. It was the end of the business relationship with Vincent . . . and, very nearly, of the life of one of the developers. In the late summer of 1993, Chris Vincent and Steve Wundke happened to be having a drink in the same Chester pub as their former partner, who was sitting in a corner of the room. The developer got up, walked towards Vincent and tapped him on the shoulder.

Vincent told him to get lost: 'I've got nothing to say to you.'

About twenty minutes later, Vincent went to the lavatory. The developer saw him walking in that direction and intercepted him at the door. Vincent walked right past him, without a word. Once more the man tapped him on the shoulder.

'Do that again, and I'll kill you,' said Vincent.

Unaware, perhaps, of Vincent's wartime experiences, the man tapped him again. Vincent swung round, grabbed him by the windpipe and began squeezing the life out of the hapless businessman. Luckily, before Vincent could complete the job he was grabbed by Stephen Wundke and three other men, who dragged him away.

'I would have killed him,' Vincent said when recounting this episode two years later. 'I'd told the bugger to leave me alone and he hadn't.'

The incident was a vivid example of Vincent's capacity for feeling wronged. The property developer's only offence was that, in a country barely staggering out of a prolonged economic recession, with a property and construction market that was still on the ropes, he had been unable to raise over £6 million for a speculative venture in the African bush. But, as he and others were to discover, Chris Vincent was apt to take other people's failures personally.

His anger may have arisen from desperation, for Mondoro was in dire straits. By March 1993 there was nothing left in the kitty. Grobbelaar's £20,000 – the sole investment up to that point – had all been spent, and the money Vincent was making from helping Wundke sell golf tours was scarcely covering his own expenses, let alone his company's. He and Wundke had taken their project to a number of venture capital companies but had not had any takers, in part because British institutions were frightened off by the Zimbabwean laws limiting foreign ownership.

Vincent had now been working on his safari project for a little over a year. He had learned an enormous amount about the tourism industry, but was still no nearer to actually owning a site. Charles Davy, one of his oldest friends, was furious at the way he had been jerked around. He told Vincent that the option was closed. From now on, the first person to put money down for his land could have it.

At this point, two men came to the rescue. One was Neil Hewlett, who realized that he, too, stood little chance of making a sale to Mondoro. So he and Keith Vincent devised another plan. Hewlett would build a camp on his farm, which Mondoro would then lease. Hewlett named his camp Acacia Palm Lodge.

The second angel of mercy was Bruce Grobbelaar. His career at Liverpool was not going well. After a dispute with the club's manager, Graeme Souness, he had been sent on loan to Stoke City. But the deal he had negotiated, which involved a share of the gate receipts as well as wages, made him, if anything, better off than he had been at Anfield. He put another £20,000 into Mondoro, taking his stake up to 20 per cent and giving Vincent some breathing space.

Almost immediately afterwards came another apparent stroke of luck – a chance meeting with a man who could solve all Mondoro's problems with one stroke of a pen. Every year Steve Wundke organized an April Fool's Day golf tournament at the Belfry. In the early hours of the morning of the 1993 tournament, Grobbelaar and Vincent were in the bar of the Belfry Hotel when Grobbelaar was approached by Stuart Dyer, a forty-five-year-old high-ranking executive with NM Financial Management, an off-shoot of the National Mutual insurance company. Dyer was a fanatical Liverpool supporter. According to Vincent, Dyer and Grobbelaar got talking. Grobbelaar began to outline his ambitions in the safari business, mentioning Mondoro and its plans. He told Dyer that he and his partner were looking for money.

'How much?' asked Dyer.

'Ten million pounds,' said Grobbelaar.

'Chicken-feed,' joked his new-found friend.

To Grobbelaar's credit, he had talked coherently enough to arouse Dyer's business instincts. And to Dyer's credit, he was able to remember the conversation when he woke up in the morning.

A formal meeting between Dyer, Grobbelaar and Vincent took place at the Belfry, the whole project was outlined and Dyer declared that he was interested in taking the matter further. He arranged to come up to Chester accompanied by an accountant and a fellow executive to go over Mondoro's business plan. Chris Vincent's projections allowed for every possible development option, along with variations in occupancy rates, costs and currency fluctuations. Whichever way he presented the scheme, it still looked like a winner. After eight years, he said, investors could expect a return on their capital of 33 per cent per annum. As Stuart Dyer was later to confirm to the Hampshire Police, Vincent had written a properly costed formal document detailing his plans for the camp and their projected return on investment. This may appear to be a trivial detail, but almost four years later it would assume considerable significance.

For his part, the accountant seemed satisfied with the projected accounts and had no financial qualms about the proposals he had been shown. It looked as if everything had been settled. True, there was no actual cash on the table, and no signed cheques lay in the bank. But a senior executive at an impeccably reputable institution was backing the development of Mondoro. More meetings were held. There were jovial, informal chats at Anfield. When the football season ended, Chris Vincent, Bruce Grobbelaar and the rest of Grobbelaar's family, including his parents-in-law, went out to Zimbabwe to get a taste of what they were trying to achieve.

The business relationship between Bruce Grobbelaar and Chris Vincent was now a friendship that involved much more than mere commerce. Vincent, after all, was the man to whom Grobbelaar would later confess all his guiltiest secrets live on videotape – and the reason for that lay less in work than in pleasure. Footballers are athletic, affluent young men who have no trouble in attracting women. They train for a few hours every morning and are then free to do as they please for the rest of the day. They have the inclination, the means and the opportunity to indulge themselves in every available temptation. In Chris Vincent, Bruce Grobbelaar found a comrade whose appetite for fun was the equal of his own. Both men were ebullient and uninhibited. They loved nothing more than turning an evening visit to a wine bar into a giant party of which they were the life and soul. They were looking for a good time. And they began their mutual search right from the start of their friendship.

# 6

## 'You Two Are Like Brothers'

In October 1992, Bruce Grobbelaar had his testimonial match. More than twenty thousand Liverpool fans came to Anfield to pay tribute to their hero, fill his coffers with the best part of £200,000, and watch a match between Liverpool and Everton. It was a tribute to Grobbelaar's standing as a sportsman that Liverpool's greatest rivals should happily agree to turn out on his behalf. And it was testimony to his popularity as a man that an entire coachload of friends had flown all the way from South Africa and then made a long and well-refreshed drive from London to Merseyside just to join him on his big day.

Grobbelaar invited Chris Vincent to come along to the game. It was Vincent's first trip to Anfield, and he was impressed to be met at the main reception desk by Bruce himself – nattily dressed in a Liverpool-red jacket – who went off to get the special guest tickets for his new pal. It was a sunny autumn afternoon and the ground had a carnival atmosphere. There were brightly coloured balloons, pretty dancing girls, and a light-hearted warm-up game featuring former greats, including Kenny Dalglish, Alan Hansen and George Best.

Then came the main event – the game against Everton. Grobbelaar ran on to a huge roar from his fans, but before taking up position in his goal he jogged across to a corner of one of the stands where a group of disabled children were sitting. Grobbelaar had donated a children's minibus to the Variety Club appeal, and he wanted the kids to know that, however important the occasion might be for him, he had not forgotten them. When the game got under way, Liverpool were awarded a penalty. Up stepped Bruce Grobbelaar himself to take it . . . and blast the ball straight at the Everton goalie, Neville Southall. A few minutes before the end Grobbelaar came off, and lapped the pitch to a standing ovation. 'They *loved* him,' Chris Vincent remembers. 'It was obvious.'

As the 1992–3 season continued, Grobbelaar began inviting Vincent to more and more games. He gradually became a familiar figure in the private lounges that were the heart of the social scene for Liverpool's most affluent supporters. The Liverpool team were sponsored by Carlsberg beer, but Candy – a local manufacturer of kitchen equipment – sponsored the club's home games. Both companies had lounges at Anfield, where they could entertain guests and clients to a lavish lunch before matches and drinks afterwards, often with players in attendance.

Candy's sales director, Ken Rutland, made his pre-match meals an event in themselves, with special guest speakers. Rutland had also sponsored Grobbelaar's Mercedes 190 – registration number H15 NET ('His Net') – and the keeper returned the favour by coming to the Candy lounge after every match.

One Saturday in November 1992, Grobbelaar met Vincent in the Candy lounge and told him he was meeting a man called Allan Gullan, the UK distributor for Zambezi lager – a Zimbabwean brew. Grobbelaar had worked out a deal which promised him a share of Zambezi's profits in return for promotional work. That night, he was going to a Liverpool night-club to work behind the bar and chat to punters: did Vincent want to come too?

A couple of hours later they were both impressing the locals by popping open two bottles of beer at a time, using their thumbnails to send the bottle-tops flying across the room. Free

T-shirts were being given out with every six beers and a queue of girls was forming to have their shirts signed by Grobbelaar . . . while they were wearing them. One of the young women there that night was the beautiful daughter of a Liverpool staff member. Unbeknownst to her father she had, said Grobbelaar, slept with two of the team, one of whom was married. Six months later, Vincent thought he saw the same woman at Anfield. He walked up to her and started chatting away, only to be met with blank stares. Within seconds, a flustered Grobbelaar arrived on the scene and made a hasty introduction. The woman in question was not the footballer's girlfriend. She was his almost-identical wife.

At one point in the Zambezi beer evening, Grobbelaar decided to entertain the people around him with a story. He put on an African accent and uttered the words, 'Dear Auntie Jane . . .' For anyone who had grown up in Rhodesia during the 1970s, this was as familiar as a line from *Blackadder* or *Monty Python* would be to an Englishman, so Chris Vincent got the reference at once. 'Dear Auntie Jane . . .' was the start of a sketch by the Rhodesian comedian Rex Tarr.

Vincent had not heard a Rex Tarr record in fifteen years, but as Grobbelaar began he collapsed in nostalgic laughter, only to follow him with another Tarr sketch – The Zulu Flying School – recalled in equal word-for-word detail. It was a perfect illustration of why he and Grobbelaar were becoming fast friends. For Grobbelaar, this was the first time since he had come to Britain that he had been able to spend convivial, boozy evenings talking to someone who really understood who he was and where he came from. In the middle of a pub, for example, he could call out, '*Eweh! Bweesa forgla!*' Vincent, getting the drinks in at the bar, would know he was saying, 'Hey you! Get me some cigarettes.' When surrounded by other people the pair of them could start speaking Shona, certain that no one else in the room – particularly the women whom they were usually discussing – could understand a word of what they were talking about.

Crucially, both men thought of themselves as African and

instinctively understood the complexities and contradictions of white African attitudes to race. Both Grobbelaar and Vincent habitually referred to 'munts', the Zimbabwean term for black people. And yet both had far more experience of living and working with black people than even the most multicultural white Briton. Vincent had fought alongside black troops in the civil war. Grobbelaar played alongside black players in the Zimbabwe national side and was as hugely popular among black Zimbabweans as he was among whites. At Liverpool one of his closest friends was the Jamaican-born midfield star John Barnes, whom he would tease by saying, 'Now we've got it right – we've got a munt to do all the work.' Barnes, though, was more than capable of defending himself, and any gag of Grobbelaar's would swiftly be answered by one that was just as sharp and just as insulting.

One afternoon at the Candy lounge Grobbelaar introduced Vincent to his wife, Debbie. Whereas many footballers' wives or girlfriends looked like off-duty Page Three girls – often exactly what they were – Debbie Grobbelaar was attractive, intelligent and sophisticated. Her looks were neat rather than drop-dead gorgeous: quite petite, slender and with short, bouffant blonde hair cut à la Princess Diana. She was always immaculately turned out in elegant suits and flat but stylish shoes. At Anfield social events she often looked a touch out of place. Debbie was not interested in football and had little in common with many of the other wives and girlfriends. So she would sit straight-backed, her ankles neatly crossed, talking to Eleanor Nicol, whose husband Steve played alongside Bruce in the Liverpool defence, or Mary Evans, the wife of Roy Evans, then assistant manager to Graeme Souness. 'She's got a plum in her mouth,' Grobbelaar would mutter in his less enchanted moments.

Like most southern African males, however, he had been brought up to behave with old-fashioned chivalry in the company of women. Whenever they lunched at the Candy lounge he would always make a point of taking Debbie's coat, hanging it up, seeing that she had everything she needed and that her drink was regularly topped up. Yet there were signs of tension in the relationship. As Grobbelaar handed Vincent the second instalment of the payment for his 10 per cent stake in Mondoro, he made one condition. 'Don't tell Debbie about this.'

A little while later, Vincent was invited to the Grobbelaar home for the first time, for a traditional South African *braai*, or barbecue. He took along a decent bottle of Cabernet Sauvignon wine and a large bunch of flowers for his hostess.

'How come your friend can bring flowers when you never get me any?' Debbie asked her husband.

Later, Bruce gave Vincent the unspoken answer to that question. In the past he had been a regular visitor to the florist's, but Debbie had once snapped, 'Why do you waste so much money on flowers?' From that day on, he never bought a single bunch.

The Grobbelaar family home was in Heswall, an exclusive area of the Wirral, just across the Mersey from Liverpool. In years to come, tabloid papers would describe it as a '£250,000 family mansion', but that description both underestimated the price – Grobbelaar told Vincent he had paid close to £300,000, at the top of the eighties' property boom – and exaggerated the scale of what was a typical home for a prosperous middle-class couple and their children.

Slightly set back off the road and protected by a hedge, the white-painted Edwardian house was reached by a short semi-circular driveway, with a garage to the left of the main building. The Grobbelaars' cars – at that time a Mercedes and a Renault Espace – were parked outside, because the garage was used for storage. The front door was flanked by double windows, with three more windows running across the house at first-floor level.

Inside, the hall ran between a smart drawing room to one side (where Grobbelaar kept his packed trophy cabinet) and a dining room to the other. Steps ran down underneath the drawing room to a cellar which contained a shower room, where Bruce would wash and shave every morning. In the dining room one wall was taken up with a miniature version of a Boer wagon, which had cabinets inside and acted as a bar. The dining table itself, seldom used for meals, was piled high with bills, accounts and junk mail. To one side stood the PC on which Debbie was completing a computer course. Beyond the dining room was a TV room, with a big-screen satellite television and a sofa which frequently acted as a cosy snoozing-spot for the family cat, which was also called Bruce. A budgie in a cage was hung tantalizingly out of Bruce's reach. Like many a suburban family, the Grobbelaars divided much of their time between the TV room and the kitchen, where the family ate their meals, and which was, naturally, kitted out by Candy.

Upstairs, the master bedroom was surprisingly small and less smartly decorated than the spare bedroom, which displayed perhaps the most unusual feature of the house – rows of shopping-bags filled with brand-new designer clothes. As a whole, though, the house was as down-to-earth as the man who had bought it. A daily, Janet – otherwise known as 'Delta Alpha' or 'Double Agent', because Bruce was sure she reported his activities back to Debbie when the latter was away – kept the place clean. But it was unashamedly lived-in, with scuffs on the paintwork and children's drawings on the kitchen wall.

His girls were Grobbelaar's pride and joy. He and Debbie, who was a couple of years his senior, had been married in the Zimbabwean town of Umtahli, from which their first daughter, Tahli, took her name. She was very much the clever, responsible elder sister. Olivia, meanwhile, who owed her name to her daddy's admiration of Olivia Newton-John, was the skinny, sporty, impish one.

'This is Mr Vincent, from Africa,' said Bruce on the day that Chris Vincent first went to his home. 'He's a safari man. He can teach you wild animal noises.'

Within minutes the girls were learning to roar like a lion, or howl like a hyena, before running away – giggling, roaring and howling as they went. The two men got to work on the barbecue, which was set up on the patio outside the kitchen.

The minor spat that Debbie and Bruce had had about Chris Vincent's flowers had long since been forgotten and the whole evening went with a swing.

At the time, the same could have been said for every aspect of Vincent's and Grobbelaar's friendship. Vincent's own enthusiasm for his safari project had infected Grobbelaar, who was taking an ever greater interest in the scheme. Vincent, in turn, had to admit that there was a lot to be said for knowing a man who could breeze into any club in the North-West safe in the knowledge that he would be treated like royalty. They would regularly go out drinking together, or playing golf. Like many footballers Grobbelaar was a keen golfer, who was better than his 12-handicap would suggest, and Vincent was just as keen. In that sport, at least, they were equally matched. At Liverpool matches, Grobbelaar adopted a new routine when first coming on to the pitch. He would turn to the part of the stand where he knew Chris Vincent was sitting, and ceremoniously flash him an exaggerated army salute. Vincent remembers John Barnes joking, 'You two are like brothers. You're both going bald. You've both got moustaches. You both drink spook 'n' diesels . . . and you both act the arse.'

They had a knack of doing it, though, in ways that always seemed to keep other people happy. One of their favourite pub games was a Chris Vincent trick called 'Drinking by Numbers', which was based on army drill. Participants had to line up along a bar at attention, before taking one step back and standing at ease. The team leader would then call out, 'Here is a full and practical demonstration of drinking by numbers. Squad will drink by numbers . . . Drink by numbers!' Then, as the leader ordered, 'One . . . two . . . three,' the drinkers would grasp their full glasses in their right hand and hold them down by the side of their right thigh, before rotating their glass-holding arms 360 degrees over their heads and back down to their sides, without spilling a drop. The glasses were then raised to the lips in a special, twisting motion before being downed in one. Once the last drop had been finished the glasses were rotated again, thrown into the air, caught and slammed on the

bar with an immediate order for another drink. As the in-
habitants of Victoria Falls told Grobbelaar when he visited
them in December 1992, the call to drink by numbers was a
sure sign that Chris Vincent was setting out on a long night of
alcoholic refreshment, but neither Grobbelaar, nor any of the
other Liverpool players with whom he socialized, ever minded
coming along for the ride.

Grobbelaar had come to Zimbabwe on this occasion for an
international match against Egypt. He and the national team
coach, Reinhard Fabish, had a relaxed relationship, but even
Fabish's tolerance might have been stretched had he known
what Grobbelaar was getting up to in Vic Falls, just a couple of
days before he was due to represent his country.

On the evening after their late-night dip into the Zambezi,
Vincent, Grobbelaar and Grobbelaar's minder Tony Milligan
hit the town once again. Leaving Explorers at closing time, they
decided to return to Elephant Hills, where there was a late-
night casino, for some further entertainment. With them was a
local businessman called Adrian Brooke, who was riding a
500cc Honda trail-bike. As they were all heading away from
Explorers, Grobbelaar, who was driving the Mazda 626 hired
the previous day by the Vincent brothers, leaned out of the
window and told Brooke, 'That thing's useless. We'll get there
before you.'

Brooke took this challenge in the spirit in which it was
intended, and roared off at top speed with the others in hot
pursuit. But as they all got closer to their destination Vincent
and Grobbelaar decided that a race was insufficiently blood-
stirring, so Vincent announced that he would climb out of the
car and on to the pillion of Brooke's bike. Grobbelaar pulled
alongside the Honda. Both car and bike were now doing
around 90 miles an hour down an unlit road on to which
wildlife was liable to roam at any minute and without warning.
There was just over half a mile of straight road in which the
entire manoeuvre had to be completed. Vincent began to edge
out of the passenger-side window. Finally he was all the way
out, with one foot on the window-sill and one hand hanging on

to the car. The other foot and hand were hanging out into the darkness, getting closer and closer to the motorbike and its rider.

In the back seat, Tony Milligan was becoming even more agitated than he had been in the helicopter. 'You Zimbabweans are fucking mad!' he yelled. No one bothered to disagree.

Now Vincent shifted his weight, leaning right out into the road, stretching his leg as far as it would go until his foot landed on the bike's passenger seat. His spare hand grabbed Adrian Brooke's shoulder. He was now like a letter X, suspended between bike and car, hurtling into the darkness. They were approaching a crest in the road. On the far side, Vincent knew, was a favourite spot for buffalo and impala. If either driver swerved to avoid an animal, let alone hit one, he himself would die instantly.

Vincent had done the car-to-bike trick before. The knack at this point was to shift his weight again, taking his hand and foot off the car and bringing them over to the bike until he was standing on the pillion. Then, when he had recovered his balance, he dropped down until he was sitting, as comfortable as you like, behind whoever was riding the bike. He was just about to do all that when he caught sight of a glint, like light bouncing off a tiny mirror, in the headlights. Both he and Grobbelaar knew at once what it was – the reflection from an animal's eyes. Grobbelaar slowed the car, forcing Vincent to let go of Brooke and hurl himself back inside the Mazda, fighting against his own forward momentum. But the deceleration was only temporary. As soon as Vincent was safe inside the car, Grobbelaar hit the gas in a desperate bid to catch up with Adrian Brooke.

They were now getting close to Elephant Hills. The turn-off was just around a bend, and in order to get through the gate a driver had almost to double-back on himself, turning sharply into the drive which stretched uphill to the hotel. Brooke took the corner at full tilt, wrestling his bike around the hairpin and into the drive. Grobbelaar followed, almost as fast, his tyres screaming and brakes smoking, showering dust and pebbles across the road like something from a Hollywood car-chase. Brooke was still in the lead but Grobbelaar was gaining, and both were fast approaching the barrier that guarded the entrance to Elephant Hills itself. A security guard, suddenly realizing that no one was going to stop, desperately raised the barrier (his efforts were in vain: it was smashed to pieces later that night by a hunter in a pick-up truck) and let the racers into the grounds.

Inside the Elephant Hills complex was a large, circular drive, with traffic-bumps laid across the road to enforce the 10 mph speed limit. Brooke hit the brakes and drove sedately up to the main entrance of the hotel, the winner. But Grobbelaar's legendary competitiveness would not allow him to give in. The Mazda hit the first bump at full speed and went flying into the air, before crashing down again with an ear-splitting crunch as its sump hit the tarmac. Then, and only then, did he brake, ramming the car almost on to its nose in a juddering emergency stop.

A shattered Tony Milligan staggered from the car and lasted half an hour in the casino before retiring to bed at around 12.30. The others kept going until 3.30, drinking all the while. When they met again at 6.00 for the morning round of golf, Milligan was still exhausted and Vincent was still drunk from the night before. Grobbelaar, however, looked perfectly rested and ready for action. After their round, Grobbelaar and Vincent took Milligan to see the Falls before catching the plane to Harare, where Zimbabwe's game was being played. The following day, Friday, Grobbelaar trained in the morning, shot a deodorant commercial in the afternoon, and sank half a dozen beers in the evening.

He had one more day's training, one well-behaved night in the Zimbabwe team hotel and then went out on Sunday afternoon and played a blinder in a game his team won 2–1. By now, Vincent was well aware of every aspect of Bruce Grobbelaar's life except one. And that would not stay secret for long.

# 7

## 'I See You've Met the Wild Thing'

On the very first evening they had met, Chris Vincent had been given a strong hint about his future business partner's sex life. He had called to arrange a meeting and been greeted by a breathless Bruce Grobbelaar on the other end of the line. But it was some while before Grobbelaar began to be frank with him about the state of his marriage and his affairs with other women.

During that first trip to Zimbabwe in December 1992, while he was staying at Elephant Hills, Grobbelaar mentioned an old girlfriend, now living in Bulawayo, whom he was trying to persuade to come up to Victoria Falls. She could not make it, but they did meet up in Harare on the Friday before the Zimbabwe–Egypt match. The woman in question had long, dark hair. She was small and slender but not particularly attractive, thought Vincent – certainly not a patch on Debbie.

Grobbelaar said that the woman was from *koodalah*, meaning 'a long time ago', and as they talked over lunch they touched each other's hands and faces with the gentle familiarity of two people who were once in love. Later Grobbelaar revealed the extent of their relationship. This mysterious woman – whose name he never mentioned – was not just another ex-girlfriend. She was the mother of his son, born before his marriage, a boy whose very existence was unknown even to his wife, though Grobbelaar would later discuss him on video tape.

If that was one revelation, there were more to come. In January 1993 Vincent was still in Zimbabwe, working on the property deals with Charles Davy and Neil Hewlett. He phoned Grobbelaar, who had returned to England but was due back in Harare the following day for another international. Vincent was planning to meet Grobbelaar at the airport to discuss the latest developments in the plans for Mondoro, but his friend asked, 'What are you doing tonight?'

Vincent said that he had arranged to go to a local club called Archipelago with Charles Davy and Jeremy Brooke, the businessman brother of Adrian Brooke, the late-night bike racer. 'Well,' said Grobbelaar, 'there's a friend of mine in Harare, and she's staying at the Sheraton. Can you give her a call?' Bruce went on to explain that his friend worked for British Airways and had flown all the way out to Zimbabwe to be there when he arrived. Then he added a brief word of warning. 'Be careful. This woman is wild. Her nickname is the Wild Thing.'

Vincent called the Sheraton as requested, and arranged to meet the mystery friend at 7.30. He was waiting in the foyer when he saw the lift stop at the mezzanine. A woman got out and walked – or rather glided – down the staircase that led to the ground floor. She was wearing high, high heels and a long black dress that clung to her body. Her dark hair was piled above her head. Her eyes were a clear, pale blue. 'Wow!' thought Vincent. If this was the Wild Thing, he was only too glad to have met her. They went off to Archipelago, where the Wild Thing's manners were, at first, as decorous as her appearance. 'You Zimbabwean men are so polite,' she purred, as Vincent and Brooke attended to her needs, fetching drinks and making small talk. Then Charles Davy arrived. He was a big, imposing, energetic man who saw no need to stand on ceremony. He took one look at the unexpected addition to the evening's party and declared, 'Now, this is a good-looking woman. What's your name?'

Davy would soon discover that this apparently frail female, barely half his size, was more than a match for him. But there was little indication of what was to come as the first few rounds of drinks were ordered and consumed. Then, without any warning, the Wild Thing leaped up on to a bar-stool, shook her slinkily clad body, waved her bare arms in the air . . . and let out a piercing scream. The three men gazed at their guest in wide-eyed amazement. What the hell was going on?

Before they had the time to answer the question, the Wild Thing had jumped back down to the ground, grabbed Charles Davy – who hated dancing – and led him off to the dance-floor. There she proceeded to writhe, shimmy and generally shake about, while her baffled partner did his level best to keep up. When they returned to the table some minutes later Davy was awash with sweat. His bald pate was glistening. His shirt was transparent. 'Flattie,' he gasped, 'you're not going to believe this . . . She bit me!'

Sure enough, there were deep tooth-marks across his arm where the Wild Thing, consumed by Bacchanalian passion, had attempted to take a chunk out of him. The Wild Thing said nothing. She just emptied another glass, let out a second, equally savage yell . . . and bit Chris Vincent on his cheek, drawing blood this time.

'Don't come near me!' cried Jeremy Brooke, running from the scene.

Gradually, everyone calmed down. There was more dancing and drinking until the time came to take the Wild Thing back to the Sheraton. It was now well past 3 a.m. and Grobbelaar was due in at 6.00. Vincent offered his services as a chauffeur and drove her to the hotel. But as he was parking, the Wild Thing suddenly burst into desperate sobbing. When asked what the matter was, she explained that her husband had left her. It was nothing to do with Bruce, she added. They were just good friends. They had known each other for eight years and there was nothing between them. In fact, Debbie Grobbelaar had got her a job at British Airways: she had been a hotel receptionist before that. Vincent sympathized and then – accompanied by

Charles Davy, who was also staying at the Sheraton – half escorted and half carried the Wild Thing into the lift and up to her room. Once inside, he laid her down on the bed, covered her with a blanket and rang room service to order a large pot of coffee, hoping to sober himself up enough to drive back to his parents' house, where he was staying.

He just about made it home that night, had an hour's sleep and got to Harare airport in time to greet Grobbelaar. The side of Vincent's face was bruised and bloodied from the excitement of the night before. His skin was pallid beneath its tan and his eyes were bloodshot. Grobbelaar took one look at the wrecked appearance of his friend, then laughed and said, 'I see you've met the Wild Thing.'

Grobbelaar was staying with two old family friends, Gordon and Pauline Crawford. For the first couple of nights he left the house, sneaked off to the Sheraton and crept back in before dawn, so that Pauline, who was very fond of Debbie, would not find out what he was up to. Then, to save himself the bother, he announced that he had to be at 'training camp': in reality the Wild Thing's hotel room.

Chris Vincent only found out what had been going on a couple of months later. Back in England, he had seen Grobbelaar's friend on a couple of occasions and they had got on well. Then, in March 1993, he and Grobbelaar were invited by Ken Rutland to a shooting competition outside Ashbourne in Derbyshire. (For his testimonial, Candy had given Grobbelaar a Browning double-barrelled shotgun with an inscribed nameplate, gold-inlaid hammers and triggers, in a presentation case.) Debbie Grobbelaar was away skiing at the time. Vincent left his car at the Grobbelaars' house and was driven to Ashbourne by Bruce in a new Volkswagen Golf he had recently received from a sponsor. It would be a social as well as sporting affair, with dinner and accommodation laid on afterwards, but both men had to be back early the following morning: Vincent for a Mondoro meeting and Grobbelaar for training.

The shoot went well and, once Grobbelaar and Vincent had changed, they went off to a pub for a quick drink before dinner.

Grobbelaar telephoned the Wild Thing and Vincent mentioned that he had seen her a few times for drinks. Seeing that his friend was listening with more than usual attention to what he was saying, and keen not to tread on his toes, Vincent asked him, 'Is there anything going on between you two?'

'Not really,' Grobbelaar replied. 'Why?'

'Well,' said Vincent, 'the Wild Thing and I are getting on really well. I think she's quite keen on me.'

Grobbelaar said nothing, but as they were heading back to their bed-and-breakfast that night, after a typical evening of eating and drinking that had gone on into the early hours, he asked Vincent, 'If we go to bed now, we'll have to get up again in about three hours and the last thing we'll want to do is get up and go. Why don't we just go now?'

'That's a lousy idea. We're pissed,' replied Vincent.

They got back to the b-and-b. A few minutes later, there was a knock on his bedroom door. It was Grobbelaar. 'Come on, let's go,' he hissed. 'We can leave some money and a note with a telephone number.' It was now just before 3 a.m. Grobbelaar, who was way past the alcohol limit, drove the seventy-odd miles across country to his friend's house in Huyton, Liverpool, in an hour and a quarter. Just short of Liverpool, he asked Vincent, 'Call the Wild Thing. Tell her we'll be there in fifteen minutes. And tell her to get some coffee on.'

When they arrived, Grobbelaar got out of the car as quickly as possible and crept up to the front door. Once inside, he closed every curtain. Then he walked out into the back garden and peered at the flats behind the house.

'What the bloody hell are you doing?' asked Vincent.

'Checking for photographers,' he said.

Once all the precautions had been taken, they went back indoors. Coffee was drunk and jokes were made, but it soon became all too clear to Vincent that he was not the main attraction. He spent the rest of the night in the spare room. Bruce Grobbelaar did not.

On the drive back to Heswall, the two men talked about the

Wild Thing. 'So . . . has this been going on for eight years, then?' asked Vincent.

'Yep,' Grobbelaar replied. There had, he said, been a two-year gap in the middle of the affair when he had not seen his lover, but then he caught sight of her one day at Anfield after a match. One look into those blue eyes and he was hooked again.

Once that confession had been made, the bond of trust between Grobbelaar and Vincent was sealed. From now on, Vincent would be Grobbelaar's ally and assistant in his constant sexual campaigns. He soon came to see that his friend was not alone in his activities.

Grobbelaar had an endless stream of naughty stories. Some were simply schoolboyish, like the one about the night in Hong Kong when the Liverpool team, who were on a tour of the Far East, had set up one of their best-known members with a beautiful dancer who was actually a man in drag.

'Have you checked it out?' Grobbelaar asked his deluded pal.

'What do you mean?'

'Have you checked that it's a woman?'

The player, who fancied himself as a ladies' man, was outraged. 'Of course it's a woman!'

'Are you sure?'

The player gave the dancer's crotch a grab. There was a lot more in his hand than there should have been. 'Christ!' he yelped, as the rest of the team collapsed in laddish hysteria.

Then there were the stories that Vincent witnessed for himself. On one occasion, in the winter of 1993, they met one of Bruce's famous team-mates at an Indian restaurant in Chester. The team-mate was sitting in a booth with two mini-skirted teenage girls, one blonde, the other a brunette. The girls were local students whom Grobbelaar and Vincent had met once before, dancing with Rob Jones, Michael Thomas and Mark Walters at a local night-club called Blimpers, a popular foot-ballers' hang-out. Everyone ordered curries, although Grobbelaar seemed more interested in the brunette than in his food. The other footballer, however, tucked into his portion before turning his attention to the blonde.

At the end of the evening Vincent agreed to give the blonde a lift back to her house in Christleton, a few miles outside Chester. The famous team-mate came too. When they got to the place where the girl was living, the footballer turned to Vincent and said, 'Hang on a minute.' Then he got out of the car and followed his new friend.

The house, which looked as though it had been converted into several flats, was set back from the road. A number of cars were parked on the forecourt, which was sheltered from the road by a hedge. Vincent had parked by the pavement on the far side of the hedge. He waited for a few minutes, surprised that the footballer, having walked the girl to her door, had not returned. Then, through the bushes, he saw something moving. He looked again. The girl was spread-eagled across the bonnet of a parked car. The footballer was on top of her. Their two bodies were moving up and down, rocking the car's suspension.

After a while, the movement stopped. A few seconds later, the footballer reappeared by Vincent's passenger door and got in. He smiled. 'Let's go!' he said, and Vincent drove him back to Chester. They stopped for a couple of drinks at Joe's Wine Bar, near the cathedral, where the footballer liked to park. Then they said goodbye, and the footballer got into his car and drove back to his wife and family.

If many of the husbands of Liverpool FC behaved badly, so did some of their wives. In 1993, for example, Liverpool played Manchester United at Old Trafford. After the game, Vincent and Grobbelaar went for a drink at the Four Seasons Hotel, close to Manchester airport. They had been there for a while when three women walked in. One of them in particular caught Chris Vincent's eye. She was wearing a tiny, black leather mini-skirt and thigh-high leather boots. 'Jesus!' gasped Vincent.

Grobbelaar looked across at the trio and grinned. 'I don't believe it. I know them.'

'Who are they?'

Grobbelaar pointed out the woman that had caught Vincent's fancy. 'That's ——'s wife,' he said, naming an ex-Liverpool player who had been transferred elsewhere. He and

Vincent wandered over and said hello. It transpired that the woman's husband was away, playing a match in Europe, so she and her friends were going out for a night on the town. Once they had had a few drinks, the women went off to a night-club.

'We should follow them,' said Grobbelaar.

'Why?' asked Vincent.

'Because when he's away, she likes to play. If we go now, we can take all three of them.'

On that occasion the two men stayed put. But one two-day binge which epitomized the way that Vincent and Grobbelaar lived took place in February 1994. At the beginning of the month, they had met two Virgin Atlantic stewardesses. One was blonde, the other brunette: both were very attractive. That first night had ended with all four going back to Grobbelaar's home – Debbie was away – where Bruce and the blonde stewardess spent the night together in the master bedroom.

On 14 February Liverpool played away to Southampton and lost 4–1. Chris Vincent had driven down to the south coast in Grobbelaar's Toyota Previa, which had an in-built fridge. This he stocked with champagne. After the game, John Barnes and Bruce Grobbelaar came up to London with Vincent, downing bubbly all the way, and checked into the Kensington Hilton Hotel. There Barnes sat with some friends from Jamaica, drinking rum. Grobbelaar and Vincent drank flaming canes – glasses of cane spirit that had been set alight. It was decided to head into the West End and continue the party at a Soho night-club. Barnes, Grobbelaar, Vincent and a female companion piled into a Mercedes, driven by a friend of Barnes. But they had only travelled a short distance when Barnes begged his friend to stop. But before he could get out of the car he was violently sick all over his trousers. Desperately, Barnes clambered across Chris Vincent, heaved himself out of the Mercedes and collapsed on to the pavement. It was a cold night and the streets were covered in snow, into which Barnes was now emptying the contents of his stomach. When there was nothing more to expel, he rubbed fresh snow all over his face, hoping to clean and refresh himself, then got back into the car. They drove on to Soho and the party continued until 5 a.m. – for everyone, that is, except John Barnes, who was left asleep in the back of the car.

A couple of hours after their night out had ended, Grobbelaar drove Vincent to Heathrow to catch the nine o'clock shuttle to Manchester, where he had a morning meeting. The errand run, he set off for Ashbourne, where he was a guest of honour at the annual day-long game of medieval football between the Uppards and Downards, locals who live on either side of the River Dove. Vincent met him there that afternoon, bringing the second, brunette stewardess with him. It was Grobbelaar's intention to bed her after the match, but at a lunch organized by Candy's Ken Rutland he met another equally enticing female.

By the early evening Vincent and the brunette were getting on splendidly, but Vincent still expected Grobbelaar to take her off his hands. If he was going to do that, however, he would have to make his move soon. So when the brunette departed for the Ladies, Vincent asked Grobbelaar, 'What are you going to do?'

Grobbelaar told him not to worry. 'You carry on. Ken's found a beauty for me. I'm going to give it one.'

Now that he knew Grobbelaar was catered for elsewhere, Vincent felt free to have the brunette for himself. Shortly after six the following morning, after two successive nights of hard drinking and sleep deprivation, he was awoken by Grobbelaar, who was fully dressed, packed and raring to go. He had to be back in Liverpool by 9.30. He was a professional footballer, after all, and he had to do his training.

Grobbelaar's promiscuity was indicative not just of his compulsive nature, but also of the stress and unhappiness that seemed to permeate his marriage. The worse the marriage became, the more he fooled around. The more he fooled around, the worse his marriage became. He took to referring to his wife as 'Mrs Hyena', a name taken from the Rex Tarr sketch 'Piccaninny Red Hooding-Ride'.

Often, when Debbie was away in Portugal or seeing her parents in the West Country with the girls, Grobbelaar and

Vincent would sit at Bruce's kitchen table late into the night, talking about his marriage and how he might escape it. He constantly complained that Debbie was giving him a hard time. She could no longer take a joke, he said, no matter how well-meant, and was upset with him for not spending enough time with his daughters. Yet he was adamant that he spent most afternoons in their company.

Debbie, meanwhile, was upset about the effect that football was having on their social life. Grobbelaar could not go out on Fridays, and when Liverpool were playing away from home he would always have to spend the night before the game in a team hotel (under Dalglish, Liverpool had gathered in a hotel before home games as well). After matches, he would always be off drinking with the lads. It left little time for her.

'I thought she had every right to bitch at him,' remembered Vincent, 'but it wasn't down to me to say so.'

Of course, Debbie's real complaint was her suspicion that Bruce was having affairs with other women. Grobbelaar would use Vincent as a combination of excuse and go-between. 'I must have heard Bruce make two hundred telephone calls to his wife,' Vincent later remarked, 'and I doubt if he ever once told her the truth.' On nights when he planned to see a girlfriend, for example, he would tell Debbie, 'I'm having a meeting with Chris.' So often did she hear this line that eventually, in under-standable frustration, she snapped, 'I don't know why you're not married to him instead of me.'

Grobbelaar's girlfriends, meanwhile, would be given Vincent's telephone number – frequently without his knowledge – which they could use to arrange meetings with Grobbelaar. Between the two men, each girl was given a nickname, like Octopussy (so-called because she had an octopus tattooed on one shoulder-blade), the Six-Footer or the Ice-Machine, an Irish lass who had encountered Grobbelaar by the ice-machine in a Dublin hotel before making love to him and – with the assistance of a girlfriend – several of his team-mates.

In the summer of 1993, when the Grobbelaar family came out to Zimbabwe on holiday, Chris Vincent was able to witness at close quarters the stress that Bruce and Debbie were under. That stress was made worse by Debbie's profound suspicions about her husband's involvement in Mondoro. Over lunch one day in Victoria Falls Debbie started chatting to Keith Vincent's wife, Maureen. 'I believe Bruce is putting a lot of money into the business,' said Maureen. 'But I don't know where the rest of the money is coming from.' For the rest of the afternoon Bruce was questioned by Debbie, who was upset by the extent to which he was becoming financially committed to the safari venture. She wanted to know all the details. How much money had he put into Mondoro? Why? How much more would he have to pay?

Grobbelaar was no happier than any other husband to receive a third-degree interrogation. But his wife was right to have her suspicions. And Grobbelaar's marriage would prove to be considerably more durable than his friendship with Vincent, let alone their business partnership. A sequence of events was about to begin that would cause its collapse and, eventually, spark off a national scandal. But before coming to that, a brief detour is required to tell the story of a young man of whom, at this stage in the proceedings, Chris Vincent was entirely unaware.

# 8

## The Man from 'Uncle'

Heng Suan Lim was born in Malaysia in 1965, to a family of Chinese descent. Within a few years his father left home and his mother was forced to send her son and his sister to an orphanage for six years. Mrs Lim worked hard, clearing dishes in a restaurant and taking in sewing as an extra part-time job. By the start of the eighties she had a better position as the assistant manager of a Kuala Lumpur night-club. She was able to rent a small flat and send for her children again. The young Lim was sixteen when he left the orphanage and returned to his family and a normal education at the Brickfields School in Kuala Lumpur, passing O- and A-Level examinations. He was a keen sportsman, captaining his school at football and playing for Malaysia's under-eighteen team in a youth tournament in South Korea. 'It was very, very important to me,' he would later say. 'I spent a lot of time playing football and training. Apart from school, the second thing on the list was football.'

At sixteen he joined Hongchin FC, a club that played in the football league run within the state of Selangor. By eighteen, Lim had made the Hongchin first team and was the side's youngest player: 'All the other players and members of the club were older than me. They took an interest in my studies and well-being.'

Sadly, though, he was not quite as successful academically as he had been on the sports field and he was unable to get the university place he wanted in Malaysia. Instead, he decided to come to Britain to study, arriving on 26 September 1986 and going to live in Stratford, East London. On the advice of a family friend called J. S. Lim (no relation), he enrolled at the London School of Accountancy.

As before, Lim tried to combine his academic work with football. Soon after arriving in England he visited Upton Park, home of West Ham United. He looked around, admiring a stadium that was far bigger than anything he was used to in Malaysia, and then wrote to West Ham, asking for a place on their staff as an apprentice. 'I remember introducing myself, outlining my credentials, including that I had been coached by Kevin Keegan in 1983.' But the Hammers were not impressed. On 6 November the club wrote back, regretting that they were unable to make use of his services. 'It came as a surprise that I got a reply,' Lim would later say. 'So I treasure that letter.'

He made no further attempt to sign up with any British professional club, nor did he join any semi-professional or even Sunday League outfit. But he did make commendable progress with his accountancy exams, passing the first set (of three) in December 1987. All the while he had been supported by his mother, with occasional help from his sister who had got a job as a stewardess for Cathay Pacific airlines. She would fly into London every month or two, stay with Lim and give him some money. But by now he was taking the first steps towards a more lucrative source of income.

In early 1987 Heng Suan Lim had dinner in London with his friend J. S. Lim and another man, Ong Chee Kew. The latter was a former player for Hongchin FC and had known Heng Suan since he first joined the club as a teenager. Though Heng Suan later claimed he did not know this, Mr Ong was also a crook, with connections to crime syndicates in Malaysia and Triads in Hong Kong. He had been prosecuted in Malaysia in 1986 for gambling offences: betting on football is illegal in that country. Clearly the experience had not put Ong off his activities, for at a dinner with the two Lims, at which Heng Suan's attempt to join West Ham was discussed, he said that it would be very useful if the younger man could pass on the odds that English bookmakers were quoting on FA Cup ties. Heng Suan was happy to comply.

A short while later, in April that year, Ong wrote to Heng Suan Lim, saying that, 'It was nice to hear from you . . . how is everything?' He went on to say that he was planning to come back to England. In the meantime, he had some advice: 'You must try your best to tackle Wimbledon and some other club. Make use of your time, for you can do it.' He also took up the subject of betting: 'For information like FA Cup, UEFA, they have odds in England. So get me the odds early . . . so I know how to bet in KL [Kuala Lumpur] . . . I'll keep in touch with you if you have good news which is urgent call me and I will pay for the call . . . I think we can make pounds and ringits soon.'

Lim knew that betting was illegal in Malaysia. But, he said, 'I thought he would be betting with friends. Chinese people all over the world have a passion for gambling.' And, of course, there was nothing illegal or reprehensible about betting on football matches in England provided, of course, that you were not one of the players, betting against your own side.

A short while later Ong wrote again, talking about the FA Cup Final that had just taken place between Spurs and Coventry. 'Hi . . . your letter was just in time. KL market was ½ and 1 for Spur [sic]. That mean Spur giving handicap ½ and 1 to Coventry.' He passed on some news about the Korean President's Cup, then insisted, 'Before I return to London, you must mix with some team which you think was possible. Don't make any promises to the players. Just make friends and talk about football and you must be careful. I will keep in touch with you. Wimbledon was a good team . . . God bless us. Do give me your phone number in your next letter. Say hello to baby [J. S. Lim] for me . . . If I make money in the coming tournament, I will send you some money to cover your expense . . . PS: When you want it to do something, please let me know and . . .' There followed a Chinese symbol which meant, 'Be careful.'

What exactly did Ong mean by asking his young friend to mix with some team, not make promises, just talk to players, and so on? Was he hoping that Lim could in some way influence their behaviour on the field? In court, Lim would claim, 'I think he meant [me] to mix with players to get inside information – something coming from the horse's mouth about their team. I should be careful relaying information to Mr Ong – on his side, not mine – because football betting was illegal [in Malaysia]. I was just helping him out. He was a relative of J. S. Lim, who had given me help, so I felt obliged to help him, even though I was busy with my studies. I might, or might not have written to him after this letter, but I am sure I never received any more letters from him. I never heard from him again.'

One important clue to Ong's motives lay in the references to 'KL market was ½ and 1 for Spur', etc. This apparently baffling code relates to the means by which Malaysians gamble on football, which is by a system of handicaps rather than odds. The system, later to take on a crucial significance, works as follows.

The team that is favourite to win a match is given a handicap of half a goal or more. If that handicap is 1, for example, they have to win by more than one goal in order for punters who back them to win their bets. If the game is drawn on the field, then the less-favoured side, for whose benefit the handicap is operating, have effectively won by one goal so far as the gamblers are concerned. So the punters backing them win their bets. They receive their stake back, plus an equal amount in winnings. If the favourites win by a single goal, their handicap cancels out the winning margin, so the gamblers' result is a draw. In that case, all the punters get their money back, but nobody wins anything. If the favourites win by more than one goal, then the people who have backed them collect their stake and the same again as their winnings.

A handicap of half a goal works the same way in that a drawn match on the field still means a gambling win for backers of the side getting the half-goal start. But in this case, any win by the favourites on the pitch – which will inevitably be by a whole goal or more – will result in their supporters getting a pay-out.

Sometimes, the bets can be split, a bit like an each-way bet on a horse. Half the bet is placed at one handicap, half at another. So, if Spurs are playing Coventry and 'the market is ½ and 1 for Spurs', the permutations are as follows. If Coventry win or draw the match, punters backing Coventry win their whole bets and Spurs supporters lose everything. If Spurs win by one goal, Coventry supporters lose their half-goal bet, but draw their whole-goal bet. So they get half their stake back. Spurs supporters win their half-goal bet, but only draw the whole-goal bet. So they receive all of their stake back, but only half their winnings. If Spurs win by more than one goal, Coventry supporters lose their entire stakes. Spurs supporters win both halves of the bet. In fact, the result was a surprise 3–2 victory for Coventry. So their fans won their bets, and Spurs supporters came away empty-handed, irrespective of the different handicaps.

Readers who find their heads spinning at that explanation need not be alarmed. The net effect of Lim's correspondence with Ong Chee Kew was that he had established for the first time a connection between himself in Britain and gamblers in Malaysia. He had become acquainted with the Malaysian gambling system – if he was not aware of it already – and he had learned that there was a value to information about English games, which could give gamblers in the Far East an edge over their opponents or bookies (and, by implication, give bookies an edge over their gamblers).

In 1987 Lim moved to North London, first to 30 The Avenue, Kilburn, and then on to 18 St Cuthbert's Road, also in Kilburn. While staying at the latter address he met his Irish girl-friend, later his wife, Cora. By now he was beginning to make a circle of friends among the Malay and Chinese communities in London, and with visiting Malaysians – many of them prominent businessmen, civil servants and politicians – whom he would help in any way he could. Lim would meet them at the airport, show them around London, take them to trade fairs and exhibitions, and go out with them for dinner and entertainment.

Though his sole sources of income were the monies he received from his mother and sister, plus the bits and bobs he picked up from odd jobs such as cleaning petrol stations, selling shoes and working as a cleaner in a pizza restaurant, Lim began to develop a taste for casinos. From 1988 he began going to them with friends, initially out of curiosity. Soon he began joining casinos, eventually becoming a member of virtually every significant gambling operation in London, and by 1990 he was a regular gambler in what he would later describe as 'a large and reckless way'. He would go out three or four nights a week. If he had associates in town for, say, ten days: 'It is possible that we would be in the casinos for seven or eight nights on the trot.' His stakes were 'sometimes £3,000, sometimes £7,000 a night'.

By then, though, he had a new and extremely significant cash supply. It came from a friend of his mother's, a wealthy Indonesian businessman called Johannes Joseph, with whom she shared a birthday. They had met in the early eighties at the night-club at which Mrs Lim was working. Heng Suan Lim had heard of Mr Joseph before coming to England but had never spoken to him until 1989, when he received a phone call from him. Joseph told the young man that he, too, had plans to send his children overseas for their studies. They had a number of telephone conversations.

'He told me that he knew my mother and knew that we were not wealthy,' said Lim. 'He said he would send me money from time to time to cover the cost of my studies. On the one hand, I was very pleased. But on the other, I was a bit sceptical because I did not know him well. I asked: is it fair to burden you with this responsibility? The standard of living in England is not cheap. He said, "Don't worry. It would be a help for your mother to know I am supporting you."'

Joseph's first cash transfer to Lim, a sum of just under £500, was made on 31 March 1989. For the rest of the year he continued to give Lim modest amounts ranging from £300 to £1,000, which totalled £6,500. He helped Lim's sister, too, buying her a home. During the first nine months of 1990 the payments to Lim continued, averaging about £1,100 per month. Sometimes the money would come directly from Mr Joseph, but on other occasions it would be routed through the Bank of Central Asia, or be sent by associates of Mr Joseph, one of whom was called Suwandi Lukito; but Joseph was always the ultimate source. At this stage there was no apparent connection between any of this money and football, let alone football gambling. For example, on 7 July 1990, when no football had been played in England for the best part of six weeks, Lim received £2,600. But it was at about that time he first encountered a man who had a great deal to do with the game: John Fashanu.

They met, they later claimed, at a shop in London. Lim was wearing a football top. Fashanu, who then had the franchise for Admiral sportswear in Nigeria, was interested in the shirt: he wanted to know what the emblem on it was, and where Lim had bought it. They started a conversation and Fashanu invited Lim to come and meet him at his office in St John's Wood – he was interested, he said, in expanding Admiral's activities into the Far East, too. At that meeting the two men discovered they had something in common – their childhood experience of life in an orphanage. From that point on they were not just business associates but close friends.

By now, Lim was known to his British friends by a name that was easier for them to remember and understand than Heng Suan. They called him Richard, a nickname he had first acquired playing football in Malaysia, apparently because he was so lion-hearted. Fashanu used to tease him about being a Chinaman with an English name. He would refer to Lim as Richie Rich or Mikey Mike. Lim, meanwhile, had his own name for his benefactor, Johannes Joseph. He called him 'uncle'.

The two men met for the first time when Joseph came to

London on 23 August 1990 for a week. The Indonesian, who was then forty-six, had flown to London alone, without his wife Elli. Mrs Lim was in town too, at Joseph's suggestion. 'He knew my mother missed me,' Lim explained. 'She had not seen me since 1986. When they were in London, Mr Joseph took care of bills, meals and shopping. From the conversations we had had before, I knew he was into businesses, but I did not appreciate how wealthy he was until I met him. Everything he wanted had got to be the best. He was a multi-millionaire. He was staying at the Hilton Park Lane, but he spent most of the time at my flat, because my mother was staying with me.' His mother, said Lim, was only too glad of the assistance he was receiving from her friend. 'It made my mother feel happier, not to be worried about me. He was relieving her of a burden.'

Until this point, Mr Joseph had purely been playing the role of a benefactor. But during this trip to London he suggested that Lim might do a small favour for him. He was, he explained, something of a gambler. Despite his European-sounding name he was actually of Chinese descent, and shared his countrymen's love of a bet. At that point, Lim was uncertain if gambling was illegal in Indonesia as well as Malaysia. But he could not see any harm in what Joseph was doing: 'He was only betting with friends and associates, not bookmakers. As I understand, he has lots of friends. Sometimes they would call up and ask if he wanted to bet on games. They would bet against each other – it's a hobby. Not just on football: boxing and tennis, too.'

What Joseph wanted was the same as Mr Ong: information. He suggested that Lim could keep track of the odds being offered on English matches and then pass them on to him. He was also interested in the team news that was released via Teletext and Ceefax: if he knew that a star player was likely to be injured, or was returning to a team after a lay-off, that would give him an edge. In short, what he was suggesting was that Lim should become a tipster. And if the tips turned out to be good ones, he would be happy to pay for them.

This was no trouble at all. Lim had retained his love of

football, sometimes playing park games with his fellow accountancy students, and keeping a close watch on everything that went on in the First Division, as it was then. 'I enjoyed English football, so providing information came naturally to me. It didn't take any extra effort to accommodate Mr Joseph's request.'

A regular system soon emerged. Joseph would send Lim the handicaps being offered in the Far East on forthcoming English matches. Lim would then compare them with the London odds, factor in any news that had emerged about players or teams, and then suggest three, four or five forecasts. He became aware that the friendly bets which his benefactor was placing were, by any normal standards, very substantial indeed. 'He would bet £15,000 per game. But if I had a good feeling about a game, I would tell him to bet more – maybe £25,000–30,000.' The sums of money flowing into Lim's account quickly started to rocket. In 1991 he received £148,000 from Mr Joseph. Of this, he would later explain, some £25,000–28,000 was passed on to a friend of Mr Joseph, who was staying in London. But be that as it may, at the age of twenty-six, while still an unqualified accountancy student, Heng Suan 'Richard' Lim was suddenly rolling in cash.

His friend John Fashanu would soon be reaping the rewards of a friendship with Johannes Joseph, too. In January, February and March 1991, Joseph visited London again. On the third occasion, between 21 and 25 March, he stayed in room 533 at the Dorchester Hotel. There he was troubled by serious toothache. Joseph needed a dentist fast, so he turned for help to his young protégé. Lim, in his turn, called his friend John Fashanu, who at once arranged an appointment for Joseph with his own dentist in Harley Street. The problem was quickly solved and, grateful for his help, Joseph invited Fashanu to dinner at the Dorchester. The two men got on well, despite the fact that Joseph spoke very little English. But Lim was able to act as an interpreter and it rapidly became clear that the entre-preneurial John Fashanu and the wealthy Johannes Joseph had many potential business interests in common. Lim would later claim that Joseph was – among other things – a commodity broker, trading in cocoa. Conveniently, Fashanu had recently started dating a beautiful student called Melissa Kassa-Mapsi, whose enormously wealthy family included many senior politicians from countries such as the Ivory Coast, the world's largest supplier of cocoa beans.

No written evidence of any business transaction between Joseph and Fashanu has ever been produced. But six months later, on 4 September 1991, in the early weeks of the 1991–2 football season, Joseph paid £12,000 to Miss Kassa-Mapsi's bank account. She then passed the money on, in cash, to John Fashanu. That same day, Joseph paid Richard Lim £9,000.

As 1992 began, a similar pattern of simultaneous payments emerged. On 21 January, Joseph paid £10,500 to Kassa-Mapsi (£10,000 of which was transferred on 29 January to the account of Fashanu's company, Fash Enterprises) and £13,000 to Lim. On 17 March, £13,000 went to Kassa-Mapsi and £2,500 to Lim. The money kept coming right through the year, irrespective of whether football was being played or not, although the size of payments did diminish in the close season. Lim, for example, received £10,000 in June 1992, £3,500 in July and £1,500 in August.

In total, Lim received £158,000 from Johannes Joseph in 1992. Of that, he said, £36,000 – received on 6 October – had been given to him to pay off the mortgage on a new flat he had bought that July in Kingscroft Road (although he actually spent the money at the gaming tables). He and his girlfriend Cora had become engaged that spring and finally married in November: Joseph gave Cora some £15,000 as a wedding present. But even allowing for those two deductions, he still received £107,000 from his Indonesian 'uncle'.

For his part, Fashanu was sent a total for the year of £94,500. Interestingly, the money – none of which was accompanied by any form of documentation indicating its commercial purpose – was all initially placed in accounts which did not bear Fashanu's name. Some £34,500 went to Miss Kassa-Mapsi's account. A further £40,000 went to an account in the name of Aloo (a female cousin of Fashanu's), controlled by

Fash. And £20,000 went to an account in the name of Peter Buckle, which had been set up by Fashanu at the National Westminster Bank. He told the bank that he had been advised to use a false name in order to protect his affairs from media intrusion. Peter Buckell was in fact a former business associate of Fashanu, who had worked as his agent when Fashanu was still at Norwich. He had no knowledge at all of the account that had been set up – as a number of telephone accounts had been, also – in a mis-spelled form of his name.

So what did Fashanu do with his money? None was ever invested in cocoa. But he spent an awful lot of it on cars. In 1991 he bought two Mercedes, a C-registration model costing £13,600, bought on 4 September, and a much smarter J-registration car – then brand-new – costing £48,500, which he purchased on 1 October. The cars were originally paid for by finance agreements, drawn up with Lombard North Central and payable by monthly instalments. In fact, they were both entirely paid off by the end of 1992. And £44,000 of the money used to pay for the cars was directly traceable from Fashanu's company Fash Enterprises, via Melissa Kassa-Mapsi, to Johannes Joseph. No tax had been paid on any of the money.

By the end of 1992, then, Heng Suan 'Richard' Lim had received roughly £300,000 from the Far East in the space of three years, and John Fashanu had received the best part of £100,000. But what had any of this to do with Chris Vincent and Bruce Grobbelaar? Up to November that year, nothing at all. But the connection was just about to be made.

For at the beginning of that month, Bruce Grobbelaar had a meeting with John Fashanu at the latter's penthouse flat. Richard Lim was present. Exactly what was said at the meeting would later become a matter of considerable controversy. It was Chris Vincent's consistent testimony that he was completely unaware of any meeting at all until several months later, in the summer of 1993, shortly after that disappointing trip with the Grobbelaar family to Zimbabwe. But then all was made clear . . .

# 9

## Enter the Short Man

The Liverpool Football Club to which Bruce Grobbelaar returned for pre-season training in July 1993 was no longer the all-conquering force of days gone by. They had last won the league title in 1990, their tenth championship in fifteen years, but that victory marked the end of the club's glory days. Kenny Dalglish had resigned as manager in February 1991 after a 4–4 draw with Everton.

Liverpool approached their former captain, Graeme Souness, to take his place. Like Dalglish, Souness was a Scot. As a player, he had possessed a rare combination of delicate skill and fearsome physical intensity. His tackles could be terrifyingly destructive. Frank Worthington, the former England striker, called him 'the dirtiest footballer of his generation', and Souness seemed to revel in the unpopularity that his ruthless determination provoked. In 1985 he published an auto-biography, *No Half Measures*. Its first words were, 'Being successful has always been more important to me than being popular.' The final sentences ran, 'I have a cupboard full of trophies and scarcely a friend on the terraces or in the dressing-rooms. Not that it bothers me.'

Nor did it bother anyone else – as long as he kept winning. At Liverpool, he had captained the team to league titles and

European Cups. As a manager, at Glasgow Rangers he had helped transform a shabby run-down giant of a club into the overwhelmingly dominant force in Scottish football, which would – under Souness and his successor Walter Smith – win nine successive Premier League titles, playing in a brand-new stadium packed with 44,000 fans. So powerful was Souness's position at Rangers, where he was also a major shareholder, that he refused Liverpool's first job offers. But in April 1991 he relented and signed a five-year contract.

Souness did not like what he found on his arrival at Liverpool. He thought the team had become lazy, that players cared more for their pay packets and the prospect of a lucrative transfer than they did for the club. A fitness fanatic who had acquired the habit of disciplined drinking and diet while playing for Sampdoria in Italy, he despised the slackness of Liverpool's training regimes and the self-indulgence of the players. And in principle he was absolutely right. The beginning of the 1990s saw a revolution in the physical demands made on footballers. The English game – smug, complacent and convinced that, if nothing else, the domestic footballer was fitter than his continental counterparts – lagged way behind its competitors abroad. Meanwhile, the stars of other sports regarded the prehistoric training methods employed by most football clubs with a mixture of amazement and contempt. British athletes and rugby players – both league and union – were at least a decade ahead of footballers in their methods of physical preparation.

Souness knew this, and he wanted his players to change their ways. Had he approached the subject tactfully, stressing the benefits to them of a new approach, he might have succeeded. But that was not his way. As the Danish international Glenn Hysen, who had skippered Liverpool under Dalglish, recalled in 1992, 'Things went wrong when Souness arrived in the spring of 1991. The atmosphere turned sour and insecurity spread. As a person, Souness is incredibly arrogant. You could never have a joke with him. There was no small talk with the players – not even about football. We were told we had to change our eating habits. No more fried food and hamburgers, but more pasta and salad. And, of course, less beer. Now I can accept that some players did drink too much . . . and a certain number of the lads ate too many fry-ups. But he could have changed things in a way which didn't destroy the spirit of the team.'

It was almost as if Souness were daring people to dislike him, and the fact that Grobbelaar had once been his Liverpool room-mate did not exclude him from the treatment dished out to everyone else.

Their conflict began at the very start of the 1992–3 season, soon after Grobbelaar had met Chris Vincent. Despite his status among the Zimbabwean people, Grobbelaar had been out of favour with the country's government. He had lost his Zimbabwean passport and been barred from playing for the national team. But when Reinhard Fabish was made the national coach, he insisted on having Grobbelaar back in the side. In a deal brokered by Canaan Banana, the first President of Zimbabwe, who was now head of the Zimbabwe FA, Grobbelaar's passport and team place were both reinstated. But he was only given two weeks' notice of his first international match.

Souness was furious. It was the start of a vital season. His first few months in charge of the club had ended with Liverpool winning the FA Cup. But their league form had been unimpressive, and the obvious instability within the team had left both fans and media needing to be convinced. To make matters worse, Souness had undergone a triple heart-bypass operation in April 1992. He had then sold the story of his health problems, along with a picture of him kissing his beautiful blonde girlfriend Karen Levy, to the *Sun*, a paper hated on Merseyside ever since it had claimed that Liverpool fans had stolen from the bodies of the dead at Hillsborough. The picture appeared on the *Sun*'s front page on the third anniversary of the disaster – a day when the Liverpool team were attending a memorial service for the dead. It was, by any standards, an act of crass tactlessness.

With all these troubles behind him, Souness was determined

to get off to a good start in the new season. And that would hardly be helped if his goalkeeper was absent in Africa. Grobbelaar stood his ground. 'If you were selected for Scotland,' he argued, 'who would you play for – Liverpool or Scotland?'

In the end, Souness had no option but to let Grobbelaar go to Zimbabwe. But he made his feelings clear by dropping him from the first team. For the first eleven games of the season Grobbelaar's place in goal went to David James, whom Souness had signed from Watford for more than £1 million. Bruce Grobbelaar, the first-choice goalie for more than a decade, could only sit and watch while he was replaced – just as he had replaced Ray Clemence eleven years beforehand. When Souness loaned him out to Stoke City early in 1993 it merely served to underline his reduced status. In the end, Grobbelaar was called back to the first team – his recall occurred unexpectedly on the morning after the April Fool's Day golf tournament at the Belfry, so he turned up for his first training session exhausted and nursing a hangover. But he must have felt like a relic of days gone by amidst the flurry of transfer activity in which Graeme Souness indulged.

By the end of the 1992–3 season he had spent £14 million on players – a figure that would eventually rise to £21.5 million by January 1994 – while off-loading stars like Peter Beardsley and Steve Staunton. Many of Souness's signings – notably Paul Stewart, an attacking midfielder acquired from Spurs – failed to make any impression at Anfield, while those that had gone were immediate hits at their new clubs. For Grobbelaar, the crucial issue was not who was coming or going, but how much they were paid. Players like Welsh striker Dean Saunders, who cost £2.9 million, were being paid up to £6,000 per week, which was far more generous than anything previously seen at Anfield. Meanwhile Grobbelaar, who had earned around £160,000 in the 1990–1 season, had actually seen his income reduced over the next two years. In the 1991–2 season, he was Liverpool's eighth best-paid player. In 1992–3 he was the eleventh. And in 1993–4, though his actual income returned to its 1990 high, his position in the club's salary ranking slipped to thirteenth. This was a slap in the face to a man who had served Liverpool for so long. To make it worse, John Barnes and Ian Rush had both had their contracts renegotiated to bring them in line with, or even ahead of, the newcomers' pay packets. Barnes was now said to be earning £9,000 per week – three times more than his old friend and team-mate Grobbelaar.

It was no secret around the club that team spirit was suffering. At one match, Grobbelaar allegedly told Vincent, the team had gone in at half-time trailing by a goal to nil. Souness, who was notorious for his half-time rages during which tea-cups would be sent hurtling across the dressing-room, started criticizing Grobbelaar for conceding the goal. The keeper was not amused. As far as he was concerned, the problem lay as much with the forwards, who had missed a series of easy chances. Pointing across the room at Dean Saunders, he shouted, 'I'm getting two-and-a-half grand a week. You paid three million for that bugger there, and he can't hit an open goal from three feet! So don't shit on me.'

For all his protests, he knew that his days as the dominant force in Liverpool's goal were numbered. Not only was David James pressing for his place, but Souness had also expressed an interest in buying the Southampton and England goalkeeper Tim Flowers. Both men were a decade or more younger than he was. Liverpool were treating Grobbelaar like a man betraying the wife who had given him the best years of her life – going behind his back in search of someone younger and, in footballing terms, sexier to play with. A bit like he was treating Debbie, in fact.

There were times, shooting the breeze over a few spook 'n' diesels at Harkers, when Grobbelaar and Vincent would joke that maybe sex would be one way of putting one over on Souness. The Liverpool players, like all footballers, made endless locker-room boasts about the top models they had supposedly slept with. Well, the lovely Karen Levy, Souness's girlfriend, was a former beauty queen, Bond girl and game-show hostess who was now working as a model. When the time came for Mondoro to put together its brochure, why not hire her to be draped decoratively around Mondoro's camp-site and then, in the romantic glow of some African twilight, seduce her? That would teach him. Or, better yet, why not invite Souness himself out on safari and ensure that he was confronted, at the closest possible range, with a charging elephant or raging lion? Souness would then be – literally, if unfeasibly – scared to death. 'The guy's ticker couldn't take it,' Grobbelaar would chortle. 'He's got a pacemaker.'

Alcohol-fuelled jokes about crazy pranks were one way of easing the tension, but with every week that passed Grobbelaar's frustration was growing, and his dissatisfaction was becoming public knowledge. On 18 September 1993 he slapped his team-mate Steve McManaman in the face after he had made a defensive error in a game against Everton. Here were players coming to blows in full view of the crowd, and everyone watching on TV. Liverpool had lost that game – their fourth defeat in five matches – and cries of 'Souness out!' were ringing out across the Kop. The fans had been unhappy with the manager since the *Sun* front-page incident. In December 1992 a newspaper poll – in the *Sun*, ironically – showed 80 per cent of Liverpool fans wanting Alan Hansen to take over from Souness. At the end of the 1992–3 season, which had ended with Liverpool failing to qualify for Europe for the first time in twenty-eight years, the press had predicted his imminent departure and he had only just survived a boardroom vote of confidence.

So when Liverpool gathered to prepare for the 1993–4 season the fault-lines within the team, and within the club as a whole, were increasingly obvious and increasingly the topic of public debate. What Grobbelaar told Vincent next, however, was a much more private matter – one that would not be revealed to any of his fellow players. One day Vincent was giving Grobbelaar a lift, near his Heswall home, when Grobbelaar mentioned that he had been approached by John Fashanu. The Wimbledon player had suggested that he might want to give professional advice to gamblers from the Far East.

They were looking for inside information on English football, and they were prepared to pay handsomely for it. All Grobbelaar had to do was to predict the likely outcome of four or five league games every week, and they would pay him a weekly retainer of between £1,500 and £2,000.

In later conversations, Grobbelaar would tell Vincent that he and Fashanu had met at the latter's London office to discuss their deal. He gave awe-struck descriptions of Fashanu's penthouse flat, located above his St John's Wood offices, which was filled with expensive furniture. 'That place is unreal,' Grobbelaar said, deeply impressed by Fashanu's success as a businessman, which he wanted to emulate. He had a deep respect for Fashanu the footballer, too, and once told Vincent, 'He scares the living shit out of our backs. They won't stand up to him.' Fashanu was physically and mentally rock-hard. Even Grobbelaar, who never lacked courage, hated having to dive at his feet. Fashanu was equally impressed by Grobbelaar's goalkeeping. More importantly, as Grobbelaar told Vincent when the latter asked why he had been approached, 'Fash says it's because I'm an African.'

Subsequent investigation of phone records would reveal that Grobbelaar had actually spoken to Heng Suan 'Richard' Lim for the first time on 5 November 1992. Lim had also been present at a meeting between Grobbelaar and Fashanu on the following day at Fash's penthouse, during, or shortly after which the subject of forecasting was first mentioned to Grobbelaar. If he was only now telling Vincent, it may have had less to do with his relationship with Fashanu or Lim than a decision that Vincent was a man he could trust. In the short term, at least, his faith would prove well justified.

'Sounds good,' said Vincent, who could see nothing wrong with the deal. It was not clear to him whether his friend would be acting for bookmakers, helping them get the odds right, or for punters, picking out the best bets. Either way, though, Grobbelaar was going to be paid for his undoubted expertise, just like a racing tipster, or a newspaper columnist advising readers about which way to bet on the football pools. Where was the problem with that?

For a few weeks after that initial discussion, there was little said about the Malaysians or John Fashanu. From time to time, when they talked on the phone, Vincent would ask Grobbelaar if he had yet been paid, but – so far as Vincent, at least, was concerned – Lim did not make an appearance until 30 September 1993. That date was one of six that would later be the subject of bitter courtroom dispute over exactly what was said and done. For now, though, here are the agreed facts of the matter.

After training that day, Grobbelaar stayed on at the Melwood training ground to be interviewed by a TV reporter, Karen Bishop, who was making a documentary about the Hillsborough stadium disaster. The filming took place about 3 p.m., and during that time Grobbelaar made two telephone calls to the offices in Bridge Street, Chester, where Chris Vincent was working. At around 3.30 Grobbelaar arrived at those offices to pick up Vincent and they drove off towards Manchester airport, via the M56.

At first, conversation centred on Karen Bishop. She had studied zoology at Oxford University. After graduating, she had gone on an expedition to South America, helping to make a film of the trip. That experience had diverted her career into television. On hearing about her interest in wildlife, Grobbelaar had mentioned Mondoro. In their budget proposals Vincent and Wundke had set aside £40,000 to make a promotional video which would show the making of the camp, the capture and transport of game for their reserve and the wonders of the surrounding scenery. Karen Bishop seemed like just the woman for the job. There and then, Vincent called her on the mobile phone and talked about the project. Bishop was very interested. They agreed to meet within the next couple of days.

They made for the Hilton Hotel on the periphery of the airport complex. In the lobby, a TV monitor gave the arrival times of incoming planes. There was a flight from Heathrow due in at 4.20. 'That must be the one,' said Grobbelaar. He was due to meet Richard Lim.

Soon Vincent saw a short, stocky young man of Chinese appearance, in a smart leather jacket, arrive in the lobby. His short hair was neatly brushed and he gave every impression of being affluent and respectable. On 28 September Lim's Barclays Bank account had received money from Johannes Joseph. On the 30th itself a further £11,500 cash had been credited to his account, source unknown. Now he was about to pass some of his money on. For when Grobbelaar, having had a private meeting with him, joined Vincent again and began driving back to Chester, he was carrying £1,000 in cash.

At 5.20 p.m., around the time that Vincent and Grobbelaar were leaving the airport, Lim's mobile phone made two attempts to call John Fashanu. Ten minutes later Fashanu called the Republican National Bank in Geneva, where he had a bank account. At 5.35, Lim called a number in Indonesia.

Grobbelaar never told Vincent what his Asian associate was called. Instead, according to Vincent, he referred to him as 'the Short Man', a reference to the lack of height which, both he and Vincent agreed, was characteristic of Far Eastern men. Over the weeks that followed the Manchester airport meeting, Vincent recalled that he and Grobbelaar talked on the telephone daily, and saw each other four or five times a week. Grobbelaar, he claimed, would come to Bridge Street in the afternoons and call the Short Man from the office, talking about matters related to football.

It is beyond dispute that a number of calls were made between the people linked with the Malaysian gamblers and their match-forecasting operation. On 1 October John Fashanu called Grobbelaar, having previously spoken to Lim. On the following day, Grobbelaar called Lim. On the 3rd, Lim called John Fashanu and his Indonesian contacts, whom he called again on the 4th prior to calling Bruce Grobbelaar.

On 6 October 1993, Bruce Grobbelaar's thirty-sixth birthday, he flew out to Zimbabwe from Heathrow for an international match. This was the second of the six crucial dates, according to Vincent's later allegations. For the time being, though, these are the facts which are agreed on all sides.

On the way down to the airport, Grobbelaar and Vincent stopped off in Wokingham to meet a businessman called Tony Taberer, owner of the Leopard Rock Hotel – arguably the finest in Zimbabwe – with whom they wanted to set up a joint marketing operation. While Tony Milligan sat in their hired Ford Fiesta, Grobbelaar and Vincent drank coffee and talked to Taberer.

Grobbelaar was booked to fly on a World Traveller economy ticket. So he got in touch with a contact at BA, who promised to make sure that he was upgraded. Thanks to another pal, Alan Jones, a marketing manager at Trust House Forte, Grobbelaar also arranged for free rooms at a Forte hotel near the airport. He would rest there before his flight, and Vincent and Milligan would stay overnight. A table had been reserved at a Chinese restaurant in another nearby hotel. Jones, Grobbelaar and his party, and a representative from Lucozade, who were looking to set up a sponsorship deal, would all have dinner there prior to Grobbelaar's 9.45 flight.

At 4.10 p.m., having reached the Forte hotel, Grobbelaar used Vincent's mobile phone to call Lim, and the two men spoke again when Lim rang Grobbelaar at 7.58. The latter then asked Vincent to drive him to Terminal 4, where his plane was due to depart. It was, perhaps, an unexpected choice of chauffeur, since Tony Milligan was his usual driver and Vincent, as his fellow diners would later agree, had been drinking steadily all afternoon and evening.

As always, Grobbelaar cut his timing as tight as possible. He and Vincent were late leaving dinner, and by the time they got to the terminal the flight was just about to board. In the rush Vincent left the car right outside the terminal entrance, despite the signs warning drivers that this was an absolute no-parking zone and cars would be towed away. Grobbelaar then grabbed his bags from the boot, which was also stuffed with the Zimbabwe team's entire allocation of team-strips, tracksuits and other assorted kit. Grobbelaar had picked it up from the British manufacturers Umbro and was having it flown out for free by Air Zimbabwe. The two men then dashed into the terminal, leaving Grobbelaar's hat, with its distinctive zebra-skin band, forgotten in the boot behind them.

They went up to a check-in counter. The girl behind the desk said, 'Hang on, we've got a VIP tag on this ticket,' and called the duty manager. The man arrived and took Grobbelaar to another desk, where the computer was started up and a First Class boarding pass issued. Before he made his way to his flight – which had, thankfully, been delayed – Grobbelaar needed to return to the car to get his hat. Vincent followed him out of the terminal.

The sight that greeted them came as a total shock. A police car was pulled up behind the Fiesta. Inside it was a cop, talking on his radio. Another officer was standing by the car, taking down details of its tax and registration. Across the way, a fire engine was on stand-by. Vincent's first reaction was that some-one had broken into the car. Within seconds, though, he realized what was really going on: as far as the security forces at Heathrow were concerned, his hire-car could contain an IRA bomb. His trained soldier's eyes picked out more police – armed ones – waiting in the background, well enough hidden to avoid alarming the public, but ready to move at a second's notice.

Grobbelaar – still mellow from the alcohol he had consumed over dinner – seemed entirely unconcerned by the presence of the policemen, and laughed and joked in an attempt to ease the situation. But the police were signally unimpressed.

'It's my car,' said Vincent, 'I'm just dropping him off.'

Grobbelaar explained who he was.

'I don't care who you are,' said one of the policemen. 'I'm giving you a ticket.'

Grobbelaar opened the boot, took out his hat and proceeded back into the terminal. Vincent returned to the dinner party and spent the night at the Forte hotel.

Grobbelaar was not the only man on the move. On 8 October, Richard Lim flew to Malaysia, travelling on to Indonesia on the 12th, before returning to Heathrow on the 14th. Over the next few weeks he made little or no attempt to call Bruce Grobbelaar, who, for his part, made no more calls to Lim in October, and only eight attempts to contact him in the whole of November.

The two men, however, continued to have a mutual friend and link in John Fashanu. On 5 November, for example, Grobbelaar made four failed attempts to contact Fashanu before getting through to him at the Hampstead home of his then girlfriend, Alexandra Williams, and speaking for five minutes. That evening Fashanu spoke to Lim. He also made two more calls to Grobbelaar's home.

Two weeks went by. Grobbelaar and Vincent continued making plans for Mondoro, visiting the World Travel Market in London in mid-November. On 18 November, Grobbelaar called Fashanu. The following day Fashanu called Lim, and Grobbelaar called Fashanu once more. And then, on 21 November 1993, Liverpool played Newcastle United at their home ground, St James's Park. This is key date number three.

Liverpool's defence had been hit by injuries. The young and inexperienced Dominic Matteo was playing at left-back, in place of Steve Nicol. Another first-team player, Mark Wright, was out, forcing Souness to play the poorly regarded Torben Piechnik in his place. Newcastle, on the other hand, had a full-strength line-up, and although the team were new to the top division, their manager Kevin Keegan had them playing with real flair and penetration.

Grobbelaar's old Liverpool team-mate, Peter Beardsley, was the creative heart of the side. Transferred by both Liverpool and Everton, whose managers had assumed his best days were behind him, the return to his home-town team had given his career an unexpected Indian summer. Alongside him was Andy Cole, then a young striker who had begun the season as a virtual unknown. Having failed to make the grade at Arsenal, he had moved to Newcastle and made an immediate impression as a wonderfully swift athlete and an instinctive goal-scorer who seemed guaranteed to hit the back of the net every time he took to the field. Together, he and Beardsley were as fine a striking partnership as English football had seen in the past decade.

On Saturday 20 November, Grobbelaar boarded the

Liverpool coach for the trip to Newcastle where the team were staying overnight before the match, which kicked off at 4 p.m. on Sunday. Afterwards, as was his usual habit, Grobbelaar would not return with the rest of his team-mates on the coach, which he hated, but would be driven back to Heswall by the ever-loyal Tony Milligan. Grobbelaar made no secret of the fact that he disliked waiting around for the coach to leave and then sitting on it for hours. Since he was the team's senior pro, and since Graeme Souness was equally keen on travelling home from games in his own Mercedes, no formal objection was raised.

On the evening of the 20th, unknown to Vincent, Grobbelaar made two attempts to speak to Richard Lim from the team hotel, at 3.22 p.m. and 7.05 p.m. He got through to Lim's number for three and a half minutes on the second occasion.

The following afternoon, the fans at St James's Park and millions more watching live on Sky Sports saw Liverpool taken apart by a brilliant first-half display from Newcastle. Brimming with confidence, playing with no thought for anything but attack, Newcastle were a goal up within the first five minutes. Robert Lee, racing down the left wing, fired a cross into the Liverpool penalty area. The ball was brilliantly placed – behind the last Liverpool defender, but too far out for Grobbelaar to come and collect. Andy Cole needed no further invitation: he dashed on to the ball and slammed it into the net past a helplessly diving Grobbelaar.

Before the first half-hour was up Cole would score twice more, both times from crosses. Grobbelaar stood no chance with any of the three goals. By the time he was able to pull off a dazzling save, throwing himself low to his right to get a hand to a shot from Scott Sellars, it was too late to save his team. In the end, a slight hamstring strain forced Grobbelaar to leave the field before the final whistle. But, ever the sportsman, he went over to Andy Cole at the end of the game and raised his opponent's hand in triumph, as if acknowledging to the crowd that he had been beaten fair and square. ·

The game ended at 5.50 p.m. Over the following hour,

Vincent made a number of attempts to reach Grobbelaar on his mobile phone. Grobbelaar was himself trying to contact Lim, making two attempts to get through to him at around 6.40 p.m. Four minutes later he called Chris Vincent's mobile. He rang him again at 9.45, by which time he was near Kendal in Cumbria, driving south towards Merseyside on the M6. Meanwhile Fashanu, too, had been trying to speak to the Malaysian, calling his home at 8.14 and then getting through to him on his mobile four minutes later.

On the following day, Monday, Grobbelaar spent part of the morning on the phone. At 8.50 a.m. he called one of Fashanu's contact numbers, leaving a message at his office in St John's Wood. Fashanu later returned the call. Grobbelaar then called Vincent's mobile phone and at 11.13 got in touch with Rathbone's, the firm of accountants who administered his testimonial fund. With these chores out of the way, he went to Manchester airport and flew to Heathrow before driving down to the Royal Mid-Surrey golf club for a relaxing round of late autumn golf.

# 10

## A Meeting at Byron Drive

It was Bruce Grobbelaar's habit to call Chris Vincent every morning on his way to training. The two men spoke on both 23 and 24 November, discussing among other things the possibility that they might travel down to London together later that week. On the 24th, Grobbelaar spoke to Rathbone's again and called Richard Lim, who had himself made seven calls that day to John Fashanu. For his part, Fashanu called an associate of Johannes Joseph called Lo Bon Swe – his first recorded call to anyone in Indonesia. The following day, the 25th, was the fourth – and in some ways the most important – of the six dates that are crucial to Chris Vincent's story.

That morning, after a flurry of telephone contacts, Grobbelaar and Vincent drove to Manchester airport, where Grobbelaar bought a Manchester–London Shuttle ticket, using a credit card and registering Vincent as 'A. Brooke'. There was nothing sinister about this subterfuge. Both men knew that Debbie Grobbelaar was deeply suspicious of Chris Vincent and of her husband's social and business relationship with him. Both men wanted to ensure that if she happened to see Bruce's card statement, and checked with friends at British Airways, she would not know that he had been travelling with Vincent. Grobbelaar had no desire to provoke a ticking-off from his wife.

In the Shuttle lounge, he and Vincent encountered two good-looking British Airways stewardesses and had a friendly, flirtatious chat with them. Then they boarded the plane for the hour-long flight. At 11.59, having landed at Heathrow, they hired a small Ford from Hertz and set off for Central London. At 12.04 Grobbelaar called Richard Lim. The connection must have been broken because he called again at 12.06. At 12.08 Lim called Fashanu's number at his girlfriend Alexandra Williams' house, using his mobile. At approximately 12.10 he paid in £22,000 to the Kilburn branch of the Leeds Building Society. At 12.16 he called Lo Bon Swe in Indonesia.

Grobbelaar's main concern, meanwhile, was finding his way to Fashanu's headquarters in Wellington Road, just by Lord's cricket ground. After a few detours and misdirections, the stands came into view. Grobbelaar and Vincent knew they were getting close, and a few seconds later they saw their destination – a red-brick office building with a revolving front door and a garage on the ground floor. 'Warm Seas' was written across the façade. At 1.25 p.m. Grobbelaar called Fashanu's office to say that he was on the way up.

He was informed that Fashanu was not at work that day. But Fash's business associate Glynn 'Mace' Mason came down to meet the two men and told them to follow him. Mace got into a waiting Mercedes 190 and led the way northwards up the Finchley Road. At 1.37 he called John Fashanu, presumably to say, 'We're on the way.' They drove through Hampstead and then round the top of Hampstead Heath before turning into The Bishops Avenue, probably the single most expensive street of housing in Britain. The two cars passed enormous multi-million-pound mansions, reserved for super-rich tycoons and Arabian princelings, before turning left into Byron Drive, a small side street but lined with equally palatial homes.

Fashanu was living with Alexandra Williams at No. 7 Byron Drive, a modern, brick-built mansion with a front door set behind a columned portico. It belonged to her Nigerian husband, Chief S. B. Williams. In the garage Vincent could see a large Mercedes and a curvy Italian sports car, possibly a Lamborghini.

Leaving Vincent in the hire-car, Grobbelaar went into the house, where he stayed for approximately thirty minutes. Lim has always denied that he was in the house, and no witness has ever testified to his presence. But at about the time that Grobbelaar and Fashanu were having their meeting – 1.58 and 2.13, to be precise – Lim was using his mobile phone to make two more calls to Lo Bon Swe in Indonesia. As with all mobile phone calls they were routed via a local cell-site, or antenna, which picked up the transmission from the mobile and sent it on to its destination. The location of the cell-site provides a rough guide to the location of the caller, since each site has a range, or 'footprint', within which it can pick up calls. These particular calls made by Lim were routed via a cell-site in Twyford Avenue, NW8. Byron Drive is within its footprint.

On emerging from the house and getting back into the car, Grobbelaar told Vincent that he and Fashanu had discussed the safari venture. 'Maybe he'd be interested in investing in it?' Vincent suggested. Then he changed the subject. 'He works with Ulrika Jonsson on *Gladiators*. Now there's something I'd like to get on safari!'

Grobbelaar now turned his mind to much more mundane matters. Coming back into Central London, he realized that there was still two and a half hours before he was due to catch the flight back to Manchester. He also remembered that he needed to buy a present for his mother-in-law, Heather Sweetland. A pair of driving-gloves would fit the bill. He decided to stop off at Harrods to buy them.

Having left the car in the NCP car-park in Basil Street Grobbelaar wandered around the great department store, pausing occasionally to sign an autograph or chat to a salesperson as if he hadn't a care in the world. He chose a pair of jeans and a tie for himself, signing his Barclaycard slip at 2.54 p.m. He tried on hats, which – like many men with thinning hair – he loved to collect. He popped into the haberdashery department and picked up his mother-in-law's gloves, which he paid for at 3.24. (By now Richard Lim was in the Rendezvous Casino at the Park Lane Hilton Hotel.)

Vincent and Grobbelaar left Harrods shortly before 4 p.m. and began to make their way out of London just as the rush hour traffic began to build up. By the time they finally got back to Heathrow to catch their 5.45 p.m. flight time was running short, so instead of returning the hire-car to the depot they left it in the short-term car-park, bay number C154, and stopped by the Hertz desk to tell them to come and get it. They boarded their plane, flew back to Manchester and went their separate ways: Grobbelaar to Debbie and the kids, Vincent to Chirk.

The following day saw a number of unusual financial transactions and an intriguing diary entry. In John Fashanu's 1993 diary, under 26 November (the space for the 25th already being full) the following entry appeared: '£50,000 = £45,000 Commission 10%'. The figure of £50,000 appeared to have been written over another number: £40,000. Beneath that was the figure £72,000. It is a mathematical fact that £72,000 less £50,000 makes £22,000: the sum that Richard Lim deposited in his account at the Leeds Building Society on 25 November.

On the morning of Friday 26 November Grobbelaar made the sole payment into his testimonial fund since its inception. Having twice phoned Rathbone's over the past few days, he went into their offices that day and handed over £5,000 in cash, telling Ian Taylor that it comprised £3,000 paid to him by QZI, the firm that owned the rights to Zambezi beer, and £2,000 repaid from Mondoro. Neither of these statements was accurate. Zambezi beer was not a success and Mondoro never gave Grobbelaar a penny. That same day Vincent – a man who scarcely ever had more than a few pounds to his name – suddenly started disposing of money. Lots and lots of money. And all of it in cash.

He began by depositing £3,700 in Mondoro's bank account. The money was actually taken to the bank by Michelle Shaw, who worked as Stephen Wundke's secretary. Wundke himself took £8,000 in cash, which he repaid to Mondoro in cheque form. The reason for this odd arrangement was that Vincent, believing that banks were obliged to inform the Inland Revenue about any cash deposits of more than £10,000, did not want to place too much cash in Mondoro's account at any one time. So without telling Wundke where his money was coming from, he persuaded him to act as a middleman.

Vincent told Wundke to expect further substantial deposits within the next few weeks. Both men, however, were due to be in southern Africa over Christmas and New Year. So before leaving the country Wundke told his colleague at Ace Golf, Ian Chilton, that an associate of Chris Vincent's might be coming to the office with a sum of money: could he look after it? Chilton asked no questions as to the quantity of money or the identity of the person. He simply agreed that, if the money arrived, he would take it home until such time as it could be dealt with.

Not all Vincent's cash went into the bank. Some £500 went to pay off a model, Amy Wilson, who had been hired to pose in a Mondoro brochure but was never actually employed. And £4,000 more was spent on tickets to Zimbabwe for Vincent and others, plus travellers' cheques for his own personal use. The final £3,000 went to settle a debt that Grobbelaar owed to a sculptor and art dealer called Pat Mavros, who had created a trophy for the testimonial match between Liverpool and Everton. Vincent and Wundke, who were still looking for big-money investors for Mondoro, had an appointment in London with the pensions arm of the Coal Board on 8 December. While he was there, Vincent contacted Mavros, who sent a driver to Vincent's hotel – the Kensington Palace – to pick up his money.

Once that was sorted, Vincent was due to meet a girl called Bernice Bala'c, whose father, Peta, was about to turn forty. Peta Bala'c had played football with Grobbelaar in South Africa, and Bruce had ordered a special football jersey, marked 'BALAC 40', as a present. He gave it to Vincent to hand on to Bernice. Bruce said that he had not seen her for years: he thought she must be about seventeen.

At around 6.30 Bernice arrived at the Kensington Palace. She was a pretty, slightly chubby blonde, wearing a long dress and a heavy overcoat and carrying several shopping bags. Vincent ordered her an orange juice. They started chatting, and moved on to alcoholic drinks. Bernice was not seventeen, but twenty-one. She was working in London for Marks and Spencer, but her family lived in Chester. Before coming to England, she said, she had grown up in South Africa. What with that and football in common, she and Chris had plenty to talk about. Bernice did not leave until 11 p.m.

She would, in time, become a key player in the drama – the catalyst for Vincent's attempt to destroy Grobbelaar. But at this point Vincent had little sense that she would ever mean much to him. Once she had gone he rang another young woman of his acquaintance and arranged to meet for a late dinner. One thing led to another. About four in the morning the telephone rang in Vincent's hotel room. It was Grobbelaar. 'I've disturbed you, haven't I?' he said, listening to Vincent's laboured breath.

'Bloody right,' said Vincent, and hung up. Thirty minutes later, the phone rang again. Grobbelaar was desperate to talk. He was sitting in his TV lounge, alone in the dark. He and Debbie had been having a row. Their marriage was going through a bad spell, he was worried that this time things might be terminal.

It was not long, though, before he was back to his usual cheerful self, as Vincent discovered on 14 December when he went down to London to watch Liverpool play Wimbledon in a Coca-Cola Cup tie. Karen Bishop, the TV documentary-maker, was coming along to the match too, and on the spur of the moment he invited Bernice Bala'c. She was off work, sick, but managed to recover enough strength to say yes to the invitation. Grobbelaar had asked Vincent about Bernice and been told, 'She's not seventeen and she's a good-looking girl!' But Vincent still had no thought of any sort of serious relationship.

At Selhurst Park, the ground shared by Wimbledon and Crystal Palace, Vincent, Bishop and Bala'c found their seats. It was freezing cold, sleet was falling and they were only just under cover. Directly in front of them were several empty rows, so when Grobbelaar ran on he spotted them immediately. Bruce saluted Vincent and then mimed 'Drinking by Numbers'. It was private signal meaning, 'I'll see you in the bar afterwards.' When the match began, Vincent was interested to see that John

Fashanu was playing for Wimbledon. This was the first time that Vincent had watched Fashanu play football. He was strong, hard and fearless, and it was obvious that Grobbelaar had been right: the Liverpool defenders were physically scared of him. The game ended in a penalty shoot-out. Grobbelaar saved two penalties, and so did the Wimbledon keeper, Hans Segers. But two of the Liverpool players missed completely, and it was Wimbledon who emerged victorious.

Afterwards, Grobbelaar joined them for a brief drink. He looked at Bernice, grinning broadly. 'The last time I saw you, you were this high.' He left the rest of his thought unspoken: now she qualified as first-class fresh. To his irritation, he could not stay long. The Liverpool team coach was heading back up north that night, and for once he had to be on it.

That night, Chris Vincent and Bernice Bala'c went back to his hotel and talked until four in the morning. The next day, he boarded a plane for Harare. He had a safari company to set up, and that was not all: he and Grobbelaar had yet another hot little project that they had found by a beach in South Africa.

# 11

## You Couldn't Fault the Keeper

On 6 January 1994 Chris Vincent left Victoria Falls and flew to Johannesburg, then on to Durban where he checked into the Holiday Inn. He was there to inspect the Prince's Grant Realty Estate, a collection of development properties grouped around a golf course on the coast about 35 miles north of Durban. The idea behind the scheme was that would-be owners would buy a plot of land roughly a quarter of an acre in size, thus becoming shareholders in the estate. They would then build their own homes in accordance with guidelines laid down by the estate. On completion of their buildings, they would be given the freehold to their plots.

Grobbelaar had been told about Prince's Grant by a cousin, Peter Springer, and the idea immediately intrigued him. The South African property market was at an extremely low ebb, as a world-wide recession coincided with local political uncertainties in the run-up to the country's first post-apartheid elections. At Prince's Grant, prime beach-front lots were available for around 200,000 Rand, then worth about £40,000. There might never again be a chance to acquire land so cheaply, and prospectuses for the scheme, maps of the area, site plans and so forth were sent to the Mondoro office at Lower Bridge Street. Vincent agreed to go and inspect Prince's Grant while he was in Zimbabwe for Christmas and the New Year and tell Grobbelaar what he thought.

The latter, of course, could not go swanning round Africa at that time of year: the holiday season was one of the professional footballer's busiest times of the year. With Grobbelaar's football matches came another intensive round of telephone calls. Between 12 and 16 December there were a number of abortive attempts at telephone contact between Grobbelaar and Richard Lim. Then on 17 December, a Friday, Grobbelaar called Fashanu at his office and Lim at his home number. Lim called Fashanu, and made contact with Grobbelaar. As a result of their conversation, he called Indonesia and then called Fashanu for a second time.

The following day Fashanu called both Grobbelaar and Lim, who again passed on a message to Indonesia. Contact between the three men, in various permutations, continued sporadically past Christmas – when Fashanu rang both Grobbelaar and Lim to wish them the compliments of the season – up to 3 January, when Grobbelaar made repeated attempts to reach Lim. He finally did so at 4.17, and the two men spoke for some ninety seconds. The following day was a Tuesday, not normally a match day. But the power of satellite television had influenced the fixture list and Liverpool were faced with a game that was always one of the highlights of their season – the home clash against Manchester United; 4 January 1994 was key date number five.

That morning Lim twice tried to contact Grobbelaar, who eventually returned the call. If they were looking forward to the big match, their anticipation was well justified. The game turned out to be a classic for both teams, for the 42,795 fans packed into a sold-out Anfield, and for all those watching on Sky Sports. Alex Ferguson, the Manchester United manager, later said it had to have been, 'If not the best, then one of the best and most enthralling games played between the two clubs. Any neutral supporter would say, "This is the best of British football. This is the kind of football I want to watch."'

It was, indeed, a perfect example of everything that is good and bad about Premier League football. The action and energy never stopped for a moment. Both teams played with total and unflagging commitment. And there were countless chances at both ends. Yet the fact that there were so many goal-scoring opportunities was in large part to a relentless succession of defensive errors by both sides.

The excitement began in the first minute, when Liverpool's Robbie Fowler shot just over the Manchester United cross-bar. But it was soon clear that the Liverpool back four of Rob Jones, Mark Wright, Neil Ruddock and Julian Dicks – all excellent players as individuals – were lacking in any mutual under-standing. To make matters worse, Wright had had barely two hours' sleep, due to family problems, and was visibly exhausted.

After eight minutes Manchester United's Eric Cantona picked the ball up on the left wing. He drove a cross to the far side of the penalty area. As Grobbelaar stood helpless on his line the United captain, Steve Bruce, ran between two defenders to head unopposed into the net. The ball powered into the space between Grobbelaar and his left-hand post. As he walked back to pick the ball out of his own goal the keeper held up his hand as if to say, 'What could I have done?'

He would soon be reaching back into the goal once again. On twenty minutes, Jamie Redknapp played a sloppy pass back towards Mark Wright. Instantly, the ball was pounced upon by the United winger Ryan Giggs. Wright came out to challenge him, but the ball bounced back off Giggs's shins, past the sprawling Wright and towards the Liverpool goal. As more defenders ran at him, Giggs took a few paces towards the edge of the Liverpool area and chipped a perfect lob over Grobbelaar, who was standing some yards out of his goal. The keeper was left flapping at the ball as it looped over him into the net once again. After the game Giggs simply said, 'I spotted Bruce Grobbelaar off his line, so I just tried to get it over him.' He succeeded brilliantly.

Now Manchester United were two goals in front, and for a while it seemed as though they would over-run Liverpool.

When, just three minutes later, United scored a third goal, Alex Ferguson thought to himself, 'We're going to win by ten.'

This time, Bruce Grobbelaar stood even less of a chance than he had on the first two occasions. Neil Ruddock fouled Roy Keane just outside the Liverpool penalty area. The defenders immediately formed the traditional wall to attempt to block any shot from the free kick. But, surprisingly, no United attackers stood anywhere near them, or made any attempt to get into the penalty box. The reason for their apparently casual attitude became clear when Denis Irwin stepped up and curled the ball over the wall and into the top right-hand corner of the goal. No goalkeeper in the world could have got a finger to it, and once again a disconsolate Grobbelaar was retrieving the ball from the netting.

It had been a hectic half-hour, but the pace of this extraordinary first half showed no signs of slacking. Within a minute of the restart, the United defence made a weak clearance. The ball rolled out to Liverpool's Nigel Clough, standing almost thirty yards out from goal. He smashed a low, first-time shot straight back the way it had come, past Schmeichel and into the bottom corner of United's goal.

'Four magnificent goals,' exclaimed Sky's Andy Gray, 'and you couldn't fault either goalkeeper for any of them.'

Fourteen minutes later it was five goals, as Clough hit a second for Liverpool after another mix-up in the United defence. Within a minute United were back attacking the Liverpool goal. Irwin, in theory a left-back, found himself in the inside-right position. Running on to a through ball, he shot with his right foot from no more than ten yards out. Grobbelaar could only parry the ball with his legs. It bounced straight into the path of Ryan Giggs. As an open goal loomed before him, Giggs swung his boot . . . and missed completely.

As the second half got under way, the end-to-end action continued unabated. Brian McClair ran through the United defence to meet the ball in the Liverpool area and chipped over Grobbelaar, who seemed to dive too soon. But the shot missed and in any case, McClair was (wrongly) given off-side. Minutes later, Giggs was put through on goal. He shot. Surely this time he had beaten Grobbelaar's dive? But no. In the last fraction of a second, when the ball seemed past him, Grobbelaar stuck out a hand and palmed it round the post for a corner.

It was an astonishing piece of goalkeeping, but there was more than one brilliant keeper on show that night. When Manchester United's Danish international Peter Schmeichel made a dramatic diving save from a shot by John Barnes, Grobbelaar led the applause, raising his arms about his head and clapping his opponent. It was a typical moment of generosity from one member of the goalkeepers' union to another. 'He's only jealous it wasn't him,' joked Andy Gray.

The Liverpool keeper would soon have his own chance to recapture the limelight, as Roy Keane chested down a cross from Eric Cantona and blasted a right-foot shot at point-blank range. Grobbelaar arched backwards and to his right. Surely he was beaten? But no, the ball hit his hand and bounced away to safety. More compliments flowed from the commentary box – Bruce was the only man keeping Liverpool in the match.

The value of his two saves became even more apparent when, with ten minutes to go, Neil Ruddock equalized with an unstoppable header from a Stig-Inge Bjornbye cross. As the final whistle went, the crowd gave both sides a standing ovation. It had been, by any standards, an extraordinary match and the moment it was over Lim called Lo Bon Swe in Indonesia, passing on the news and speaking to him for five and a half minutes. Two hours later, at 11.30 p.m., Lim did something unusual. Instead of calling Bruce Grobbelaar's mobile phone, as was his normal practice, he put in a call direct to the Grobbelaar home for a conversation that lasted no more than fifteen seconds.

Chris Vincent, of course, had no idea of the drama unfolding at Anfield. On 8 January he met Charles de Chamoy, the agent for Prince's Grant, and together they visited the site. As far as Vincent was concerned the development was spectacular, and three plots in particular, right on the shoreline, caught his eye.

He called Grobbelaar at home in Heswall and, as the goal-keeper studied his plans, Vincent talked through the various options available to them. According to Vincent, they agreed that the best bet was to try to buy all three plots. Two were adjacent to one another and would form the setting for a single magnificent home. The other, reckoned Vincent, could be sold at a later date and might – if prices moved as he expected – pay for the whole deal. This turned out to be an accurate assessment: the third plot, then on the market at 212,000 Rand (roughly £42,500) was eventually sold in April 1994 for 650,000 Rand, or £130,000. As so often with Vincent's and Grobbelaar's plans, the idea was fine – the problem was making it work.

By Vincent's account – which would later be challenged, and must therefore be regarded with due scepticism – Grobbelaar agreed that Vincent should buy the three properties, which would cost some £120,000. 'Should I sign the contract in your name?' asked Vincent.

'No,' said Grobbelaar. 'I don't want Debbie to find out. Sign as the company.'

Vincent agreed. 'We'll have to form a South African company eventually. But in the meantime, I'll sign as Mondoro.'

He put the phone down and told de Chamoy that the deal was on. The South African asked him how long he would need in order to get the necessary money together. Vincent told him two to three months. But, as a gesture of goodwill, he wrote out a company cheque for £1,000.

Vincent and Grobbelaar did not meet again until 22 January, a Saturday, when Liverpool were playing at home against Manchester City. Vincent drove Grobbelaar to Melwood, the Liverpool training ground, where the team met up before home games. The two men discussed their property venture in South Africa, and the need to raise enough money to complete that deal, as well as the original Mondoro scheme. Vincent then went back to Chester and picked up Bernice Bala'c, whom he was taking to Anfield for the match.

For Bernice, this was her first taste of footballing high life.

Vincent had told her that they would be visiting the executive lounges before watching the game. Afterwards they would have a few drinks at the ground before going on to dinner. Debbie Grobbelaar was away, so Bruce would be free to join them for the evening's entertainments. Bernice's first concern, naturally enough, was to work out what she should wear. She settled on black jeans, a beige wool top, a black waistcoat and a long string of fake pearls. In her bag, she packed a pair of more elegant black leggings for the evening's events.

When Chris Vincent saw her, he was bowled over. Since their last encounter at the Wimbledon game Bernice had been ill and, unable to eat, had lost twenty pounds. Before, she had been a pretty girl; now, she was stunning. Delighted by the transformation, he drove her to Anfield. In the Candy lounge the atmosphere was one of masculine good humour and self-satisfaction as Candy staff, their clients and prosperous local businessmen made the best of this enjoyable status symbol. Vincent seemed to be a familiar figure, well known to many of the people there. But beneath the bonhomie Bernice sensed a certain unease.

'People would come up and say hello, and I couldn't tell who was genuine and who wasn't. Everyone was back-slapping, but the scene seemed quite fake. Janet, the Grobbelaars' au pair, was there with her nephew, and she sat next to me during the game. Ian Rush's wife Jackie arrived, just as the crowd were cheering because he'd scored a goal. She looked quite smart and dressed up, wearing a long skirt and a jacket with shoulder pads that I recognized from Wallis. Janet saw her and passed some comment about how she didn't like her. But the next minute it was, "Hi Jackie, how *are* you?" Not many wives go to games, except for really important matches, and I remember thinking how hard it must be for them – the competition must be awful.'

For Bernice, the most interesting thing about the game, which Liverpool won 2–1, was Jamie Redknapp, whose boyish looks and shock of floppy black hair made him the team's pin-up. Afterwards she met Bruce Grobbelaar again, when he came up to the Candy lounge and stayed for about an hour and a half. When the time came to leave, Bruce, Chris and Bernice were making their way out when they were approached by an acquaintance called Alan Murphy, who ran a successful local paper business. He started chatting to Bernice, insisting that, 'The next time you want to see a game, get hold of me. I've got a box here and you're more than welcome to come.'

Outside Anfield, they were surrounded by young fans begging for Bruce's autograph. 'I loved watching the kids,' remembers Bernice. 'You could see the heroism they felt for him. Now this was their chance. Their eyes would be wide, and it was almost as if they couldn't get the words out to say, "Please can I have your autograph, Mr Grobbelaar."' Grobbelaar walked along, chatting to Vincent, and signing as he went. When they reached the car they set off for Bentley's, a wine-bar in the Albert Dock which was popular with the Liverpool players. On the way, the two men talked over their plans for setting up businesses in Zimbabwe and South Africa. As usual, they were full of optimism for the future. 'They were always enthusiastic, always laughing,' says Bernice Bala'c. 'You couldn't be with them for five minutes without laughing too.' In a bid to join the conversation, once they had reached the wine-bar she asked whether Grobbelaar was planning to move back to South Africa once his footballing days were over. When he said yes, she asked, 'What does your wife think about that?'

Grobbelaar grimaced. 'Aaahhh . . .' he murmured.

'Oops, wrong question,' said Bernice.

Any embarrassment was short-lived, as the calm, early evening atmosphere at Bentley's was shattered by the howl of a hyena, followed by the bark of a baboon. The noises came from Neil Ruddock and Jamie Redknapp – both had been taught their animal impersonations by Chris and Bruce – who had turned up along with a posse of other players including Steve McManaman, Don Hutchison and Dominic Matteo.

Grobbelaar bought a round of drinks for the new arrivals, like an indulgent uncle treating a gaggle of high-spirited nephews. Within minutes the party was in full swing. As Bernice persuaded Jamie Redknapp to sign her match ticket, and Bruce Grobbelaar disappeared to make a telephone call, Chris Vincent gave another masterclass in Zimbabwean behaviour to an eager Neil Ruddock. A quick guide to authentic-sounding lion noises was followed by instructions in Drinking by Numbers. Ruddock found it hard, even impossible, to swing his arm in the required manner without spilling his glass and its contents all over the floor. Amidst mounting hilarity more and more drinks were ordered, until Ruddock – his thirst still entirely unquenched – was surrounded by the contents of six or seven glasses.

Amidst the chaos, there was conversation about a Jungleman charity golf tournament Grobbelaar was helping to organize in Zimbabwe the following June. Liverpool were going on a post-season tour of South Africa, and several of the players were talking of staying on for a week to play some golf and have a nice holiday by Victoria Falls.

By about 8.30 people were moving on. The players were the first to leave, but as Bruce, Chris and Bernice drove away from Bentley's a few minutes later they passed a taxi filled with all the Liverpool lads, who cheered and shouted out of the cab's windows as they went by. Grobbelaar, meanwhile, said he needed to drop something off at a friend's party. This turned out to be the fortieth birthday celebrations of Phil Thompson, the former Liverpool centre-half, who had been a team-mate of Bruce's during the club's glory days. Thompson, now a football pundit for Sky Sports, stood with his wife and two of their four sons greeting guests at the door of the function room where the party was being held. Bernice complimented Mrs Thompson on her boys and jokingly said to Grobbelaar – whose children, of course, are girls – that he ought to get the recipe for sons off the Thompsons.

'I already know the recipe,' said Grobbelaar, leaving Bernice feeling baffled and embarrassed in equal proportions. For Chris Vincent, however, the remark made perfect sense. He already knew about Grobbelaar's illegitimate son, apparently sired during his National Service days in the mid-1970s. One day, as Bruce would later say on tape, the lad would turn up on his doorstep asking for money. Bernice, however, was rapidly getting the feeling that all was not what it seemed in Bruce Grobbelaar's private life. Before the night was out, that impression would be further underlined.

Mrs Thompson seemed unperturbed by the arrival of one of her husband's old team-mates and two uninvited extra guests. As the men proceeded to the bar, she hospitably introduced Bernice to a table-full of Liverpool wives, all bedecked in sequins, shoulder pads and big hair. They too did their best to make the younger woman feel at home, asking where she worked and reacting with delight when she replied that she was an executive at Marks and Spencer. Conversation turned to Mrs T – what, they asked, had she bought Phil for his birthday present? A romantic holiday for two to Menorca, she replied, to much appreciative cooing.

Chris Vincent, meanwhile, was talking to more former Liverpool heroes, including Kenny Dalglish and Alan Hansen, and spreading the word about the Jungleman golf tournament. Hansen, in particular, seemed keen on the idea, which increasingly looked as though it would be packed with sporting celebrities.

Soon it was time to move on once again, because Grobbelaar had another social appointment. They had been invited, he said, to a party full of women – it would be rude not to go. The trio climbed back into Chris Vincent's Rover 214, this time with Grobbelaar at the wheel, and set off for their next destination. At one point they took a wrong turning off a roundabout and found themselves heading along a dual carriageway. Grobbelaar's response to the situation was instant. He stopped the car, then began reversing the way they had come, towards the roundabout. Going backwards in the wrong direction, down a major road, Bernice was terrified. The two men, however, were nearly helpless with laughter.

Soon they were at the hotel where the party was being held, pausing briefly at the bar for a quick drink. Someone approached Grobbelaar and told him that a dark-haired woman was waiting for him downstairs. He and Vincent looked at one another, laughed and called out, 'Wild Thing!' As they went downstairs to the party, Bernice saw a small, slim woman with astonishing turquoise eyes and dark, permed hair appear and put her arm around Bruce. Within seconds she was shouting and swearing at Grobbelaar. Then she turned on Chris Vincent and started verbally attacking him, pointing a finger in his face as she did so. Finally, spotting Bernice, she turned to Grobbelaar and hissed, 'Who is this? Is she your latest?'

As the argument continued, Bernice was led away by the host of the party, Alan Murphy, whom she had briefly met that afternoon at Anfield. Once again, her job with Marks and Sparks was a useful talking point. It emerged that Murphy made various kinds of paper, including newsprint and toilet tissue, and St Michael was one of his customers. The party was being held for his staff, 90 per cent of whom were, as promised, female.

Bernice went to get a drink. At the bar, some women asked her who had been shouting at Grobbelaar. Just a friend of his, she said. The women were surprised. They had got the impression that there was more to the relationship than friendship. The mysterious but argumentative brunette had been telling them that Grobbelaar was going to leave his wife, marry her and settle with her in Zimbabwe.

As the party went on, it became clear that the trio that had started the evening was now a quartet. The Wild Thing was dancing and drinking with Grobbelaar as though nothing had happened. It transpired that she had expected him to take her to Phil Thompson's, and had spent all afternoon getting ready. When she was later instructed – via a telephone call from Bentley's – to meet him at a toilet-paper factory's staff party, she was not best pleased, and she held Chris Vincent equally responsible for her situation. It was not long, however, before the Wild Thing and Bruce were back in the party spirit. Chris and Bernice started dancing too, before the two women danced together, staggering off the dance-floor and on to the carpet with their arms around one another's waists, doing a combination of aerobics and the can-can.

Once everyone had sat down again, a conversation ensued about a gigantic bottle of champagne which was sitting, unattended, on a nearby table. This had been a prize in the party's raffle, but Vincent and Grobbelaar declared that they were not sure it was genuine. There was only one way to find out what the bottle might actually contain, and that was to open it. Despite the fact that it was someone else's prize, this they duly did. Sure enough, the mega-magnum contained several bottles' worth of genuine bubbly. The champagne was still nowhere near finished by one o'clock, when it was decided that the time had come to leave. So it was taken out to the car, in which all four party-goers then set off for the Wild Thing's house: Grobbelaar held the giant bottle between his knees while his friend slumped in the back with her arm around Bernice, occasionally yelling unintelligibly at the top of her voice.

Eventually they reached the Wild Thing's semi-detached thirties home. Grobbelaar got out of the car and crawled on his hands and knees to the front door, his usual method for ensuring that no one could see him. The others, still conventionally on foot, went in and coffee was brewed. It was not long, though, before Bernice found herself on the move again, heading off with Chris to a nearby garage to get some cigarettes. On the way, Bernice asked him what on earth was going on. He explained that he was trying to give his best friend the chance to sort out a few problems in private. When they got back to the house there was a Michael Bolton record playing on a stereo system in the dining room, but whoever had been listening to the music had disappeared. The ground floor was deserted and Grobbelaar's purple jacket was hanging at the foot of the stairs.

Bernice and Chris made some coffee and talked about what to do next. In the kitchen, tickets to Liverpool matches at Anfield were pinned to a noticeboard. By now Bernice was keen to get home to Chester, but Vincent felt unwilling to desert Bruce, who had no other means of transport. In any case, he and Grobbelaar were due to spend Sunday discussing their business affairs. As they talked, Bernice noticed a diary lying open next to a telephone. By it were a series of photographs showing Bruce and the Wild Thing with their arms around one another. The diary itself contained constant references to meetings with and telephone calls to Bruce. The relationship had obviously been going on for some time.

Suddenly there came the sound of someone making their way downstairs. The Wild Thing appeared. She was wrapped in a sheet which fell open, revealing all too graphically that she was wearing nothing underneath.

'Hi,' said Bernice, trying to look her in the eye.

'I take it my mate's sleeping?' said Vincent.

Yes, she said, he was fast asleep upstairs.

Bernice turned towards Chris Vincent. 'Are you going to wait for him till broad daylight?' she enquired.

It was now nearly four in the morning, and her patience was beginning to run out. Vincent agreed that he ought to take her home. They reached Chester at five o'clock. Once he had seen Bernice to the door of her parents' home, Vincent turned around and drove back to the Wild Thing's home to pick up Bruce Grobbelaar and take him back to the Wirral. These were the duties of a mate, and Chris Vincent took them very seriously indeed.

# 12

## Midnight Rendezvous

Over the next two weeks Grobbelaar and Vincent continued in their usual routine. On Sunday 23 January they met as planned. They played snooker, had a few drinks and talked about the South African situation. Over the next few days, Grobbelaar made his usual Monday and Thursday visits to Mondoro's Bridge Street office and shared the usual drinks at Harkers. By the end of January, he had dramatic news to report from Anfield: Graeme Souness had finally resigned as manager of Liverpool and been replaced by his former assistant, Roy Evans.

On 28 January Grobbelaar attempted to contact Richard Lim. But the Malaysian was out of the country, having left for the Far East on the 16th. He would not return until the morning of 4 February, having flown overnight from Kuala Lumpur. There is no record of any call from Lim to Grobbelaar during his stay in the Far East (nor of any other calls coming into the UK from Malaysia or Indonesia at any time during this entire story). But according to Vincent, on 2 or 3 February Grobbelaar told him, 'We're at Norwich this weekend and I have to see the Short Man before the game. Can you come to Norwich on Friday, then take me down to London on Friday night?'

That request signalled the sixth and final event which needs to be considered in detail, even if – for the time being – some aspects of it must be left unspoken.

Grobbelaar wanted Vincent to stay in the same hotel as the Liverpool team – something he had never done before – and Vincent was only too happy to oblige. But by Friday morning, when Grobbelaar got on the team bus, he still had not been told where the team would be spending the night. He promised to call Vincent on his mobile phone as soon as he knew where they were supposed to be meeting. In the meantime, Vincent set off on the long cross-country trek from Chester to Norwich. En route, he heard that Liverpool were checking into the Sprowston Manor Hotel. He called Lower Bridge Street and asked Michelle Shaw to book him into the same hotel for the night. It took some time for Vincent to find the hotel, but eventually, late on Friday afternoon, he arrived, checked in and met Grobbelaar. The latter explained that he would have to have an early dinner with the rest of the Liverpool team. Once that was over he would try to sneak away and they would set off for London.

During the day there had been a series of calls between Lim, Fashanu and Lo Bon Swe. At 3.09 p.m. Grobbelaar called Richard Lim, who then made another call to Lo Bon Swe. This was a Friday afternoon, roughly twenty-four hours before a full Saturday programme of Premier League football. If Lim was passing on a series of tips from Bruce Grobbelaar to his backers in the Far East, this would be as good a time as any to do it.

Back in Norwich, Vincent had dinner by himself, then watched some television. Some time later, Grobbelaar came to his room. At 9.05 he called Lim – or the Short Man, as he still was to Vincent – on his mobile, speaking for a little over two minutes. But before they left for London Grobbelaar had one more call to make, this time to his Liverpool room-mate, Steve Nicol. 'Has anyone been around, yet?' Grobbelaar asked the Scottish international defender. 'If anyone does come looking for me, tell them I'm with Chris doing some safari stuff. We're going to slink off for a few beers.'

With the precaution taken, Grobbelaar planned his getaway. Chris Vincent would leave by the hotel's front door and drive round to a side entrance, from which Grobbelaar would then emerge. Vincent did as planned, reached the side entrance and waited for several minutes, but no one emerged. Finally Grobbelaar arrived, running round from the front of the hotel and getting into the car with an urgent, 'Let's go!' It turned out that the hotel's side door had been locked. Grobbelaar had been forced to go to the foyer and stand out of sight until the receptionist left her desk and went back into her office. Then, like a boarding-school boy trying to get away to a midnight feast without being spotted by Matron, he dashed through the foyer and raced across to the waiting car. He would do the driving, he said. Vincent could handle the return leg.

They set off towards the M11 motorway. After stopping at a service station to pick up the 'Cokes and smokes' that were their staple diet, Grobbelaar put the accelerator to the floor and, with the speedometer nudging 100 miles per hour, headed for London. As always, he kept his mobile phone busy. At 10 p.m., by which time the car was near Ely in Cambridgeshire, Grobbelaar called the Short Man, telling him that he expected to reach London in about two hours. Then he dialled the Wild Thing, and – with Vincent joining in from the passenger seat – a typically loud, three-way conversation ensued.

More calls between the car and Richard Lim confirmed that they were all heading for their rendezvous at the Park Lane Hilton Hotel. Once Vincent and Grobbelaar got to London, however, their plans began to go wrong. At King's Cross, Grobbelaar got stuck in the one-way system and found himself heading towards the City of London rather than the West End. As he and Vincent cursed their mistake they searched desperately for a way back towards the Hilton, before regaining their bearings and heading towards Marble Arch. A final call to the Short Man established that they would soon be arriving, and arrangements were made for Grobbelaar's meeting. Lim, meanwhile, was near the Brompton Road in Knightsbridge, from where he made two calls to his contacts in Indonesia.

It was now roughly midnight. According to Vincent – in an account that would later be, if not disproved, certainly much mocked – Grobbelaar was getting nervous. He had, he said, told the Short Man that he would be hiring a driver for the night. He told Vincent to put a hat on, so that he had the authentic look of a chauffeur. The only hat available was a folding panama. Vincent objected that anyone driving a small red hire-car, wearing a panama hat in the middle of the night, would look less like a chauffeur and more like a prat. But he put it on, anyway.

As they reached the Hilton, they saw that the road outside the main entrance was packed with Rolls Royces, Mercedes and other imposing limousines, all of them driven by genuine, peak-capped chauffeurs. Grobbelaar jumped out and ran into the hotel. Vincent drove around to the back of the hotel, where there was a rear entrance, and waited for Grobbelaar out of sight of the crowds. Grobbelaar's presence in the Hilton was confirmed by at least two of the hotel's employees. Some time later he returned to the car, carrying an envelope filled with £1,500 in cash. He told Vincent that he needed to get some rest before tomorrow's match, so he leaned back in the passenger seat and grabbed an hour or so's sleep while Vincent drove him back to Norwich.

They reached their destination at around 3.30 a.m. At the hotel, Vincent parked the car and went on ahead into the foyer to make sure that the coast was clear. Grobbelaar followed once Vincent had signalled that all was well. The next morning they sat together in the hotel foyer and had a cup of tea. Rob Jones stopped to say hello. John Barnes sat chatting with Vincent for half an hour or so, talking about the safari business. None of the players had the faintest idea that their goalkeeper had been down to London and back while they were sleeping in their hotel beds.

When the time came for the team to make their way to Carrow Road, Norwich City's compact little ground, Grobbelaar gave Vincent a match ticket and told him to follow the team coach. The keeper also informed the police, who would be acting as escorts, that Vincent was with Liverpool. So the coach and its accompanying car drove into Norwich with police outriders, much to Vincent's delight. Nor was he the only associate of Grobbelaar's at Carrow Road. Richard Lim, who had twice called Indonesia about fifteen minutes before the kick-off, was also in the stands. He had come up from London specially to see the game, which turned out to have enough twists and turns to make it worth the journey.

Norwich scored first, with Grobbelaar helpless as Mark Wright – desperately trying to beat a Norwich forward to a cross, played in from the Norwich right wing towards Grobbelaar's near post – succeeded only in knocking the ball towards another Norwich player, who gratefully bundled it into the net. The Canaries would have gone two-up in the forty-second minute had not Grobbelaar pulled off a typical reflex save, sprawling in front of a shot by Jeremy Goss and stopping it with his legs. Instead, the second half began with a Liverpool equalizer. Norwich then hit the net once again to make the score 2–1. Chris Sutton, a twenty-year-old striker who had been one of the finds of the season, ran on to a through ball which sat up invitingly in front of him. While the ball was still in mid-bounce Sutton volleyed it into the top right-hand corner of the goal, past Grobbelaar's outstretched arms. Liverpool, though, were not beaten. With the resilience for which they were famous they came right back and equalized for a second time. So the match ended with honours even and the fans feeling that they had been given more than their money's worth of entertainment.

Vincent had planned to drive Grobbelaar back to Chester, where they had agreed to meet Bernice Bala'c and her family for a drink at Harkers. But Grobbelaar was unable to get away from the rest of the team as quickly as usual. When Vincent phoned him in the Liverpool dressing room, he arranged for Vincent to follow the Liverpool coach to a service station on the A1. Grobbelaar would leave his team-mates and join him there. In due course Grobbelaar emerged from the coach accompanied by Nigel Clough, who needed a lift in the direction of

Derby where his family lived. Once he had been dropped off Grobbelaar took over at the wheel, driving with characteristic speed. They reached Chester and Harkers, twenty minutes before closing time, and had a quick drink.

It seemed like business as usual, but in fact it was more like the end of an era. The moment that Grobbelaar had long dreaded, when he would lose his Liverpool place to his younger rival, David James, was imminent. Grobbelaar would play his last game for the Liverpool first team on 19 February. In the six months after that, his contract with Richard Lim, which had promised an easy, regular supplement to his footballing income, would dwindle away to virtually nothing. Meanwhile, though there would still be a few good times to come, the friendship between Bruce Grobbelaar and Chris Vincent was also moving towards its endgame.

# 13

## Acacia Palm Lodge

Throughout the months during which Bruce had become involved with John Fashanu and the Short Man, Chris Vincent had been trying to set up Mondoro's operations in Zimbabwe. Stuart Dyer – the NM Financial Management executive – still came to every Liverpool game at Anfield, and conducted meetings with Vincent, Grobbelaar and Wundke, but despite his enthusiasm had not produced any actual cash. The delays had become a standing joke for Vincent and Wundke, but their sense of humour was beginning to wear thin. Then came more bad news. Dyer's company was being taken over by another institution, Friends Provident. He told Vincent and Wundke that they would have to be patient for a little while longer yet.

Despite the delays, all was still not lost. If Dyer fell through, Wundke had a possible alternative: Chris Fleet, a wealthy stockbroker who managed his mother's portfolio. He, Dyer, Wundke and a host of wives, children and friends came out to Victoria Falls between Christmas 1993 and the New Year. By now the Vincent brothers had become adept at showing would-be investors the sights, and Fleet for one was highly impressed. 'Count me in,' he said, when he returned to the UK, adding that he would personally invest up to £500,000.

No sooner had Chris Vincent got back to Chester then he

received some more good news. His brother Keith called. He had been out to see Neil Hewlett's camp, Acacia Palm Lodge. 'I promise you,' he told Chris, 'it's the best in Africa.' Even more encouragingly, Hewlett would soon be ready to lease the site to Mondoro.

Chris Vincent and Stephen Wundke decided on yet another new plan. Instead of trying to raise millions right from the off, they would drum up just enough cash to run Hewlett's camp. Once they had made a success of that, they would then have a track record with which to impress major investors. They reckoned they needed a minimum of £275,000 to get the camp going. Ideally, though, they wanted £400,000 to do the job properly. With the operation scaled down in this way, both Fleet and Dyer were willing to come in on a personal basis. Fleet wrote out a cheque for £50,000, although it was never cashed, and Dyer promised £100,000. Another investor, a prominent industrialist, pledged £50,000, to be paid as soon as he had personally seen the camp and been satisfied that it was going to work.

Vincent now went to see Grobbelaar. He had £200,000 in the pipeline, but he still needed twice that to run the business with any margin for error. That was going to have to be raised from somewhere. There was another problem, too: Neil Hewlett was asking for £10,000 per month rental for his camp, which could only sleep eight guests. That meant that the prices would have to be high, which in turn required five-star facilities and the guarantee of the all-important Big Five species, particularly lion and elephant. Chris and Keith Vincent faxed one another back and forth between Chester and Victoria Falls. Keith assured his brother that Hewlett was promising to introduce lions, and on that basis Vincent agreed to send Hewlett a £30,000 deposit on the first three months' rental. To cover that payment, he asked his investors for their money. Fleet would not let him cash his £50,000 cheque, but a deposit of that sum was made to Mondoro's bank account, transferred by Stephen Wundke from his mother's account. On 15 March Stuart Dyer wrote out his cheque for £100,000, although he asked Vincent not to cash it for six weeks because he wanted to cover it by cashing in some unit trusts. On 31 March a Mondoro cheque for £30,000 was sent, as promised, to Hewlett's account at a branch of Lloyd's Bank in Guernsey.

Crucially, however, no lease agreement had actually been signed, although one had been drawn up in Chester by Tim Parker, a solicitor who acted for Stephen Wundke. But Keith Vincent was able to come to Britain at the end of March, bringing with him photographs of the camp and documents confirming the basis on which Mondoro were agreeing to rent it – specifically that there would be lions and elephants on the property. Keith attended the 1994 April Fool's Day golf tournament at the Belfry and listened with delight as Stuart Dyer and Chris Fleet appeared to compete with one another as each claimed he would be the first to raise the £6 million needed to buy Mondoro its own estate. He went back to Zimbabwe feeling sure that everything was going to be fine. On 18 April Chris Vincent and Bernice Bala'c followed him. They were going out to set up the camp and prepare for their first guests. Finally, after all the long, frustrating months of inaction, Mondoro was getting down to business.

Bernice Bala'c's presence requires some explanation. She had been living with a boyfriend, an Australian, in West London. But in the weeks after her long night out with Vincent and Grobbelaar, which had ended at the Wild Thing's house, she and Vincent had begun seeing one another on a more regular basis. She would meet him at his flat in Chirk, or at his hotel in London, whenever he was in town. They went to more Liverpool games together, and she got to know both Bruce and Debbie Grobbelaar. Eventually Vincent offered her a job as his assistant at the camp, and at the beginning of March they went to Zimbabwe together. They spent some time with Chris's parents. For all Chris's talk of the coldness between himself and his father, Bernice was impressed by the Vincents' huge house in Harare, their warm hospitality and the good-humoured atmosphere. She and Chris met up with Bruce Grobbelaar, who had flown out for another international, and they all flew back to England together. But there were, she recalled, less whole-some aspects to the trip.

One night at the Elephant Hills Country Club they made love for the first time. It was the start of a physical relationship that would continue, on and off, until the summer of 1995. Vincent's feelings for Bernice became a crucial element in his eventual conflict with both his brother and Bruce Grobbelaar. But she later maintained that she had never intended the relationship to be a sexual one. 'It was disastrous,' she said of their first night in bed together. 'I was so uncomfortable about the whole situation. I hadn't thought about Chris at all in that way, and there was no physical attraction whatever.' Her view of him was that he was an incredible enthusiast and motivator, who brought out the best in her at work. He was generous, warm-hearted and a wonderful friend. But once the sun went down, that same psychological intensity could become over-whelming. Throughout her time in Zimbabwe, including the three months during which she worked at Acacia Palm Lodge, 'I was pressured into doing things that I didn't want to do.' The same pattern continued throughout their relationship. Vincent, she claimed, would put her under constant pressure to have sex with him. 'I tried so hard to break away from this whole thing so many times,' she said. 'But there were times when I would grit my teeth and think, "I'd better make the best of it."' It was easier, she said, to let him have his way than waste even more energy arguing.

Bernice gave this account in the living room of my home in Sussex, while Chris Vincent was in another part of the house no more than fifty feet away. Like a diplomat shuttling between two warring leaders, I then walked along the corridor and put the allegations to Vincent. He can, indeed, be an extremely forceful character, particularly when in pursuit of something he wants. But he was outraged that Bernice should have described their relationship as she did. If she had been so offended by his advances on their first trip to Zimbabwe, he argued, why did she continue to visit him, go out with him and Grobbelaar, or work with him in Zimbabwe? And why, on 9 March, two days after returning from Zimbabwe for the first time, did Bernice send him a card (which he then produced and showed to me), printed with the words 'A Poem for an Extra Special Friend', thanking him for 'one of the most exciting and enjoyable weeks of my life'.

Whatever the truth of the situation, in the weeks after their trip to Zimbabwe Chris and Bernice had long late-night telephone calls and occasional meetings in London. On 9 April they went to the Grand National with Bruce Grobbelaar and Sally Kershaw, an interior designer who had been working on designs for the rooms at Acacia Palm Lodge. The girls changed for the races at Grobbelaar's home. As a former employee of Marks and Spencer Bernice was amused to see that the spare room, where she and Sally got dressed, was decorated with a pale blue and yellow M&S fabric called 'Charleston Gardens'. She was struck, as Chris Vincent had been, by the rows of bags packed with designer clothing that were lined up along the walls of the room. But she felt uneasy using another woman's home when she was not there, particularly since Bruce was at Anfield, as Liverpool played the morning football match that traditionally precedes the National.

Grobbelaar met them after the match. At Aintree they were entertained by Ken Rutland and Candy. Champagne was drunk, bets were placed and the odd bit of money was won. At one point Bernice showed Bruce some pictures she had taken a few days beforehand when they had all gone out for a night at the Castle Tavern, a South African pub on Shepherd's Bush Green in West London, after Liverpool's Premier League game against Wimbledon. 'I'm going to sell these to the *Sun*!' she joked.

Grobbelaar laughed. 'Go ahead,' he said.

That night Bernice would get another taste of the Grobbelaar lifestyle. She, Sally, Chris and Bruce spent the night at a country house hotel called Cardon Park. Sally and Bernice sat up until eight in the morning drinking champagne. Chris Vincent retired early with a stomach upset. Bruce spent the night with Octopussy, one of his many girlfriends.

Ten days later Bernice was in Zimbabwe at the start of a new life. She could hardly have picked a more spectacular location for it. Acacia Palm Lodge consisted of four guest cottages, grouped around a central reception and dining area and small swimming pool. Tall trees dappled the property in shade. All the buildings were thatched, with high ceilings supported by massive wooden posts. Inside, the walls were white, with terra-cotta tiles on the floor. The total effect was a perfect combination of simple African charm and upmarket sophistication.

Almost from the moment he arrived, however, Chris Vincent found himself in conflict with Neil Hewlett. He and Bernice were welcomed to the camp with drinks and a lavish lunch hosted by Hewlett, his wife Patty and daughter Kerry. But it soon became clear that, although the camp itself was almost complete, there were niggling details that still needed to be sorted out. For example, the staff accommodation had not been built as promised. Also, Vincent felt that the camp's hot-water boilers were too small to cope with the demands of guests who might all want to take showers at roughly the same time – after returning from a game-drive, for example. Such water as they did produce was so hot that it melted the PVC pipes Hewlett had installed.

These were, perhaps, the sort of teething problems one would expect to encounter at the start of any project. More intractable was the staffing situation. The workers at the camp had all originally been employed by Hewlett and still felt that they owed their loyalty to him. They told him everything that went on in the camp, to the point where – as Bernice discovered – he even knew what she was eating for breakfast or dinner.

Finally, and most importantly of all, it was abundantly clear that Hewlett was reluctant to introduce lions or leopards on to his land. It transpired that a herd of kudu – a species of large antelope – liked to feed at sunset on an open plain in front of Hewlett's own camp, a collection of buildings elsewhere on the estate. Hewlett's family had become very fond of the kudu. But if any predators were introduced, they would naturally go hunting where their prey was thickest. This would mean that the Hewletts' idyllic view of grazing kudu would be disturbed by big cats eating their pets for tea. The women in Neil Hewlett's life made it clear to him that this would not be tolerated. Throughout the time that Vincent and Bala'c were at Acacia Palm, any leopards, cheetahs or hyenas found by Hewlett's men were liable to be shot. But without any lions on the doorstep, guests at Acacia Palm would have to be trucked to the Hwange National Park. This severely limited the camp's selling power and meant that the price would have to be cut. If that happened, Vincent insisted, the rent would have to come down too.

Over the last week of April the camp filled up with Mondoro's associates, investors, friends and family. It all seemed cosy enough on the surface, but in the few days that Vincent had been in Zimbabwe Mondoro was already beginning to fray at the edges. Stephen Wundke had been asking Chris Fleet to reimburse him the £50,000 that had been transferred to Mondoro from his mother's account. But Fleet was getting nervous: why was he the only person, other than Grobbelaar, who had actually put money into the company? And where, exactly, was Grobbelaar's money coming from? Wundke and Fleet went to see him to make sure that he really was going to invest £150,000, as Vincent had told them. But Grobbelaar was unable to reassure them. 'Where the hell am I going to find 150 grand?' he asked.

With those words, Grobbelaar effectively ended Chris Vincent's long-term hopes of running the Mondoro Wildlife Corporation. Convinced that they had been fed a pack of lies, Wundke and Fleet decided to restructure the company. Fleet would take it over and invest the capital necessary to run the business. Wundke would become the managing director of Mondoro Wildlife Corporation, Jersey. Chris Vincent would be offered £1,500 a month to be the camp manager. Having started the project as an entrepreneur, Vincent would be reduced to nothing more than a hired hand.

None of this was revealed during the time that Wundke and

Fleet were in Zimbabwe, but it was clear that something was going on. Arguments broke out between the Vincent brothers, Wundke and Fleet, closely followed by reconciliations and assurances of financial support. Fleet – who had decamped to Elephant Hills – was complaining that he had not received the 3 per cent shareholding in Mondoro to which his (uncashed) £50,000 cheque should have entitled him. Wundke was telling Keith Vincent that he could run Mondoro in Zimbabwe, while he, Wundke, looked after things in the UK. Over the telephone from Heswall, Grobbelaar was assuring the Vincents that of course he was in for all the money he had promised – he had just not been able to say so in front of Debbie.

Neil Hewlett was watching the comings and goings with a combination of curiosity, concern and a determination that, whatever happened, he would not be the loser. All in all, it was a crazy way to run a business.

Once the camp was clear of all the visitors, Chris and Bernice got down to the serious matter of preparing for the first paying guests, who arrived towards the end of May. Arguments over lions and leopards continued, but for all their disagreements Hewlett and Vincent did begin work on another deal which would – once 'consultancy fees' had been paid to the appropriate officials – have given them the right to set up additional camps in the Hwange National Park, some of the finest safari country in the world.

They also agreed that Vincent would buy Hewlett's Toyota Landcruiser truck, which had been converted for use as an open-top safari vehicle, for £24,500. The first £4,000 would be due on 1 June, with the balance payable one month later. Vincent was still expecting to receive £100,000 as soon as Stuart Dyer's cheque was cashed. But, just to be on the safe side, he spoke to Grobbelaar to make sure that he would guarantee the payment if all else failed. Sure, he said, he would pay for it out of his testimonial fund.

On 29 May Grobbelaar and Steve Nicol arrived at Acacia Palm with their families. Neil Hewlett wasted no time, greeting Grobbelaar with the words, 'Hi, Bruce. It's such an honour to meet a man of your stature.' Then they sat down for tea, at which Hewlett launched a stinging attack on Chris Vincent's management of the camp. Vincent responded with equal venom. Grobbelaar did his best to calm them down – physically restraining Vincent at one point – but Hewlett had planted in his mind the idea that Vincent was falling down on the job. Hewlett then came to the next item on the agenda: his truck. He wanted his down payment. Grobbelaar pulled out his cheque-book. 'What do we owe you?' he asked, and splashed out £5,000. He then signed a contract guaranteeing the rest of the money owing on the truck.

If Vincent was feeling irascible, it was partly because he had now been informed, via a fax from Stephen Wundke, of the plans to take over Mondoro. The following day, he had a meet-ing with Grobbelaar and his brother Keith, at which they decided to stick to the original plan. For the time being, both Vincents and Grobbelaar were still on the same side. The mood of togetherness was evident as everyone gathered around the camp-fire at Acacia Palm. Bruce and Chris played the guitar and sang songs, while Bruce's mother Beryl looked on in delight. She still wore the very first medal he had ever won, playing for the Vancouver Whitecaps, on a chain around her neck. The thought that her son's Liverpool days were over brought a tear to Beryl's eyes, but she cheered up when he took her in his arms and gave her an enormous hug. Even Debbie Grobbelaar had a few drinks and relaxed, perhaps because she and Bruce seemed to have decided to kiss and make up. Chris and Bernice could see the *joie de vivre* that had attracted Bruce to her in the first place.

'I've seen the error of my ways,' Grobbelaar told Vincent. 'We're very happy, and I'm going to give Debbie 100 per cent support and be a model husband.'

Behind the scenes, however, Grobbelaar's problems were mounting up. His contract with Liverpool had ended and he and Roy Evans had been unable to agree on a new one: Grobbelaar wanted a guaranteed two-year deal, but Evans was only prepared to offer a single season's work. There were possible openings at Newcastle and Coventry, both of which were managed by ex-Liverpool players, and at Southampton. But in the meantime he was unemployed.

To make matters worse, he had been caught drink-driving. In June, when he appeared before magistrates in Wrexham, his lawyer claimed: 'My client is unemployed . . . he has no income coming in. The only savings he has are for his children's schooling. His incomings have exceeded his outgoings by £500 per month.' His testimonial fund was running low. He was, by any objective standard, in no position to guarantee the future of any business. Yet that was his position at Mondoro.

Grobbelaar had one further financial burden to carry. He had helped organize the Jungleman golf tournament at the Elephant Hills Country Club at the beginning of June. The tournament was raising money to help send handicapped Zimbabwean athletes to the Special Olympics. Eighteen people, including the Grobbelaars and the Nicols, had flown out from England. Elephant Hills had agreed to pay for the celebrities, but the rest were having to pay their own way. Their bookings were arranged and paid for by Keith Vincent, using the account of Wilderness Safaris, the firm his wife, Maureen, worked for. The total bill came to 56,000 Zimbabwean dollars – roughly £5,000. There was no reason why Keith should not have done this. He was in partnership with Wilderness's owner, Colin Bell, in various businesses in Victoria Falls. By using that account, he gave himself thirty days' free credit. By the time the thirty days were up, he reasoned, he would have been paid back by Grobbelaar, who was in charge of the whole party – and he would then reimburse Wilderness.

The tournament went well, and was followed by a dinner-dance. Once again, Grobbelaar and Vincent entertained everyone with their songs. Bruce then sang the Liverpool anthem, 'You'll Never Walk Alone', and was followed by Steve Nicol, who made an emotional speech in praise of his old friend and team-mate. Dry eyes were in short supply all round.

Among the guests at the Jungleman tournament was Alan Murphy, the millionaire papermill owner whose party Bruce,

Chris, Bernice and the Wild Thing had attended five months beforehand. With him were his wife and sixteen-year-old daughter Davinia, who would go on to become an actress in the Channel 4 series *Hollyoaks*. A ravishingly pretty blonde, and the apple of her father's eye, she wandered around the tournament in a minuscule bikini topped by a sleeveless, see-through white blouse.

After dinner Chris, Bernice and Davinia set off for Downtime, a night-club under the Illala Lodge Hotel. Over the preceding few days Bernice and Davinia had established a delicately balanced relationship: as the two prettiest girls in the neighbourhood they were part bosom-buddies, part rivals. Davinia also had something – or someone – Bernice would have liked: Jamie Redknapp.

'I knew her as "Jamie Redknapp's girlfriend" before I even knew her name,' recalls Bernice. 'Russell Osman [the ex-England defender who was also taking part in the tournament] kept cracking jokes about, "Has Jamie called yet?" And he had.'

As she sat by the bar at Downtime in another revealing outfit, Davinia referred to Jamie. Affecting an innocent ignorance, Bernice asked, 'Sorry, who?'

'Jamie Redknapp,' said Davinia, a little miffed that her celebrity boyfriend should have gone unrecognized.

'Oh,' went Bernice, 'is he a footballer, or something?'

Determined to get the best of this sweet-faced girly skirmish, Davinia explained that Jamie was indeed a very fine and famous footballer. She liked the best of everything, she said. 'When I go and buy jeans, I just can't help buying Armani.' When she chose men, she did so on the same principle (quite so: her next would be Ryan Giggs).

Chris Vincent, meanwhile, had promised Alan Murphy that he would keep an eye on the magnate's beloved daughter and bring her safely home. By 2 a.m. he was feeling exhausted, and in dire need of a good night's sleep. He tried to persuade the girls to leave with him. But just as he was putting his case two hunky members of a touring rugby club, enjoying a

post-match celebration, approached the bar. They gazed ador-
ingly at Davinia and Bernice and burst into song, imitating Tom
Cruise's performance of 'You've Lost That Loving Feeling' from
*Top Gun*. There was no chance of prising the blondes away
from these boys, so Vincent gave up the unequal battle and
headed back to Elephant Hills. For him, he thought, the
Jungleman event was over. But he was wrong.

When the time came to settle the bill Grobbelaar told Keith
Vincent, 'Chris will fix it.' It was not the only financial problem
bothering Keith. Becoming increasingly worried about
Mondoro's perennial lack of money, he wanted to know where
Grobbelaar was going to find the £200,000 he was supposed to
be investing. According to Chris Vincent – and this was to be a
fact that would later be disputed and discussed at great length
in court – he decided to let Keith in on a secret which he had
hitherto mentioned to nobody else. 'You didn't hear this from
me,' he said, 'but Bruce has got this deal with some guys
from the Far East. They work some betting scam. Don't worry.
He's going to be paid big bucks.'

Keith Vincent would later verbally confirm to a detective
constable from the Hampshire Police that Chris had made this
claim, but he was not willing to sign a formal statement to that
effect even though he later repeated the allegation to me. In
Chris Vincent's account, his brother was not pleased by what he
had been told. But despite his unease, a brief peace descended
on Acacia Palm Lodge. There were guests to look after –
genuine, bill-paying guests – and a camp to run.

True, there was always the odd squabble. Maureen Vincent
found out that Bernice Bala'c was supposed to be earning £800
per month, which was more than twice as much as she made
working for Wilderness. On the other hand, Maureen was
actually paid, which Bernice had not been. Still, she passed her
dissatisfaction on to her husband, who felt as aggrieved as she
did, and another little crack opened up in the company.

Those cracks would soon widen. At the end of June Chris
and Bernice flew to Johannesburg to meet Bruce Grobbelaar,
who had been playing as a guest with a team in Cape Town.

The news that Grobbelaar brought from Britain was mixed. He did not have any money for Bernice, who had still not been paid, but he would sort it all out. And he had spoken to Stuart Dyer, who promised once again that his £100,000 cheque could soon be cashed. Grobbelaar and Vincent then had a meeting with Colin Bell, the Wilderness Safaris boss, who was keen to come in on the Hwange National Park deal. They agreed to split their new camps fifty-fifty between Mondoro and Wilderness, with Mondoro supplying the sites and Bell putting up the money needed to develop them.

Bell was happy to do business with them, but less happy with what he was told about the situation at Acacia Palm Lodge. He advised Vincent to get out while he could. But Vincent was determined to press on. He still had plenty of clients booked up, even if he could only charge them £100 a night instead of the £300 he could have asked if the Big Five animals had been on the property. And for weeks he had been hammering out an agreement with Hewlett to lower the rent he was paying on the camp, in line with the reduced revenues. His problem, as it had been with every business he had ever tried to run, was operating capital. The balance of the money on the Toyota was soon due, and there was nothing in the bank. Meanwhile, bills were piling up at the supermarket that supplied the camp, and at Hertz, from whom he was hiring his car.

Then, on or around 24 June 1994, came another crisis. The first that Chris Vincent or Bernice Bala'c knew of it was when one of Hewlett's most trusted staff, Rapson, drove into the camp in a Toyota truck. He was carrying a 30-06 Winchester rifle. He told Vincent that poachers had been spotted on Hewlett's land. Rapson went to the staff accommodation and picked up two more men, Major and Jamieson, both of whom were expert trackers. The three men then disappeared in the truck.

Later that day, between 5 and 5.30 p.m., Neil Hewlett appeared at the camp. Chris and Bernice were standing by the outdoor barbecue. 'What happened to the poachers?' asked Vincent.

Hewlett replied that there had been six of them. His men had picked up tracks indicating that men had been coming in and out of the property over a two- or three-day period. They had clearly killed and butchered kudu. Rapson, Major and Jamieson had found three of the men. They had been shot.

'What – dead?' asked Vincent.

Hewlett said that yes, they had been shot dead.

Bernice was shocked, 'People have been shot?'

Vincent, though, was concerned with the practicalities. In Zimbabwe it is legal to shoot poachers who have tried to resist or escape arrest, provided that (a) the authorities have been informed of their presence on one's land, in advance of any further action; (b) the poachers are armed; and (c) there is clear evidence that they have already killed an animal.

Hewlett walked away, and Bernice – still appalled by the whole story – started firing questions at Chris. 'You don't just shoot people, do you?'

Later on, Chris telephoned his brother and told him what had happened. Keith's response was instant. 'Pack your bags and get off the property.'

'I don't know for sure that he actually did it,' said Chris. 'It could just be Hewlett talking his usual shit.'

Subsequently, while being interviewed by the Hampshire Police, Vincent made a statement about the alleged killings. The police passed their information on to Interpol. They were later told that Hewlett's property had been searched and no bodies found.

The poachers incident was the least of Chris and Bernice's worries. By the beginning of July the conflict with Hewlett – who still had not received either a signed lease or payment for his truck – was becoming serious. Hewlett drafted a memo to Vincent complaining about his conduct: it concluded, 'Your activities with the Mondoro Wildlife Corporation are bordering on the criminal.' Vincent replied in equally strong terms, saying that Hewlett had failed to introduce the promised wild animals, and pointing out that Hewlett could have signed the original lease document several months ago.

Just to complicate matters, Bruce Grobbelaar called from

Cape Town with bad news. Hewlett had telephoned Debbie. 'I don't want to interfere,' he had said, 'but your husband has signed for a truck that cost £20,000, and I want to know when I'm going to get paid.' Debbie, needless to say, had not been best pleased. When her husband had got home from the round of golf he had been playing, she asked him, 'What's going on?'

Everything was falling apart. Keith Vincent, convinced that his brother was responsible for the unpaid debts of the Jungleman golf day, had resigned as a director of Mondoro, although he retained his share of the potentially far more lucrative Hwange deal. On 9 July Chris received a fax from Bruce Grobbelaar in Cape Town. He, too, was resigning. He would sort out the compensation for his shares at a later date, he wrote. 'I remember thinking, "That's it. It's all over,"' Bernice Bala'c recalled when I spoke to her a year later. To make matters worse, she had received news that her mother was ill. On 10 July she flew back to London. She did not return until the 20th.

While she was away, Chris and Keith Vincent had their final falling-out. In April they had met Stephen Boler, an extremely wealthy kitchen manufacturer, based in Britain and well up the *Sunday Times* list of the nation's 500 richest individuals, who wished to buy a large tract of safari land. But because he was not a Zimbabwean, Boler needed a local partner. The Vincents knew of just such a piece of land – Charles Davy's still unsold estate. In exchange for setting up the deal and managing the estate they would receive a substantial stake; Bruce Grobbelaar would also have a share.

In mid-July, Boler sent his son out to Africa to look at t he land. While he was there, Chris Vincent asked him to get his father to give Bernice the money she needed to fly back to Africa. Keith was furious. 'You could fuck up the whole deal,' he shouted. 'I don't give a fuck if that woman never comes back again.' Chris was outraged that his brother, his one great ally throughout the whole of his life, could have referred to 'his' woman in that way. He never spoke a civil word to him again.

While all that was going on, Chris kept calling Stuart Dyer, desperately trying to get his permission to cash the £100,000. On Monday 18 July Vincent phoned Dyer once again. 'Has the money gone through yet?' he asked.

'No,' said Dyer.

'Why not?'

'Because Bruce called me last week and told me not to put any money into Mondoro.'

Now Bruce Grobbelaar and Neil Hewlett started having daily telephone conversations. Hewlett offered Bruce a 3 per cent stake in the whole 14,000-acre property, in exchange for £40,000 cash and 50 per cent of Grobbelaar's holiday flat in Portugal. Alternatively he could, with Stuart Dyer's help, buy the camp and 700 acres, plus full traversing rights to the rest of the estate, for £400,000.

Vincent, who as yet knew nothing of these negotiations, was desperately casting around for help. Out of the blue, some arrived. He bumped into Jeremy Brooke, who had been with Chris and Charles Davy on the night they met the Wild Thing. Brooke was running Sheerwater, an adventure holiday company he had helped to set up. He told Vincent he was short of accommodation over the next few months. He would, he said, pay 750,000 Zimbabwean dollars for 800 bed/nights at Acacia Palm Lodge. That was the best part of £65,000 – more than enough to allow Vincent to buy Hewlett's truck and run the camp without any help from anyone else.

The following weekend, Brooke decided to get even more involved. Sheerwater would negotiate a lease agreement for the camp with Hewlett, and insist as part of the deal that he leave the property. Vincent thought that the chances of Hewlett agreeing to that were nil. But when the idea was put to Hewlett on 25 July he did not dismiss it.

'I'll give you an answer in the morning,' said Hewlett. 'I'm honour-bound to speak to Bruce Grobbelaar first because I've given him an option on the property.'

Next morning, Hewlett told Vincent he had decided to decline the Sheerwater offer. He and Patty wished to stay on their farm. But they were prepared to let Chris and Bernice stay on to manage the camp for them – salary £250 per month.

Vincent spoke to Stuart Dyer again and was told that Grobbelaar would be coming out to Zimbabwe at the beginning of August. Bruce had been in Kuala Lumpur, playing in a tournament for a local Malaysian team. Despite all that had happened, Vincent still believed that he could get out of the mess with his business intact. On his arrival in Harare, on 2 August, Grobbelaar was not met, as per usual, by Chris Vincent, but by Neil and Kerry Hewlett, and Kerry's boyfriend, Justin Swart. They all flew up to Victoria Falls together. When Grobbelaar reached the camp, Chris was out. So he gave Bernice a big hug and chatted to her for three-quarters of an hour. 'I could see he was on a mission,' she recalls.

'You should sit down with Chris and hear everything from him,' said Bernice.

'No,' said Grobbelaar, 'it's too late. We couldn't sort it out.'

Bernice told him that things at the camp were going well: they had guests and were beginning to earn some money. But Grobbelaar seemed not to hear her.

'What's happened to this business?' he asked. 'It's two and a half years down the road and we've got nothing.'

When Chris returned to the camp, the customary bonhomie between him and Grobbelaar had vanished. They shook hands coldly. Vincent did his best to tell Grobbelaar what had been going on and persuade him that Mondoro still had a future.

'Do you want out?' he asked.

'No, no, no,' Grobbelaar assured him. Then he added: 'I'm sure we can sort this out.'

Vincent said that the two of them had to sit down with Neil Hewlett in the morning. He offered to show Grobbelaar his accounts, to prove that none of his money had been wasted. But before they saw Hewlett, Chris had one final accusation to make: 'The man is a lying, cheating crook.'

Three hours later, Grobbelaar returned from his own meeting with Hewlett. He pulled Chris Vincent aside and took his hand. 'Don't worry,' he said. 'It's all sorted out for tomorrow.'

Vincent was delighted. He assumed that Grobbelaar would pay the money owed on the truck and that he could get on with running the camp. A meeting was set for 3 p.m. on 3 August.

The next morning, Bruce went off to play golf. Chris paced up and down, chain-smoking. When Bernice tried to get him to relax, he said, 'Bruce can't side with Hewlett. He's got to side with me.'

At three o'clock Hewlett arrived at the camp, angry and icily formal. 'Good afternoon, Mr Vincent. Where is Mr Grobbelaar?'

Bruce was still out. No one knew where. Hewlett drove off again.

Through all this, there had been clients in the camp. At 6 p.m. they returned from their day's expedition, and Chris and Bernice did their best to be relaxed and hospitable. But just as they were settling down to eat Hewlett's truck arrived, driven by Kerry Hewlett's boyfriend, Justin Swart. The meeting was now at Neil Hewlett's private camp. Grobbelaar was waiting for them there along with Maureen Vincent – Keith's wife – and the three Hewletts – Neil, Patty and Kerry.

Hewlett went straight into the offensive. 'Right, Mr Vincent, I believe you said to Mr Grobbelaar yesterday that I was a lying, cheating, bastard . . .'

'Yes,' said Vincent, knowing now that he had been ambushed. But Hewlett wanted to ram the point home. He leaned across to Kerry and said, 'Would you get my tape-recorder?'

Wherever Neil Hewlett went he was likely to be carrying a large green desk diary, in which he made constant notes, and a small Olympus dictaphone. When Kerry returned, Hewlett turned the machine on and started recording.

'Bruce,' he began, 'is it true that Chris last night stated that he would have nothing to do with me because I was a lying, cheating bastard, or words very similar to that?'

'Very similar to that,' agreed Grobbelaar.

Hewlett turned to Vincent. 'Chris, did you say that?'

Vincent was beaten. 'I'm not prepared to answer that unless I'm in the presence of a solicitor.'

The meeting went on for some time more. Hewlett had complaints he wanted to get off his chest, as had Maureen Vincent. Patty Hewlett did her best to seem reasonable. 'You know, Bruce,' she said, 'we've tried so hard with Chris.'

Hewlett ended it all by saying, 'Chris, that's it. Tomorrow, you pack up and go.'

That night, as they were packing, Chris told Bernice that he had always believed Bruce Grobbelaar would come through for them in the end because he had no choice. 'I've got so much shit against him, I could pin his arse to the wall,' he raged. Later, Bernice would recall the occasion with vivid clarity. 'I had been aware of a problem with finance, but Chris had said to me that he and Bruce had a big business deal that was going to materialize in October. Then, after the meeting with Hewlett, Bruce stayed at the Hewletts' and Chris and I came back to the camp. I started packing. I remember very clearly Chris had a shotgun in his hand. He was neurotic, raging. I was shaking. Here he was, in this state, with a gun in his hand and there was ammo around the place. He did calm down eventually. Even after the meeting, he said he believed that he and Bruce could patch it up. And it was that night he told me that Bruce was throwing games.'

The fact that Vincent made that claim does not make it true. He might very well have been inventing an allegation against a man with whom he was clearly very angry, intending to smear him. At the very best, Bernice's recollection is nothing more than hearsay. But this was the second alleged occasion on which Chris Vincent mentioned, however fleetingly, the possibility that there had been something illicit about Bruce Grobbelaar's activities. And the context in which he said it, as recalled by both Vincent and Bala'c, is illuminating. Vincent was not talking about getting his revenge. He was claiming that Grobbelaar would never dare to hurt him in the first place.

The following morning, Hewlett told Bernice that she could continue to work at the camp. 'Obviously I can only offer you minimal money, but you're welcome to stay if you wish.' She turned down the offer. Going into the kitchens, she noticed that the stock had vanished, removed by Hewlett's men. He now had all the furniture, uniforms and equipment bought by Mondoro. He had his truck back, plus the £5,000 that Grobbelaar had paid as a first instalment. And because the £30,000 down payment had covered rental on the camp for June, July and August, he had one month's rent in the bank.

Vincent, meanwhile, owed around £600 to Jay's, the local supermarket where he bought his stock. He also owed £3,000 to Hertz for the rent of his car. Mondoro's local debts amounted to some £14,000. Added to that, Grobbelaar's total loss on Mondoro, and related deals, was a little under £60,000. He paid out a total of £40,000 from his testimonial, plus around £12,000 in November and December 1993, plus £5,000 for the Toyota Landcruiser.

Now Grobbelaar had to get back to England. He had signed for Southampton and the season was about to begin. It was decided that Bernice would go with him; understandably, she just wanted to get home to her mum and dad. When Vincent and Grobbelaar parted, Vincent was in tears. 'I'm just sorry it ended this way,' he sobbed.

Bruce and Bernice flew to Harare and spent the night of 4 August at Gordon and Pauline Crawford's house. Harry Weir was there, an old family friend who had been landlord to both Bruce Grobbelaar and Peta Bala'c when they had been starting their careers as footballers in Durban, South Africa. They sat around discussing what had gone wrong, and how Vincent was to blame. Bruce called Debbie, who was at the family's holiday home in Portugal. 'Bernice is here with me,' he said. 'It's all over.' He looked devastated. Next, he spoke to his daughters. It was Tahli's birthday in two days' time and the girls were sad that their daddy wasn't going to be with them. 'Daddy's got to get a job,' Bruce explained.

The following day he met Keith Vincent, who had come down to Harare to see him, still wanting the money he was owed from the Jungleman tournament. They discussed the various deals in which they were still involved. It was agreed that, as soon as any of them generated any cash, Bernice would be paid all her back salary. If that took too long, Bruce would pay her himself. In the meantime, Bruce gave her 300 Zimbabwean dollars and told her to go shopping.

Later that day, Bernice got a call from Chris Vincent. He would be at Harare airport to see her, he said. 'Just keep calm, and don't react to anything he says,' advised Grobbelaar. At the airport, where there were more emotional scenes between Grobbelaar and Vincent, Chris gave Bernice 500 Rand, the last money he had in the world, to pay for her train ticket from Gatwick to Chester.

Two days later, Bruce Grobbelaar met Bernice and her father, Peta Bala'c, for a drink at Harkers. 'Oh Peta, I'm so sorry,' said Bruce.

'I don't want to hear those words,' said Bala'c. 'It wasn't your fault. My main concern is that Bernice hasn't been paid and we can't pay off her debts.'

Grobbelaar understood the situation. 'I will personally pay her,' he said, and they settled on a date of 20 August. Grobbelaar said that Bernice should relax. Maybe she could go and see her grandparents in Devon. Or she could stay with Harry Weir, who had a house in Torquay.

There was one other thing he wanted to say. 'I'm having nothing to do with Chris any more.'

# 14

## The Turning of the Worm

On Monday, 8 August, Chris Vincent took his golf clubs to the pro shop at a Harare golf club and sold them for 4,500 Zimbabwean dollars. He picked up a plane ticket to England, paid for with a (worthless) Mondoro cheque, and got on the evening flight to London. His dreams of running a successful safari camp lay in ruins, as did his relationship with his own family. The high hopes and good spirits of months gone by had been replaced by an atmosphere of universal venom. On the Sunday night he had told his father that he was penniless – could he possibly lend him some money? His father replied, 'Your brother was here. I had a long discussion with him and he told me not to lend you any fucking money. So the answer is no.'

By then, Chris and Keith Vincent had already talked. Chris had told his brother that he had spoken to Grobbelaar and had agreed to hand over all his interests in Mondoro, and the Hwange and Davy deals, on condition that Bernice was paid the £5,500 owing to her in back pay. Keith agreed that he too had been told about that deal and was happy to proceed, provided that Chris sent him a letter confirming their verbal agreement. Chris wrote to him, as requested, on the Monday morning. That afternoon Keith phoned his brother, complaining that he still had not been reimbursed for the money he had laid out on the Jungleman golf tournament.

Chris was neither sympathetic nor even interested. That evening, as he sat on the plane back to England, he wrote in his diary, 'Somehow, I don't think I'm going to have any contact with my father, Keith or Maureen ever again. I feel so badly let down.'

When he arrived in England on Tuesday morning Vincent's immediate priority was to earn some money. Aside from the £400 he had made by selling his golf clubs, he did not have a penny in the world. His first call was to Tony Taberer, the Wokingham-based businessman whom he had met with Grobbelaar several months beforehand. Vincent knew that Taberer had a travel agency, and an agency in Zimbabwe for American Airlines. Did he want to go into business packaging holidays to Zimbabwe?

Taberer was on his way to Florida, via Gatwick. He told Vincent to stay at the airport: he would meet him before his flight. Their meeting went well, but Taberer wanted a proposal in writing. When Vincent got back to his flat in Chirk that evening, having stopped off in Chester to see Bernice, he set to work on his business proposal.

The following week saw Vincent in London and Wokingham, meeting Tony Taberer's son, Paul, who was also his group accountant. At the same time, Vincent still had hopes of pulling off a last-minute coup by buying out Neil Hewlett and taking back his camp. Even as Mondoro was collapsing, Vincent had been telephoning Stuart Dyer, who still seemed prepared to invest £400,000 in buying and refurbishing Acacia Palm Lodge. On 15 August they had spoken again. 'I'm out of money,' Vincent told Dyer. 'I need £1,500 to see me through for a month, to put the deal together.'

Dyer told Vincent that he would meet him in London at the Friends Provident offices near the Old Bailey. They would have lunch and Vincent could pick up his money. However, when Vincent got to the office he found a note apologizing for Dyer's absence, but telling him not to worry: the cheque would be sorted out soon. He waited ten days or more, but nothing happened. By the end of the month, there was still no money. Vincent was now going three or four days at a time without food, desperately trying to eke out his resources. He arranged with Dyer to meet him in Portsmouth. This time they really would have lunch. This time he really would be paid.

By the time Vincent reached Portsmouth, on 30 August, he had £4 in his pocket and a quarter of a tank of petrol in his car. Stuart Dyer met him in the reception area of his office. He was clearly not interested in advancing Vincent £1,500, still less in investing £400,000 in his business. But Dyer agreed to walk down the road to a bank, where he withdrew £100 from a cash machine and gave Vincent £90.

Viewed dispassionately, Dyer's actions seem entirely reasonable. He must have had a strong suspicion that if he paid out £1,500 he was unlikely ever to see it again. Mondoro had swallowed every penny put into it, without producing anything in return – hardly the best basis for a further six-figure investment. If it cost £90 to get Vincent off his back, so be it.

For Vincent, though, the situation was truly desperate. Half-starved, in no physical or emotional state to act rationally or efficiently, he was at his wits' end. He called Bernice Bala'c from Portsmouth and told her what had happened. 'I remember hanging up the phone thinking, "What now?" I was beside myself. I didn't know where to go or what to do. I had nothing left in life, and the only mate I'd got was even worse off than I was. I went and bought something to eat. I hadn't had any food for three days. I'd actually been looking forward to lunch. For me, when Dyer didn't come up with the money that was the final bullet going into a loaded gun. Now the chamber was full.'

Bernice, meanwhile, had been doing her best to avoid him. Her mother would tell her to have Chris Vincent over for a meal. 'I can't stand by and see someone go without,' she would say.

'I don't want to see him,' Bernice would snap back.

Vincent later recalled: 'Every time I'd phone Bernice she'd

say, "Have you got any money for me?" I'd say I just wanted to chat with her. She'd say, "Why? This whole thing has got nothing to do with me. I'm bitter with all of you."'

If ever Vincent came over, she would greet him sullenly, 'Why are you here?'

'Don't cook him a meal,' she would tell her mother. 'He's not staying.'

Since her return from Zimbabwe, she too had waited in vain for money. Her £5,000 had been promised for 20 August, but the date came and went without any sign of the cash. On the 22nd, she called Bruce Grobbelaar on his mobile phone. They were cut off in mid-conversation. He did not call her back.

Two days later they spoke again. He was on a coach, en route to Aston Villa for a match. 'I've just rung up to speak about the situation, so it can be sorted out,' said Bernice.

'What situation?' asked Grobbelaar.

'My life is a wreck.'

'Oh . . .' mused Grobbelaar, 'that situation.'

They spoke again on 30 August. 'This is really not going down well, is it?' said Grobbelaar. Then he asked Bernice, 'What do you need?'

She told him that she needed an immediate £3,000 to pay all her credit cards and other debts. The following day he spoke to her again from the airport – he was flying out to Africa, he said, to sort everything out. He would pay her when he got back. By now Bernice, too, was falling apart. Scarcely eating, constantly in tears, she could not understand how a group of adults could act so spitefully towards each other and, by extension, her.

She turned for help to Stephen Wundke, but he was not sympathetic. These things happened in business, he said. This time it had happened to her. Of course, he added, she could go to a lawyer and get the police to sort everything out, and then Chris Vincent would end up in jail.

'For what?' asked Bernice.

For taking money from Chris Fleet under false pretences, replied Wundke.

Once again Bernice was baffled. Why had no one sat down and gone through the Mondoro accounts? Surely there was some money around, if only the £35,000 that had been paid to Neil Hewlett – he had kicked them out long before their next rent was due. Why had he not been asked to pay back some of the excess?

On 2 September Vincent spoke to Tony Taberer for the final time. The businessman was sorry, but he could not begin to think about any new deals for a year at least. With that, Vincent's final hopes were dashed. By now he was living off a daily ration of a can of corned beef and half a loaf of bread. His rent was being paid by the DSS, but he could not draw any cash benefits. On the few occasions when he went to Chester to visit Bernice, he would offset the £6 cost of the journey by going without food for the day. The only way he was keeping any sort of grip on his mind was by going for long walks in the Welsh hills. But the more he walked, the hungrier he became.

One day towards the beginning of September, Vincent went to see a doctor in Chirk. He told the GP that his business had gone bust and his life was in ruins. Now he said, he was feeling homicidal towards his former business partners. He had, he said, shot plenty of people. It would not be difficult to do it again.

The doctor recommended a counsellor. What Vincent needed even more badly than advice, however, was food. 'I seriously thought of trying to get myself checked into the local hospital, just so I could get fed.'

Instead, he had to sustain himself with thoughts of revenge. As he walked the hills, he kept returning to the idea that Grobbelaar had betrayed him. As with Dyer, a dispassionate observer might well sympathize with Grobbelaar. He had given Chris Vincent tens of thousands of pounds without receiving a single penny back. He was the one who had lost out. Vincent might now be bust, but he had been equally bust when Grobbelaar first met him. And any material comfort he had enjoyed in the meantime had been thanks to Grobbelaar's generosity.

But that was not how Chris Vincent was ever likely to see it. In his world, you were either with him – 100 per cent, no arguments, no ifs or buts – or against him. Any change of side, no matter how temporary, could never be seen as a simple difference of opinion. It was a stab in the back. And the only way in which one could deal with such a betrayal was to exact a full and final revenge.

For now Vincent was retreating in his mind to the one thing at which he had been an undeniable success, and to the time in his life that had left the greatest and most permanent mark on his character. He was going back to war. Now he started thinking like a soldier.

As a recruit, Vincent had been told that there was no point hitting an enemy with a single bullet, because he might still be in a fit state to fire back. You had to keep firing until he was well and truly dead. During the Rhodesian civil war he had been shot at by enemies who missed, or merely left him wounded. In return, he had pumped their bodies so full of bullets that they performed a grotesque St Vitus dance as they jerked around on the dusty soil. Now Grobbelaar had left him wounded. He would not make the same mistake. He would finish his enemy off. But how?

On 5 September he visited Bernice. It was a cold, grey, overcast day. When Vincent saw the state she was in, he was profoundly shocked. As she sat in her parents' living room, dressed in maroon tracksuit bottoms and a white T-shirt, she was little more than skin and bones. 'She looked as if she'd spent the last six weeks in Auschwitz,' he recalls. 'She was constantly on the verge of tears. After an hour, I just had to go.' Bernice's suffering was the last straw. Vincent felt that Grobbelaar had hurt not only him – a grown man who could look after himself – but also a young woman who was in no position to strike back. By going to her aid, he was giving his plans a moral justification that went beyond mere personal revenge.

As he sat on the 6.14 train back to Chirk, he considered the specific means by which he would wreak his revenge. He intended to go to the newspapers with a story which he believed would destroy Bruce Grobbelaar. He tried to imagine the consequences – the effect his claims would have on Grobbelaar's wife, his children, his fans, on football as a whole. And then there was one final question: who on earth would ever believe him? Vincent spent the night awake. He thought back on all the good times he had had with Grobbelaar. Then he recalled the last, bitter days in Zimbabwe. Above all, he thought of the way Bernice had looked that afternoon – the way she too had been betrayed. He fell asleep at about five in the morning. When he awoke, he knew that whatever he was going to do he had to do it now.

He went to the local newsagent and rifled through the papers, looking for their telephone numbers. Then he started walking out of Chirk, up the Ceirog Valley, towards a telephone kiosk about a mile out of town. It was a cold day, the sun struggling to fight its way through breaks in the cloud, casting occasional shadows from the great oak trees standing by the side of the road. Just before the telephone kiosk was a humpbacked bridge spanning the River Ceirog. Vincent stopped there for fifteen minutes, sitting by the river. Finally he told himself, 'Now!' He walked to the phone box. His heart was pounding, his palms damp with sweat. He felt as he had done fifteen years beforehand, waiting in an ambush, convinced his heart was beating so loudly that the enemy must be sure to hear it.

The first number he dialled was that of the *Sun*. When he got through to the paper's Wapping office, he was put through to the news desk. He told the voice on the other end of the line that he had a story involving football players and bribery. But he only had ten pence left in the phone: could they call back? Ten seconds later they did. Vincent repeated his claim, adding that the players involved were well-known internationals. The *Sun* wanted names. He would not give them any. Nor would he give his own name or location, except to say that he was somewhere in North Wales. Vincent did not want to give his story away for nothing. But all the *Sun* man had to go on was a vague claim, made by an anonymous caller from an unknown phone a long way from London.

'Hang on,' said the journalist. 'I'm going to put you through to a reporter called John Troup, in our Manchester office.'

The call was transferred and a second conversation, identical to the first, ensued. Eventually, Troup insisted that if he did not have some idea of the identities of the people involved in the story he could not take it any further. So Vincent told him: Bruce Grobbelaar. He was, he said, a close friend and associate of the ex-Liverpool goalkeeper. And, as a further element of the story, he had the names of a number of women with whom Grobbelaar had been conducting affairs.

'Where are you?' asked Troup.

Vincent told him, giving his address in Chirk – Top Flat, The Mount, Trevor Road.

Troup said he would be there in ninety minutes, driving a red BMW 3-Series, registration G268 CKA. Then he hung up.

Now Vincent was shaking. He had set a process in motion that might be impossible to stop. Back at his flat, he took out a sheaf of documents – share certificates, faxes and correspondence – that might establish his credibility. Then, like a good soldier, ever determined to avoid capture or detection, he went 200 yards up the road and found a hiding-place from which he could watch, unseen, as Troup arrived.

At 3.30 the reporter arrived. The man who got out of the BMW was about five foot ten inches tall, dark-haired and slightly overweight, with a round, bespectacled face. Vincent walked up the road towards him, said hello, and led him up the stairs to his flat. The two men settled down in the living room, Troup on the end of the sofa, with Vincent at right-angles to him in an armchair.

Vincent began by saying that he wanted to make a financial deal. Specifically, he needed cash immediately. If the *Sun* could not give him the means to feed himself within forty-eight hours, he was going to another newspaper.

Troup explained that his paper had a regular procedure on such occasions. He produced a standard letter of agreement that committed both Vincent and the *Sun* to absolute confidentiality, and assured Vincent that he would be paid an appropriate sum in the event of a story emerging from their discussions. Both men signed the letter.

Vincent then ran through the bare bones of his story. For at very most the third time, he made an allegation that would reverberate for years to come. Grobbelaar, he said, had been involved with a Far Eastern gambling syndicate, whose UK contacts included John Fashanu. The syndicate's aim, he said, was to make fortunes by fixing the results of football matches.

He described how Grobbelaar had gone to meet his Malaysian contact, the Short Man, at Manchester airport: the first of the six key occasions. On the way to the meeting, claimed Vincent, Grobbelaar had told him that he was going to discuss the possibility of moving from forecasting the results of matches to influencing those results. On the way back to Chester, he claimed, Grobbelaar had told Vincent that he had agreed to the scheme: he would do his best to make sure that Liverpool lost.

The significance of the second key date, the 6 October trip to Gatwick airport, was now revealed: Grobbelaar, said Vincent, had met the Short Man in the departures terminal and received another payment. Most devastatingly of all, Vincent claimed that Grobbelaar had agreed to throw the game played between Newcastle and Liverpool the previous November. When Liverpool had lost 3–0, he had been paid £40,000. This money had been collected, in cash, from a house in Hampstead at which John Fashanu had been present: Vincent claimed to have seen him with his own eyes.

Those were the third and fourth disputed incidents. The fifth involved the classic 3–3 draw between Liverpool and Manchester United. This, too, had been intended as a fix, said Vincent, but Grobbelaar had been unable to secure the right result. The same had happened on the sixth key date, the game against Norwich. Vincent had driven Grobbelaar down to London to meet his paymaster and possibly Fashanu as well. On the following day, Grobbelaar was supposed to have ensured that Liverpool lost to Norwich. Once again, he had been unable to do so.

An enormous amount of extra detail would be added to these allegations over the months ahead. They would be repeated as evidence, challenged and examined in a series of court proceedings. But their core was the claim that Bruce Grobbelaar, one of Anfield's all-time greatest heroes, had been paid to lose.

Vincent also made allegations about Grobbelaar's extramarital flings with a number of different women. Troup's first reaction, Vincent would later recall, was that the women were the story he wanted. The football stuff was great, he said, but it could never be proved. The sex, on the other hand, they could run within a week or so. He would speak to his news editor in Manchester, Peter Sherlock, and get back to Vincent in a couple of days.

Shortly after the meeting – the exact date is uncertain – Troup roughed out a brief memo, intended purely for the *Sun*'s internal purposes, giving his editors the outline of the story. This first written account differed somewhat from the story as eventually published. For example, it conflated the trip to Byron Drive on 25 November 1993 with the drive down from Norwich to the Park Lane Hilton on the night of 4–5 February 1994. 'Chris drove through the night to meet Fash at an office block near Lords,' wrote Troup. 'The three of them then drove to a house where Fashanu met the syndicate's UK go-between, known by Grobbelaar as the Short Man. Grob was introduced to syndicate members and given his money.'

It was not until 8 September that Troup called Vincent again, agreeing to pick him up in Chirk and drive him to the *Sun*'s Manchester offices. There would be £150 waiting for him at the local branch of Thomas Cook – all the *Sun*'s cash payments, it emerged, had to be authorized by London and then sent via

Thomas Cook: nothing could be done without approval from Wapping.

The two men reached Manchester at about 4.30. Troup was still sceptical about the football bribery angle – there was no way they could make the story stand up. Vincent, however, had been thinking about that problem and had come up with a solution. If he could persuade Grobbelaar to talk about what he had done, then they might be able to extract a usable confession. But what bait could they use to make Grobbelaar want to talk? Over the course of the afternoon, Vincent worked out a plan. He would invent a bogus gambling syndicate, working on the same lines as the one he had already described. If Grobbelaar could be bribed by one group of criminals, he asked, why not by another?

But Troup was still sceptical. 'I'll call Grobbelaar and arrange a meeting,' said Vincent, trying to find a means of convincing him that the plan could work. Troup agreed, and led Vincent to a private office where he wired a tape-recorder to the telephone. Vincent dialled Grobbelaar's mobile number. When the phone was picked up, he just asked, 'Howzit?'

Grobbelaar did not need to be told who was calling. 'How are you?' he asked. 'Where are you? Here . . . let me give you my number. I'm staying at the Hilton Hotel in Southampton. It's 0703 702 700, room 407.'

Vincent agreed to call him back on the hotel number. By the time he put down the phone, Troup was convinced of one thing: this man clearly knew Bruce Grobbelaar just as well as he claimed. Vincent called the Hilton and was put through to Grobbelaar.

'Listen, we should get together in the next couple of weeks. I've got some business things you should hear about,' said Vincent.

Grobbelaar replied, 'Fine . . . fine.' He added that Southampton were playing Spurs at White Hart Lane on 12 September. They would be staying at a hotel before the game. When Grobbelaar knew where that was, he would call and arrange a meeting.

The phone call had been tense, like a husband and wife trying to establish peace terms after a marital spat. Grobbelaar, it seemed, wanted the friendship to continue, but both men were affected by the knowledge of what had happened in Zimbabwe. Vincent was nervous for another reason. He was setting up his closest friend for a devastating journalistic sting.

Troup, on the other hand, had visibly relaxed. He made a quick call to the Hilton, just to confirm that Grobbelaar was indeed staying in room 407. Once assured that he was, Troup gave Vincent the £150 and arranged for him to be driven back to Chirk. They agreed to travel down to London together on Monday 12 September for the meeting with Grobbelaar.

But when Troup and Vincent set off at 9.30 that morning, they still had no idea where the meeting would be. They drove down the M6 and M1 to the Watford Gap services. There, Troup went off in search of food, while Vincent called Grobbelaar, who was on his team coach, from a phone booth. They agreed to meet at 2 p.m. in the Swallow Hotel at Waltham Abbey. 'When you get there,' said Grobbelaar, 'I'll be in my room.'

Sure enough, the Southampton coach was clearly visible in the hotel car park when Troup and Vincent reached Waltham Abbey. They still had some time to kill, so retired to a nearby pub to run through their plans for the meeting. In the saloon bar, Troup produced a tape-machine. 'It'll run for thirty minutes,' he said, 'and then it'll go beep.' Vincent was not impressed. He pointed out that he was totally deaf in one ear, and had only partial hearing in the other. He would never be able to hear the beep. Bruce Grobbelaar, on the other hand, had nothing wrong with his hearing at all. So, whatever else happened, their conversation had to be less than half an hour long. It was not an auspicious start to their project.

To make matters worse, Troup had recovered all his former scepticism about the bribery angle. In common with many, many people who would later hear Vincent's story, he simply did not believe that match-fixing was possible, let alone that it actually went on. When Vincent told him that he was expecting to be paid between £40,000 and £100,000, he scoffed. 'We'd only pay that for a royal story, and probably not even then.'

Troup took Vincent to the Swallow Hotel and dropped him off, agreeing to pick him up later. Vincent was wearing a grey windcheater jacket. He slipped the tape-recorder into an inside pocket, arranging it so that it could be turned on easily. Inside the hotel, he was confronted with a circular reception area from which passages radiated to all the rooms. Ahead of him was a bar surrounded by tables. To the left was a flight of steps leading up to a landing, or mezzanine, on which there were more tables, settees and chairs. He called Grobbelaar from the reception desk and was told to wait there. Now that he knew his target was on the way, Vincent switched on the tape-recorder and checked the time. It was 2.05.

A moment later Grobbelaar appeared, dressed in a polo shirt, tracksuit bottoms and trainers. They went up the stairs together to the mezzanine and sat down, with Grobbelaar on Vincent's left – the side of his deaf ear. Vincent – by now petrified that he would be found out – took off his jacket, with the tape-machine still in it, and placed it next to him on the couch.

For his part Grobbelaar seemed tense, and upset by Vincent's obvious loss of weight, his air of tension and defeat. They began talking about Grobbelaar's move to Southampton, what the club was like, where he was staying. Then, Vincent would later allege, he asked whether Grobbelaar was still doing business with the Short Man.

According to Vincent, Grobbelaar said no. He had only just joined Southampton. It was too soon.

Undeterred, Vincent went on. He had met some guys at Chester races, he said. They had indicated that they wanted to get into betting on football. He had told them that he had a friend who might be interested in helping their bets pay out.

Grobbelaar looked alarmed. 'No, not at the moment,' he said. According to Vincent – in an account which Grobbelaar emphatically denies, and which is certainly inaccurate in that the Short Man has never been jailed, anywhere in the world –

Grobbelaar continued, 'While I was out in Kuala Lumpur [playing in the pre-season tournament], the Short Man was in jail. His boss was in jail. Three directors of the club were in jail. That's one of the reasons Fash had to move from Wimbledon. People were getting too close.'

'They're prepared to pay good money,' Vincent persisted. Then he asked, 'Who else do you know who'd be interested in this?'

'The only people who know about it are yourself, myself, Fash and the Short Man,' said Grobbelaar. Once again, this response is purely Vincent's, disputed, account.

By now Vincent was keen to make his getaway. In his version of the tale he had captured Grobbelaar on tape, even if no details of any match-fixing had been specified. He had got him to mention Fashanu and the Short Man. That surely should be enough. He was just about to take his leave when he saw a sight that chilled his blood. John Troup was walking towards them across the hotel foyer. For a moment it seemed as though Troup was going to burst in on them. But then he settled himself at the bar. Clearly, he had just come to check that the meeting was going according to plan.

Above him, the two men continued their conversation. Vincent said he had come to town for a couple of job interviews. Grobbelaar asked if he had seen Bernice. No, said Vincent, playing the whole thing down, he had only spoken to her.

'There's not a day that goes past that I don't think about Mondoro,' said Grobbelaar. 'I don't know who to believe.'

They talked for a few minutes more, then Grobbelaar got up, saying, 'We didn't have this meeting. Milligan's about to arrive.'

They got up and went downstairs. As they walked across the foyer, Troup left his seat by the bar and walked right past them, taking a good look at Grobbelaar. Vincent was inwardly furious. He knew that Grobbelaar was observant. He wouldn't forget Troup's face, and if he ever saw it again he would be bound to be suspicious.

Vincent said goodbye to Grobbelaar and went out into the

car-park, expecting to see Troup waiting for him. Now there was a new worry. Milligan was an ex-policeman. If he saw Vincent getting into a car, Vincent was worried he might call up his old mates on the force and get them to trace the registration number.

But Troup was not there. Milligan, on the other hand, was – his metallic light green Citroen was pulling into the car-park. Vincent hid behind a Land Rover Discovery to avoid being spotted. As he was standing there, Don Hutchison, who had recently been transferred from Liverpool to West Ham, turned up. He immediately recognized the balding, moustachioed figure standing behind the Discovery and bade him a cheerful hello.

Vincent fled the car-park and stood by the side of the road, expecting Troup to turn up at any moment. For twenty minutes or more he waited. Nothing happened.

Finally the red BMW came in view, stopped and let Vincent in. They drove back to the pub and played the tape. After all the drama and tension, the results were disappointing. Most of the conversation was lost under a blanket of background noise – people talking, plates crashing and so forth. But a few phrases stood out, like 'the Short Man' and 'that's one of the reasons Fash had to leave Wimbledon'.

There was, at any rate, enough to persuade Troup that there was something to Vincent's story. They drove to Wellington Road, so that Vincent could point out the Warm Seas building where he and Grobbelaar had first gone to meet Fashanu. Troup went in to check the company names on the plaque inside the front door. When he emerged, his face was wreathed in a beaming smile. One of the names was Fash Enterprises.

Next Troup, directed by Vincent, drove up the Finchley Road to Byron Drive. They saw the house where the £40,000 had allegedly been handed over. Troup took down the address, and then they headed out to the M1 and Manchester. Troup was now convinced that both Grobbelaar and Fashanu had been up to no good. When they got to Chirk, he said he would call the next day.

Like any good news man, John Troup could smell a good story like a rat can smell a drain. Now the rat-pack was about to be let loose. And Bruce Grobbelaar had no idea that he was to be its prey.

# 15

## 'I Just Wanted to Give It One . . .'

Despite his apparent enthusiasm it was not until 29 September, more than a fortnight after the meeting at Waltham Abbey, that John Troup made contact with Vincent again. By now, Vincent had mapped out the whole of his allegation. Troup, though, was in no immediate position to take the story any further. He was sent to Northern Ireland to work on another assignment, leaving Chris Vincent to kick his heels in Chirk. Once again, Vincent was penniless. So, day after day, he would call the *Sun*'s Manchester offices, asking when Troup would return and demanding further payments. Eventually, after Vincent had threatened once again to go to another newspaper, he was given another £150.

In Chester, Bernice Bala'c was still trying to get her money from Bruce Grobbelaar. She had told her bank and her credit card companies that she was due to get some money soon, but they were becoming impatient. On 6 September, just as Vincent was preparing to call the *Sun*, she tried to contact Grobbelaar on his mobile phone. When that proved impossible she called his home number, hoping to catch Debbie and ask her when her husband would be back.

Bernice was only too well aware that Bruce kept his business and private affairs as hidden from his wife as possible. She had witnessed at first hand occasions when she and Vincent would drop Grobbelaar off at his house in the early hours of the morning before letting the car freewheel away down the road, lest Debbie be wakened by the engine and her suspicions be aroused. Now she was given a first-hand account of how the situation was seen from Debbie's side of the fence.

Debbie knew that Bernice and Bruce had talked about money. But, she added, she and her husband were still paying off bills that had been run up by Chris Vincent. So far as Debbie was concerned, he was the true villain. 'I don't know why they employed you,' said Debbie, switching to Bernice. 'You were much too expensive and they couldn't afford you there.'

The younger woman attempted to justify herself and her (unpaid) salary, but Debbie Grobbelaar pointed out, 'Bruce is not a bottomless pit.' With a husband who had come within a whisker of being unemployed, a house to maintain and two children to educate and feed, Debbie Grobbelaar had reason to feel unsympathetic.

'It's a bit of a lost cause, isn't it?' said Mrs Bala'c as her daughter finally ended the conversation. Indeed it was. Over the next few weeks Bernice – by now aware that Chris Vincent had taken his story to the papers – made further attempts to contact Grobbelaar, finally speaking to him on 20 September. But all her attempts to persuade him to repay her, as he had promised to do, proved fruitless.

Grobbelaar, meanwhile, had continued with his football career. On 24 September he played for Southampton against Coventry. The previous Thursday, the 22nd, Richard Lim had spoken to Grobbelaar on the telephone, having made four unsuccessful attempts to get through to him. On the 23rd, Lim spoke to Lo Bon Swe in Indonesia. He then called Grobbelaar and, and on finishing that conversation, called Lo Bon Swe again. That same day Lim called Fashanu, who immediately called Grobbelaar and then got straight back to Lim. On the morning of the game Lim called Indonesia, speaking for more than nine minutes. Then came the contest itself: despite conceding an early goal, when Grobbelaar got a hand to a lob from

Dion Dublin but could not keep it out of the net, the Saints won 3–1. Richard Lim was at the game.

Meanwhile, the men from the *Sun* were finally getting down to business. Troup and Vincent spoke on 29 September and agreed a strategy for dealing with Grobbelaar. Vincent would go to Southampton, claiming that he was being interviewed for a job with a Swiss company called Buhler-Maig – a genuine firm, based outside Zurich, which manufactures food-processing equipment. He would tell Grobbelaar that he was lined up to become their UK sales representative and was in Southampton to meet their executives and undergo a series of medicals. He would then elaborate on the bogus betting scam he had mentioned at the Swallow Hotel. If possible, he had to make Grobbelaar accept some money live on camera, so that the paper could produce visible evidence of his willingness to accept cash for throwing football matches.

Assisting John Troup was another young star of the *Sun*, Guy Patrick. He was smaller and thinner than his partner, with a schoolboyish air about him – the cunning, cheeky lad who had sneaked some fags into class and was going to smoke them behind the bike-shed at break.

The two made a well-matched pair. Troup was a first-class news man, adept at unearthing stories. Patrick's knack was interviewing the tearful mistresses of politicians and TV stars, gaining their confidence for exactly as long as it took to get the story, and then moving on to the next target. Born into Fleet Street – his father worked at the *Daily Mirror* – Patrick was a young man on the make, flashing his designer clothes and barking into his mobile phone.

'It must cost a fortune to look as scruffy as you do,' quipped Vincent soon after they had met. But the banter barely disguised the mutual tension, suspicion and outright dislike that was swiftly to characterize the relationship between himself and the representatives of the mighty 'Currant Bun'.

Vincent and the two reporters drove down to Southampton on Monday 3 October, talking, as men do when they have little else in common, about sport. Patrick wanted to be filled in on the whole story. Both reporters emphasized again that the crucial thing was to tape Grobbelaar *in flagrante delicto*, cash in hand, metaphorical trousers down.

The *Sun*'s travel agents, Show Travel, book staff who are on the road into Forte hotels. So, once at their destination, the three men found that they had been booked into the Forte Posthouse. A modern, three-star hotel, it catered to middle managers and families. Downstairs, a restaurant-cum-bar called Traders enticed hungry guests with an outdoors-y décor of stripped floorboards and wooden panelling that was an all-purpose combination of Wild West cantina, African hunting lodge and Alpine chalet, complete with antique ski equipment on the walls. Neon signs promised American beer. Puddings were self-served from a place called Dessert Island.

The bedrooms were modern, clean, but hardly luxurious. There was no room-service, nor could bar-tabs or restaurant bills be charged to a room account. This was a problem. Vincent had to be kept out of sight when he was not meeting Grobbelaar. Certainly, he could not afford to be seen in Troup's or Patrick's company. So they needed a hotel which could keep him fed and watered in his room. Food was less important: by now he was in fighting mode, fuelled by little more than nicotine, Coke and milk.

It was unanimously decided that a move was in order. Directly across the road from the Posthouse stood the De Vere Grand Harbour Hotel, an altogether swankier five-star establishment that looked like a post-modernist ziggurat of grey stone and gleaming glass. This was more like the sort of place where a smart Swiss company might house a would-be executive, and so – keeping a room at the Posthouse from which long-range camera shots could be taken, should Grobbelaar ever turn up at the De Vere – the *Sun* team moved in.

To everyone's delight, this new home-from-home gave guests a chargecard with which meals and drinks could be billed to room accounts. The journalists were operating under strict rules governing the amount they could spend on themselves, but Vincent was free to do as he liked. As a consequence his card became a ticket to free drinks, both for the 'sting' team and for hotel guests who would gather round Vincent in the bar as he regaled them with stories about Africa.

By the Tuesday, the full squad of *Sun* operatives had started arriving. Nigel Cairns was the chief photographer on the story, a short, cheery, balding man with the rare knack of getting scoop photographs without behaving obnoxiously in the process. The surveillance equipment turned up in an ancient white Transit van, driven by a young man whom Vincent swiftly nicknamed the Dweeb. This was Conrad Brown, son of Gerry Brown, a Fleet Street stalwart who had uncovered the private life of Idi Amin, confronted Frank Bough with evidence of his predilections for professional sex and illicit drugs, exposed Pamella Bordes and helped set up the Victoria Station stake-out that uncovered the payment of £2,000 from Jeffrey Archer to the prostitute Monica Coghlan.

Now his boy had gone into the business, complete with a van-load of cameras, bugs and tape-recorders which he carted, case by case, into the De Vere Grand Harbour, enraging Vincent as he did so: they were supposed to be operating discreetly and, if possible, undercover.

Brown-alias-Dweeb had a number of briefcases, holdalls and so on in which a camera could be hidden. Vincent's fear was that Grobbelaar, who was familiar with most of his kit, might have his suspicions aroused by an odd-looking piece of luggage. Eventually, however, he settled on an anonymous black holdall, inside which was a wooden frame to which a video-camera could be mounted. The camera itself had a tiny, ¼-inch lens that viewed the world through a brass-ringed stud-hole on the side of the bag. So long as it was positioned away from any light that might reflect on the lens, the camera was undetectable.

Vincent carried the holdall into the hotel so that it was clearly associated with him, and then placed it in the luggage-rack in his room on top of his suitcase. To ensure that there was an accurate sound-recording of everything that was said between Vincent and Grobbelaar, his room was bugged with three devices – one behind the headboard of his bed, one under the table, and another behind his TV.

He was also given a Motorola mobile phone that was actually a transmitting microphone. He could take it with him to any meeting with Grobbelaar, and, provided that Conrad Brown was within range, he would be able to pick up anything that was said.

All through Tuesday, Brown, dressed in denims and Doc Marten boots, traipsed through the exclusive halls of the Grand Harbour Hotel as he made the journey between Vincent's room and his van, fetching and carrying his kit. Troup and Patrick were well aware that their bosses back at Wapping would very soon be wanting to see a story in return for running a mini-convention at Southampton's most expensive hotel. They kept pressing Vincent to set up a meeting with Grobbelaar.

But Vincent knew that Grobbelaar, once he had agreed to meet, might very well turn up fifteen minutes later. He refused to make a move until all the surveillance systems were installed, tested and fully up-and-running. The best time to get their man, Vincent insisted, was first thing in the morning, some time between 9 and 9.30. By then he would have woken up, but he would not yet have set off for training. That meant leaving the call until Wednesday morning. Troup and Patrick were furious, but Vincent was adamant: no call would be made before Wednesday.

While they waited for the sting to take place, Vincent and the *Sun* team refined their story. The bogus syndicate would offer Grobbelaar £2,000 as the first instalment on a regular retainer, plus a one-off payment of £100,000 if he agreed to name a match that he would throw. The reporters were also keen to make Grobbelaar discuss his supposed activities from the previous season. Vincent told them that this would be no problem. Somewhat reassured, John Troup went off to the nearest branch of Thomas Cook and picked up £2,000 in cash that had been wired to him from Wapping. He then accompanied Chris Vincent as the latter put the money in his room-safe – using the code 1701, Bernice Bala'c's birthday –

and watched to make sure that the Zimbabwean did not just pocket the two grand and do a runner. He also passed on the latest instruction from the *Sun*'s lawyers: it was not, after all, necessary for Grobbelaar actually to take the money. Clear verbal evidence of his willingness to be corrupted would be all they would need to defend an accusation of libel, and it would save £2,000.

Wednesday came and went. Vincent could not contact Grobbelaar. Tempers shortened. More calls were made between the hacks and their editorial bosses. More drinks, meals and even massages – the De Vere has a luxurious gym, spa and beauty-treatment complex – were charged to Vincent's room, though he, by now consumed with nerves, was unable to eat more than a Greek salad and a bowl of soup every day.

One of the reasons for his tension was the need to make a firm contract with the *Sun*. He wanted £100,000 for his story. The paper reiterated that such a sum would be out of the question – £20,000 was their limit. Telephone negotiations buzzed backwards and forwards between Southampton and Wapping. In the end a deal was struck at £30,000, a sum of money that would fade into insignificance compared with the millions that would later be expended as a result of what happened next.

For finally, on Thursday 6 October 1994 – Bruce Grobbelaar's thirty-seventh birthday – Vincent managed to get through to his old friend on his mobile phone. He told him he was staying at the De Vere Grand Harbour.

'Oh, yeah,' said Grobbelaar. 'I was there the other day.'

'Do you want to come over for a beer some time?'

'Yeah, great, it's my birthday . . . Look, I've got to play golf after training. Why don't I come round for a beer about half-past three, four o'clock?'

'Great,' said Vincent. They arranged to meet that afternoon in the hotel lounge. Grobbelaar was on the way. At last the trap was set.

By Vincent's account, the Southampton star Matthew Le Tissier dropped Grobbelaar off at the hotel at about half-past four that afternoon. The two former friends sat in the lounge and ordered some tea. At first the atmosphere was tense, but then Grobbelaar, keen to change the mood, said, '*Ach*, it's my birthday . . . we'd better have a spook 'n' diesel.'

Once a couple of these rum and cokes had gone down the hatch, the atmosphere mellowed out a bit. At one point, the Wild Thing called up to wish Bruce a happy birthday. 'Do you know who's here with me?' asked Grobbelaar, handing the phone to Vincent. It was not the first time that Vincent had spoken to the Wild Thing since his return from Zimbabwe. A few weeks beforehand he had rung her to try to persuade her to pay him £250, which she owed him after her last trip to Africa. The Wild Thing had replied, rather testily, that she was short of cash, having just bought a new car. 'I hear it all went wrong,' she said.

'It's all very sad,' Chris replied.

'Well,' she said, 'there's always two sides to every story.'

Never was a truer but more futile word spoken. Still, all seemed well now. She was talking to Vincent. He was talking to Grobbelaar. It was almost like old times.

Grobbelaar certainly seemed to think so, and he discussed the state of his life and marriage with all his customary frankness. After a while, he disappeared to the Gents. On his way, he passed a group of smartly-suited, thirtysomething business-women who began chattering among themselves. 'Is that . . . ?' 'Yes, I think so . . .'

On his way back from the lavatory Grobbelaar was ambushed by the women, who signalled him to join them. This he gladly did, staying with them for ten or fifteen minutes. By the time he returned to Vincent's table he was in high spirits, and willingly agreed to head upstairs to play some snooker. The two men walked up to the first floor where another, smaller bar was conveniently placed outside the hotel games room. There they befriended a waitress, setting up an arrangement whereby they only had to open the door of the games room, call out to her, and the next two drinks would automatically arrive. With that supply-line established, they went in to play snooker.

Vincent took the bugged mobile phone with him, presuming that it would be able to record whatever happened next.

What follows is Vincent's account, given to me in August 1995, much of which he repeated in his evidence to the *Sun*'s lawyers, the police and then in court. Bruce Grobbelaar has always categorically denied it, and it should be noted that although Lim did try to make contact with Grobbelaar three times on the evening of 6 October, and then again at 1.05 a.m. on the 7th, no conclusive evidence exists of any proper conversation between the two men at the time suggested by Vincent.

In any event, Vincent recalled that Grobbelaar won the first two frames, amusing himself between shots by making Bruce Lee-style kung-fu gestures with his cue. Another couple of frames went by, and then Grobbelaar's phone rang. He went to answer it and his first words were, 'Hello, Bubka . . .'

It was the Short Man. Vincent could not believe his luck. Grobbelaar started talking to him about the previous weekend's game, against Coventry, which Southampton had won. Vincent, eager to appear discreet, moved to the far side of the room.

The moment the call was over, Grobbelaar said, 'Do you know who that was? The Short Man.' He went on to explain that the Short Man had called him a week beforehand and asked about the Coventry game.

'It's a Wimbledon for Southampton,' Grobbelaar had said, meaning that his team would win. The Short Man had said no, his people were betting on a loss. Grobbelaar said that he had pushed a harmless Dion Dublin header into the back of his own net within two minutes of the kick-off, but all to no avail – Southampton had scored three goals in reply.

So far as Vincent was concerned, everything was going splendidly. He and Grobbelaar were having a fine time playing snooker, drinking spook 'n' diesels and nattering away about the infuriating difficulties involved in trying to fix a football match. But then disaster struck. A father and his teenage son came into the room, picked up a pair of cues and started setting up the balls for a game. All conversation about the Short Man had to stop.

Instead, they switched to Grobbelaar's second favourite subject, women. Grobbelaar himself had been as busy as ever. He had met a girl called Lindy White on the plane, coming back from his last trip to Zimbabwe. He had been in an aisle seat and she had been on the other side of the aisle. At one point in the flight, she had got up to go the loo. On her return, she had bent down to pick something up from the floor. Grobbelaar was lost in admiration. 'When you see its body . . .', he told Vincent, '. . . I just wanted to give it one there and then.' 'It', or rather Miss White, was coming to stay with him at the weekend. In the meantime, an attractive blonde in her mid-twenties was sitting at the bar just outside the snooker room. With half a dozen frames, and a lot more drinks, under their belts, Grobbelaar and Vincent stopped by the bar to have another spook 'n' diesel and give her the once-over.

While they were there, the phone rang – a call for Mr Vincent. It was John Troup. There had been a problem. The *Sun* team had assumed that Vincent and Grobbelaar would meet downstairs at teatime and then go straight up to Vincent's room. So as soon as he had gone down for his rendezvous, they had gone into his room and switched on the video-camera. But the two men had spent such a long time chatting and playing snooker that the tape in the camera had run out. They therefore had to get into his room and rewind the tape. So, at all costs, he must keep Grobbelaar down in the bar for the next few minutes.

The *Sun* men had one further confession. The bogus Motorola phone could only transmit the material it was picking up over a very short distance, and while Grobbelaar and Vincent had been drinking in the lounge, or playing snooker, they had been too far away from the gadget's receiver. Guy Patrick had been shadowing Bruce and Chris – sitting at the far side of the lounge, or in the bar outside the snooker room – but he had not actually heard anything they had said. As a result the journalists had not recorded, or even heard, anything of any use.

Vincent could not believe it. As far as he was concerned, Grobbelaar had taken a call from the Short Man, owned up to attempting to throw the Coventry match, discussed John Fashanu's activities in terms which cannot be described here – and the *Sun* had missed the lot. Vincent ended the call and resumed his conversation with Grobbelaar. The two men discussed their next move. Grobbelaar said he knew a good Italian restaurant in the New Forest town of Brockenhurst where they could pick up some dinner (although what he did not know was that the owner's son was a reporter on the *Sun*).

Sounds good, replied Vincent, adding – as casually as he could – that he had some Mondoro papers for Grobbelaar to sign. Why didn't he come up to Vincent's room, get the paperwork over and done with and then they could go out after that? Grobbelaar, unaware that Vincent's real intention was to get him within range of a video-camera, agreed, and wandered up to his doom.

# 16

## Roll the Tapes

Vincent's view of the events of the next few hours, days and weeks was founded on one straightforward principle. 'I was on a mission. And the mission was to fix this bastard.' On the evening of 6 October 1994, he went into action.

The two men walked into Vincent's room and on to video-tape. Grobbelaar was wearing dark trousers and a pale grey rugby-shirt. The smaller, slighter Vincent was in dark trousers, a green cardigan and a light-coloured shirt, open at the neck. The setting was a typical upmarket hotel room: cream walls, blue-green drapes – in front of which stood a table and two matching armchairs – a dusty pink carpet with a slightly darker, diamond-patterned over-check, a double bed covered in a multicoloured, striped bedspread.

Vincent was suffering from an ulcer, which had been aggravated by his alcoholic intake. He offered Grobbelaar a Zantac pill but the latter turned it down, saying that it was a banned substance. As Vincent picked out some Mondoro documents, a more businesslike, even tense atmosphere replaced the laddish good mood of the snooker room and bar. Grobbelaar reached for his mobile phone and made a call: 'Hello . . . may I speak to Lindy, please?' He was calling the girl from the Zimbabwe flight. While he waited for her to come to the phone he turned to Vincent: 'We need more *foghla* [cigarettes].'

Now Lindy was on the line, wishing Grobbelaar a happy birthday. He was pleased that she had remembered, but less delighted when she revealed that she could not make their planned assignation that weekend. 'That's a pity,' he said. 'Shall we just leave it till next week? Yeah . . . next week for sure.' No, he couldn't manage next weekend. He was recording an interview with Jimmy Tarbuck. 'I'll give you a call next week,' he concluded, adding to Vincent as he switched the phone off, 'That was Lindy . . . Lindy White.'

The talk switched from play to work. Vincent pulled out the papers covering his departure from Mondoro that he and Grobbelaar – who between them owned 90 per cent of the shares – had to sign. He had just introduced the subject when his own telephone started ringing. Once again it was John Troup. There was another problem. They had managed to rewind the tape, but the Dweeb had run out of batteries for the video-camera. It might come to a grinding halt at any moment. So Vincent had to call the meeting off and reschedule the whole thing for another time. He mouthed to Grobbelaar that it was his would-be employers calling to arrange the next morning's interview. His own thoughts were directed towards his actual paymasters on the *Sun*: 'I could have shot the bastards.'

Grobbelaar seemed keen to get up and make a move towards dinner, even walking towards the door. His suggestion was that he and Vincent should have another drink, then go out for dinner, spend the night at his flat in Lymington and head back into Southampton on the train in the morning (he could not drive because of his recent ban). For a moment it looked as though everything would be over for the night – at least as far as the *Sun*'s plans went – but then Vincent decided to himself, 'Fuck it . . . let's go for it.'

He turned to Grobbelaar and said, 'Shall we graze here?'

No, replied the other man, he'd rather go to the Italian place. Then he added, 'There's some fucking fresh in there.'

'Did you see that fresh in the bar there?' asked Vincent.

'That's why we're going to have a drink in the bar,' confirmed Grobbelaar. 'You can ask her if she's got a car. She can take us.'

'Good idea,' said Vincent. They were just about to leave the room when Grobbelaar, as if wanting to get something off his chest, turned back and said, 'Whatever's going on, I just want to get it sorted out, squared. There's been a whole lot of flak flying around . . . she [Debbie] thinks I've been fucking . . . I said, listen, if that's the way you feel, fine. That's why I'm down here. It's a separation job . . . In the two years we've been working together, we were always fucking playing. She's thought she's found out from her mates that I've been fucking around, but she can't get any evidence. I told her, if you think I'm like that, we must wind up now.'

Grobbelaar continued to complain about the state of his marriage, but Vincent wanted to get down to business. 'You got that call down there before the other buggers arrived. Was that the Short Man?'

'Yeah,' replied Grobbelaar.

'You remember those guys I talked about,' Vincent continued. 'I went back to them. I didn't give any names—'

Grobbelaar interrupted him. 'I'm upset with you for telling your brother.'

'Well, he asked, "Why doesn't Bruce pay me?"' explained Vincent.

'Because I'm waiting for the cash,' replied Grobbelaar. 'If the ball doesn't play, it doesn't play. In the Man United game alone, do you know how much money I lost? One hundred and twenty-five fucking thousand pounds in cash . . . Man United.'

'What happened there?' asked Vincent.

'Three–one up at Anfield, three–all draw.'

Vincent changed the subject. 'What made you choose the Newcastle game?'

'I chose the Newcastle game because I knew I could do business there.'

'Was that because they came into the Premier League last year?'

Grobbelaar explained: 'They had big bucks on it, so I got the cash.' Then he returned to the other match: 'United. Three–one at half-time, 2–3, 3–3. I could have done something, because in the second half I made a fucking blinding . . . two blinding saves, but I was diving the wrong fucking way.' He wagged a finger at Vincent as if to emphasize the point: 'It's true as the fucking living God, I dived the fucking hell . . .' He made a whooshing sound and turned his head to the left, as if following the ball. 'It just went and it fucking hit my hand.'

'Like the Norwich game, where it hit your feet?' asked Vincent, remembering the way he had saved the shot by Jeremy Goss.

'Exactly. I just can't help thinking, the thing is, I don't like to lose. So it's instinct, fucking . . .'

Grobbelaar's words died away as he stroked his face and moustache ruminatively. Vincent decided to press home, tempting Grobbelaar with the prospect of easy money.

'They're prepared to give you two grand every two weeks on the basis that you pick one game.'

'What's two grand?' asked Grobbelaar dismissively.

'It's two grand every two weeks until you pick a game, and if you dip in [lose] on that game – 100 Gs.'

Now Grobbelaar seemed interested. 'I didn't know that . . . you didn't say it.' He pondered the subject as Vincent went into some more details about his imaginary associates – how he had met them at Chester races, how the scheme would work. 'All you do is leave a date on an answering machine,' he said.

'A date . . . where's the answering machine?'

'The guys can meet you.'

'I don't want to meet, because then they'll know who it is.'

Vincent picked up the envelope containing the *Sun*'s £2,000 and waved it in front of Grobbelaar. 'They've given me two grand, because if you're going to do the business they're serious.' By the way, he added, did Grobbelaar want his money to be handed over in person, or would he prefer an envelope drop?

Suddenly Grobbelaar seemed uneasy. 'I want to know how many people know, because this could be the fucking end of it . . . There's fucking investigators all over and I'll tell you what – they are heavy into it. Lou Macari got done badly. He bet that his team [Swindon Town] was going to lose . . . he was banned from managing for one year.'

Macari – whose punishment was, in fact, a £1,000 fine – wasn't the only person to have been nabbed, by Grobbelaar's account. 'Do you think I went out to Kuala Lumpur on the off-chance?' he asked Vincent. 'Absolutely not. Because the Short Man had said, "Any time you want to go to the Far East, you and your wife can go – I'll sort it out." I got an offer to go to Kuala Lumpur to play for Selangor, which is the state Kuala Lumpur is in—'

'While you were out there—' interjected Vincent, but Grobbelaar continued, 'Two players in jail, another two directors of Singapore in jail.'

He gave a brief outline of the tournament. There had been two groups of three teams, each with one local side and two guest clubs. In Grobbelaar's group there were Dundee United and Bayern Munich, in the other Leeds United and the South American side Flamengo. The group winners would play each other in a final.

In their first game, Selangor drew against Dundee (although, said the ever-competitive Grobbelaar, 'We should've fucking won'). But before the match against the German team, 'The manager was shitting himself, because they're riding high money that they'll get Bayern Munich in the final, plus another foreign side.' The locals, in other words, had to lose so that Bayern could qualify. 'The manager pulled all the [Malaysian] internationals out of the side and played the second team. He said to the guest players, "Thanks, but you're injured, and you've got a broken nose, and I don't want to play you" . . . and we lost 3–1. What the fuck, you know . . . it wasn't by chance I went over there. It was set up, to see how I was.'

'Is this the Short Man's boss?' asked Vincent.

'I don't know,' came the reply. 'But the boss man there, if it is the same person, he's fucking big in Malaysia. He'll say, that man . . . pow!' He made a chopping motion with his hand. 'That's it. Finished!'

Once again, conversation drifted back to the new offer. Once again Grobbelaar went over the details: 'I pick the games? How many per year?'

'One per season.'

'I could go right to the end of the season and pick the fucking last game?'

'Uh-huh,' Vincent agreed. 'My thought was, if the Short Man was back in business with you, then if you wanted, you could pick the same game for both . . . 200 Gs.'

'I could fucking retire,' Grobbelaar murmured.

Vincent embroidered his tale a little more, throwing in the names of his two new partners, 'Richard and Guy'.

'Richard and Guy,' mused Grobbelaar. 'But how many other fucking partners are there? The Short Man has only got one other person, and that's JF. The rest are out of the country.'

Now Grobbelaar began to mimic a man talking into two phones at once, as he explained the mechanics of the Malaysians' operation: 'The Short Man sits on one phone and talks to me, and he talks to overseas, and that's all he does. But [your] people are in the country. Go back to them and say, "Listen, the person wants to know how many people know about it." Tell them I don't want any bullshit . . . How many people are going to know?'

'OK.'

'And what they do for a living . . . that's another thing.'

'What,' asked Vincent, 'does the Short Man do?'

'He doesn't do anything. He just goes back and forth.'

'Sorting out?'

'Yeah,' and then, apropos of nothing in particular, he added, 'JF drives around in the top fucking Merc . . . You know that night we went to the Ipswich game . . .'

'Norwich,' Vincent corrected him.

'Was it Norwich? *Ja,* Norwich . . . He had a fucking Rolex on his arm. I said, "Give it to me, I want to weigh it." It was the fucking business – three grand's worth of watch. "This is yours, the next time you do the business. We don't talk shit," he says. "You do the business and that's yours."'

'Do they allow you to pick the games?' asked Vincent.

Grobbelaar said, 'No, that's what they don't, because . . . the last one, I said to him on the Thursday, "Change it, we're going to do the business." He said, "No, we've already done it, so make sure." And he was there. He said to me tonight, "You had no chance," and then he adopted an Oriental accent: "You had no chance, Grobbelaar."'

Now it seemed certain: the *Sun* had their story and Vincent had his man. 'Shall we gap it?' he said.

They left the room and the tape-machines. The girl at the bar was talking to a man Vincent had befriended over the past few days, a clinical psychologist. With no chance of a score, Grobbelaar restricted himself to a single spook 'n' diesel before he and Vincent took a taxi to the Italian restaurant in Brockenhurst.

All through this last stage of the evening he kept coming back to his main concerns: how many people knew about the plan? Who were they? Over plates of tagliatelle they downed a bottle of wine, followed by another after-dinner drink at the bar while they were waiting for a taxi to Lymington.

Grobbelaar's flat was their final stop for the evening. It overlooked the car-park, near the marina at Lymington. Furnished, and kept in good order by the fastidious Grobbelaar, it had one bedroom, containing a single and a double bed. On the answerphone there were four birthday messages from Debbie and another from the Wild Thing. There were about thirty birthday cards sitting in a pile. He pulled out one from the Wild Thing, then some more from fans, his two daughters, and finally his wife. Next he walked out on to the balcony. 'I'm going to bring that Lindy White down here and give it one,' he promised.

The two men went to bed – the owner in the double, the

visitor in the single. Next morning, they took the train into Southampton. Bruce Grobbelaar spent the whole trip signing autographs for young admirers. When they got into town, Chris Vincent took a taxi back to the De Vere Grand Harbour Hotel where he met the men from the *Sun*.

# 17

## 'How Clandestine Is This?'

Over the next few days, the journalists transcribed the video-tape and sent the text back to a delighted Peter Sherlock in Manchester. Vincent, meanwhile, insisted on keeping the £2,000 he had been given as a bribe for Grobbelaar, which he took as an advance on his £30,000 payment. Any resistance to his request was met with the simple but effective statement that he had put the money in his room-safe and he was the only person who knew the combination. So either they gave him the cash, or he would leave it to rot. In the great scheme of things, a squabble over an envelope full of cash was not a particular problem. The main thing was that the material garnered from the videotape was spectacular. Still, the paper wanted more.

At first, it seemed that there would be no trouble in setting up another taped encounter. On Friday morning, Grobbelaar and Vincent had spoken again on the phone. Grobbelaar, pleased that he and his mate were back on terms, and eager to do business with him, was ready to set up more meetings. But that Saturday he injured his cheekbone in a collision with his team-mate Francis Benali. Hospital reports suggested that he would be off for at least two weeks, which he was planning to spend – contrary to his talk of 'a separation job' – at home in

Heswall with Debbie and the girls. Under no circumstances would Vincent be a welcome guest in Mrs Grobbelaar's house, so for the time being the *Sun*'s plans would have to be put on ice.

On the Sunday, Vincent travelled to Chester to see Bernice Bala'c. Calculating that he needed £80 per week to get him through the next fortnight, he kept £160 for himself and gave her £1,840. This was the first, but by no means the last nor the largest, of several payments and gifts he would bestow on 'his' girl.

Ten days after Grobbelaar's injury Troup and Patrick contacted Vincent, urging him to set up another meeting with his former business partner. He called Bruce and was told that he would be going back to Southampton on 21 October with his family, who would then be going off for a short half-term holiday at Center Parcs. So he would be happy to meet at any time from the 24th onwards. With that in mind, Vincent and his accompanying journalists travelled down to Southampton on the 23rd, staying in the distressingly downmarket Polygon Hotel (where, to their horror, the bar ran out of beer) before moving into the De Vere Grand Harbour on the afternoon of the 24th.

As soon as they were installed, Vincent called Grobbelaar. The latter was driving up to Crawley to talk to a publisher about a series of children's books he was interested in producing. Vincent claimed he had been checking out the two businessmen who wanted to run a match-fixing ring. 'One guy,' he said, 'comes from an island close to the guys you do business with ... Hotel Kilo.' (Or HK – Hong Kong, in other, less dramatic, words.) Grobbelaar replied that he would be back in Southampton soon after six and he would see Vincent in the hotel at seven.

At around 7.30 Grobbelaar arrived and had a drink with Vincent in the upstairs bar. His eyes still bruised and swollen from his injury, he was accompanied by a new minder called Martin Johnson, a quietly spoken man in his early forties, so it was impossible for him to talk about the football business.

They played some frames of snooker and then went out for a pizza at a local Italian restaurant. Vincent later claimed that when he popped off for a pee, Grobbelaar followed him. 'What's the story with these guys?' he asked, as they stood before a steaming urinal.

Vincent told him it was too dangerous to talk – there were people around. Besides, he needed to go through it in detail when they had a bit more time to spare (and when, he thought to himself, there was a tape-recorder running).

Grobbelaar was insistent – he wanted to know.

'No,' said Vincent, 'I heard footsteps. Someone's coming.'

Reluctantly, Grobbelaar abandoned his enquiries and followed Vincent back upstairs. After a few more drinks back at the hotel, they agreed to meet the following morning at eleven.

The next day, 25 October, Grobbelaar called Vincent from a Southampton hospital, where he had been having a protective mask fitted, to say that he was on his way. This time, to ensure complete privacy, they agreed to meet in Vincent's room. Grobbelaar's arrival was captured by photographers stationed in the Forte Posthouse just across the road. John Troup also watched him arrive, from the shelter of Conrad Brown's van. The latter, along with Guy Patrick, was closeted in the room next door to Vincent's.

From the beginning of the meeting, the mood between the two men was far more relaxed than it had been when first they talked. Grobbelaar, dressed in a black tracksuit with a vivid V-shaped pattern in red, white and yellow emblazoned across his chest, sauntered in and began describing the way his face had been covered in clingfilm before having plaster poured over it to create a mould for the mask. 'I had to sit for twenty minutes like that, breathing through a bloody tube!'

But once the small talk was put aside, and the first of many Marlboros lit, the conversation soon switched to the bogus syndicate Vincent had invented. One point had dawned on Grobbelaar: he wanted to remain anonymous, but, 'As soon as you tell them, "That team will lose", they'll know who it is.'

Then, switching subjects as was his habit, he announced, 'The Short Man's back.' As if oblivious to the fact that he had already told the story during their previous meeting, he went back over the recent Coventry match. 'He told me, "I've been trying to get hold of you. What about this one – is it a Wimbledon or a Leeds?" He was using W or L – he could have said Whisky or Lima. I said it's a Wimbledon, for us. He said, "We've already done it." He's telling me. "You're going to lose the game." So, two minutes into the game, I pushed the ball into the back of the net. That was the Coventry game . . . and then we come steamrollering back!' The last two sentences were delivered amidst hoots of laughter. 'One–nil at half-time,' he went on, 'then we win 3–1.'

'I wondered if you'd done a deal with the Short Man,' said Vincent, who now began to describe his new paymasters. One, he said, was a property developer who controlled companies that were quoted on the Hong Kong exchange. He mentioned the Sporting Index, which had introduced spread betting into Britain, in which gamblers punted on specific results.

Grobbelaar butted in, explaining that the Malaysian syndicates also liked to bet on specific scores rather than general results. 'I tell you how they're betting, the Short Man. Put a bet on and the team has to lose by a certain number of goals. For the Coventry game, it's just by one and then we clean up. If it's a draw . . . what did he use for a draw? . . . he didn't use Delta . . . if it's a Dundee, we're going to lose all our money, because sometimes, if it's a draw, they retain all the money they put on. So I've got to know if they're going to lose all their money if it's a draw, or just . . .'

Vincent suggested that, with the Sporting Index, you could place new bets at half-time. Bearing that in mind, he had asked his contacts, 'What happens if my guy makes sure they're two-down at half-time?'

'Did you say, "Let in?"' asked a worried Grobbelaar.

'No . . . "Make sure".'

'He must know it's a goalkeeper.'

Vincent continued on the theme of the half-time bet.

Grobbelaar explained: 'They can actually take the money at half-time and say, "Right, we've won that much money,"' but the subtleties of the betting system were not his major concern. 'I'm still fucking worried,' he said.

And so the conversation continued, with Vincent dangling the prospect of at least £100,000 before Grobbelaar's eyes, while the goalkeeper vacillated. 'It's too dangerous,' he said. 'But I'll look at it.'

When Vincent – inspired by the *Sun*'s payment procedures – said that he could arrange cash to be sent via Thomas Cook, Grobbelaar replied: 'If you do that, they'll find out it's me . . . The thing I was going to do,' he said, shaking a finger at Vincent, 'was put it in a box, and just put it in a locker . . . not in a bank, because they'll fucking find it . . . just put it in greenbacks, and then I'm going to take the fucking full lot and go . . .' (here he made a whooshing sound, accompanied by a flying gesture with his hand) '. . . out of the country to Zims or South Africa. And I'm not going to put it in a bank, I'm going to buy property.'

'What's the biggest pay-out you've had from the Short Man so far?' asked Vincent.

'Forty.'

'But for Manchester United, you'd have got . . . ?'

'One hundred and twenty.'

Vincent looked suitably impressed, before remarking, 'They must be shitting off now, because Fash is off [injured] as well.'

Grobbelaar agreed that there was, indeed, excrement in the air. 'That's why he wants me back as soon as he can, and he wants [the match against] Leeds. I said, "No." I said, "Man City, at Man City." . . . Then I would collect the greenbacks from the Short Man and go straight out, because I'm going [to Zimbabwe] three days later. I'm taking the greenbacks and fucking off . . .'

Another pause, another change of tack: 'You see the thing is . . . my problem, if they find out it's me, there's going to be an investigation and there's deep shit. I was very annoyed with you because your brother actually said—'

'He said, "What the fuck is going on?"' Vincent interrupted. But Grobbelaar was still concerned.

'If I get caught, I'm out . . .'

'South Africa, here we come,' said his ex-partner.

'. . . Then the family fucking life is gone . . . they'll be putting my family under fucking severe . . . because then they'll be looked on as fucking crooks as well.'

'Obviously Debbie doesn't know about this,' said Vincent, supportively.

'Fuck all. But if there is an investigation on it, then obviously she is going to ask questions . . .'

By now, all Grobbelaar's earlier mood of relaxation had gone. He stood up, as if trying to walk off his tension. 'My missus doesn't know that we're talking. Milligan knows I've seen you a couple of times and he says, "You fucking know what he's like" . . .'

It was almost as if the two men were conducting a clandestine affair. 'We've got to be bloody careful,' said Vincent.

Then, confirming that he for one did not see himself as having been responsible for Chris Vincent's downfall in Zimbabwe, Grobbelaar went on, 'Because, what happened in Zimbabwe . . . I still don't know the full story. To this day, I'm still fucking worried. I'm trying to work out what happened to the fucking cash, what happened to this, what happened to that, who's fucking pulled the fucking plug . . . I don't know, because you haven't really explained to me.'

'I haven't had the opportunity. Hewlett—' began Vincent, but was quickly interrupted as Grobbelaar agreed: 'I know that Hewlett's trying to stitch every fucker up . . . I know that now, right?'

But, he suggested, there was a way in which the whole sorry saga might yet have a happy ending. 'I know the way that things could turn around in your favour, and I might give you an opportunity to do that. These greenbacks . . . you could pick them up every week and put them in a box . . . Bang, bang, bang . . . and accumulate it and account for it. Don't fucking use it, don't even touch it, because if there's a time when they say, "I've paid this fucker some money, and it's gone missing," and they put the cops on to me, I'm going to say, "Hey . . ." ' he lifted his hands in a gesture of outraged innocence . . . '"I've got no fucking money. You tell me where the fucking money is."'

Vincent responded enthusiastically. He was only too happy to mind Grobbelaar's money. Speaking of the whole imaginary plan, he said, 'I see it as a way of giving you back the cash you put into the business.'

'Yes,' agreed Grobbelaar, 'and you could come right in my missus's eyes, right? You say, "Here is your money back – this is the money I've earned, and this is the money I'm paying you back." That'll clear the air on that side, and it'll clear the air with your brother.'

'I appreciate what you're saying,' agreed Vincent. 'We could sort the whole thing out.'

This, ironically, was the emotional heart of the conversation. For all the talk about football and corruption, and for all the presence of the *Sun*'s recorders and reporters, the two men were both trying to come to terms with what had happened in Zimbabwe. A friendship that had meant an enormous amount to both of them had disintegrated into bitterness. Their attempts to explain and to rationalize what had happened to Mondoro, and to repair the damage, increasingly came to dominate their conversations.

Both men were speaking from the heart when they talked about Mondoro. Grobbelaar had mentioned Vincent's brother, had said that Chris could sort things out with him. 'But Keith is one of the ones who's going along with Hewlett,' Vincent protested. 'Keith, and Wundke and Fleet.'

A few minutes earlier, Grobbelaar had reached out and pulled a wastepaper basket from its home beneath a side table, across the carpet to his feet. Now, as if repeating his own name in Afrikaans, in which it sounds just like a man with a heavy cold trying to clear the phlegm from his throat – Hhhrrobbeluh! – he summoned a great gob from deep inside his chest. The glistening mass of spittle hung from his lower lip for a second, then dropped into the basket.

During the several seconds the procedure had taken to execute, Vincent had been talking about Keith. Now, though, Grobbelaar cut straight to the chase.

'What happened to the cash?'

'Thirty-five and a half thousand went to Hewlett,' said Vincent.

'And we've got fuck all to show for it.'

'Fuck all. He fucking gave us one right up the fucking arse.'

Grobbelaar began to reply, 'I just want to fucking . . .' but then, as was his way, he switched subjects in mid-sentence. 'How do you know who this fucker's been talking to?'

He meant the man behind Vincent's syndicate. Vincent responded by going off at a tangent, describing the palatial circumstances in which the man lived. 'It's got to be worth at least a million, with half a million pounds' worth of engraved staircases. He likes sure-fire bets.' The house he was actually describing was the De Beer's diamond company's house in Cadogan Square where Vincent's father liked to stay on his visits to London. It featured an extravagant hand-carved staircase, rising through the full height of the building.

Grobbelaar was not interested in property. 'You've got to go back to him and say, "How clandestine is this?" Because if it ever breaks, it's going to be fucking—'

'Take off to all four corners of the earth,' said Vincent, completing the sentence.

'My family . . .' began Grobbelaar.

This was a crucial moment. Months later, as we went through every moment of his meetings with Grobbelaar, Vincent swore that, 'If he'd said, "No, I won't do it. They'd be on the street," I'd have pulled the plug at that moment.'

But Grobbelaar did not say no. Instead, he went on, 'If the shit ever hits the fan, I don't think I'd have a fucking marriage. I'd just say, "Debbie, there's the lot. I'll fuck off."'

'Do you have enough bucks for them to be looked after?' wondered Vincent.

'I've got the house – I'd make that over to them – and the property in Portugal, and the fucking testimonial.'

'Obviously there's a risk . . .'

'There's a fucking big risk and that's what I'm worried about. If at any time . . . you're going to have to tell them this – that's why the money's going in a box . . . if at any time I feel that it's not on, the money will go straight back.'

'I'll just say that there'll be a game towards the end of the season,' said Vincent.

'I want to sign fuck all,' emphasized Grobbelaar.

'You'll nominate which team is going to lose,' continued Vincent. But suddenly the goalkeeper was distracted by a news report on the television, which had been on in the background throughout their conversation. A man dressed in a Spiderman outfit was trying to scale a skyscraper. 'Look at this fucking idiot!' exclaimed Grobbelaar, breaking the tension. 'Climbing the building without any ropes or anything – disabled as well. He's fucking mad!'

'Where do we take it from here?' asked Vincent, trying to bring things back down to earth. 'Does the Short Man bet only on you losing?'

'He asks me if it's a win or a—'

Vincent interrupted. 'So he bets both ways. So this is a similar type of thing.'

'It's all the same,' said Grobbelaar.

Vincent began, 'The people in the Far East must be—'

'Heavy,' Grobbelaar concluded. 'It's fucking frightening . . . Do you think I went out to Kuala Lumpur for the fucking games? I was getting sussed out by the Short Man's people, to see what type of person I am . . . if I'm genuine. I like to win. I don't like to fucking lose.' The following day, he added, he would be playing with a mask on. His broken cheekbone must have been painful and – despite the artificial protection – desperately vulnerable, but his pride, his professionalism and his raw courage all insisted that he carry out his job.

'What are you going to do about this lot now?' asked

Vincent. There was a long pause. Then Grobbelaar made his decision. 'To say it's on at this stage.'

But no sooner had those words been spoken than he hesitated again, raising a series of objections. What if they found out who he was? What if he gave them a match which did not involve him at all ... say, Leicester at Manchester United?

'Because then you're fucking him around,' said Grobbelaar, 'and he won't like it. Then you've got to wear a bullet-proof vest – that's how big it is. You can get fucking . . .' he made his fingers into a gun and pointed them at Vincent . . . 'Pow! One of those jobs. This is how dangerous it is. When you're playing with that much money, it's fucking dangerous.' Then he returned to a familiar theme. Who were these people Vincent was talking about? Where did they come from? Were they white? What did they look like?

'English . . . bloody smart,' said Vincent.

'Plum-in-the-mouth boys,' snorted Grobbelaar derisively.

'No,' Vincent disagreed. 'I think they've made their bucks through—'

'Through devious means,' said Grobbelaar, continuing his image of ruthless gangsters. 'That means . . .' Once again he pointed his fingers, gun-style, and pulled an imaginary trigger.

'Let me put it this way . . .' Vincent began.

'They don't hesitate to put anybody away,' said Grobbelaar. Even so, he added, 'I will go with these guys until the end of the season. I know which game I will pick . . . Liverpool, at Liverpool. Or Man United at Man United. That's in March.

'How quick afterwards would I get paid?' he asked, before switching almost immediately to the down-side of the deal. 'There's been these things in other countries and fuckers have been banned for life, footballers and baseballers . . . and then the depression sets in, and all that shit, and that's fucking hard to swallow.' He sighed, 'I still think the best way to make money for us, or for myself, was to go into the wildlife industry, and still to this day, I think it's . . .'

'It's such a shame,' said Vincent.

'I'm still fucking sick about it, really,' said Grobbelaar, as they went back over Mondoro, naming the people who could yet buy out Hewlett and restore their right to run a camp at Acacia Palm Lodge. For the second time he emphasized that this could be Vincent's chance to rescue his reputation in Zimbabwe, where, as Vincent agreed, 'My name is like mud these days.' He needed 'a hundred grunters [£100,000]', said Grobbelaar. More like three or four, said Vincent. Once more they dissected Neil Hewlett's supposed betrayals over the camp, the Hwange deal and the Bolers' would-be property purchase.

'Hewlett got to you because he told you things about me,' Vincent told Grobbelaar, as the latter made another one of his extravagant spits. 'He had every munt in that camp paid to tell him everything that happened every day.'

Vincent had a catalogue of complaints he wanted to voice. But Grobbelaar interrupted, with a note of finality: 'We'll do it this season. Tell him that it's on and I'm going to pick one game.' For the umpteenth time Grobbelaar emphasized the need for secrecy, and underlined the plan to lock his money away where no one could get at it – 'I don't know where you're going to put it, because I don't want this fucking cash to go missing.'

Then he and Vincent tried to work out how much he would make from the deal. He had been told he would make £2,000 every two weeks.

'So, how many weeks have we got left until the end of the season?' Grobbelaar asked.

'I don't know.'

'Sorry, till January.'

Vincent worked it out. 'There's nine until Christmas, so ten till the end of the year, four in January . . . fourteen.'

'Fourteen,' Grobbelaar repeated.

'That's twenty-eight grand,' suggested Vincent, forgetting his own story. It was two grand a fortnight, not a week. But Grobbelaar did not appear to spot the mistake.

'Twenty-eight grand,' he murmured.

## ☉ World Exclusive ☉

# GROBBELAAR TOOK BRIBES TO FIX GAMES

*Stunned . . Grobbelaar is confronted yesterday*    Picture: NIGEL CAIRNS

By JOHN TROUP and GUY PATRICK

SOCCER star Bruce Grobbelaar is exposed by The Sun today for taking massive bribes to throw key matches.

The flamboyant keeper pocketed £40,000 to lose a game while playing for Liverpool.

Greedy Grobbelaar, 37, was offered £175,000 to let in goals in another two Premiership fixtures.

He was caught on video boasting how he cheated to help a powerful and shadowy Far East syndicate pull off betting stings.

Grobbelaar, now with Southampton, was ashen-faced when Sun reporters confronted him at Gatwick Airport last night.

He said the revelations would probably "destroy me, my career, my marriage and existence here."

Then he claimed: "I have never tried to throw a game in my life"

Grobbelaar, who has worn a protective mask in recent matches after breaking his cheek, was due to fly to Harare for games with his national team Zimbabwe. But he vanished from the terminal without catching his plane.

The Sun had recorded him telling how he collected cash from the syndicate's mysterious go-between nicknamed The Short Man. The

*Continued on Page Two*

**Full amazing story: Pages 2, 3, 4, 5 & 6**

9 November 1994: the *Sun* front page that started an eight-year legal war. The final verdict: Grobbelaar had indeed accepted bribes. But had he fixed games? The Law Lords said no. *SUN*

Pictured in Zimbabwe (*above*), and (*left and below*) on holiday with Vincent, the woman he loved and lost: Bernice Bala'c.

ABOVE: Chris Vincent, a remarkably successful ladies' man.

'By the end of January,' said Vincent the salesman.

'Then there's three . . . three . . .'

'Till the beginning of March,' intruded Vincent, bafflingly. There are, after all, four weeks in February. Grobbelaar ignored him. 'That's another two, another four . . . that's twenty-eight, thirty-two . . . it'll be about thirty-four to the game. The Liverpool game should be 34.'

Vincent decided to ice his cake and put a metaphorical cherry on top. Making it up as he went along, he said, 'They've told me you're going to get 100K, plus ten per cent of whatever they make on top of that. If they make a million bucks, that's another hundred Gs coming to you. Two million – 200Gs.'

'Is that genuine?' asked Grobbelaar. The thought of cash brought him back to an old subject. 'I want to know where you're going to put the greenbacks.'

Vincent was into the home stretch and beginning to relax. 'I haven't a fucking clue at this stage. There's time to organize a lock-up in fucking Selfridges.'

'No,' snapped Grobbelaar, 'that's too dangerous. There'll be cameras on you all the fucking time.'

They were winding down now, discussing Grobbelaar's scheme to launch a Jungleman series of children's books, set in Africa, all about a magical young hero who could turn himself into any kind of animal. For one final time, Grobbelaar returned to the question of what to do with all the money. He was keen not to be personally connected to the deal.

'I might actually have to have another person to take it from you. The only one link in the chain is that I'm going to have to be with my brother.' This was Peter, who worked as a supervisor at a McDonald's restaurant at Heathrow airport. He did not seem to be an ideal choice, as Grobbelaar soon explained. 'It's the worst evil, because if I fall out with my brother he'll fucking blab.' They were considering circumstances that did not and could not arise. But there seemed to be reasons for Bruce's distrust. 'This is what I learned from the last Short Man. I've given my *boet* [Afrikaans for 'brother'] some cash, which he was supposed to give back to me. But he fucking—'

What he f—ing did was never discovered. This was an unmissable opportunity for Vincent to sound off about his great bugbear. 'As far as I'm concerned with my family, I don't have one any more.'

Grobbelaar was genuinely shocked. 'You can't say that.'

But Vincent was having none of it. The sheer hurt he felt at the way he had been treated – or, at any rate, believed he had – poured out. 'They bent me over and gave me one right up the fucking nought. I didn't know that Keith . . . I was just so disappointed. They had me right in the back with a fucking lance.' He explained how Keith had turned his parents against him.

'You've got to speak to them on your own, without anybody there,' said Grobbelaar.

Vincent had already tried that, and failed. 'When I pitched up in Harare [my father] said, "You've fucked things right up and I think you're a cunt, so get out of here." I had fuck all . . . nothing,' he moaned to Grobbelaar. 'My father's got so much kite in the UK and I said, "Please, I need some bucks to get myself sorted out when I get back there," and he told me to fuck off, because Keith had told him not to give me any money. So then I said fine . . . I went four days without food.'

It was a heartrending tale, but Grobbelaar had other matters on his mind. Leaning forward towards Vincent, he said, 'You're going to have to use another name when you leave a message on the answerphone, because if my missus finds out—'

Vincent had a ready solution. 'You know who I sound like on the phone? Allan Lamb.'

'Yeah,' said Grobbelaar, happy to take the name of the ex-England cricketer in vain. 'Just say Allan.' Then he had a better idea. 'He's got a brother . . . what's his name? Just use Charlie Lamb.'

'Why don't we use Charlie Vermaak . . . CV?'

Grobbelaar was satisfied. 'Charles Vermaak . . . Yeah, an old school chullie [mate] of mine is a Vermaak anyway. Fine.'

He got up and began to make his way from the room. If the words of the conversation were to be believed, Grobbelaar seemed to have agreed his terms. In return for a fortnightly payment of £2,000, plus £100,000, plus 10 per cent of any profits, he would do his best to ensure a Southampton defeat at a nominated game – probably against Manchester United or Liverpool. Chris Vincent, alias Charles Vermaak, would act as his go-between and banker. Vincent would redeem himself in front of Grobbelaar, Debbie and the Vincent family. Everything seemed to be well set.

Once the footballer had left the hotel, Vincent contacted the *Sun* journalists. As he had done after the previous meeting, he attempted to hang on to the £2,000 – although without success on this occasion. They arranged that Vincent would check out of the hotel, then wait in the lounge for Nigel Cairns, the *Sun* photographer, to pick him up.

At around 12.30, as Vincent was sitting waiting for Cairns, Grobbelaar came back to the hotel. This was an unforeseen and potentially disastrous situation. If Grobbelaar saw Vincent and Cairns together, their cover would be blown. Vincent watched with mounting horror as Grobbelaar walked towards him. But luckily, Cairns too had spotted Grobbelaar's arrival, and had alerted his colleagues. They paged Vincent, who went to the reception desk where he was told that a taxi had been ordered for him. On his return to the lounge he sat with Grobbelaar, who was accompanied by his new driver, Martin. As soon as the latter got up to get some tea and sandwiches, Grobbelaar leaned forward and – according to Vincent, whose claim is not corroborated by any taped evidence – confirmed, 'I'll do the Liverpool game at Liverpool.'

The final detail had been settled. After ten or fifteen minutes, Vincent caught his cab. Grobbelaar and Martin left a little while later. Amazingly, the *Sun* men had not told Vincent or the driver where they were supposed to go, so Vincent called John Troup on his mobile and arranged to meet at Southampton station. This was a high-risk rendezvous, since Grobbelaar, banned from driving, often used the train to get back to his flat in Lymington. Vincent got to the station and waited there for another nerve-racking quarter of an hour. Eventually, after more phone calls, it was established that he and Troup were waiting at different entrances. Finally, they met up again and took a train to Winchester, where they would review the results of their latest escapade.

# 18

## The Final Encounter

Booked into a Forte hotel close to Winchester Cathedral, Vincent, Troup and Patrick went through the tapes of the second meeting. The journalists transcribed the material and sent it to their offices in Manchester. There were more arguments over money, as Vincent made his demands and Troup did his best to resist. Eventually they settled on a £400 sweetener, just to tide Vincent over. The latter had a great deal of tension he needed to get out of his system. He hit the pubs of Winchester and got himself thoroughly unwound.

On the following day, 26 October, Vincent was informed that the time had come to present all the Grobbelaar material to the *Sun*'s lawyers and, even more importantly, to its then editor, Stuart Higgins. In 1987 Higgins had been immortalized in the mythology of the *Sun* when the previous editor, Kelvin MacKenzie, had given him one of his infamous bollockings. Higgins had not fought back, which merely infuriated his boss still further. MacKenzie concluded his tirade by shouting, 'You just sit there, soaking it all up . . . You're like a sponge. A fucking human sponge.'

This outburst gave MacKenzie an idea. The next day Higgins' face appeared on page 5 of the paper. 'Want someone to yell at? Scream at? Fume at?' asked the copy next to it. 'Ring

Higgy the human sponge, he'll soak it up.' 'Higgy,' said the piece, which printed his direct-line telephone number at Wapping, 'LOVES loudmouths. Can't LIVE without a tongue-lashing . . . So pick up the phone and fume, folks. His Wimpishness is waiting for your calls with a silly-billy grin on his face and honeyed words of love in his heart . . . the fool.'

For days, Higgy the human sponge had to endure the rantings of foam-flecked *Sun* readers, who insulted him, sneered at him and, in one case, threatened to ram 'the rough end of a pineapple' up his nether regions. But Higgins was both tougher and shrewder than he looked. Far from cracking under the strain, he survived, prospered and moved up the *Sun*'s ranks. Seven years later, when Kelvin MacKenzie departed for a career in satellite and cable television, Stuart Higgins was appointed editor of the country's most powerful newspaper.

Chris Vincent was another who would discover that there was little to be gained by shouting at Higgins. For now, though, he and the two hacks went up to London and checked into the Britannia International Hotel in Marsh Wall, Docklands, not far from the *Sun*'s Wapping headquarters. Troup and Patrick went to their office, telling Vincent to stay at the hotel and keep his head down. He swam and worked out in the hotel gym. By nine in the evening, the two reporters were back. They had good news . . . and bad news. The good news was that their lawyers thought that the story was libel-proof. They did not have to make any allegations against Grobbelaar – he had said it all for himself. But there was a catch. Grobbelaar had mentioned the fact that he was going to throw the game against Manchester City. It was due to be played on 5 November. If they waited until then, they could catch him red-handed.

Vincent's reply was swift and to the point. 'I told them to fuck right off.'

He knew that Bernice Bala'c desperately needed cash to appease her bank and creditors. So he told the *Sun* that he was not prepared to cooperate further unless he was paid some more money. Once again, he threatened to go to another newspaper. Troup consulted with Stuart Higgins and a further £200 was produced. It was also agreed that this money, along with that which he had already received, would be paid in addition to his agreed £30,000.

They would all go back to Southampton the following week for one final taped meeting with Grobbelaar. That settled, the *Sun* spent the next two days going over their material while Vincent went sightseeing in London. On the Friday evening Troup and Patrick went back home to Manchester, leaving Vincent at the Britannia Hotel.

On Sunday the 30th he left London and took the train to Chester to see Bernice, desperate to rekindle their friendship. He returned that night, expecting to find instructions from the *Sun*. But it was not until Monday that he was told that they would all be returning to Southampton on the following day – Tuesday 1 November.

Troup and Patrick would go there direct from Manchester. Vincent was given a first-class rail ticket from London. They would set him up in an apartment, using the cover story that he had got his new job and been given a company flat. On the Wednesday morning they moved over to Vincent's new home, Flat 40, Osbourne House, Grosvenor Square. It was a ground-floor apartment in a modern, Georgian-style block laid out in a U-shape around a gravel courtyard dotted with bushes.

Although the flat was small, with just one bedroom, it was well equipped with smart furniture, a kitchen and every possible appliance – just the sort of place a successful company might arrange for a newly arrived executive. Few companies, however, would give the place the sort of make-over that the *Sun* now provided. Gerry Brown – father of Dweeb – arrived to wire the place for sound and vision. He worked with a pro-fessionalism and assurance by which Vincent, for once, was mightily impressed. In the drawers underneath the bed he placed an eight-hour tape-recorder. Cables were laid under the carpet to microphones dotted around the living room. A mini hi-fi system, which had a camera concealed within it, was installed.

All day, Troup had been trying to persuade Vincent to call

Grobbelaar and arrange an immediate meeting. Vincent had resisted, not wanting to do anything until he knew that the flat had been properly bugged. His caution turned out to be well justified because when the whole system was installed and tested – disaster! It didn't work. The tape-recorder was malfunctioning. Brown tried to call his son, at first with no success. Eventually, Conrad was tracked down and ordered to bring a second tape-recorder down to Southampton a.s.a.p. Eventually he arrived, put the new machine in place and made the whole set-up work. By now, though, it was past ten at night. Any meeting would have to wait until the following day.

When Vincent first called Grobbelaar on the morning of 3 November he was not at home. Wanting to retain an element of surprise, Vincent did not leave a message on the machine but tried again an hour or so later, this time getting through. Grobbelaar was packing up his flat prior to moving to a new cottage. He was in high spirits, sounding as though he thought that his friendship with Vincent had been restored to full health.

'You know who was here last weekend?' he asked, apparently unaware that this conversation, like the ones at the De Vere Hotel, was being taped. 'The Six-Footer. Do you know how old she is?'

Vincent guessed that the woman in question might be anywhere between twenty-two and thirty.

'Twenty-two,' said Grobbelaar, delightedly. 'I brought it here and gave it the big one, on the balcony.'

'Like a dog?' enquired Vincent.

'Correct,' confirmed his pal.

The two men met up for a relaxed, bantering pub lunch. Vincent apologized that he would not spend the afternoon helping Grobbelaar with his house-moving, but he had a number of business meetings to attend. They agreed to get together again that evening at Shooters, a bar in a waterside development called Town Quay, close to Southampton Docks.

As it happened, Shooters was closed for a private party, so they moved on to another nearby bar called Bojangles.

Grobbelaar was now less interested in the football side of his dealings with Vincent – which could not, in any case, be discussed, as Martin had come with him to the bar – than in Zimbabwe. He still wanted to get to the bottom of what had happened to Acacia Palm Lodge. But after a couple of beers Martin could not drink any more for fear of getting caught drink-driving, and Grobbelaar decided that he would dispense with his services for the evening.

'I'll go with Chris,' he said. Vincent was driving a maroon-coloured Vauxhall Cavalier, hired for him by the *Sun* as his supposed company car.

Once Martin was out of earshot, Vincent reminded Grobbelaar that he still had the £2,000 that was his first payment from the new gambling syndicate. 'I can't keep carrying it around for ever,' he said. The money was at his flat. Why didn't they go there? Then he could hand over the cash and show off his new place. They drove the short distance to Grosvenor Square and their third, and final, taped meeting.

When, on the morning of 4 November, John Troup first watched the video-recording of the previous night's encounter, his first words were, 'Fuck me! This is some monologue, this.'

Indeed it was. Secure in the knowledge that the case against Grobbelaar had already been established, Vincent was now free to let rip on the subjects close to his heart – Mondoro, his business partners, his family and Grobbelaar himself. But before he got under way, there was one small detail to sort out.

'Jesus, smart flat,' said Grobbelaar admiringly when he first walked in. Vincent fetched him a glass of wine. Then he fired off a quick warning shot to the effect that, 'Keith and Maureen were talking out of their backsides,' and – having ensured that Grobbelaar, smartly dressed in a shirt and tie, was standing by the sofa, directly in line with the camera hidden in the mini hi-fi – handed over the envelope containing £2,000.

'There you go, sir. I've just been carrying it around the fucking countryside.'

Grobbelaar took the envelope, looked at it briefly and threw it on to the sofa. He sat down, pulling on the first of many cigarettes. Vincent sat down for a while, but soon rose to his feet, pacing up and down, gesticulating, his voice becoming ever louder, ever more emotional. Some idea of his intensity can be gleaned from a simple statistic: throughout the conversation, Vincent averaged seventeen 'fucks' or 'fuckings' per minute.

Given half a chance, Grobbelaar swore at roughly the same pace, but his voice was calmer, deeper and more conciliatory throughout. Now that his football business had been sorted out he could relax, setting himself up as the mediator between Chris and the rest of the world.

Vincent was on a mission from the *Sun*, who wanted him to gather incriminating material against Grobbelaar. Grobbelaar would later claim that he too was on a mission – to collect evidence against Vincent. But for the vast majority of the third meeting what can actually be heard are two friends trying to put their friendship back together, with Grobbelaar in particular doing everything he can to be conciliatory and let bygones be bygones. And, just like the old days, there was always time for their traditional leisure pursuits. At one point, footsteps could be heard outside – the unmistakable tippy-tapping of a woman's shoes. Like a hound that had caught the scent of its prey, Grobbelaar stiffened, turned his head.

Vincent notices the gesture. 'There's fresh around, yeah. But I haven't seen it yet.'

After another long oration from Vincent about Mondoro, Grobbelaar tried to persuade him to stop raking over the past in his mind: 'You're starting a new life now.'

Vincent appeared to agree. 'I took about a month or six weeks to recover, and then I just said, right . . . finished.'

Grobbelaar lit another cigarette, then spoke: 'I'm still wanting a part of Africa. I will get that objective sooner or later, right?' They kept talking about the camp, returning relentlessly to all the usual suspects: Hewlett, Keith, his wife Maureen. According to Grobbelaar, 'The first time we went out there [to the camp], she poisoned my missus's mind about you. Her words were that you nearly destroyed her marriage.'

'If Keith hasn't got any balls, I'm not responsible for that,' snorted Vincent.

'Exactly,' said Grobbelaar. 'The whole scenario is, they poisoned my mind against you. I'll tell you straight. Before talking to you here, I was guilty of saying that you weren't the person I thought you were.'

Vincent looked as if he were about to interrupt, but Grobbelaar held up his hands as if to stop him and went on: 'I do understand now, when you came to see me at the Swallow Hotel . . . I've never seen a man lose so much of his confidence. I never thought you'd do that. And now you've got your confidence back.'

'I've got a job now,' said Vincent.

'But there,' continued Grobbelaar, 'I saw a man die. I didn't like what I saw . . . I don't want our friendship to be taken away.'

Grobbelaar strongly agreed that the camp had been a good idea and that they had been running it in the right way. Money, he said, had never been their prime objective: 'That's what I told you in the beginning. The reason I'm putting the money in is so when I'm retired I can say, thank you very much . . .' Just whom he would say this to was never made clear. The world? Debbie? Vincent was too far into his own self-justification to pause for anyone else's information.

'I was getting shot at,' he said, referring to his days in the Rhodesian Army, in which his brother Keith had been too young to serve.

'I was there when we got shot at,' agreed Grobbelaar. 'I volunteered when National Servicemen were used as guinea-pigs, as fucking Fire Force.'

Vincent nodded appreciatively. 'This wine's actually fucking good.' Then he underlined once again the pain he felt at the way his family had treated him. He explained how the final fight with his father had its roots in his father's refusal to come and see him receive his Bronze Cross.

'But there's your mother,' said Grobbelaar. 'You've got somebody there.'

The real crunch for Chris, though, was that he had gone to his father looking for help – and been refused. He found this incomprehensible. If someone ever came to him, they would get the shirt off his back.

Grobbelaar agreed, 'To this day, I know I'll get a knock on the door from my son,' he said. 'And if he says, "You owe me some fucking bucks" . . . well, I do. I did pay for his clothing and feeding, up until [his mother] got married, and that's when it came quits.' Several years down the line, he said, the time was bound to come when he would be asked to cough up another instalment.

Here was a strong suggestion that Grobbelaar's illegitimate son existed, but the *Sun* were never able to find the boy, who would by then have been about eighteen. Soon after the Grobbelaar story broke, they ran an advertisement in the paper asking for anyone who had had a child by a Liverpool goal-keeper to contact them. Sure enough, a woman came forward, and a team was sent to interview and photograph her. When they got to her home, they discovered she did indeed have a child whose father was a goalkeeper. But that goalkeeper was not Bruce Grobbelaar.

That, though, was all a matter for the future. For now, Chris Vincent was trying to explain to Grobbelaar how he felt. As far as he was concerned, everything that had happened in Zimbabwe was behind him. He had come back to England determined to start a new life, with a new job, new home and a new circle of friends. But Vincent's words rang hollow, for the wounds caused by the collapse of Mondoro, and the personal conflicts arising from that, were still all too evident. Along the way, he mentioned that people in Victoria Falls still felt that he had taken them to the cleaners.

Grobbelaar seemed surprised: 'We didn't take anyone to the cleaners.'

Vincent explained that there were still unpaid bills amounting to more than 30,000 Zimbabwean dollars – around £3,000. One of these debts, for 5,000 Zimbabwean dollars, was to Jay's Supermarket. Jay Gopal, who ran the place, had always been incredibly helpful to Vincent, who said he was determined to pay him back £500 from his first monthly pay cheque.

Grobbelaar immediately offered to go halves. In fact, he went on, pointing to the envelope full of cash, why didn't Chris pay him the money directly out of that? 'You know what I'm going to do?' he went on. 'Fly out [to Zimbabwe] on Tuesday or Wednesday, take a 'copter out there and see what Hewlett's reaction is when I walk into the camp. Do you think I should do it? I don't want to hide. I want to go and face these fuckers.'

'I've had to say, it's finished,' said Vincent. 'I've just said, Vincent: you've got to make yourself a new life. You've got to find yourself a job, something you like doing. You've got to find somewhere to live, find a new circle of friends. You've just got to start from Square One.'

This was, as later events would prove, fantastically good advice. Sadly, however, he did not follow it. In fact, within seconds he was back on the subject of the camp – how great it could have been, and how appallingly it went wrong. 'All I was trying to do was run the best fucking safari camp . . . and we did.'

'We did,' agreed Grobbelaar. 'My mother . . . when we sang that song [at the Jungleman dinner] she fucking cried. And that really opened my missus's eyes. We were fucking right. Even now, my missus says to me, "Where's Chris?" And I say I don't know, because I can't say to her . . .'

'Have you told anybody that you and I have spoken?' asked Vincent.

'I said to Moany Tilligan . . .' Grobbelaar replied.

Vincent went back to the money. He was due to pick up another two grand next Tuesday or Wednesday: 'Do you want me to drop it off at the airport?'

Grobbelaar, too, returned to the subject of football. 'I'll tell you something. I'm doing a Short Man at the weekend. He's supposed to be ringing me tonight, but I'm not available.'

'Is it a big one?' asked Vincent.

'It's going to be double what he was going to give.'

'What . . . eighty?'

'It'll be about that,' said Grobbelaar. Then he paused. 'No, fifty. But hopefully the fifty will be ready for when I go. I'm not sure what to do. I think I'll keep the fifty and lock it in my trunk, keep it in greenbacks. And then, when I've got an inkling of what to do with it, I'll do it.'

'I'd take it with you, if I was you,' said Vincent.

'Yeah, that's what I'm going to do,' replied Grobbelaar.

'I'll speak to these guys tomorrow.'

'Don't tell them I'm doing anything.'

Vincent told him not to worry. 'They can't do anything till next year anyway . . . their tax year ends on 31 December and then they've got big cash they can get rid of.'

They talked for a while longer, and Grobbelaar said he was thinking of investing in a golf course in South Africa. Then the conversation petered to a close as the two men wandered to and from the bathroom and got ready to go out to dinner. Before they left, there was one last detail that had to be seen to: Grobbelaar had put down the envelope containing the £2,000. Now Vincent gave it to him again. Grobbelaar put it in the pocket of his leather bomber-jacket. The cash had been accepted. The two men left the flat.

They then drove in Vincent's hire-car to the same Italian restaurant in Brockenhurst, the Palio, where they had eaten after the first taped meeting at the De Vere Grand Harbour Hotel. En route, Grobbelaar – almost as if he sensed that there was something wrong – took the money out of his pocket and put it in the glove-compartment of the car. As they drove through the Hampshire countryside, he insisted, 'You must phone your brother.'

Vincent refused. 'If you ever see my brother, tell him I'll be the best friend in the world to anyone until they shoot me in the back. And then I'll be the most evil son-of-a-bitch on the planet.'

Grobbelaar was clearly shaken. 'I wonder what you think of me now?' he asked, before changing the subject as quickly as possible.

They enjoyed a friendly dinner. At about 11.20 they left the restaurant and Vincent drove Grobbelaar back to his flat in Lymington. Shortly before midnight, Vincent claims that the telephone rang. The call that followed, according to his allegation, must have come from Richard Lim. Yet no such call was traced to his mobile or domestic telephone accounts. So the only possible assumptions are that either he made it from a different telephone – at a casino, for example, or one belonging to a friend – or that he never made it at all and that Vincent invented the call as a means of bolstering what was on the *Sun*'s videotape. It should also be noted that both Lim and Grobbelaar denied ever using the nickname 'Bubka', although viewers of *I'm a Celebrity . . . Get Me Out of Here!* will recall that John Fashanu frequently called his fellow competitors 'Bubbelah', a term of endearment that was soon picked up by Phil Tuffnell as well.

Vincent, however, maintains that Grobbelaar said, 'Hello, Bubka. This weekend . . . ?'

Vincent then allegedly heard a one-sided conversation, as the two men went over the details for Saturday's game. Southampton were due to lose. 'By how many?' asked Grobbelaar, asking about the goal-difference he had to maintain.

He was given the information. '*Ja*, OK . . . and how much?'

A figure was mentioned. 'Fine. I'll speak to you later about sorting it out.'

When the call was over, Vincent asked, 'Was that the Short Man?'

'Yes,' Grobbelaar allegedly confirmed. 'This weekend, Man City, by one goal. But they're going back to paying small money – £25,000.'

Whatever the truth about that call, Vincent left soon afterwards, saying goodbye to Grobbelaar for the final time. He drove back to Southampton and, at around 1 a.m., met John Troup and the other *Sun* staff at their base in the Dolphin Hotel. Gerry Brown picked up a video-monitor and took it with him as they went back to Vincent's flat to watch the tape.

They were not best pleased by the emphasis on Zimbabwe, speeding through most of the recording at fast-forward. But there were a few choice morsels – Grobbelaar's mention of his son, the unprompted reference to the Short Man business at the weekend, and, best of all, his acceptance of a bribe. Now, they felt certain, they had really got their man.

For the *Sun* journalists, the manner in which the trap had been set and sprung was a purely professional affair. For all the jokes about the Dweeb, they had done a remarkably slick and thorough job, proving – if proof were needed – that there is no news hound in the world to compare with a British tabloid hack. But what of Vincent? He had set up his best mate for a fall. Yet the conversation on the tapes proved that Grobbelaar was clearly concerned for his friend. He wanted Vincent to recover his morale, his self-confidence and his standing with his family and friends. He kept offering to help him out. How, then, could Vincent look him in the eye, knowing what was really going on?

In the late summer of 1995, as we were working our way through the many hours of interviews that formed the initial basis for this book, I put this point to Chris Vincent, knowing that if I did not press him on it, others surely would. The conversation that ensued felt very much like our own version of one of those *Sun* tapes.

What, I asked, would it have taken for Vincent to have told Grobbelaar that he was working for the *Sun*?

'It would have taken him to apologize, to realize what he's done, and actually come straight out and say, "I've fucked you up badly, and it's all my fault."'

But did Grobbelaar really know that he had fucked you up?

'If he didn't by the end of that meeting, he was stupid.'

But even at that stage, you could have stopped.

Vincent was adamant. 'The point is, why must I be his conscience? He must work out that he actually betrayed the trust between us, and it's going to take him to say, "I'm helluva sorry that I went and told Hewlett what you and I discussed and I'm a complete prat for having done it." He sits in a meeting and says, "I let those guys poison my mind against you." But it's like all the shit that happened in Zimbabwe is not his fault. It's all Hewlett's fault, and Keith's fault, and Fleet's fault, and Wundke's fault. It's not his fault. When it is. He's the son-of-a-bitch who signed for the truck. He's the son-of-a-bitch who agreed to put the money in out of his testimonial fund until we cashed Dyer's cheque. He's the guy that stopped Dyer sending the money to me. He's the guy that promised to pay Keith the bloody money for the Jungleman. It was his golf tournament. Everything points to him. He was the guy who was cheating on his wife. So all the way down the line, every-thing points to him.'

So what would Vincent have done if Grobbelaar had said sorry?

'I'd have said, "Well, the first thing you've got to do is give me five-and-a-half grand to go and pay Bernice, and give it to me right now, in greenbacks. And the whole thing I've been telling you about is complete bullshit, because I've been trying to set you up right here. If you want to carry on dealing with the Short Man, that's fine, but I want greenbacks." In other words, he's got to make a severe plan with me now.'

That would be blackmail.

'Correct.'

I wondered what would happen if, a few years from now, when all the court cases and anything that might follow from them were done and dusted, he were to meet Grobbelaar in the street. What would he say?

'I would just say, "Are we even now? You took everything I'd worked for my whole life away from me, and then proceeded to continue stitching up other people." For me it's quits then. And if he walked up and said, "I believe you've got a safari camp. I've got three hundred thousand sitting in the bank, do you want it?" I would speak to him about it.' Then Vincent began to take a calmer view of the situation. 'The guy fucked up badly, but I'm more angry with my family – because they're family – than I am with him. I just think that he's a prat for not recognizing that I was his best friend, and I was trying to help him. He didn't sit down with his best friend and say, "What's going on here?" And then when I give him a chance to do that, in that third meeting in Southampton, he still doesn't. He says, "I'll give you the opportunity to put things right." Who does he think he is? He fucked up in the first place. All he had to do was say sorry and fix it. And fixing it would just have been to take five and a half thousand pounds and give it to Bernice. And I'd have said, "Fine, we're quits."'

But Grobbelaar did not say sorry. He did not hand over the five grand to Bernice. So Vincent got his revenge, and his money, by the only other means available to him – the *Sun*.

# 19

## Scoop!

In any newspaper investigation, the most nerve-racking point for the journalists involved is when the moment comes to 'front-up' the subject of their enquiries. For days, weeks or even months, information has been gathered from every possible source, by every possible means. At times this may have been an exciting, even dangerous, process. But nothing compares to the nerve it takes to look someone in the eye and say – or at least suggest – 'You're nicked.'

For John Troup and Guy Patrick, their moment of truth with Bruce Grobbelaar occurred at around 4.30 p.m. on 8 November 1994. They had been working on their story since 6 September. They had a live witness, taped evidence and photographs. The only thing they did not have was an admission or denial from the man at the centre of it all. They had to get a quote from Grobbelaar at all costs. They knew that the time to catch him would be when he made his departure to Zimbabwe from Gatwick airport. They would have one, and only one, opportunity to speak to him. That being the case, the front-up that followed was little short of a masterpiece.

Before that could happen, however, there was one final detail the *Sun* wanted to capture – Grobbelaar's purported attempt to throw the Manchester City–Southampton match. Vincent,

Troup and Patrick went up to Manchester on 4 November. The following day the reporters went to the match, accompanied by a team of photographers who were briefed to cover Grobbelaar from every possible angle. To the journalists' frustration, the game ended in a 3–3 draw. In the months and years to come, videotapes of the game would be examined by football experts who had not been shown copies of the *Sun* videotapes. On the basis of what they saw during the ninety minutes of the match, none of them would detect any deliberate errors by Grobbelaar. But the *Sun* team, who had seen and heard Grobbelaar telling Vincent that he was 'doing a Short Man', were on the look-out for incriminating evidence and were bound to interpret events in that light.

They felt sure, for example, that Grobbelaar had dived over the ball to let in the third goal. They also believed that – towards the end of the match when the draw seemed certain – he had sent a goal-kick straight to the feet of a Man City forward, Adie Mike, who promptly shot wide of the goal.

Nigel Cairns, the photographer who had worked with Vincent, Troup and Patrick in Southampton, was assigned to cover the game. He later told me: 'I've done a game every Saturday for the past twenty-two years. And if you're at the wrong end when a goal is scored, the saving shot you always take is the goalkeeper of the scoring team, celebrating. But when Southampton got their first goal Bruce just stood there ashen-faced. On the other goals, he was shaking his head.'

Yet Grobbelaar also made two good saves, one at close range from Garry Flitcroft, who shot the ball straight at Grobbelaar after the latter had advanced from his line to narrow the angle. Were they the actions of a man trying to throw a game?

At the end of the match, Cairns – who knew what his paper had planned for the following week – was convinced that he had witnessed Grobbelaar's last-ever performance. Surely, he thought, the FA would ban him as soon as the story came out. He decided to follow him off the park. 'Bruce put his arm round [Manchester City's] Paul Walsh and congratulated him,' Cairns remembered. Walsh had ended with two goals to his name and the incident was similar to Grobbelaar's raising Andy Cole's arm after the Newcastle game. But what did that imply? Was it evidence of any dubious intent on Grobbelaar's part? Or was it simply the reaction of a wholehearted sportsman who always gave of his very best, but was man enough to recognize the skills of his opponents?

The following day Chris Vincent went back to his flat in Chirk, where he had packed up all his possessions on the assumption that he might need to make a quick getaway after the story broke. Nigel Cairns accompanied him, and photographed him revealing the cubby-hole under the bath where he had hidden the £20,000 he had allegedly been given after the Newcastle match.

There had been some talk of confronting Grobbelaar at his home, where he was spending the weekend with Debbie and the girls, trying to repair his marriage. But it was decided that it would be better to get him as he left for Zimbabwe. He had told Vincent he was going out there to play in an international, but there was still some uncertainty about exactly which flight he would take.

From a phone-box in Chirk Vincent called Grobbelaar, who told him that he was planning to leave the UK on Tuesday. His flight left at 5 p.m. They arranged to meet at the Air Zimbabwe desk at Gatwick airport at 3 p.m., supposedly so that Vincent could hand over the second £2,000 payment from his mythical syndicate.

Later on Sunday afternoon, Vincent drove to Chester to see Bernice Bala'c. She remembers that he looked exhausted. He told her that the story was going to be hitting the streets within the next few days. 'It's going to open a can of worms,' he said. 'And lions, tigers, elephants and God knows what else are going to come out of that can as well.'

Back in Manchester, the tabloid juggernaut was really picking up momentum. Troup and Patrick had begun the work of turning their transcribed tapes into usable stories. The Vincent–Grobbelaar conversations were a goldmine which would soon produce three successive front-page splashes and half a dozen inside spreads – the sort of haul that can make a reporter's career.

Monday saw Vincent in the *Sun*'s offices, signing a two-page affidavit to cover allegations that referred to incidents not dealt with on tape – visiting Manchester and Heathrow airports with Grobbelaar to pick up money; the meeting at Fashanu's house; the journey to the Hilton Hotel before the Norwich game; and so on.

By now, Troup and Patrick were becoming understandably nervous. Guy Patrick still feared that the whole story was a set-up. He would not believe that matches could be fixed or that such wealthy syndicates could operate so secretly. His incredulity foreshadowed what many supposed experts would say when the story broke, but in an increasingly heated argument Troup insisted that they had not been sold a pup: the story was legitimate and he was sticking by it.

As the general mood became ever more edgy, Vincent asked Peter Sherlock, the local editor, what would happen to him when the solids hit the fan. He was told not to worry. The *Sun* would make sure he was well looked after. There were bound to be FA and even police investigations, and Grobbelaar was likely to try to sue for libel. Since the paper would need his help throughout the post-publication period, they would put him on the payroll. 'You've got to trust us,' Sherlock said.

In the same spirit of mutual cooperation, he and Vincent agreed a further £2,000 deal for the telephone numbers of several Grobbelaar girlfriends, including the Wild Thing, the two Virgin Atlantic stewardesses and the Ice Machine. He also told them that Kate Read – the Six-Footer – could be found at the Castle Tavern in Shepherd's Bush, West London.

Later in the day, Vincent, Troup and Patrick caught the train down to London. From the moment when he had first called the *Sun*, Vincent had found it impossible to concentrate on reading a book or even a magazine. So he kept himself occupied by fiddling with a lock-knife – a sharp, pointed knife used in the chipboard industry to check board density. Worried that his meetings with Grobbelaar might end in violence, Vincent had taught himself to lock and unlock the knife while it was still in his trouser-pocket. He could now whip it from his trousers, flick the blade open and be ready to defend himself within a second.

As he sat in the first-class compartment of the InterCity 125 Vincent worked on his technique, endlessly opening and closing the blade. Given the atmosphere of tension that had descended upon the trio, the sight of a proven killer amusing himself by toying with a deadly weapon was the very last thing that John Troup and Guy Patrick needed to calm their nerves.

That evening they checked into the elegant, old-fashioned surroundings of Brown's Hotel in Dover Street, just off Piccadilly. Vincent was put into journalistic purdah, and told not to leave his room until Grobbelaar had been fronted-up and the story put to bed. He began smoking and pacing his room: he would scarcely stop doing either of those things for the next thirty-six hours.

By 11 a.m. on Tuesday, Gatwick airport had been turned into a stake-out zone: half a dozen photographers were covering entrances, exits and the Air Zimbabwe desk. A room had been hired in an airport hotel and filled with computer equipment and portable scanners that enabled photographers to wire their negatives direct to Wapping, via telephone lines. Back at the North Terminal, John Troup, Guy Patrick and Gerry Brown were wired-up and in position. They knew that Grobbelaar would go to the airline desk and ask for 'Pat' – the local manager responsible for ensuring his upgrade to Business Class. All he had to do now was turn up.

At 1 p.m. Grobbelaar arrived at Gatwick. But he did not do what was expected of him. Instead, he walked straight through the terminal, caught a cab and disappeared. The *Sun*'s reporters were horrified. They called Vincent. 'What the fuck is he doing?'

'Don't worry, he's probably gone to see a girl. He'll be back.'

But he did not come back. Three more hours went by. More calls, of ever-increasing desperation, were made between

Gatwick and Brown's Hotel. At 4.30, just as Vincent was calling Nigel Cairns for the umpteenth time, the word came through. Grobbelaar had reappeared. He was walking towards the Air Zimbabwe desk in the company of Martin Johnson. Troup and Patrick were following him. They had caught him. The front-up had begun.

'Bruce Grobbelaar?' asked Guy Patrick, with a properly formal, even respectful tone to his voice. 'Guy Patrick and John Troup from the *Sun* newspaper, sir.'

Grobbelaar acknowledged their presence, before Patrick spoke words which must be the contemporary British equivalent to a knock on the door from the KGB, or a midnight visit from the Gestapo: 'We have a series of grave allegations which the paper intends publishing tomorrow. We wondered if we could have just two minutes with you . . .'

There was something almost apologetic about the way that Patrick revealed that his paper had been compiling evidence that, well . . . 'It sounds awful, but you threw a game at a Premier League match last season. You received £40,000.'

Troup cut in, playing Mr Nasty. He named the Short Man, informed Grobbelaar that they knew about the games he had tried, but failed, to throw, then played his ace: 'We have video evidence . . .'

Now it was getting tough. They presented Grobbelaar with a picture of himself receiving the £2,000 from Chris Vincent. Grobbelaar was standing like a soldier 'at ease', with his hands clasped behind his back, bouncing on the balls of his feet. He claimed that he had not taken the money, but the reporters piled on the pressure: the meetings at the De Vere Hotel; his claims that he had dived the wrong way against Manchester United; his quote that, 'That's as true as fucking honest God'; the game against Coventry City. Repeatedly they told him, 'We've got it on tape.'

Slowly the truth of his situation began to dawn on Grobbelaar. 'Have you got a videotape?'

Oh yes, they had a tape all right, and from three different meetings. They named Chris Vincent and detailed the deal he and Grobbelaar had made, underlining once again, 'And those meetings were filmed.'

'I met him, yes,' blustered Grobbelaar. 'But I made it clear to him that that would never be able to become [*sic*], because if I ever get caught, I'm in big trouble.'

Both reporters started questioning Grobbelaar at once. 'Why did you take the £2,000 off him, then?' asked Patrick.

'I didn't.'

'Why would you say, "If I ever got caught"?' insisted Troup.

Grobbelaar tried to protest that he had thrown the money away.

Troup: 'But you put it straight in your pocket.'

Patrick: 'You put it in your pocket and you walked out of that flat.'

Troup: 'We can prove all of that as well.'

Grobbelaar changed tack, claiming that he had put the money 'in safeguard', in case 'that person' – i.e. Vincent – tried to incriminate him. He had only met him, he said, to discuss the Mondoro deal.

The *Sun* knew different. They went straight to the second meeting, on the day his mask had been fitted. They pointed out that he had begun by saying, 'Tell me the deal with these guys.'

Grobbelaar backed down a fraction. Yes, he had been approached about a syndicate that could make sure-fire money, but he had said that there was nothing sure-fire in the world.

'No, you didn't,' said Patrick. 'You said, and I quote, "The deal's on. Go back and tell them it's on. One game this season." That's what you said. That's what's going in the paper tomorrow.'

At that point, Grobbelaar asked if they could move to a quieter seating area where fewer people could overhear their conversation: 'I know you got a tape on you,' he sighed.

As more and more of the evidence emerged, Grobbelaar painted a picture of his dealings with Chris Vincent. The latter, he said, had blown between £55,000 and £60,000 of his money in a business in Zimbabwe. He had just wanted to find out where all the money had gone. Vincent approached him with an idea of fixing matches. But, he insisted, 'I've never tried to throw a game in my life.'

It was no good, insisted the reporters. They had him on tape. They had him talking to the Short Man. They had him boasting and joking about his deals and his unintended saves. If he was so appalled by Vincent's proposal, they asked him, why hadn't he simply told him to get lost?

'I have done that on numerous—' Grobbelaar began.

But Troup wasn't going to let him escape. 'We know that you haven't done that, because we've actually been there.'

They had been at Maine Road on Saturday, too. And bearing in mind what a fine goalkeeper Grobbelaar was, they were of the opinion that he could have saved the third goal and need not later have kicked the ball straight to Adie Mike.

'You can run your story, if that is what you want to do,' said Grobbelaar. 'What you will do is destroy myself, destroy my career, destroy my marriage and my existence here. What you get out of it, I don't know.'

'Are you denying it all, though?' asked Troup.

'Yes, I'm totally denying it.'

So they started again. Why did he have the meetings with Vincent? Why not tell him to get lost?

Grobbelaar pleaded. 'This will end my whole bloody marriage . . . I thought I was just getting back.' He made a final attempt to counter-attack. He said he had always known his meetings with Vincent were being taped. He had had a good look around and seen the camera at once.

'Where was it?'

'Up on the right-hand side.'

'Wrong.'

Grobbelaar tried again: 'Either one in the kitchen or one in the ceiling.'

'Wrong.'

The pressure was unrelenting. Patrick said, 'Can I ask you something? I know it's a slightly personal question, but are you faithful to your wife?'

Of course Grobbelaar said yes. And of course they started listing the girlfriends.

Again Grobbelaar tried to switch subjects. He said he had people, both in this country and in Zimbabwe, looking into Vincent's bribery allegations. He named 'Ian Bloomfield' of the Manchester Police. Subsequent enquiries indicated that there was no Ian Bloomfield on the Manchester force.

When the reporters mentioned John Fashanu, Grobbelaar said that he and Fash were working together to set up an agency to get footballers over to Britain from Africa, using Fashanu's Nigerian connections.

Patrick was not interested. 'Do you think it's a particularly sensible thing for a man in your position, and idolized as you are, to talk about throwing games if you haven't done it?'

Back they went to Grobbelaar's acceptance of Vincent's offer, and his determination to keep the whole thing secret from his wife. Why did he take the money? Why did he say he'd dived the wrong way? They'd taped him. They'd taped him three times. Why did he do these things? If he wanted to set up Vincent, why wasn't he taping him? Why?

It must have seemed to Grobbelaar that this was as bad as anything could possibly be. Until it got worse. His mobile rang. It was Debbie, calling from Heswall. The *Sun* – as tough as ever – had caught the Grobbelaars in a pincer movement. All the time that their men had been waiting at Gatwick, a second team had been keeping the family home under surveillance. As soon as Bruce Grobbelaar had been caught by Troup and Patrick, they had gone after Debbie. A reporter called Charles Yates had rung her front door-bell. As soon as the door opened he asked, 'Do you know your husband has been throwing football matches?'

'No, no, no,' repeated Debbie. 'He wouldn't do that. No.'

Yates followed the same line as Troup and Patrick had done. He told Debbie Grobbelaar that his paper had been investigating the story for two months, in collusion with Chris Vincent.

'I've heard of him from years ago,' said Debbie. 'I'm sorry, but I'm absolutely flabbergasted. I can't believe what you are saying. I don't really want to talk to you any more.'

She closed the door in Yates's face. But he was not to be silenced so easily. 'We have proof that your husband has been unfaithful,' shouted the *Sun* man, as his terrified prey burst into tears and reached for the telephone to call her spouse.

The conversation did not last long. 'You spoke to a reporter there?' asked an incredulous Bruce. 'I'm sitting with them now . . . it's all to do with Chris Vincent.'

She told him that they had photographed her, and asked about the accusations that had been made about him.

'I said that I have never done that in my life,' her husband insisted. 'I've told them exactly what Mr Vincent was up to in the beginning.' He had to go, he said. He'd call her. Yes . . . they probably did have a tape. But he'd sort it out . . . In the meantime, could she get hold of his solicitor, Dave Hewitt . . . just phone him . . . OK, OK . . . and finally, 'I'll speak to you later. Bye.'

Imagine being in Bruce Grobbelaar's shoes. His best mate had sold him out to the *Sun*. They had an apparent confession preserved forever on videotape. And now he had to explain it all to his wife.

'Does your editor want the £2,000 back? Because I've got it,' pleaded Grobbelaar as his tormentors went through their questions once again. At 5.09 he rang Wapping and was put through to the *Sun*'s editor, Stuart Higgins. As a posse of *Sun* photographers clustered around him, their flash-guns blasting, Grobbelaar tried to put his case at the start of a nine-minute conversation. 'Listen, I've got your two reporters here,' he began, not knowing that his words would, a few hours later, be printed verbatim in the *Sun*. Grobbelaar went on to repeat his claim that he was a totally honest person who had never thrown a game in his life, and that these allegations would ruin his marriage and his career. Referring to Chris Vincent as 'a certain person', he again admitted that he had been approached by him to take part in a 'sure-fire thing', but had said that the fortnightly £2,000 should be put in a box because he would not have anything to do with it.

Higgins remained polite throughout the conversation, first calling Grobbelaar 'sir' before switching to a more informal 'Bruce'. But, as with Troup and Patrick, his questions gradually closed in on Grobbelaar, allowing him less and less possibility of escape on anything other than the *Sun*'s terms. Without referring to Manchester United by name, he talked about 'the other match' where Grobbelaar had blown the chance of making £135,000 (he was £10,000 out, but no one was counting).

'If you've got that on tape, you've got that on tape,' replied Grobbelaar. 'But I never threw that game. If you look at the evidence, I made two blinding saves.'

Higgins had another question: if the *Sun*'s allegations were false, why would Grobbelaar worry about their effect on his life?

The answer was confused but comprehensible. 'Well, because of people trying to blame and put false pretences on other people to actually believe it. And it's probably going to happen. You know what papers are like.'

Well, Stuart Higgins knew, but Grobbelaar probably did not. Because he failed to understand that the tabloid press loves nothing more than a repentant sinner. And Stuart Higgins now gave him the opportunity to plea-bargain for his reputation.

'I know what the papers are like,' he said, 'and I have to say that from our point of view, we only print what we believe. The evidence in this case is totally overwhelming. If we can reach an accommodation with you, in that you want to say that something happened on a lower scale, or that you regret it deeply and want to apologize to somebody . . .'

'Who have I got to apologize to?' replied Grobbelaar.

'I would submit, with the greatest respect, Bruce,' suggested Higgins, 'at least twenty thousand Liverpool fans, and your team-mates.'

'There's no allegation at all saying that I've ever got to apologize to them. The serious thing is that I never did anything.'

Once the call to Higgins was concluded (with a number of references to John Fashanu, whose name was kept out of the paper's reports on the following day), Grobbelaar departed, accompanied by some airport security men who were acting as minders. Awaiting him on the Air Zimbabwe flight were two more *Sun* staff, who had been booked on to the flight in case he somehow evaded the team at the airport. Their brief was to front him up at Harare airport, when the plane landed on Wednesday morning.

Troup and Patrick were sure Grobbelaar had boarded the plane, but Vincent, trapped in his Mayfair hotel room, was less certain. He called Grobbelaar's mobile. It rang, which meant that its owner must still be on British soil.

Vincent called Patrick at Gatwick. 'Grobbelaar didn't get on that flight.'

The response was less than sympathetic. 'We're busy here. Fuck off.'

'Don't you tell me to fuck off,' exploded Vincent, 'or I'll come and blow your fucking head off.'

Mindful, perhaps, that a threat from Chris Vincent was not to be ignored lightly, Patrick relented. He called Grobbelaar, who answered, saying, 'I'm just getting on a flight.' But he was not jetting out to Zimbabwe. He was speeding back to Manchester to calm his wife and consult with his lawyers.

John Fashanu, meanwhile, had quickly discovered that something was going on. Rumours had been spreading suggesting that the *Sun* – with whom he had a contract as a star columnist – were planning a big scoop about football match-fixing. At 5.37 he made the first of two calls to a former team-mate, the Wimbledon goalkeeper Hans Segers. He left messages on Grobbelaar's phone. He made three calls to Richard Lim's mobile phone. At 10.23 he called Lim again. Eighteen minutes later, he left messages with both Grobbelaar and Segers. At 10.46, after another failed attempt, Fashanu finally got through to Bruce Grobbelaar and the two men spoke for a little over three minutes. The calls continued into the night. Lim and Fashanu spoke at 11.30 and midnight. At 1.43 Fashanu called out to Indonesia. At 5.45 he was on the phone again to Lim. Ten minutes after that, he was trying Grobbelaar again.

The calls had one direct upshot. On 9 November Richard Lim left Britain and flew to Malaysia. He later testified that he had been making arrangements to do so anyway, intending to fly out on the 11th or 12th, so as to supervise the arrival of a Bentley which he had ordered and shipped from Britain on behalf of a member of the Malaysian royal family. He was due to meet the car at the dockside and organize any payment of duty, clearance through customs and so on. Then John Fashanu called.

According to Lim, 'I received a call [on 8 November] from John informing that there would be a story involving Bruce, relating to a football or sex scandal. He did not know any details, but said he would call back. He did, and said it involved match-fixing and that there was some effort to link all of us – me, Bruce and Fash – and say what we did: to turn it into a more serious allegation. I was surprised, I remember saying to Fash, do we really need to clarify this matter with anyone? Fash told me it was a press matter, leave it to them for now. "Since you are going [to Malaysia], you might as well go now, in case the media get heavy."'

Debbie, meanwhile, had escaped the *Sun*'s siege at Heswall by leaving through the back door and taking refuge with her neighbours. The only person to go inside the Grobbelaars' home over the next few days was Janet, the family's cleaner.

Grobbelaar would spend the next two nights in England, before flying out to Zimbabwe on Thursday evening pursued by a horde of reporters. Troup and Patrick, meanwhile, filed their stories by around 8.30 in the evening, leaving them to the *Sun*'s 'back bench' of sub-editors to hammer into printable shape.

Two hours later, they were back in Brown's. Vincent was allowed out of his luxurious cell to join them in the bar, where cocktails were knocked back and calls placed to Wapping, ordering up the first finished copies. These were a while in coming. In order to ensure that none of its tabloid competitors could share its scoop, the *Sun* carried no mention whatever of

Grobbelaar in its first edition. But by 11.30 the presses were rolling with a new front page.

For once, the *Sun* did not play games with its headline. There were no cries of 'Gotcha!', no jokes about hamsters, no puns or sniggers, just the bold, unambiguous assertion: 'GROBBELAAR TOOK BRIBES TO FIX GAMES'. Troup and Patrick's story was equally to the point. 'Soccer star Bruce Grobbelaar is exposed by the *Sun* today for taking massive bribes to throw key matches.' The 'full amazing story' continued on pages 2, 3, 4, 5 and 6.

For fear of provoking libel actions, newspaper lawyers will often insist that scandalous news stories of this kind are littered with evasions and obscure allusions to activities that might have occurred, or words that might have been said. But with the sole exception that John Fashanu's name was omitted and replaced by the coy parenthesis that 'The *Sun* named another famous footballer,' the stories continued the astonishing frankness of the front page. 'Grob – I let in 3 goals and picked up £40,000', ran the page 2 headline. On page 3, in the space normally occupied by a topless, pouting lovely stood a grinning Grobbelaar. '3–0, but he's laughing now', said the caption, as three more photographs captured each of Andy Cole's goals. Chris Vincent was pictured in the bathroom of his flat in Chirk. Next to him, in bold type, were the words, 'Bruce gave me £20,000 . . . I hid it in my bath.'

On the following spread, a blizzard of asterisks blew across a partial transcript of the Southampton videotapes, as the paper revealed how 'f***ing worried' Grobbelaar had been about what might happen 'if the s**t ever hit the fan'. Well, it was hitting it now. A huge colour picture on page 5 showed Vincent handing Grobbelaar the fateful £2,000 envelope. Once again, there was no pussyfooting. In capital letters, the *Sun* declared: 'SOCCER BRIBE SENSATION – Moment Cheat grabbed £2,000'. Page 6 contained an editorial headlined, 'He fouled the field of dreams', along with a transcript of the Grobbelaar–Higgins phone call. It was not until page 7 that readers could finally feast their eyes on 'Prime Cutie' Teri Clark, twenty-two, whose brother worked on a meat counter and who consequently possessed 'a nice bit of rump, two lean legs and a tasty topside'.

This explosive package arrived at Brown's at about 1.30 a.m. For the two young journalists whose by-lines dominated this world exclusive story it was a moment of undiluted triumph, which was only increased by the knowledge that there was a great deal more to come.

Vincent's feelings, as he looked at the results of his handiwork, were far more ambivalent. At first he could barely read the words. He was, both literally and figuratively, tired and emotional – shattered by the constant tension, uncertainty and stress that had engulfed him since the fateful week in August when Mondoro had fallen apart. He had one more drink and went back up to his room. But although he was desperately in need of rest, sleep was impossible. Once again he returned to his routine of pacing up and down his room, chain-smoking Marlboros. Around 4 a.m., knowing that South Africa was two hours ahead of the UK, he started phoning acquaintances there to see if the story had broken on any of the morning news programmes.

Lim, too, was keeping up with events. 'When I read the *Sun* on 9 November, I was very perplexed by its contents, simply because I felt they described the Short Man and I could see that it was me – for example, going to the Hilton – but in other paragraphs they said the Short Man was the representative of a syndicate, all sorts of things, and I felt very concerned. Of course it was untrue.'

# 20

## 'My Client Protests His Innocence'

In the hours after the *Sun* first published its revelations, the rest of the media did their best to catch up with, and jump on, the bandwagon that had just started rolling. For a day or two rumours had been circulating of a big bribery scandal in the football world, but no one had expected this.

The story that insiders had anticipated concerned the Wimbledon–Everton match at the end of the 1993–4 season. Needing a win to stay in the Premier League, Everton had scraped through 3–2, with a late, soft goal. Sheffield United had been relegated in their place. When, on Tuesday afternoon, the then Wimbledon chairman Sam Hammam had been approached by one reporter, he had pleaded, 'Everyone thinks I threw the game because I'm a friend of Bill Kenwright [the theatrical producer and passionate Evertonian].' But, he pointed out, he had promised his whole team an all-expenses-paid trip to Las Vegas for themselves and their partners if they finished in the top six of the Premier League and qualified for Europe. The loss had cost them their holiday.

The Wimbledon–Everton game was, in fact, one of the matches that the Crown would later allege had been thrown by Hans Segers. But that revelation was still months away. For now, the focus was all on Grobbelaar. By eight in the morning the Football

Association headquarters in Lancaster Gate was besieged by reporters, waiting for any reaction from the authorities.

At about two in the afternoon a short, exhausted-looking man, with a sandy-red moustache, dark glasses and a black scarf, paused as he was walking along the pavement just opposite the FA. It was Chris Vincent. The *Sun* had now moved him into a safe apartment in Gloucester Terrace, just a few yards away. A couple of hours later Troup and Patrick arrived at his flat, bringing the first £10,000 instalment of his payment from the *Sun*. He immediately went out shopping in Regent Street and spent a considerable proportion of it on an expensive Swiss watch, and matching gold and diamond earrings and a ring, all for Bernice. He would later pay her a total of £8,600, which represented the salary she would have had from Mondoro had she worked for the company until the end of November. He ended up giving her money and presents worth £13,500, plus a return air fare to Australia.

She, in return, travelled down to London and, for the next six weeks, bore the burden of his emotions. As he later put it, 'In July 1994 my three best friends were Bruce, Keith and Bernice. Keith had blown himself out. I was now blowing out Bruce. Here was my last remaining close friend that I could discuss things with. I just wanted to say, "I'll always be your mate." The average person has got a family, friends, a girlfriend or a boyfriend, and they can devote x-amount of emotion and affection to all of them. She was now getting everything I would have given to everyone else. It must have been overwhelming.'

They sat in the flat, talking into the early hours. The weight of Vincent's emotions made Bernice feel claustrophobic. To make matters worse, she was confused and uncertain about the action Vincent had taken in betraying his former friend.

'It was such a shame that it had to end this way, knowing what a great friendship they'd had,' she later recalled. 'I felt as though I was being asked to pick sides. I told Chris that I supported him as a friend, but I couldn't support what he'd done, and I didn't want to look as if I was picking sides, as if I was saying that Bruce had done it. Because I didn't know whether he had or not. I genuinely believe that Bruce didn't know how he had messed up with Chris. If they'd had one decent conversation together, before the meeting with Hewlett, it would have been so different. I saw a picture of Debbie and the girls in the paper and thought, "This should not be happening."'

Vincent, too, felt sympathetic towards Debbie Grobbelaar, although he had been the immediate cause of her misfortune. 'I was sorry for her. She'd been bullshitted all down the line and she'd be as flabbergasted as the rest of the world.'

That evening, Vincent filmed an interview with GMTV. On the following day, 10 November, Bruce Grobbelaar flew out to Zimbabwe. At Gatwick he bought two bottles of Courvoisier brandy from the duty-free shop. Reporters asked him, 'Are you going to drink those before the game, or after?'

'After the game, what do you think?' replied Grobbelaar. He disappeared towards the departure gate, pursued by a female *Sun* reporter. 'Keep running. It's good for your legs,' he called out to her, laughing. He was asked if he had a message for his fans. 'Yes, say hello,' he replied.

He was smuggled aboard the Air Zimbabwe flight and hidden in the cockpit. Forty-five minutes after take-off, he appeared in the cabin. When the plane landed at Harare there was bedlam. More reporters were following Grobbelaar than had covered the country's independence celebrations. Accompanied by one of his two solicitors, Brian Canavan, Grobbelaar read out a brief statement: 'Good morning and welcome to Zimbabwe. I'm going to enjoy the game on Sunday, but I know that some of you are not here for the football. I'd like to say, regarding the allegations made against me, that I totally refute them.'

At the national stadium, where the team were training, he posed for pictures with Coventry City's Zimbabwean forward, Peter Ndlovu, who put on Grobbelaar's protective mask while the keeper looked on in mock horror. Afterwards he was asked how Debbie was dealing with the scandal. He paused and looked at the ground for several seconds. Then he said, 'It's been very hard for her. It's been very hard for all my family.'

Zimbabwe won the match against Zambia 2–1, before their leader, President Mugabe, the world's press and forty thousand fans who waved banners proclaiming, 'We love you Bruce,' and periodically chanted, 'Bruce is God.'

Meanwhile, at about this time in the Far East, Johannes Joseph, Lo Bon Swe and three associates were taking a trip to Christmas Island, a holiday destination in the Indian Ocean about 350 miles south of the Indonesian capital, Jakarta. They visited a casino and spent 29.3 million Australian dollars (roughly £14 million) on gambling chips. Of this, they gambled about 7 million dollars. Their largest single win was attributed to Lo Bon Swe, who raked in 2.3 million dollars (roughly £1.1 million) on a single punt. One thing was perfectly obvious: when these men gambled, they gambled big.

Back in England, Southampton Football Club was equally protective. Lawrie McMenemy, the club's director of football, told reporters that his club was a family. And when a family is in trouble, it unites. He had asked Grobbelaar whether there was any truth to the allegations and been told that there was not. And that was good enough for him.

At training before the club's home match against Arsenal, Grobbelaar looked as relaxed and self-confident as ever, happily posing for photographers. And on the Saturday morning he received more media support from Hans Segers, who raised the subject of the rumours about the Wimbledon–Everton match that had been circulating prior to the *Sun*'s revelations. 'For a few crazy hours,' he confessed, 'people had been ringing my home, asking if it was me.' Since Segers was not the man under investigation, he was happy to put in a word for a man who was. The Arsenal game would be a tough test of character, but, 'I believe he will be mentally prepared. Good goalkeepers can block it all out, and Bruce is the most experienced of the lot.'

Sure enough, Grobbelaar kept a clean sheet. The Arsenal fans waved joke notes from the 'Bank of Grobbland', inscribed 'I promise to let in one goal in return for Fifty Pounds', but he was not intimidated and Southampton won 1–0.

'Everyone in life should have their opportunity to prove their innocence,' declaimed the Saints' manager, Alan Ball, after the match. Over the months to come, as first press allegations, then criminal charges mounted up, Southampton Football Club and its employees would remain steadfastly loyal to Bruce Grobbelaar. Even after Ball had ceased to be the club's manager and moved to Manchester City, he would tell a reporter who asked him how he had coped with the Grobbelaar scandal that it had been, 'Dead easy. Dead honest.'

'He arrived back from Zimbabwe,' Ball continued, 'and I got him in here and said, "Sit down, I'm going to ask you a man's question. I want one answer." I asked him the question. He gave me the answer. I said, "Right, I'll back you all the way. You've got a pal." It was difficult with the media following us everywhere, but I had no hesitation in backing him and I still do to this day.'

Ball's replacement, a genial, good-natured Geordie called Dave Merrington, who had long had charge of Southampton's youth side, echoed those sentiments. Long after Grobbelaar had been charged, and the process of remand hearings was under way, Merrington continued to praise Grobbelaar's enthusiasm and his positive effect on team morale. The only time his support weakened was when Grobbelaar returned home from a trip to Zimbabwe on a Tuesday, having told the club that he would be back on the preceding Friday. Southampton were left without a reserve keeper for a Premier League match, and reacted by publicly censuring Grobbelaar and fining him two weeks' wages.

His club colleagues were not the only ones who found the allegations that Grobbelaar had ever thrown a match, still less the Newcastle game, hard to believe. Gerald Ashby, the highly experienced referee who had taken charge of the Newcastle–Liverpool match said, 'I'm amazed. There was nothing in the game that raised any suspicions in my mind. I remember the game for the attacking play, especially from Newcastle. I just admired the way that Andy Cole put away his hat-trick.'

Others, though, had less reason to applaud. For Liverpool striker Paul Stewart the match was an unhappy watershed in his career. After the game, Graeme Souness told him that he had no part in his plans for the club. He spent some time on loan to Wolves, then languished in the reserves before being given a free transfer at the beginning of 1996. 'Perhaps I should be blaming Bruce Grobbelaar for wrecking my career at Liverpool,' he said. 'When something like this happens, it's hard for players to take it all in.'

Stewart was not the only Liverpudlian whose first-team career ended at Newcastle. It was also the last time that poor Torben Peichnik found his name on the team-sheet. Within months he was on his way to the Danish club AGF Aarhus, also on a free transfer. 'Don't remind me of that game,' he begged reporters who approached him after the Grobbelaar scandal was exposed. 'I was made the scapegoat for it. But,' he added, 'Bruce couldn't have done anything about those three goals. He had no chance.'

Others were less forgiving. On 13 November 1994 two of Grobbelaar's girlfriends, twenty-seven-year-old Rachel Potter and twenty-two-year-old Kate Read, were pictured on the front page of the *News of the World*, wearing Liverpool goalkeeper's strips and holding up red cards. The headline next to them read: 'World Exclusive: CHEATING GROB SCORED IN BED WITH US (And we didn't even have to bribe him)'.

Read was the Six-Footer of whom Grobbelaar had boasted to Vincent: 'I brought it here and gave it the big one out on the balcony.' Not wanting to besmirch their serious sports corruption story with smut, or to appear needlessly vengeful, the *Sun* team had handed over all the material relating to Grobbelaar's sex-life to their News International colleagues on the legendary News of the Screws. Reporters confronted Kate Read and showed her a transcript of the tape in which Grobbelaar boasted to Vincent. She burst into tears. 'For a start,' she later revealed to the paper's millions of readers, 'it was untrue – we did not have sex on his balcony. Secondly, I could not believe he'd talk about me like that. I thought he cared about me. But there he is, bragging about me like I'm a cheap little tart and he's a teenage boy. I thought he was better than that.'

Even if Grobbelaar had not made love to her on his balcony, there were plenty of places where he had. Their affair, Read revealed, had begun in Zimbabwe during the summer of 1993, while she was working as a barmaid in Harare and Grobbelaar was in town for World Cup game. Nothing happened after their first date, but when Bruce returned to the country a fortnight later she got in touch with him again. They went out, kissed and cuddled in public – he had no worries about being seen misbehaving in Zimbabwe, she said, where he was a national hero – and then went back to his hotel room, where the keeper revealed to her that, 'He has an absolutely fantastic body . . . He was very tender and caring and made sure I was relaxed and enjoying myself. The sex was wonderful, heavenly. I cannot fault him in that department.' Six weeks later, when Grobbelaar was back in Zimbabwe – at roughly the time when he was on that unhappy holiday with Debbie and the girls – he 'popped round for sex with Kate' again, and she was happy to oblige. She felt Bruce really cared about her.

Read's revelations contained a number of remarks that tied in with Vincent's recollections of life with Grobbelaar. The bragging, for example, was par for the course. Furthermore, she said that although Grobbelaar never mentioned his wife by name, he made it clear that their relationship was under severe strain and that they argued every day. His daughters, however, 'meant everything to him'.

The affair resumed after Bruce had been transferred to Southampton. Kate contacted her lover through the club. One day, immediately after Debbie and the girls had left to go back to Heswall, he returned her call and they met on the train between Southampton and Lymington. But whereas Grobbelaar had been relaxed and openly affectionate in

Zimbabwe, he was impassive, cautious, acting as if he barely knew her – displaying exactly the same sort of caution, in fact, as he had done when he visited the Wild Thing's house several months beforehand.

For her part, Rachel Potter claimed Grobbelaar had told her that he had let in a goal against Crystal Palace, and been sent off in a European Cup Winners' Cup game against ·Spartak Moscow, because he had been distracted by thinking about her. A passionate Liverpool fan, Potter had met Grobbelaar in March 1992. She told the *News of the World* that she and Bruce had twice made love when he was staying at hotels with the Liverpool team. On the night they met, which had ended with no more than a kiss on the cheek, Grobbelaar had repeatedly called Potter at home after she had left the Croydon hotel where he was staying. One of the calls, though, had been hurriedly cut off: Debbie was trying to get through to him on another line. On another occasion he called her from the Liverpool team coach: 'He began making filthy suggestions about what he wanted to do with me,' said Potter. 'I was disgusted. And it was made worse because he was saying it in front of his team-mates on the coach.'

Once again, the standard rules of engagement applied. When Rachel was invited to the players' lounge at Anfield Bruce did not pay her any public attention because Debbie was in the room. Eventually he called her at three the following morning, sounding very drunk and apologizing that he had not been able to get away to be with her.

If the *News of the World*'s front half was berating Grobbelaar for being 'a sex-hungry love rat who cheated on his devoted wife Debbie', the paper's sports pages were boasting their own exclusive: 'Grob my week of torment', in which the keeper revealed that, 'The last 100 hours have been a living hell. It has been the toughest part of my life and the worst week for my family.'

Presumably the week took an even bigger turn for the worse when his family read the rest of the paper. Elsewhere, though, people who could not have given a damn about Grobbelaar's sexual prowess were looking into his affairs. Within forty-eight hours of the scandal breaking the FA announced an investigation into the bribery allegations, as did the Hampshire and Merseyside Police.

# 21

# Aftermath

The joint police inquiry was led by Detective Superintendent Roger Hoddinott – head of Hampshire CID and brother of the country's Chief Constable, John Hoddinott – and Merseyside's DS John Robbins. Hoddinott, who eventually took sole charge of the case, is a Southampton fan, and no lover of greedy footballers.

For the officers who were chosen for the case – on the simple basis that they were the ones available when it first came up – it was a wonderful opportunity to impress their superiors. As one detective told me during the course of the investigation, 'Lots of people go through an entire career without a case like this. The main difficulty is not talking about it with colleagues. Everybody wants to know what's going on.'

For Roger Hoddinott, this was also a chance to make a name for himself in the last years of his life on the force. When the story broke, he told Guy Phillips of Meridian TV, 'He's on our doorstep. There's probably nothing in it, but I'll take a look. If all this does is stop one other conceited footballer from trying to cheat, I'll feel I've done my job.'

If that made his approach seem casual, it soon became clear that it was anything but that. Operation Navaho, as the investigation was called, involved more than fifty officers at its peak.

Policemen were drafted in from all over the county, and a team of twelve stayed with the case right the way through to the committal hearing in March 1996. One of them was Detective Sergeant Glyniss Turner, a small, neat, dark-haired detective who exuded efficiency and shrewdness. Along with her partner DC Peter Gulliver – her total opposite, being tall, blond, male and laid-back – she would be Chris Vincent's police contact throughout the investigation, repeatedly interviewing him over the following eighteen months.

Vincent's first contact with Glyniss Turner was made on 16 November. He had made a formal statement to the *Sun*'s solicitors, Farrer and Co., and was asked to repeat its contents to her and a Merseyside detective. Over the next fortnight, as the *Sun* moved him and Bernice down to the West Country, a series of progressively more intensive interviews were conducted by Turner and Inspector Tom Tobin, a round-faced, balding Oxford graduate. In an attempt to catch Vincent out they would ask questions that had no connection with each other, jumping from time to time and place to place, coming back to the same subject in a dozen different ways.

The police were not the only ones who would need Vincent's evidence. If the *Sun* were to fight off the libel writs being fired at them by Grobbelaar's lawyers, they needed to be sure of Vincent's cooperation. It would cost them £1,000 a week, he said. They refused to pay the money. Vincent came back with another suggestion: £500 a week, plus a house and car. It did not seem like an outrageous request to him. Thanks to his information, the *Sun* had been handed a week's worth of front pages, with more to come.

Bernice, meanwhile, was trying to stay out of the spotlight. Ever since the first day's headlines had appeared, the Bala'cs' telephone had rung off the hook as reporters tried to track her down. So her family had to let the answering-machine pick up every incoming call, and enquiries as to Bernice's whereabouts, even from family friends, had been treated with caution. On her first morning back home in Chester Bernice was just getting dressed when the telephone rang.

For once, she picked up the receiver and said, 'Hello.'

There was no answer.

She replaced the handset. A few moments later, the doorbell went. A man was standing there, wearing a suit and carrying a briefcase. He claimed to work for Grobbelaar's solicitors.

'Is Mr Bala'c in?' he asked.

'No,' said Bernice, 'Can I help you?'

'Is Mrs Bala'c in?' continued the solicitors.

'No,' repeated Bernice, adding, 'You're Bruce's lawyer, aren't you?'

'And you're Bernice,' he said.

The young woman, alone in the house, felt intimidated. She told the man that she did not want to talk to him. 'I'll call my father and let him know you called.'

'Actually, I'd rather talk to you,' said the lawyer.

Bernice called her father, who advised her to tell her visitor to go away.

'I have – he won't go,' said Bernice.

'Don't panic,' said her father. 'Just tell him to go. Call me back if he doesn't.'

But the man did not go. In fact he stayed for more than an hour, asking questions about Mondoro. It was clear from what he said that Grobbelaar's defence was going to be that Vincent's whole story was an attempt to frame him in revenge for what had happened in Zimbabwe.

On the way out, the man remarked, 'I gather you're leaving in a couple of days. Have a nice trip.'

'Yeah . . . See you some time,' Bernice said.

He smiled. 'You never know. It might be where you're going to next.'

There was, to Bernice, nothing friendly about his remark. Instead it felt as if she had been warned. She was planning to fly to Australia for Christmas and spend some time there with friends. Now the enemy knew where she was going. She could not get away from them.

She and Chris Vincent flew out to Australia, via Bali and Singapore, where they had a holiday that veered from fun, to passion, to intense, bitter argument. A similar sense of conflict was poisoning Vincent's relations with the *Sun*, who were rapidly distancing themselves from him and any prospect of a continued business relationship. On 24 January 1995, soon after his return from Australia, he had a meeting with a number of *Sun* representatives in the office of the editor, Stuart Higgins. He was told that the paper had been advised by its lawyers that it could not enter into any further agreements with him, since that would amount to paying a prospective witness in their libel action against Grobbelaar. It was against their rules.

'Your rules would look fucking stupid if you had an AK47 shoved up your nose,' raged Vincent.

The conversation continued, inconclusively, for a few more minutes. Finally Vincent asked, 'Stuart, are you prepared to make a deal with me?'

Higgins shrugged. 'My hands are tied.'

Now Vincent leaped to his feet, pulled £3 in change from his pocket and flung it down in front of him. 'This is my last fucking money in the world,' he shouted. 'What are you going to do about it?'

What Higgins did was to call his security guards and have Vincent ejected from the building.

So began six months of half-life, in which Vincent frequently found himself down to his last few pence. There were times when he wandered the streets of London all night, spending hours over drinks in 24-hour cafés, just so he could stay in the warm. He once even finished a half cup of cappuccino left behind at a Waterloo Station buffet by a young woman with coffee-money to spare.

He eked out an existence by selling scripts of his story to an increasingly sceptical press, persuading journalists to pay for a glimpse of what he had to offer, like some dancer in a media peep-show. A Sunday newspaper, for example, paid £6,000 to see his police statement and the *Sun* video. When he had money he would stay in hotels, or fly abroad on holiday. When he did not he would rely upon friends, or even the police. In the second half of July they sent him off to a vicarage on the Isle of Wight normally used as a halfway house for disturbed and criminal teenagers.

The place was kept by the vicar, whose wife had died some years earlier. His housekeeping, sadly, lacked a woman's touch. 'I was scared to put my bare feet on the bedroom floor because the carpets were so dirty,' recalled Vincent, who is a neat and fastidious man where personal hygiene is concerned. The dinner plates were covered with congealed old food, and the garden was overgrown with weeds. Unable to put up with his surroundings, Vincent would walk for seven or eight hours a day, exploring the island around him. He had been lent £80 by a sympathetic TV journalist, but all the money was spent on food, the fare at the vicarage being inedible.

The police were by now having mixed feelings about his value. On the one hand they felt that he was an extraordinary witness, whose evidence kept checking out. Thanks to his leads, they had been able to put together a pattern of telephone calls and cash transfers that appeared to substantiate his allegations. On the other hand they were fed up with his constant demands for money and special treatment. 'We've got a hundred witnesses. You're not crucial,' one furious detective inspector told him.

But that was not strictly true. Vincent was crucial. And both sides knew it. Bruce Grobbelaar was first arrested at 7 a.m. on 14 March by a team of detectives who caught him at his cottage in Lymington. He was taken to Southampton for questioning. At the same time officers in Tamworth, Staffordshire, arrested John Fashanu. They took him to Birmingham, where he met every question with a curt 'No comment.' In London, two teams of detectives picked up his new wife Melissa Kassa-Mapsi and the Malaysian businessman Heng Suan 'Richard' Lim. In Fleet, Hampshire, they arrested Hans Segers, the very same Wimbledon goalie who had been protesting his baffled innocence back in November. It was thanks to Vincent's description of the meeting at Byron Drive that the police had been able to connect Fashanu to the case. Going deeper into his bank and company accounts, they found a dizzying maze of transactions. 'We are looking at every financial aspect of this case, including the finances of Mr Fashanu,' said a police source on the day of the arrests. 'We are talking about a very complex web of financial dealings which will take a considerable time to unravel.'

Vincent had never known the real name of Fashanu's associate, the so-called Short Man. Heng Suan Lim (his nickname of Richard was not publicly revealed until the trial) was described by neighbours as a nice, respectable young man, 'who always went around with a smile on his face'. The same would have been said for the police had it not been for a leak which tipped off the media in advance, so that detectives arriving at Grobbelaar's home found it ringed with reporters and cameramen. A little while later two neighbourhood bobbies, seeing the crowds, came along to clear the obstruction from the highway. They were told that Bruce Grobbelaar was in the house, being read his rights. The bobbies did not believe it. They strolled up to the front door, only to be sent away with a flea in their ear by the plain-clothes men and women within. But their discomfort was as nothing compared to that suffered by Chief Constable Hoddinott.

At 10.00 o'clock that morning, he was touring the BBC South studios in Southampton when a monitor happened to show an ITV bulletin, filmed by Meridian TV, about Grobbelaar's arrest. A BBC executive asked Hoddinott why Meridian had been informed of the arrest while his people had not. The policeman had to confess that no one at all had been informed – or at least, they shouldn't have been. Over the next three months, two detectives – one a Special Branch officer – interviewed more than one hundred people in a fruitless search for the source of the leak.

The difficulty of keeping a watertight investigation was one which plagued Operation Navaho. The police would spend months gathering information, only to find the same material getting to newspapers within a matter of hours. Vincent was warned not to hide any guilty secrets from the police. They promised that if he did, there would be others who could pay to uncover them.

This was no mere figure of speech, as Vincent was to discover. In its April 1995 edition, *Business Age* magazine published a feature on John Fashanu headlined, 'Is he telling the truth?' The writer, Anil Bhoyrul (who would later achieve journalistic fame as one of the *Daily Mirror*'s City Slicker columnists), had interviewed Fashanu a year beforehand for *Business Age*. On 16 March 1995, two days after Fashanu's arrest, he faxed a letter to Fash requesting another interview. Bhoyrul reminded him that he had claimed he was being 'stitched up' and suggested that he might welcome the chance to put his side of the story across. As writers often do when trying to reel an interview in, he did his best to engage Fashanu's sympathy, promising to show him his text in advance of publication and wishing him all the best for the future: 'I've no doubt the eventual outcome of recent events will be in your favour,' he concluded.

The letter worked. Bhoyrul got his interview and Fashanu got his positive spin. The article described Vincent as 'a sworn enemy of Grobbelaar [and] a discredited businessman' who had been paid 'at least £100,000 by News International for his testimony'. Bhoyrul explained how he had spoken to Fashanu over three lengthy interviews: 'Often emotional, touching the bounds of rage and tearfulness, each session was always interrupted either by fans, the press or police.'

Fashanu's central claim was that Grobbelaar had approached him, rather than the other way around, because, 'He was having big financial problems with his safari park project and wanted me to find some investors for the project.' Grobbelaar, Bhoyrul explained, had invested heavily and lost £40,000. 'With losses of £120,000 between them, Vincent suggested Grobbelaar should approach Fashanu,' wrote Bhoyrul, adding: 'Fashanu now says, "Vincent was not only being offered £100,000 to frame Bruce, but was on a £50,000 bonus for every other player he got involved. Getting me into this was perfect – I know all the right people. I mean, I know practically everyone in the world. As far as Vincent was concerned, I was the perfect name for him to pick up his £50,000 bonus, because I'm a high profile black footballer and I'm a television star."'

Fashanu then claimed to have met Grobbelaar at 'an apartment in Hyde Park'. He said he wanted information on some Zimbabwean players, including Peter Ndlovu 'who now plays for Coventry City'. This, he said, was his normal procedure: 'I find out who the good players in Africa are before anyone else and then I bring them over to England.' This, he swore, was 'the first time I ever met Bruce'.

'At the same time,' commented the sympathetic Bhoyrul, 'News International were busy secretly videotaping many of Grobbelaar's meetings. Nevertheless, there was little evidence that either player was involved in a match-fixing plot. But . . . Fashanu is the past-master at digging his own grave. He admits he did it again. Having decided not to personally invest in Grobbelaar's safari park, he said he knew someone who might – Malaysian businessman Heng Suan Lim. Fashanu then took on the role of middle-man, introducing Suan Lim to Bruce Grobbelaar. Chris Vincent's story of a Far Eastern betting ring was suddenly given credibility . . .'

'Is he telling the truth?' was the headline. Good question. The first meeting between Grobbelaar and Fashanu had taken place in November 1992. As Grobbelaar told Vincent, it was at Fashanu's apartment near Lord's. At that stage, though Vincent and Grobbelaar were certainly looking for investors in Mondoro, the company was not in debt – certainly not to the tune of £120,000. Heng Suan Lim was at that meeting, and the subject of Mondoro may have been discussed. By common admission, however, the deal that followed the conversation had nothing to do with safari parks, but was concerned with forecasting the results of football matches for the Far Eastern gamblers to whom Lim relayed information. Vincent – who was paid £33,000, not £100,000, by the *Sun* – could not have been trying to entrap Fashanu at that stage, because he did not make contact with the paper until September 1994. Finally, the *Sun*, who did not at any stage offer Vincent £50,000 – or any money at all – for additional names, were not videotaping Grobbelaar's meetings, and would not start to do so until October 1994. On the other hand, Fashanu's suggestion that he put Grobbelaar in touch with Heng Suan Lim was an interesting one, given that Grobbelaar was at that stage still staunchly denying that he had ever met the Malaysian.

Intrigued by what the article contained, Chris Vincent called Anil Bhoyrul and asked if he would like to interview him, too. For a fee of £5,000 he spoke to Bhoyrul, showed him both his police statement and the *Sun* videotape of his meetings with Grobbelaar, and posed for photographs. According to both Bhoyrul and his then-editor Tom Rubython, the deal gave Business and Fortune Holdings, a subsidiary of *Business Age*, the right to Vincent's story in all media, including books: when Vincent signed his original agreement with me, he was (though I had no idea of it for years to come) in breach of that agreement.

In any event, on the advice of the magazine's lawyers, his interview with *Business Age* was never published, but the money Vincent received enabled him to go to South Africa for six weeks. On 16 May, at 7.17 in the evening, Vincent was staying with some friends, Paul and Karen Gallow, in Johannesburg, when the telephone rang. Vincent picked it up. He could hear a 'pip!', indicating an overseas call. He assumed it must be Bernice.

'Hello,' he said. There was no answer. He repeated, four or five more times, 'Hello . . . hello . . .'

There was a long silence, and then came the sound of a voice. 'This is your worst nightmare,' said the voice. 'You have been found out and you are not going to live much longer.' Then the line went dead.

Vincent immediately called the Hampshire Police and reported the incident. He was asked whether he would press charges if the call was traced, and replied that he would. Then he phoned Bernice and told her exactly what had happened.

'You must have thought this would happen,' she said.

'Yes,' replied Vincent, 'I was just wondering when.'

Meanwhile, 4 July was looming on the horizon, the date that Messrs Grobbelaar, Fashanu, Segers and Lim were due to appear at a number of Hampshire police stations, possibly to face charges. And, as it approached, some unusual events were taking place.

Back in April, Anil Bhoyrul had a conversation with a young woman called Shaa Wasmund, whom he had met through a colleague at work. Wasmund was a brilliant and ambitious young PR executive who had made her name representing Chris Eubank. Now, she said, she was a confidante of John Fashanu. Bhoyrul expressed an interest in interviewing Fashanu for a third time. Wasmund told him that Fashanu's lawyers had advised him not to speak to the press. In early June, by which time he had spoken to Vincent and heard his side of the story, Bhoyrul spoke to Wasmund again. This time the response was more positive.

On 9 June, Wasmund called Bhoyrul and asked him to go to her house at 4 Prebend Street in Islington, North London, which was also the headquarters of her company Nautilus Communications. She told him that John Fashanu wanted to meet him, but that the meeting would be private and off-the-record. On no account should he bring a tape-recorder. Bhoyrul went to Prebend Street by taxi. Wasmund then drove him in her Honda Civic to Warm Seas. En route, Bhoyrul tried to find out what he could expect to get from the meeting: should he try to pin Fashanu down about his side of the story? Wasmund told him to take it easy. This, she said, was the start of a long process. He wasn't going to get anything he could print today.

When they got to Warm Seas they were met by Fashanu and the ever-present Mace. Wasmund walked straight up to Fashanu and greeted him with a hug. But before Bhoyrul had time to say or do anything, Mace had walked up to him and silently carried out a brisk body search. Mace then produced a device which Bhoyrul later described as looking like a walkie-talkie, with lots of flashing lights and an aerial. This odd-looking box – later recovered by the police – was a bug-detector which Mace swept up and down Bhoyrul's body. As the journalist was about to discover, Fashanu was convinced that his business and media enemies were having him watched and that conversations were bugged.

Once the security check had been completed, the conversation began. Fashanu was not happy with Bhoyrul's article, nor a follow-up published in the May 1995 *Business Age*, which said that he and Vincent had been close associates (which, of course, they had not). Bhoyrul apologized and then mentioned that the whole case seemed to hang on what Vincent was saying. He also added that his evidence had been checked and cross-checked and seemed to stand up.

'Well,' said Fashanu, 'you've met him. What do you think?'

As the conversation went on, Fashanu's position became clearer. From his perspective, there was no evidence against him other than Vincent's evidence, in which he only made one appearance. He also claimed that people were trying to frame him, although he refused to specify who they might be. The conversation ended with Fashanu agreeing to a proper interview with Bhoyrul on 5 July, the day after he was due to see the police – providing, of course, that he was free to give it. Bhoyrul and Wasmund then went out to dinner.

A few days later – 13 or 14 June – Wasmund came to Bhoyrul's home and once again the conversation turned to Chris Vincent. Her opinion seemed to be that Fashanu would get off because Vincent's evidence was so unreliable.

On 15 June, Wasmund had three mobile-phone conversations with John Fashanu: a three-minute chat at 10.12 a.m., followed by two much briefer conversations at 10.53 a.m. and 8.22 p.m. An hour after the third call, at about 9.30, she called Bhoyrul and told him to come over to her house. He would, she said, find it very interesting.

When Bhoyrul got to the house he found Wasmund outside. She was test-driving a new Jeep and invited him for a spin around the block. As they returned to the house, a black

Mercedes was pulling up. It was driven by John Fashanu. They all went inside. Fashanu was carrying a briefcase containing the same bug-detector Mace had used at Warm Seas a few days earlier. Fash took it out and began walking round Wasmund's one-bedroom flat, pointed the device at pieces of furniture and corners of rooms, just in case there were listening devices planted there. He then beckoned Wasmund and Bhoyrul into the kitchenette at the far left of the open-plan lounge, turned the lights down so that they could not be seen, and told Wasmund to put on some music. A stop-start conversation then followed – stopping between tracks on the CD, starting up again as soon as the music recommenced.

Fashanu did not want to be overheard, and it's easy to understand why. According to testimony given by Bhoyrul to the police on 5 July 1995 and repeated later that month in an affidavit given by him to the *Sun* as part of the newspaper's evidence in its libel action against Bruce Grobbelaar (which was already under way by the summer of 1995), the discussion was dominated by the subject of Chris Vincent, his evidence and what could be done to make it less effective.

Wasmund got the ball rolling by emphasizing once again how the whole case was based on Vincent's testimony. More than once she remarked: 'We all know John is innocent.' She said she had told Fashanu that he needed an article in the press in which Vincent spoke more positively about him. Fash had opposed Wasmund but now, he said, he had become convinced that she was right. He asked Bhoyrul what his relationship with Vincent was like: how often did he see him? And where was he now? 'Johannesburg,' said Bhoyrul.

Fashanu wondered whether Bhoyrul would want to go and interview Vincent in South Africa. Wasmund asked how much he thought Vincent would charge, to which Bhoyrul replied that it would be at least £5,000. Wasmund continued: she wanted him to ask Vincent whether he had anything against Fashanu – whether he wanted him to go down.

Bhoyrul asked, 'What do you mean, change his entire statement?'

'If that's what it adds up to in his answers,' said Wasmund. 'Then you've got a good story.'

'What, like a splash: "Vincent Says I Hope Fash Gets Off!"?'

'Yes, something like that.'

By now, Bhoyrul was beginning to have serious concerns about Fashanu's intentions. He said that he wanted no part of the scheme. So Fashanu changed tack. He turned to Wasmund and asked, 'Why don't *you* go?'

Bhoyrul laughed, 'You've got to be kidding! What would you say? You're working for John Fashanu and you want him to change his story? If I was Chris Vincent I'd want a lot more than five grand if I knew where you lot were coming from.'

Bhoyrul – like any reporter, still curious to see how the story developed – ended the meeting by saying that he would get Vincent to contact Wasmund. Over the next three days, Wasmund called him repeatedly, asking if he had been in touch. But it was not until 19 June that Chris Vincent happened to call him. Bhoyrul told Vincent that a journalist was trying to contact him and gave him Wasmund's number.

Over the next ten days, Bhoyrul was at the hub of a series of calls relating to events as they unfolded between Vincent and Wasmund. By now, he was worried that his journalistic interest in the intrigue might have made him too involved in a potentially damaging situation. So he asked his editor Tom Rubython for advice. Rubython told him to pull out of the story immediately.

Next question: should Bhoyrul approach the police? Possibly. But not before he had called the *Sun*.

Bhoyrul got in touch with Guy Patrick and John Troup and told them his entire story. On 30 June, in Troup's presence, he called Shaa Wasmund and had a flirtatious conversation. A flirtatious, taped conversation.

Wasmund said that Vincent had called her up and offered to buy her lunch – the first time, they both agreed, he had ever been known to part with his money. 'He must really like you,' laughed Bhoyrul. They chatted on, agreeing that Vincent was a 'sleazeball'. Wasmund said that she had met Vincent and explained that if he could come up with good material that supported Fashanu's case, Fash would use it in a libel action against the *Sun*. 'I just made it clear to him that libel cases are very financially remunerative and anybody who's involved in them usually benefits quite substantially – so he understood what I was saying.'

On Sunday 2 July, Bhoyrul met Wasmund for breakfast at Joe's Café, a small restaurant near to the Joseph store in Brompton Cross, South Kensington. According to Bhoyrul, Wasmund claimed that Vincent had effectively changed his statement in ways that would help Fashanu. She also suggested that he, Bhoyrul, might get 'an early Christmas present'. The entire conversation was videotaped by the *Sun*, but, as on a number of previous occasions, the tape was not clear enough to be of any value.

But what of Chris Vincent? He had been in southern Africa, spending a few happy weeks on safari before he heard from Anil Bhoyrul. By his recollection, Bhoyrul said that he had been approached by a journalist called Charlotte Evans who was keen to get in touch with Vincent to interview him. Vincent was given a number. He called Evans, who said that she was planning to fly out to South Africa to speak to him. Vincent told her that his rate for a conversation was £5,000. 'No cash . . . no speak.'

Charlotte Evans was a name that Shaa Wasmund occasionally used when working as a writer. She would stick to it throughout her dealings with Vincent. After a few days of telephone negotiation, Evans/Wasmund agreed that Vincent would fly back to England, all expenses paid. On 23 June she spoke to John Fashanu on the phone at 1.56 p.m. Half an hour later, she transferred £1,000 to Chris Vincent in South Africa. Having stayed in Johannesburg long enough to see the rugby World Cup final, Vincent flew back to Britain on an overnight South African Airways charter flight to Stansted.

On the plane, awaiting take-off, he got talking to two men from Ipswich. When he said that he came from Zimbabwe, they replied that they had spotted another Zimbabwean at the airport, Bruce Grobbelaar. He had been standing in the same check-in line. In fact, he was probably on the plane. Ever eager to give events their most dramatic interpretation, Vincent summoned a stewardess and explained who he was. 'If Bruce Grobbelaar is on this flight, you'd better get one of us off it,' he said. The passenger list was checked. Grobbelaar was not on the flight. But he might just be on one of two other SAA charters that were flying back to the UK at roughly the same time. When they got to Stansted there was another SAA jumbo on the tarmac. Vincent told the crew of his plane that he was not getting off without a police escort.

Two officers armed with Heckler and Koch sub-machine-guns were summoned to the gate where the 747 was docked and marched with Vincent through the terminal. Their routine was impressively smooth. At any one time one policeman would be ten to fifteen metres ahead of Vincent, giving no indication that he was the passenger under guard. The second man would walk a few metres behind. At corners the lead man would wait, looking out for any danger. The second policeman would then take over at the front while the first one slipped in behind. In fact there was no need whatever for Vincent to worry. Grobbelaar was on the third flight, several minutes behind them. In any case, there was never the slightest evidence that he had done, or tried to do, anything whatsoever to hurt Chris Vincent, however sorely one might think he must have been tempted.

Vincent arrived in England on the morning of 26 June. He called the woman he knew as Charlotte Evans from the airport and was told to take a cab into town. She had reserved a room for him at the Royal Norfolk Hotel in Bayswater, close to Paddington Station. When he reached the hotel shortly after midday, 'Evans' was waiting for him. She was a young woman in her twenties, quite short, with long dark hair pulled back in a ponytail and held by a scrunchie. She wore a simple sleeveless brown mini-dress and high espadrilles.

At 12.48, Shaa Wasmund, alias Charlotte Evans, called John Fashanu and spoke to him for 4 minutes 30 seconds.

She and Vincent went for lunch at an Italian restaurant. Evans said she was writing an article for the *Daily Mirror* praising Fashanu, his work for Unicef, his role on *Gladiators* and so on. Vincent said that he would tell her what he knew about Fashanu for £3,000 – of which he had already received £1,000 – plus his travel and hotel expenses, which had amounted to some £1,500. To Vincent, the woman he knew as Charlotte Evans was very different from the journalists he had met previously in his travels around Fleet Street. According to his account, she told him: 'During the course of the interview I'll be asking questions about how it was reported in the *Sun* that you saw John Fashanu coming out of his house [when he met with Grobbelaar]. Maybe you could say you weren't sure it was Fashanu. Maybe it was just a tall black man.'

Vincent replied that he could only tell her what he saw. He said he would be stupid to change his story, because there were construction workers there that day [if there were any such workers, none were ever traced] who would be able to verify that it was Fashanu, anyway. Evans seemed unsure about whether to accept his reasoning. She said she would phone him again to arrange another meeting. At 3.20 p.m. she made the first of three successive phone calls to John Fashanu, totalling four minutes in all.

Vincent became convinced that this was a set-up, and that Evans was working for Fashanu. He called the *Sun*, to see if they wanted the story. They did not, and just to emphasize the point they called the police to alert them. But Vincent had beaten them to it, leaving a message for Glyniss Turner and Peter Gulliver before he contacted Wapping.

The following morning, the 27th, the phone calls began again. At 11.05 Wasmund contacted Fashanu and they spoke for 2 minutes 30 seconds. Just before 1.00 p.m., she called the Royal Norfolk Hotel. Five minutes later, Vincent called her back. They arranged to meet again outside the Oxford Street entrance to Selfridges. Wasmund then called Fashanu.

When Vincent got to Selfridges, Wasmund told him, 'We've got to go somewhere quiet for the interview.' They went back to her metallic grey two-door Honda car and drove north to Regent's Park, looking for an open space, checking around to see if anyone could possibly see or hear their conversation. Then she stopped the car and, without getting out, said, 'Let's do the interview.'

Vincent asked to see her money.

Wasmund pulled out a white envelope filled with £50 notes. She counted out £2,000, checking three or four times to make sure she had the right amount, then put £500 change back in the envelope, saying that she would pay still more the next day. Vincent counted the notes and then gave them back to her.

She started the interview. Vincent later claimed that he stuck to material he had already given to the *Sun*. Wasmund told him that she had met Fashanu, who was trying to gather evidence for a libel action against the *Sun*, which had described him as 'Fash the Cash'. She had, in fact, popped round to see his assistant that same day, and had been reassured that Fashanu had no grudge against Vincent and would be happy if he joined him in his fight against the *Sun*.

Vincent replied that if Fashanu was not charged with any offence, and wanted to take the *Sun* to the cleaners, he would be more than happy to help. 'But,' he repeated, 'I saw John Fashanu and Bruce Grobbelaar at the house together. All I can tell you is what I saw, and I can't change that. It doesn't do me any good to bullshit.'

After forty-five minutes the interview ended and the two of them went for ice-creams and a walk in the park. When they returned to the car, Vincent picked up his £2,000.

Back at the Royal Norfolk, Vincent was faxed a series of letters written to 'Charlotte Evans' by various organizations with whom she had worked as a journalist.

Meanwhile, a team from Hampshire Police led by Detective Inspector Rod Davies, who had assumed day-to-day control of the case, had come up to London on 27 June to investigate whether Fashanu was attempting to bribe Vincent and thus pervert the course of justice. Davies set up an operations room in the British Transport Police offices at Paddington Station.

Vincent gave a formal statement of what had happened between himself and Wasmund/Evans. Then Davies asked Vincent to hand over all the money he had on him: the £2,000 he had been given by Wasmund, plus the small amount remaining from his trip to South Africa.

Vincent was appalled. 'What have I got to live on?' he pleaded.

Davies was entirely unmoved. 'We've got to have that money. It's evidence.'

So Vincent gave him all his cash. Once again, he was stony broke. Davies, however, had more pressing matters on his mind. Would Vincent agree to be wired when he next met Wasmund? Certainly, he said.

On the morning of 28 June Vincent met Davies and his team again to discuss their strategy. He was due to see Shaa Wasmund to get expenses and do another interview. This time, he was told, it was vital that he talked Wasmund into being explicit about what she wanted him to do. If possible, she should name specific amounts that she or Fashanu were prepared to pay for specific services. If that happened, he must not commit himself to anything. He should just say, 'I'll think about it.' Then he should try to arrange a meeting to pick up the cash from John Fashanu in person, so that he could be caught red-handed. Davies told Vincent, 'We believe that certain people will do anything to taint you as a witness and we have information to that effect. We believe that this woman is a key part of this.'

Vincent spent the day trying to get in touch with Wasmund. She was out of town, and not due back until six in the evening.

As 5 p.m. he was wired up. A Nagra tape-machine was placed in the small of his back and attached by a nylon belt. It contained a reel of quarter-inch tape which could record for more than three hours in complete silence. From the machine emerged three wires. Two of them led to microphones stuck to his chest, near his armpits. The third was attached to a remote-control switch. You pulled to turn the machine on, and pushed for off. Finally, the whole device was sealed, so that any evidence it collected could not be tampered with. Then Vincent went back to his hotel to wait for Shaa Wasmund's call.

She was late getting into town. Their meeting was delayed, first until 9.30, then until 10, and then until the following day. Back he went to the room at Paddington Station to be unwired by the tired, frustrated police.

At 9.15 a.m. on 29 June Wasmund called Vincent again and arranged to meet him by the Angel, Islington underground station at 12.15. Vincent, who had been rewired, got there by 11.50. Wasmund did not arrive for a further fifty minutes. Then he saw a familiar sun-dress coming down the pavement towards him. It was Shaa Wasmund, carrying the same white envelope from which she had extracted the £2,000 when they had spoken in Regent's Park.

Vincent spoke into his armpit microphone. 'The tape is on, I'm leaving the Angel, and I can see the subject approaching.'

She said she knew a café where they could talk, two or three blocks away. They settled in a corner table at the back of the room and she apologized for her absence on the previous day. She'd been in Birmingham and had not returned until 2 a.m. She said the name of the *Mirror* journalist with whom she was working was Chris Tyler (a name that later turned out to be false – no one called Chris Tyler worked for the *Daily Mirror*, either on staff or as a freelance). The *Mirror*'s story about John Fashanu was, she said, due to run on 3 July, just prior to Fashanu reporting to the police, as he and Grobbelaar had to do, on the 4th.

Wasmund said she was no longer interested in doing a piece about Grobbelaar, but she would be happy to meet again to sort out Vincent's expenses which now stood at about £2,000. In the meantime she gave him £500.

It was a frustrating meeting for the police. Wasmund, who seemed far more relaxed than during her previous meetings, happily chatted about Fashanu, mentioning once again that he had no axe to grind with Vincent. She also reiterated – as she would later tell Bhoyrul – that Fashanu was interested in running a libel action against the *Sun*. 'My hero!' replied Vincent, who was by now in full *Sun*-hating mode himself. 'I'd like to smack Patrick around the ears one of these times,' he snarled.

'John's a good man,' said Wasmund, who mentioned his work for Unicef and the faith that organization had shown in him. She presented him as a man wronged by the media – 'Higgins will lose his job,' she said, referring to the editor of the *Sun* – and the police. 'The police in this country have a bad reputation at the moment, always making mistakes like the Guildford Four and the Birmingham Six.' All in all, she doubted whether there was enough evidence for Fashanu to be charged: 'I really think it's highly unlikely from all I've heard,' she said.

At no time did Wasmund make any offer of a bribe, or any overt suggestion that Vincent should change his evidence. She was very careful to say that she never spoke to John Fashanu directly, only to his assistant. But, she concluded, 'It would probably be very good for you and John to meet up or even to talk via the phone when you can . . . The sums involved in that kind of libel for both of you are phenomenal. I'm sure that would adequately see your safari park up and running. At the end of the day, that's what you've got to remember, because that's what it's all about.'

'As I said, I'd rather have a safari park . . .' agreed Vincent.

Wasmund drove the point home. 'Exactly. Why did you do all this? Because you were in business with somebody and you'd pissed two years' hard work in setting up a safari park and they stabbed you in the back . . . Sometimes fate has a funny way of dealing with things. This safari park will get the go-ahead because you sue the *Sun* for libel. At the end of the day, it doesn't matter where the money comes from.'

Shortly after 1 p.m., Vincent and Wasmund parted company. At 1.12, Wasmund called John Fashanu. They spoke for 1 minute 34 seconds.

Vincent returned to Paddington. This time he was allowed to keep the £500 to pay his bill at the Royal Norfolk Hotel. The operation had not gone as well as he had hoped, but the police did not seem unduly bothered, any more than they had been surprised by the initial approach that was made to him.

'You wouldn't believe what we get told,' explained Inspector Davies. 'People talk, then other people talk and then we know.' Davies was sure, however, that whatever anyone may or may not have said over the telephone, Vincent was not in any serious danger. 'These guys have got far too much to lose,' he said. 'If anything happens to you, they're the first people we'd pick up. Anyway, judging by what's happened so far, we'd know about it before they did anything, and we'd inform you about it.'

No charges were brought against any of the four men arrested for alleged match-fixing when they reported to the police on 4 July. But at 7.45 on the morning of 6 July, the police arrested John Fashanu, Shaa Wasmund and Tony Shepherd – her co-director at Nautilus Communications – with a view to bringing charges of attempting to pervert the course of justice. Police searched both Fashanu's premises at Cavendish House (where his bug-detector was among the items of evidence seized) and Wasmund's Prebend Street flat. At the latter they found a number of items, including a customer copy of the Western Union money transfer to Chris Vincent, which had been sent in the name of Charlotte Evans.

From Islington Wasmund was driven to the Civic Centre Police Station Southampton, where she was interviewed between 8.30 and 10 p.m. She was interviewed again the following day from 1.13 to 4.45 p.m. After considerable internal debate among police officers and officials from the Crown Prosecution Service, however, it was decided not to press charges in this case.

Vincent meanwhile had gone to Windsor and checked into the Hart and Garter Hotel. It would be his home on and off – whenever he had enough money to pay the bill – for most of the next twelve months. There, in early July, he reflected on his situation. It was not a happy one. In the previous seven months he had been given £46,000 tax-free, and spent the lot. Yet after all this time, no charges had been brought against Grobbelaar and the rest. Vincent was desperate for that to happen, because he felt that it would validate his actions and prove to the world that there was some genuine substance to his allegations. In the meantime he had been strung along for months, constantly being promised that something would happen, but always being disappointed in the end.

Grobbelaar, meanwhile, had been far from idle. His libel case against the *Sun* had been proceeding since 21 December 1994, when his lawyers had issued his first Statement of Claim. The *Sun* submitted their defence on 4 January. Both sides then proceeded to gather evidence. On 6 July 1995 Grobbelaar served his formal reply to the *Sun*'s defence. It contained three outright falsehoods of considerable significance, told by Grobbelaar to his solicitors and reproduced by them in good faith. The first was that the 'Short Man' referred to in his conversations with Chris Vincent was 'purely a figment of my imagination'. The second was that he denied making a visit to see John Fashanu on 25 November 1993. The third was that he denied the trip from Norwich to the Hilton Hotel, London, on 5 February 1994 (when, of course, he met the very Short Man whom he claimed to have been imaginary).

Grobbelaar was clearly in confident mood. As if to underline the fact (and reinforce Vincent's frustration) he was featured on television in an advertisement for Sainsbury's supermarkets, for which he was paid an estimated £100,000. Grob was seen dropping a big juicy watermelon, for which the store then refunded him. The very fact that the ad was both made and aired appeared to illustrate that the public did not believe that the match-fixing stories could possibly be true. 'We had no complaints at all,' a Sainsbury's spokeswoman later told me. 'People just appreciated the humour.'

It would soon be clear, however, that the accusations against Grobbelaar and his alleged co-conspirators were anything but a joke. For on Monday 24 July – a blazingly hot day in the middle of Britain's finest summer for three hundred years – Bruce Grobbelaar, John Fashanu, Hans Segers, Heng Suan Lim and Melissa Kassa-Mapsi were jointly charged with conspiracy under Section One of the Criminal Act, 1977. The charge alleged that in 'London, or elsewhere between February 1st 1991 and March 15th 1995 they conspired together and with others known and unknown to give and corruptly to accept gifts of money as inducements improperly to influence the outcome of football matches or as rewards for having so done.' Each of the five faced further specific charges under Section One of the Prevention of Corruption Act, 1906. Grobbelaar was charged with four offences, Fashanu and Lim with two each, and one apiece for Segers and Kassa-Mapsi.

All of the defendants vigorously protested their innocence. 'I feel fine,' declared Grobbelaar, on whose behalf Dave Hewitt said, 'From the outset Bruce has denied any involvement whatsoever with any criminal activity and he maintains that denial today.' Fashanu's solicitor, Henri Brandman, stated that, 'John continues to protest his innocence in the strongest possible terms. He looks forward to clearing his name.' 'I'm gobsmacked,' said Segers. 'I had no idea I was going to be charged until I got to the police station.'

Soon afterwards, John Fashanu announced his retirement from football. But he continued to present *Gladiators*, both in England and Australia, his cheery TV persona unblemished by the charges hanging over him. Both Segers and Grobbelaar stayed with their respective clubs, which continued to support them publicly, but neither played any significant part in the 1995–6 season.

# 22

## 'I'll Go to the Ultimate Ends'

Chris Vincent, meanwhile, came to stay with me at my home near the South Downs. We needed to spend a fortnight or so conducting the interviews that would form the foundations for this book, and it seemed as easy to put him in the spare room as to drive back and forth to Windsor every day – particularly since my house was free, whereas the Hart and Garter was not.

He arrived with a suitcase full of clothes and a great bundle of personal papers. These included his CV; testimonial letters from teachers and employers; his army papers, including his citation for the Bronze Star; a thick bundle of newspaper cuttings about the case; hundreds of photographs of himself, Bruce and Bernice fooling around in Cheshire, London and Zimbabwe; photographs of the Mondoro camp, the land around it and the animals on the property (kudu well to the fore); and – something of which he was very proud – a business plan setting out the original concept of his safari camp, including the purchase of land, its location, the cost of running a camp and likely returns over one, three and five years, given various rates of occupancy. When this document was created I cannot say, although the fact that it related to land purchase, rather than leasing, must put it relatively early in the Mondoro scheme of things. But I can absolutely testify to having seen it –

a fact which would later assume a significance of which I was, at this point, entirely unaware.

Down to the country, too, came Bernice Bala'c. She was slim, blonde and lightly tanned – she looked, to be specific, like a marginally less curvaceous Cameron Diaz. Her personality seemed equally charming: well mannered, enthusiastic and eager to please. Her presence served a number of functions. She could give supporting eye-witness evidence to much of what Chris had to say. Although she had no direct knowledge whatever of the key incidents in the match-fixing allegations, she had been out with Chris and Bruce, had witnessed their friendship first-hand, had been present through most of Mondoro's final months and had been party to some of the events surrounding Chris's involvement with the *Sun*.

But there were hidden agendas which soon became all too apparent. Chris had evidently been desperately in love with Bernice. As he himself said, he had no contact with his family and his deepest friendship had been torn apart; she was all he had left. When he brought Bernice down to stay with me – she slept, it should be noted, on a sofa-bed in a different room from him – he must still have hoped that he could win her round.

For her part, Bernice was keen to ensure the exact opposite. She had already suffered an enormous amount of strain as a result of both the collapse of Mondoro and the events that followed, plus considerable intrusion on her privacy from reporters looking for follow-up angles to support or (more often) discredit the *Sun*'s investigations. The last thing she needed was to be portrayed as Chris Vincent's sexy, adoring blonde girlfriend – a fact which she made perfectly clear as the fortnight's stay became three weeks, then four, and then dragged on over two months.

The increasing tension between Chris and Bernice cast a pall over the entire household. Their arguments could be heard raging through the walls of their rooms. Eventually Bernice would leave, discovering when she came to pack that some of the expensive jewellery Chris had given her the day after the *Sun* story broke had gone missing: we never found it.

Bernice has always said that my family reminded her of the Grobbelaars: my wife, Clare, was as cool and elegant as Debbie; our two daughters were like Tahli and Olivia; even the general chaos of our domestic life – right down to the children's pictures stuck to the fridge door – was the same. There was another similarity: both Mrs Thomas and Mrs Grobbelaar took a very, very dim view of their husbands' business dealings with Christopher Vincent.

If the two women were ever to get together they would have the wax dolls and voodoo pins out in no time, because Clare was getting intuitive wobblies about Chris from the moment he walked through our door. Partly, she just hated sharing our house for weeks on end with a couple whose psychodrama became more convoluted with every day that passed. Partly, she resented the fact that I had handed over £3,000 – soon to become £4,000 – which now appeared to be financing treats for Bernice, like flying lessons at a nearby aerodrome. But most of all, she was being driven mad by the fact that every single one of her alarm bells was ringing fit to bust and her husband was refusing to listen to her.

I was too busy listening to Chris Vincent. As any journalist or policeman who was ever interviewed him will agree, Chris has an astonishing memory. He does not just say what happened. He can remember times, telephone numbers, exact conversations. He was also obsessed. He could, and did, talk for hours, and hours, and hours . . . and endless bloody hours. We would sit there for days on end, Chris surviving on a diet of Cokes, smokes and pints of milk, as his life story poured out in all its wounded bitterness, from the earliest psychological wounds he suffered at his father's hands, via his army and business exploits – he loved telling his war stories, in all their vivid, gory detail – through the long and tortured saga of Mondoro, to the heart of his allegations.

The story he told me was substantially the same as the evidence he gave to the police and subsequently, under oath, in two trials. What follows is his account, and it must be remembered that every single allegation of corrupt activity was challenged in court by the defence and rejected by criminal and civil juries. Where there is specific independent evidence to challenge Vincent's account I have done my best to include it, without disrupting Vincent's story to the point where it becomes unintelligible.

The starting point was the meeting with Richard Lim at the Manchester Hilton on 30 September 1993. Vincent described his reactions on the fateful drive to Manchester airport, when Grobbelaar, he claimed, told him that the 'guys from the Far East' were prepared to pay him 'big bucks' to fix games.

Vincent said that he replied: 'What, so Liverpool lose? But how do you do that?'

Grobbelaar's response, he said, was to snort, 'I've been a goalkeeper for fourteen years. I'm one of the best in the world. If I'm a yard off my line, no one will ever know.'

In Vincent's account, Grobbelaar had wound down the window and spat out of the car, narrowly missing another driver's windshield. 'Jesus!' he laughed. 'I'd better be more careful!'

As he told his story, I asked Vincent how he had reacted to these alleged revelations. If Grobbelaar had really said what he claimed, why had he not objected, or told him not to be so foolish?

Vincent's answer was that he knew what Grobbelaar had in mind was highly immoral, but if that was what he wanted to do it was his business. Like Grobbelaar, he had become used to the corruption that governed every aspect of life in Africa, where bribes and backhanders were an essential means of getting things done. That, of itself, did not shock him.

On a sporting level, his interests were golf, rugby and cricket. As he put it, 'If it had been Ian Botham, and he had been offered money to throw a Test Match, it would have been different, because I'm a supporter of Ian Botham and a supporter of cricket. I'd have told him to fuck off, not to touch it with a bargepole. But at that time I couldn't give a monkey's about English football. I didn't know anything about the football-gambling laws in this country, or football corruption.

If I'd known then what I know now, my choice would have been simple: either, as soon as we get to Manchester airport, get straight out of the car, pick up a phone, call the FA or the coppers and say, "Come here now. This boy's up to shit." Or look after my best friend.'

Whatever the circumstances, the lesson that had been drummed into Chris Vincent all through his army years, to the point that it had become the key to his personal values, was this. You don't run out on a mate. You stand and fight together. His only question to Grobbelaar, he said, was 'Why am I here?'

'Because if anybody sees me, we can just say I'm on safari business with you.'

Vincent then described how he sat and listened while Grobbelaar explained his plan. 'I've got three or four years left. I'm going to make as much as I can, then I'm fucking off to Africa.' He told Vincent that a man had flown up from London on the Shuttle to give him some money and discuss possible games he could throw. They would be meeting at the airport Hilton. In an account that would later be the subject of fierce courtroom debate, Vincent claimed that Grobbelaar had asked him where the best place was to pick up his money: he wanted somewhere discreet.

'Go to the toilet,' said Vincent.

Vincent testified that Lim arrived and disappeared with Grobbelaar into the hotel bar. Within a few minutes the two men re-emerged and walked across the foyer to the Gents. A short while later, Grobbelaar appeared again and began walking briskly past the reception desk towards the front door, nodding at Vincent to get him to follow. When he and Vincent got back into the car he pulled a standard, white A4-width envelope from the waistband of his trousers and twisted round to put it in a briefcase on the passenger seat behind him. Then he put the car into gear and sped towards the open road.

Once they were back on the motorway, said Vincent, Grobbelaar went into more detail about his meeting with the individual he had now christened the Short Man. He had been offered £40,000 as the fee for throwing a game. Once again, he went back to his long-term aims. 'I'm going to go to South Africa and buy property, but I'm not telling the missus. In three or four years I'll go to Debbie and say, "I came to this country with £10. Now I'm going back to Africa. You can have the house, the flat in Portugal, the testimonial fund. I'm going back to Africa . . . and I'm taking £10 with me."'

It soon became clear that, if his own evidence was to be believed, Vincent had been happily complicit in Grobbelaar's schemes. When Grobbelaar had, allegedly, met the Short Man at Heathrow Airport on 6 October 1993, Vincent had been happy to act as his chauffeur, look-out and bag-man. He had, he said, watched as Grobbelaar – easily distinguishable in his bright, mustard-coloured jacket – walked towards the terminal entrance, through which the Short Man appeared. The two men did not even bother to shake hands. They had a conversation lasting no more than fifteen or twenty seconds before the Short Man put his hand inside his leather jacket – a brown one, this time – and pulled out an envelope, identical to the one Vincent had seen at Manchester Airport. Grobbelaar then walked back out through the door and Vincent followed him out of the terminal.

When Grobbelaar and Vincent re-emerged, to find their car surrounded by police, who suspected a terrorist bomb threat, Grobbelaar had been unfazed. As an officer started writing out the parking ticket, Grobbelaar moved round to the boot of the car, which he opened, as if about to get something out. Taking care to keep the envelope hidden from the police, he tore off the top and began counting the money inside.

'There should be a grand there,' he told Vincent, his voice suddenly tense. 'You take £450 to give to Milligan. I need £300 . . .' The whole process of counting and dividing the money was too complicated and time-consuming. 'Look,' he said, shoving the envelope into Vincent's hands, 'you take the lot.' And with that, he had gone back into the terminal to catch his flight.

Vincent claimed that there had been only £750 in the envelope, but if Grobbelaar was disappointed at the syndicate's lack of generosity he didn't seem to show it. On his return from Zimbabwe, the calls to and from the Short Man became ever more frequent. If there was anyone else, apart from Chris Vincent, in the room when the Short Man called, Grobbelaar would answer him with a brusque 'I'll call you later.' But he confided completely in Vincent, often speaking to the Short Man in front of him, or thinking out loud about which game to choose for his first fix. 'The Short Man's asked me about this weekend,' he'd say, as games with Arsenal and Leeds went by without any decision.

Then, ten days before Liverpool were due to play Newcastle, he told Vincent, 'It's next weekend. We're going up north. It's going to be a "London" for us.' In other words – according to the alleged code for 'win', 'lose' or 'draw' – he would lose. Soon afterwards, the deal was confirmed. 'Next weekend I'm doing the business at Newcastle.'

There was going to be a lot of pressure on Grobbelaar to perform. The Malaysians were going to be staking hundreds of thousands of pounds. They had to be sure that he was going to deliver his end of the deal. But how?

It has been established by the highest court in the land that Bruce Grobbelaar did not deliberately let in any goals, when playing for Liverpool or Southampton. But in all the time that I spent with Chris Vincent, even he never suggested that this was what Grobbelaar had actually done. Instead, he said, Grobbelaar had planned to pick games that he thought his team would lose anyway, and then use his on-field influence to make that more likely.

From Grobbelaar's perspective, there were therefore good reasons for choosing the Newcastle game. Under normal circumstances Liverpool – the dominant English team of the previous fifteen years – would be likely to beat newly promoted Newcastle, and the betting odds would reflect that. But Grobbelaar knew that Liverpool's increasingly unreliable defence had been further weakened by injuries, and experienced campaigners had been replaced by men whom Grobbelaar did not respect, like 'that bloody idiot Torben Piechnik'. Not only did Grobbelaar think that the Dane was no good, but he could also ensure that he was made worse by being ordered out of position.

This last point is a crucial element. For a goalkeeper does more than block shots. He also directs the defenders in front of him, telling them where to go, which spaces to cover, which oncoming forward to pick up. A good keeper makes the penalty area his personal domain and regards himself as fully entitled to criticize any of his team-mates who make a mistake inside it.

Grobbelaar would not hesitate to use his authority to the full, but in the old days his team-mates had been equally sure of themselves. Men like Phil Thompson or Alan Hansen were unlikely to let themselves be ordered into positions they did not want to occupy. They'd spent long enough at the very top of the game to be able to use their own judgement. But less experienced players were a more malleable proposition. They might do what they were told.

According to Vincent, Grobbelaar reckoned that he would only have to place his defenders a few feet out of position to give opposing forwards a fractional advantage. If the forwards were good enough, that fraction would be all they would need. They could home in on the goal and leave Grobbelaar with no chance of stopping them, and no public blame for letting them in. Any criticism would fall squarely on his defenders' shoulders.

As it happened, Newcastle's form was so good, and their attacking play so potent, that even these methods proved unnecessary. The Magpies won fair and square. Grobbelaar did not have to do anything to assist them. But he would collect his corrupt winnings anyway, just as if he had done.

When the game ended, with Newcastle 3–0 victors, Vincent was keen to find out how Grobbelaar was feeling. He gave his friend about forty minutes to change and then tried calling him, but to no avail: the phone was switched off. At the sixth or seventh attempt he got through. The call was certainly made: telephone records prove it. The content of the conversation, as reported by Vincent and reproduced below, was of course denied by Grobbelaar.

'I'm in the car with Milligan,' said Grobbelaar, indicating that he couldn't talk.

'Good result, eh?' said Vincent.

'*Ja*, good one,' came the satisfied reply.

As events proved, this was the only time, in five supposedly fixed matches, when Grobbelaar was able to lose. Even if they were offering to pay him huge amounts of money, the Malaysian gambling syndicates did virtually nothing to improve their chances of winning. They would have been better off tossing a coin and placing their money on a heads-or-tails basis. So why bother? Perhaps because they were playing for huge stakes.

After the Newcastle game, Grobbelaar told Chris Vincent (according to Vincent, that is) that the syndicate had won £3.2 million on the Newcastle game alone. If the bets they placed on the four other Grobbelaar games had come off, their winnings might have topped £15 million. These are vast sums, but they were well within the compass of men who were prepared to spend £14 million on a single casino visit. And if that kind of money is at stake, the incentive for corruption must be very real indeed.

This was corruption to which Chris Vincent raised no objection whatever. Vincent freely admitted that he had no scruples about taking the money that he claimed Grobbelaar would receive as a result of Liverpool's loss. 'My best mate and business partner was saying he could make £40,000 every time he chucked a game, and he'd put it into our business.' He was also, he said, excited by Fashanu's supposed part in the proceedings. Fashanu had powerful connections in Africa. He was linked to the United Nations. One way and another, he could do their safari business a great deal of good. According to Vincent, the handover of cash had taken place during the meeting at Byron Drive.

Vincent's account of the meeting, as given to me, the police and two courts, contained a number of details which differed from the version of events described earlier in this book. Vincent said that when he and Bruce had reached the house on that November afternoon – he was not, at the time, sure of the exact date – Grobbelaar got out of the car, holding his briefcase. He told Vincent to stay where he was. Next to the garage was a set of French windows. Grobbelaar tried the handle, but it was locked. Vincent slipped across to the driver's seat, put the car into reverse and kept his hand over the ignition key. If anything happened, he was ready for a quick getaway.

At the front of the house, a portico sheltered the main entrance. By it, children's toys were scattered – a tricycle and little trolley. Now John Fashanu emerged from the door, wearing dark jeans and a short-sleeved polo shirt. He shouted out, 'Bruce!'

But according to evidence given under oath in court by both Grobbelaar and Tabetha Samvura, a Zimbabwean maid working at the house, Fashanu did not come to the door: Samvura said that she opened it and let both Grobbelaar and Mace into the house. Fashanu then greeted them inside. Mace told the court, 'I went to the front door to ring the bell and Mr Grobbelaar joined me. The door was answered by a maid and Mr Grobbelaar went inside. Mr Fashanu was in the hallway. I didn't go in.'

The way Vincent saw it, however, Grobbelaar walked over and shook Fashanu's hand while both men were still outside the house. Vincent claimed that, seeing Fash for the first time, he had been struck by the size and power of the man: no wonder other players were terrified by him. He was obviously as hard as nails. It was also clear from the way the two men greeted each other that they were close – two Africans, thought Vincent, who were both on the same wavelength.

The two men went inside the house and Vincent briefly saw them walk past a window before they disappeared from view. He claimed Grobbelaar later told him that Fashanu had asked, 'Who's the guy in the car?'

'That's my safari partner,' Grobbelaar had answered. 'He comes from Africa, too. He knows how to—' he drew his hand across his mouth – '*nyarara*.'

For ten or fifteen minutes after Grobbelaar went into the house, said Vincent, there was no sign of life. Then Grobbelaar emerged, alone this time, and walked towards the car, still carrying his case. He went straight up to the driver's door, opened it and slung the case on to the back seat. 'I'll drive,' he said. 'Let's get out of here quick.'

That Grobbelaar drove away with Vincent is undisputed by everyone, bar Miss Samvura, who testified that Mace had been waiting outside to collect him. It is only fair to say that both Vincent and Mace are small white men with somewhat rodent-like features: to a black Zimbabwean they might well be hard to distinguish.

Back to Vincent's account: as they began to put distance between themselves and Byron Drive, Grobbelaar slowly unwound. 'Get my briefcase,' he ordered Vincent. 'There's an envelope there. Open it and count what's inside.'

Vincent turned around and flicked open the case. There before him was a thick, tightly filled brown envelope, about a foot long. In it was £40,000, divided into sixteen bundles of fifty £50 notes, sealed in plastic bags and wrapped in a band marked 'Midland Bank, Marble Arch, London'. The bands, said Vincent, were marked with 'the previous day's date'. This last detail is either a mistake or a pure invention: police investigations confirmed that the Midland Bank, Marble Arch, did not supply anyone with £40,000 in cash on 24 November, the day before the meeting at Byron Drive. It is possible that only one or two of the bundles were marked in that way: Vincent's account seemed to differ from one occasion to another on this point.

Be that as it may, he said that Grobbelaar started to give instructions about what to do with the money, listing all the bills he had to pay and asking Vincent to add them up. He still owed £6,500 for his Mercedes. Milligan needed £2,500 and there was a further £3,000 that had to be paid to Pat Mavros, the dealer who had supplied the prize statue donated to the winning team in his testimonial match. Various other payments were mentioned. What did they add up to?

Vincent told him: £17,000.

'Right,' said Grobbelaar, 'I'll give you £20,000. Put it in your briefcase. I'll put the other 20K in mine.'

Now that the business side of things had been sorted out, he began to relax. 'You should have been inside that house,' he said. The furniture had been amazing, and included a long dining table made from a massive piece of solid wood.

'Who was there?' asked Vincent.

'JF and the Short Man's boss,' replied Grobbelaar. Once again, this certainly was not right. Telephone evidence indicates that Lim could have been in Byron Drive, though he, Grobbelaar, Mace and Samvura all deny it. But his boss was Johannes Joseph. He was not even in Britain, let alone Byron Drive, at the time.

Vincent said he had more questions about Fashanu. 'How long has he been doing this?'

'About a year,' Grobbelaar allegedly replied. 'He told me he's made between £400,000 and £800,000 for chucking football games.'

One should bear in mind that the Crown at no time tried to link John Fashanu with any specific matches which he might have attempted to throw. In the prosecution's version of events, his role was that of a middle-man. And even by the prosecution's account, the monies paid to him by Johannes Joseph – over four years, not one – amounted to something over £200,000, far less than the sums Vincent described.

Nevertheless, Vincent said he had hoped that Grobbelaar's activities could make hundreds of thousands of pounds for Mondoro. When asked, during the research for his book, how he felt about taking what he said was bent money, he replied, 'Well, I wasn't bending it. To be honest, at that point I knew what Bruce was doing was highly immoral. But I didn't know it was illegal. He was going to give me vast amounts of money to get rid of in southern Africa. I'd already signed a deal on his behalf. I'm protecting my mate's arse . . . To me, this bullshit with the football was irrelevant to the safari business. He's giving me money and saying, "Here, take this and use it in Zimbabwe" . . . I don't give a fuck where it comes from.'

How could he take Grobbelaar's money at one point, and

then claim that there was a moral justification for 'exposing' his alleged activities at a later date?

Vincent came up with an analogy. 'Imagine you're in business with a guy for two and a half years, and he's your best friend, and then you discover that all the money he's given you had come from drug-dealing with twelve-year-olds. You've got a choice. You can either run him in, or look after his arse. So you look after his arse. Then he fires you out the window. Now the rules have changed.'

Well, it's morality, Jim, but not as we know it.

Irrespective of where Grobbelaar was finding the money to put into Mondoro, the simple truth is that Vincent's chief motive was expediency. He needed cash and he was not too bothered where it came from. And needing cash was a recurrent motif where he was concerned.

As well as borrowing £4,000 from me in the summer of 1995, he cadged a further £12,000 from another friend. But somehow, the money never seemed to last. He would regularly ring me up, asking for more – requests which only served to heighten the tension that Clare (quite rightly, in retrospect) felt about the whole business. As the autumn passed and Christmas approached, his requests became more desperate and our conversations more heated.

At one level, I felt a basic human sympathy for a fellow man who was frequently penniless (although I increasingly began to wonder why he did not simply work for a living, like the rest of us). But on another level I came increasingly to resent his disruptive influence: the fall-outs that led to the collapse of Mondoro became all too comprehensible as all the individuals and companies involved in this book became ever more fractious with one another, two close friendships came close to breaking point, and my ten-year marriage came under intolerable strain.

Then, just before Christmas 1995, Chris – who had become increasingly desperate in the face of his poverty – and I had a bizarre telephone conversation. He had managed to track me down to the office of the *Mail on Sunday*'s *Night and Day* magazine, where I had been writing a weekly column. He started by stating that he was going to come down to my house and seize all his personal documents, plus the tapes of our conversations and all my notebooks. I told him that the tapes and the notebooks were my personal property and I would not release them. But if he wanted his papers, I would be happy to give them to him at any location of his choosing.

No, he insisted, he was coming down to my house. We argued for a while: under no circumstances was I letting him anywhere near my wife and children – enough damage had been caused already on that front. Eventually he agreed, but then started talking about how he was sick of the whole book project, sick of the way the British did business (his chief complaint being that there were too many promises and not enough cash). He was going to walk away from the whole thing.

I told him that I intended to write the book for which I had signed a contract, whether he was part of it or not. Chris exploded that he would never allow that: 'I will go to the ultimate ends to stop you,' he shouted.

I asked him if he was threatening me – and if so, with what? If he was threatening legal action, he could forget it: I would win. If he was threatening physical action, I was calling the police right now. So which was it?

'I'm just saying I will go the ultimate ends to prevent you doing that book,' he repeated.

The conversation continued for a short while longer, to the amazement of *Night and Day* colleagues listening to my end of it in their office. Then, my work done, I went off to do some Christmas shopping. Later that month I sent him postal orders totalling £100 so that he could at least buy himself a decent Christmas dinner. Some while later I also returned his personal papers, including the photographs and the business plan. It did not seem like a big deal at the time. I always assumed that I could get them back if necessary. It proved to be a misjudgement of major proportions.

As 1996 began, I was writing the first draft of this book. In March, Vincent gave evidence in the committal proceedings which determined that the case would go on to a full trial. But that trial, originally expected to take place in the first half of the year, kept being delayed. Chris was – and he can hardly be blamed for this – desperately frustrated by the long wait. It had already been well over a year since he first broke the story and he wanted to get the whole thing behind him. Despite that, as the spring and summer of 1996 wore on he seemed in remarkably good form. He had found a billet in a house outside Windsor owned by a professional golfer, and was even doing a spot of caddying for him.

He was also, he told me, working hard to revive his safari camp idea. He said he had found some Arab investors willing to spend up to sixteen million dollars on buying land and constructing a camp. Muslim law, he said, prevented them from charging interest on the loan, so he had agreed that any money they put into the project would be used to buy shares in a joint company, which would then be bought back for an agreed price – conveniently equivalent to the sum applicable if the money had been earning interest – at a later date.

Vincent had news on the Grobbelaar front, too. He had, he said, spoken to representatives from Tri-Star Pictures, and to some of Rupert Murdoch's top film executives. There was huge Hollywood interest in filming his story. Someone had suggested Tom Selleck to play Grobbelaar. And Mel Gibson to play Chris Vincent. As unlikely as that casting sounded – personally I would see Chris Vincent as more of a Gary Oldman or Tim Roth kind of character – I was pleased by how much better he was getting on. Roughly a year on from the start of our project, we met a few times in Windsor to discuss his reactions to my draft. He promised to send me a detailed list of corrections. None came. We talked a couple of times on the phone and he promised that they were on the way. I was getting concerned because he had told me that he was due to leave the country for South Africa shortly. So on 1 October 1996 I put in another call to the house where he was staying.

The telephone was answered by a policeman. The house was being searched. Chris Vincent had just been arrested at the offices of Ian Wilson, John Fashanu's TV and media agent. It would later be alleged that Vincent had placed a call to Fashanu's office on 26 September, asking to speak to one of Fashanu's representatives: Wilson had been nominated. Fashanu then informed his solicitor of Vincent's approach. Vincent met Wilson and, in a taped conversation, asked for £500,000. In return, he would not give evidence in the forthcoming trial but would go 'where Jesus couldn't find me'. His offer was reported to the police. At a second meeting with Wilson, on 1 October, Vincent asked for £300,000 within the hearing of a police officer. When he was charged, Vincent said, 'I am not guilty.' The police later discovered that he had booked, but not paid for, a £30,000 holiday to South Africa, the Seychelles, Singapore, Australia, New Zealand, Bali, Tahiti, Buenos Aires, Barbados and Antigua.

Chris Vincent was charged with attempting to pervert the course of justice – charges which he denied – and remanded in custody in Winchester Prison. One irony was thus heaped upon another: having caught Bruce Grobbelaar in a taped sting, he had himself been trapped on tape. His defence would be roughly the same as Bruce Grobbelaar's had been when confronted by the *Sun* reporters: what he said had all been false – he was doing it in order to entrap John Fashanu. But there was one big difference: the only person in jail was Chris Vincent.

He was held only a few hundred yards up the road from the courtroom where both his and Bruce Grobbelaar's cases were due to be heard. I visited him there one grim, drizzly afternoon in November. It was not an experience I would recommend. Prosperous, law-abiding, middle-class folk have no concept of the terminally depressing awfulness of prison. Outside, girlfriends, wives, mums and nippers hang around a stark, graffiti-stained Portakabin, bare-legged and corned beef-skinned, chain-smoking, blatantly poverty-stricken.

Then a screw opens the main gate, the previous batch of visitors file out into the gloom, and the numbers are called out that will admit the next lot, one by one, into the world behind that great black door. You are frisked and sent through a metal-detector. Your hand is placed against a metal plate which takes some sort of impression: you only get out again by giving the matching impression at the end of the visit. Then you walk into the nick.

Forget all those images from American movies: lovers talking to one another on microphones, pressing their hands against the panes of glass that part them. In England it is far more prosaic: a dining-hall, plastic chairs, Formica-topped tables and scalding tea in plastic cups, twenty pence a time. Chris, an outdoorsman who always kept himself fit and ruddy-faced, looked as though he had been bleached. When he called out his usual greeting – 'Howzit?' – and gave his characteristic grin, he still had an air of surface jollity, but his eyes were dulled and his teeth were horribly stained. No one ever tells you this about prison, but inmates have to provide their own toothpaste, soap and shaving gear. If you have no money – and Chris did not – you don't get to be clean. It is, I think, an unforgivable humiliation.

We talked about this book, and his situation: Chris was banged up while the men he had accused were walking free. Still, he felt confident that he would have his revenge when the time came to give evidence. He could do a decent job of it, he thought, but he was worried: no one from the police or the Crown Prosecution Service had been to see him, or provided him with his witness statements. It had been so long since the whole fuss began that even he was beginning to forget things. He would soon be forcibly reminded.

# 23

## 'Would All Those Concerned in the Case of Grobbelaar and Others . . .'

Over the course of several weeks, a trial becomes its own community. One might imagine that all the various camps – defence, prosecution, police, defendants, media and so on – would keep pretty much to themselves. But in fact they are constantly intermingled, and that was particularly so from the very start of the case that the *Sun* had taken to calling the Trial of the Century. In the brief mid-morning or mid-afternoon recesses people would gather in the broad corridor outside courtroom number 3, Winchester Crown Court, sharing impressions of the way things were going, discussing tactics, asking questions or giving off-the-record briefings. At lunch, the court canteen would frequently find four or five members of the jury on one table, a bunch of hacks swapping journalistic war stories on another, and John Fashanu holding court on a third.

Because the case was held in Winchester and most of the participants came from London, nights were spent in hotels and evenings in pubs. Four of Heng Suan Lim's team set up a pub quiz team. They called themselves The Short Man. After they had won £100 in two consecutive Tuesday night triumphs at the Exchange, one of their favourite haunts close to the court, they were challenged by a team of *Sun* journalists and photographers. Their name? The Bung-Busters.

Once a pint or two had been drunk, or a brandy sipped – one of the major legal players was said to have run up a £1,500 Armagnac bill at a hostelry close to the cathedral by the time the trial ended – barristers gave reporters their private views of the case. Some were completely unrepeatable in any public forum. Others were light-hearted ('Wooden feet – and head likewise,' said one counsel of a player). Others were wildly upbeat.

After one particularly effective day in court, one of the lead defence counsel was offering to bet all-comers a bottle of champagne that he had just got his client off. 'I've hit the gravy train!' said a lawyer whose presence at such a high-profile case had ensured a stream of equally prominent clients. Even junior counsel took great pleasure in buying journalists drinks, rubbing in the fact that – thanks to their stupendous fees – they could easily afford to do so. Three of the defendants were on legal aid, the generosity of which was underlined when, towards the end of the trial, figures were published showing that Hans Segers' barrister, Desmond De Silva QC, had earned in excess of £400,000 in the past year from legal aid cases. Rodney Klevan QC, acting for Bruce Grobbelaar, was also named among the profession's top twenty earners from that source.

They were not being paid for their conviviality, of course, but for their skill in the courtroom itself. The Winchester court building is hidden from casual passers-by at the far end of an open cobbled square, accessible via a little side street off the main road. At the entrance to the square a knot of TV and newspaper cameramen would gather every day to capture pictures of the trial's main participants entering and leaving court. One day's pictures always seemed remarkably like another's, but still the snappers lingered, as if to suggest that the proceedings had not really taken place unless some record of their existence was captured on film or videotape. The defendants and their families always made a great display of ignoring the lenses stuck in their faces, but there must have been something comforting in the ritual for them, too. What was it, after all, if not continuing confirmation of their personal significance?

Once past the cameras, anyone wishing to go to court had to cross the square and climb some stone steps which led up to a squat, modern building whose façade, in which recessed windows were separated by jutting bulwarks of concrete and flint, suggested a twentieth-century interpretation of a medieval castle. It was a neat stylistic joke, for the courts are surrounded by legal and council offices housed in Victorian Gothic blocks – another century's play on the myth of the Middle Ages.

To get to the court itself, one had to climb more stairs. Once past the security check and metal-detector, one turned left up a staircase towards a broad landing looking down on to the high entrance hall, off which could be found two of the case's most popular meeting places – the canteen and the Gents. Yet more stairs led up to the floor where Court No. 3 – the scene of the next several weeks' drama – was to be found. Its entrance was two-thirds of the way along a broad hallway, lined on one side by settees. To the right as one walked along the hall was Court No. 5, a former magistrates' court due for refurbishment but deemed suitable in the meantime to be used as an annexe for the ladies and gentlemen of the press.

This room was filled with long tables at which the hacks sat, scribbling furiously as they took down the words transmitted by audio feed from the court itself. They were faced by a dais where a court official watched over them like a schoolteacher invigilating in an examination hall from which the pupils – rascals all – were liable at any moment to disappear as they dashed off to file the latest revelations to their news desks. However respectfully witnesses and lawyers may have been treated in court, they were never safe from the scathing commentary uttered in the privacy of Court No. 5.

That, though, was a mere side-show. What of the main event? To the left of the hallway, one short, final staircase led up to the double swing-doors that provided entry to Court No. 3. It was a suitably imposing setting for the drama that was to take place, being 50 or 60 feet square and about 30 feet high.

Against the rear wall stood the dock, which looked across the room to Mr Justice Tuckey, ensconced in a tall red leather seat and surrounded by volumes of evidence and video-monitors.

The accused always sat in the same order: Lim nearest the door, then Fashanu, Segers and Grobbelaar. Between the dock and the judge on the floor of the courtroom were the lawyers, in four rows of benches and desks, each containing between four and six men (there were never more than one or two women amongst the lawyers). The front rank, facing the judge, was reserved for junior barristers. In the second row sat the leading counsel for the prosecution, Mr Calvert-Smith, whose tatty old wig, quite denuded of its curls, gave him an air of genteel impoverishment; Mr De Silva, very tall, very bulky, with a sallow, yellow-ochre complexion (perhaps he was simply nicotine-stained: his first action upon leaving the court was always to reach for a comforting fag); and Mr Klevan, his QC's frock-coat with its deep cuffs and black frogging merely adding to his Georgian appearance.

Behind these old lions came the younger guns: Lim's man Jerome Lynch, whose balding close-cropped pate and lush moustache made him – as he would later remind the jury – a dead ringer for Grobbelaar himself. Having made a series of simulated TV trials for Channel 4, Lynch was en route to becoming something of a media star. As he remarked, 'I said to Bruce, the time will come when he knows he's really made it, because people will say, "Aren't you Jerome Lynch?"'

Acting for John Fashanu was Trevor Burke. He was the quietest and youngest-looking of the four defence counsel, with a boyish face beneath wavy greying hair, but in many ways he was the toughest. As the case proceeded, he revealed a streak of ruthlessness in his pursuit of his client's interests that made him the most likely to clash with the judge, but which arguably gave his case the most intellectual coherence of all the defences presented to the jury.

Burke had been retained by one of the men who could frequently be found in the last row of legal benches – John Fashanu's solicitor, Henri Brandman. An East End boy (his own preferred description) and life-long West Ham United fan, the forty-one-year-old Brandman was to celebrities what Red Adair is to oil rigs: the guy who puts out fires. When, on 23 January 1995, Gillian Taylforth, the *EastEnders* actress, accidentally deposited her BMW in the front garden of 23 Clarendon Road, Borehamwood, while driving under the influence of three glasses of wine and another of champagne, Henri Brandman pleaded her case at Watford magistrates' court. On 7 November 1990, when the boxer Terry Marsh was acquitted of the charge of attempting to murder his ex-manager Frank Warren, it was his solicitor Henri Brandman who stood before reporters outside the Old Bailey to tell them, 'Terry wishes to thank all his family and friends who have supported and stood by him through his ordeal.'

Other Brandman clients include Nigel Benn (cleared of assault in 1997) and Paul Ince (cleared of assault in 1995). When Michael Watson, the boxer brain-damaged during a world title fight in 1991, sued the British Board of Boxing Control, it was Henri Brandman who helped him do it. When the luscious TV starlet Emma Noble – later to marry John Major's son James – wanted to ensure that no future boyfriends sold their stories to the papers as two previous lovers had done, it was Henri Brandman who drew up what the *Sun* called her 'kiss-and-no-tell' contract.

Brandman's short, balding figure was frequently to be seen at his client's trial. His immense affability never wavered, even when dealing with journalists who, as he well knew, were working hard to uncover further potentially embarrassing revelations should John Fashanu be found guilty. But then, as one experienced tabloid reporter at Winchester put it, 'Henri knows how to play the game. He knows what the red-tops [the *Sun*, *Mirror* and *Star*] want and he knows how to deliver it. He understands that we're just doing our job and he's just doing his job. I think he's as good as Max Clifford at giving us a good soundbite and he's totally above board as well.'

Speaking of red-tops, to the right of the dock, ranged length-ways along the side wall, were the press benches; to their right, the police seats; right again, the witness box. Ranged directly across the courtroom from the witness box, so as to provide a direct view of whoever was in it, were the jury benches. And on the morning of 14 January, with the press benches packed and a hum of anticipation in the air, it was the composition of that jury to which the court would have to turn its attention before the case itself could begin.

A line of about twenty-five men and women filed into the room. Justice Tuckey told them that this case would probably go on into March, although it should be over by Easter. Because it was likely to be a long trial it had been necessary to call a large number of potential jurors, Tuckey said, adding that the case had already received wide publicity. 'If you believe you could not try the case fairly, please say so and you will be excused.' If jurors were fans or employees of any of the clubs for which the defendants had played; if they were employees of the *Sun*; or if they had any close connections with any of the accused, they should say so now.

As he delivered these words, Tuckey was being examined by everyone in the room, much as the players and spectators at a Cup Final might run an eye over the referee. Would he be lenient or tough? Would he favour one side or the other? Would he keep up with play, or would there be niggling little off-the-ball incidents that would escape his notice?

Many of those questions were answered, as they usually are, within minutes of the legal kick-off. The Hon. Sir Simon Lane Tuckey – aged fifty-five, ruggedly handsome, educated in (appropriately enough) Zimbabwe and listing as his recreations sailing and tennis – had entered the courtroom with all the bounce and energy of an upmarket chat-show host springing into the studio. Clearly, this was no desiccated old buffer who might enquire in tremulous tones, 'Who, or what, is a Gazza?' Tuckey was one of nature's house captains: posh enough to impress, without being remotely Hooray Henry. He was dry, droll, obviously in charge. So, one thought, no problems there.

The would-be jurors' names were called out and answered either with an affirmative, 'Yes,' followed by a walk to the jury-box, or by an excuse for non-attendance. A mother with a ten-year-old daughter, a pub licensee who could not afford to be away from his bar; a passionate Liverpool supporter and a woman who had recently suffered a bereavement were all told they could go. A middle-aged gentleman in a jacket and tie revealed that he was happy to do his duty, but that he had an unmissable appointment on 24 March. 'We'll take a bet on you,' quipped Tuckey amidst much laughter, and the man took his place in the jury-box.

It took about half an hour to select nine men and three women. The youngest juror, a woman, must have been in her mid-twenties; the eldest, male and female, in their sixties. As the case went on, their views would be the subject of constant speculation by lawyers, policemen and press alike. At least one man, it was universally agreed, was irretrievably lost to the prosecution within hours of the start of the case. Another was lost to the case altogether and removed. The rest were far harder to read.

Over the following seven weeks they would be confronted by a mass of evidence, much of it contained in a bewildering variety of documents. Though there were moments when either side (most often the prosecution) would lose the jury's attention, it could not be denied that they gave the proceedings the care and consideration they deserved. Nor did they act in the face of any overwhelmingly compelling evidence presented by either side.

When the jury was summoned on the morning of Tuesday 14 January the general expectation, particularly among the tabloid press-men, was that they would convict: the *Sun* videotapes would surely see to that. By the time the judge dismissed them on the morning of Monday 3 March the universal opinion among all those who had sat through the case was that they had no idea which way the decision would go.

But that is to get ahead of the story. With the jury appointed, the charges against the defendants were formally read out: 'Heng Suan (otherwise Richard) Lim, John Fashanu, Hans Cornelius Segers and Bruce David Grobbelaar are charged as follows . . . Count One: Conspiracy to give and accept corrupt payments, contrary to Section 1(1) of the Criminal Law Act, 1977.' The particulars of the offence alleged that Lim, Fashanu and Segers, 'on diverse days between the first day of February 1991 and the ninth day of November 1994 conspired together and with others known and unknown corruptly to give and corruptly to accept gifts of money to influence or attempt to influence the outcome of football matches or as rewards for having done so'.

The second count, also of conspiracy to give and accept corrupt payments, was made against Lim, Fashanu and Grobbelaar, stating: 'On diverse days between the first day of November 1992 and the ninth day of November 1994 [they] conspired together and with others known and unknown', in the manner described above.

Finally there was a third count of corruption, against Grobbelaar alone, that, 'On the third day of November 1994 being an agent of Southampton Football Club [he] corruptly accepted from Christopher James Edward Vincent the sum of £2,000 as an inducement or reward for doing an act in relation to the affairs or business of his principal, namely for improperly influencing or attempting to influence the outcome of a football match or matches.'

With the charges read, and a warning about reporting procedures delivered to the media by Justice Tuckey, on the assumption that 'some members of the press may be more accustomed to reporting from the field than the court,' David Calvert-Smith rose to his feet and began the case for the Crown. 'You'll soon get to know us pretty well, I'm afraid,' he told the jury, gesturing towards his fellow barristers. And, it would rapidly become clear, there was something else the jury would get to know – the charts.

'The charts' – two words which would soon strike dread into all who heard them – were a series of twenty-three documents gathered in ring-bound A3 and A4 folders. They contained a number of graphs depicting the amounts of money transferred to, from and between the various defendants and their contacts in the Far East; more graphs detailing the number of telephone calls between the defendants, by month and year; and an over-sized diary dealing with crucial dates in the period covered by the charges, in which were listed the times and durations of telephone calls, key movements by the defendants, all deposits or withdrawals of cash, plus dates, times, venues and scores of all relevant football matches. The charts were colour-coded with highlighter ink: green for Grobbelaar, blue for Lim, pink for Segers and red for Fashanu. Jurors would spend hours leafing through them, at first with bafflement, then with familiarity, and then with resignation as yet another reference was made to their contents.

Along with the charts, the 'jury bundle' with which each juror was equipped contained a Schedule of Admissions – a list of all the matters of fact agreed upon by both sides. Some of these were entirely banal: it was agreed, for example, that Bruce Grobbelaar had, indeed, been the Liverpool FC goalkeeper. Others were more significant: to many people's surprise, there was no argument about the existence of hundreds of thousands of pounds sent from sources in Indonesia and Malaysia to accounts held by, or on behalf of, John Fashanu and Richard Lim. There was, of course, intense dispute about what those monies were for.

The jurors were also given transcripts of the various taped conversations between Vincent and Grobbelaar, and between Grobbelaar and the *Sun* reporters. Each set of documents was separated from the others by coloured card inserts, and much time on the first day was expended while the jury struggled to put the right papers behind the appropriate coloured card, as directed by the judge. Once again, the parallel with school – a primary, this time – was all too evident.

Calvert-Smith introduced the jury to all this bumf in his quiet, apologetic way, while the journalists sat in their box, pens poised above their notebooks, waiting for the moment when the fun would begin. Surely he would soon let rip, reminding the twelve men and women of the multiple betrayals implicit in the charges – the steadfast team-mates whose hard work and mutual trust had been undermined by treachery in their midst; the loyal fans who had spent their money and cheered themselves hoarse, unaware that their heroes were plotting against the teams they loved; the wee kiddies whose innocent hero-worship had been abused; the very spirit of the game that had been defiled. British football, we were expecting to hear, might not be the most skilful in the world, but it is the most wholehearted. Just think of all those clichés – of the lads digging in, battling hard, giving 110 per cent for the full ninety minutes. Yes, even the clichés had been betrayed.

There was not a hack in the room who could not have whipped up a few stirring paragraphs with which David Calvert-Smith could begin his speech, all packed full of snappily damning phrases for the following day's headline-writers to get their teeth into. But despite a strong sporting background he chose to embark upon a calm, ordered, unemotional recitation of facts. Over the next three days he would present a complicated, hugely detailed case in a manner that would demonstrate complete mastery of his brief and of all the many documents in which it was encapsulated. But he would miss the chance to seize the emotional initiative, to win the hearts as well as the minds of the jury – and it was an omission that would cost the Crown dear.

Not that his recital was without interest. We soon learned that Bruce Grobbelaar had earned around £160,000 from Liverpool in the 1990–1 season, rather less in the two following years, and about the same in 1993–4. We learned that Fashanu earned approximately £200,000 per annum at Wimbledon, and was paid a signing-on fee of another £200,000 when he joined Aston Villa in the summer of 1994. Segers, it was clear, was rather less fortunate. His gross annual income from football averaged around £80,000 – hardly chicken-feed, but hardly riches either.

Calvert-Smith talked about the 'large, unexplainable sums of money' that Fashanu had received from Indonesia. He alleged that Lim was the English representative of a Far Eastern gambling syndicate. Both Fashanu and Lim, he alleged, had handed over sums of money to the other two defendants. Grobbelaar had admitted that he was party to the conspiracy on tape.

Then came a passage that was to assume crucial significance. 'You may be asking yourselves how one player can guarantee the result of a match. Of course he can't. He may never have the opportunity. His team-mates or the opposition may frustrate him – that's what happened when Liverpool played Manchester United in January 1994. There is a limit to what any person can do in front of forty to fifty thousand spectators and the millions watching on TV. You can't simply let the ball run through your legs. But goalkeepers do make mistakes and the odd deliberate mistake may escape attention . . .

Here I saw one of the female jurors shake her head in disapproval. But of what: the act itself, or Calvert-Smith's suggestion of it?

'If you are a betting man,' the prosecutor continued, 'the goalkeeper is the most obvious single man in the team to approach.' Now came the key point: 'If money was corruptly given and received on the grounds that players would try to influence results, it doesn't matter if the result owed little, everything or nothing to the actual assistance of corrupt players.' It was the agreement to fix, not any fixing itself, that provided grounds for a charge of conspiracy.

But had there been any such agreement? Well, one witness claimed that there had – Christopher James Edward Vincent. Now came Calvert-Smith's warnings as to his character, his attempts to make money from the case, the potential benefits that might accrue to him from a successful prosecution, and the charge of attempting to pervert the course of justice which he faced. Here, too, the prosecution faced severe difficulties.

In many respects, Vincent was an extraordinarily good witness. Police officers had been astonished by the degree to which his claims could be corroborated by independent evidence from telephone companies, credit-card slips and even human witnesses. But by stressing his failings of character so early in the proceedings, Calvert-Smith had somewhat sold the pass. Of course, he wanted the jury to be aware of the allegations the defence would be likely to throw against Vincent, in the hope that their shock value might be blunted and their effect discounted in advance. But he gave the jury nothing positive with which to set against this beyond the assertion that, 'Although he is a witness for whom you may have no sympathy, in fact what he says is borne out by the evidence.'

Since it was clear that Vincent was going to get a thorough going-over from the defence (although quite how thorough no one can have imagined), it might have been as well to emphasize the brighter side to his character as far as possible: his heroism and skill as a soldier, his energy and enthusiasm (however misplaced) as a businessman, his loyalty as a friend until he himself was betrayed. You might think that an excessively rosy picture of Chris Vincent's character. But in a court of law one of the functions of a barrister is to put the best possible gloss on the people whom he represents, or upon whom he is relying to put his case.

Far more significant, though, was a factor over which David Calvert-Smith had no control. The Hampshire Police had decided not to bring charges against John Fashanu and Shaa Wasmund for attempting to pervert the course of justice.

In the autumn of 1995, that seemed like a sensible decision. By January 1997, it had taken on a very different complexion. For no mention of the matter could be made in court – quite properly, since it would be grossly unfair to discuss serious allegations against John Fashanu without giving him the opportunity to mount a full defence against them. But the charges levelled against Chris Vincent, of which a great deal was made in court (and against which he had no chance, at that time, to defend himself), might have been looked at in a very different light had jurors been aware of the events of June 1995.

Even so, there seemed to be plenty to be going on with. 'You must be bored stiff by now, but it's important,' said David Calvert-Smith, two-thirds of the way through his long, long speech. He was not far wrong. On the very first day, I found myself sitting in the public gallery directly behind a ravishing blue-eyed blonde, dressed in a stretchy black mini-skirt, a fitted black pinstripe jacket and black suede high-heels with gold, heart-shaped buckles. Mid-way through the afternoon, she leaned across to the neatly dressed man sitting next to her and whispered in his ear. I could clearly see her mouth the words, 'This is so boring.'

The blonde was Astrid Segers, who would rapidly become a permanent fixture at the trial, along with Debbie Grobbelaar (whatever might have been said or printed about Bruce Grobbelaar's behaviour and the state of his marriage, Debbie's support for him throughout his court ordeal was absolutely unswerving: she barely missed a single day of proceedings). Perhaps Astrid was upset that her husband had not featured much in Calvert-Smith's early remarks, but that omission would soon be rectified. As tedious as the speech may have been – and even the judge jokingly remarked at one point that he would have to show Calvert-Smith the red card if he went on much longer – and as difficult as it must have been for the jury to assimilate the enormous mountain of information, it gradually became apparent that there were some extraordinary stories hidden away among those endless telephone calls.

The most bizarre of all was Hans Segers' account to the police of how he had come by large amounts of non-footballing money. He said he had a Swiss bank account containing about £160,000 which had been made from his outside activities, principally a company called Ties International and a goal-keeping school in Wokingham. He kept his money in Switzerland for tax reasons.

The police had protested that neither of those two businesses made much money. So where had the Swiss money come from? Segers told them he had made it in Holland, before coming to England in 1984. The cash had been transferred to Switzerland from another account in Jersey, where he had held £250,000.

OK . . . where had that come from? Stealing high-price cars, he said. He had done it with his cousin, who was now dead. The exchange that followed was not given to the court until a few days after the opening speech, but I include it here for simplicity's sake.

Detective Sergeant Brian Mitchell (who was an inspector by the time of the trial) told Segers, 'I have some difficulty believing that at the age of seventeen you were such a prolific and successful car thief. It sounds a little far-fetched.'

Segers: 'I have some tough friends out there.'

Mitchell: 'How did you normally steal the vehicles?'

Segers: 'Contact, ignition.'

Mitchell: 'How did you do that?'

Segers: 'Well, I was the driver.'

Mitchell: 'So who did it?'

Segers: 'He did.'

Mitchell: 'You don't know how to do it, but you make £100,000 stealing cars . . . How did you break in?'

Segers: 'Smash a window.'

Mitchell: 'That's not very professional.'

Segers continued with his story. He had transferred his car-money from Jersey to Switzerland in bundles of cash, which were delivered to him by someone from the Jersey bank at the Excelsior Hotel near Heathrow. He was not, he said, a close friend of John Fashanu and did not speak to him very often on the phone, although Fashanu had advised him on his tie business. The name Lim, or Richard Lim, meant nothing to him.

Mitchell had not been impressed. 'Your body-language tells me you're worried . . . about what? Your demeanour has changed. Your face has gone red. You're twitching, holding your hands tightly – as though you're someone who's got something to hide.'

Well, perhaps he had. Hans Segers, it transpired, had made seven cash deposits into his so-called 'Gloves' account at the Republican National Bank of New York. His account was actually held in Geneva, but he made the deposits at the bank's London branch at 46 Berkeley Square in wealthy Mayfair.

The money Segers had paid in during 1993 and 1994 totalled £104,000. Every one of the payments had been made during, or just after the close of, the football season. The last of them was just one day before Grobbelaar's encounter with the *Sun* reporters at Gatwick airport. On one occasion, a payment of

£6,000 had been virtually simultaneous with one by John Fashanu of £31,500 into the same bank. On another, a £14,000 payment followed a day after Fashanu had deposited £30,000, again into the same branch of the same bank.

Each of Segers' seven deposits, and the events surrounding it, was described in detail by Calvert-Smith, as were all the activities surrounding the disputed Grobbelaar games. The latter have already been dealt with elsewhere in this book, but to give a flavour of the case against Fashanu, Lim and Segers, this is how Calvert-Smith described the sequence of events surrounding a payment of £19,000 in cash, made by Hans Segers into his RNB account on 13 May 1994.

The prosecutor explained that it followed the last game of Wimbledon's season on 7 May, in which they had lost 3–2 to Everton. This was, of course, the very game that Segers had talked about soon after the Grobbelaar story broke, saying that people had thought it had been fixed. The match had been of crucial importance, because it enabled Everton to stay in the Premiership.

There had been some brief contact between Segers and Lim on 29 April. On 5 May John Fashanu twice called Lim, who then called Indonesia. Fashanu then called his bank in Geneva, and he and Lim exchanged two more calls that day.

On 6 May, Hans Segers was staying at the Lord Daresbury Hotel, Widnes, prior to the game, in which John Fashanu did not play. At 10.50 a.m. Lim left a message on Segers' mobile phone. Lim then called Indonesia, then Fashanu, then Indonesia again, then Fashanu again, then made two more calls to Indonesia.

At 17.14 Segers called John Fashanu's mobile phone. At 17.24 Fashanu called Lim, who immediately put in yet another call to Indonesia.

At 20.09 a call was made from Segers' hotel room to a Fashanu number held in the name of Peter Buckle. That number immediately called Lim and spoke for two and a half minutes. Within three minutes of the end of that call, Lim called Hans Segers' mobile and spoke to him for three minutes and six seconds.

At 12.42 on 7 May, the day of the Everton–Wimbledon match, Lim called Johannes Joseph's associate, Lo Bon Swe, in Indonesia. Two hours later, fifteen minutes before kick-off, he called Mr Lo again. Everton won the match, thanks to a last-gasp goal when a soft, mis-hit shot bounced over Segers' outstretched arm.

At 16.50, almost immediately after the final whistle, Lim called Indonesia. At 22.10 that night, Fashanu's mobile made two attempts to contact Lim. Fashanu's 'Buckle' phone then called Benny Santoso, another agreed associate of Johannes Joseph.

On 10 May there were two telephone conversations between Lim and Segers.

On 11 May Fashanu's Buckle number again called Lim.

On 13 May Segers called the Buckle number from a mobile phone within the Lodge Road cell-site, London NW8, close to Fashanu's office and penthouse. 'Is that coincidence?' asked Calvert-Smith. 'Segers is there an hour before he pays his cash in. He calls a number in the same area, as if to say, "I'm here."'

At 13.43, Lim called from the same Lodge Road site to Indonesia. He made another call at 14.01. So he and Segers were, at the very least, within the same cell-site at roughly the same time. By 14.23, however, Lim was in London W10, but using his phone to call John Fashanu.

Eight minutes later, at 14.31, Hans Segers went into the Republican National Bank to deposit £19,000. 'Are those calls coincidental?' asked Calvert-Smith. 'Or are they connected to Mr Segers' visit to the bank to pay in all that cash?'

At 23.30, he then revealed, John Fashanu's telephone called Johannes Joseph in Indonesia.

This, then, was the flavour of the case against Segers, Fashanu and Lim. 'We don't have a Vincent figure,' said Calvert-Smith. 'All the Crown can do is say, look, here are these payments, here are these telephone contacts about which Mr Segers has lied, here are these matches Wimbledon have lost and telephone contacts around the time of those matches: can you draw the inference that the money, the telephone calls and the matches are linked?'

Good question. The job of the prosecution would now be to

ensure that the jury drew exactly that inference. The job of the defence – their throats soothed by the cough sweets which one thoughtful lady juror had passed to a defence barrister when she noticed that his voice was hoarse – would be to cast doubt on that inference and to suggest alternative explanations.

And so battle commenced. Chris Vincent told his story – somewhat hesitantly, since he was clearly not on top form – and was then eviscerated by Rodney Klevan. Glynn Mason, or 'Mace', was produced by the prosecution to testify that he had indeed accompanied Bruce Grobbelaar and Chris Vincent to 7 Byron Drive on 25 November 1993. But from the prosecution's point of view the value of evidence from this small, thin man, with a beaky nose and slightly protuberant teeth was somewhat undermined by his palpable loyalty to his friend and employer, John Fashanu. No sooner was his account – which utterly refuted any possibility that he had seen any cash transaction between Fashanu and Grobbelaar – concluded than he returned to his natural habitat, close by Fashanu's side at every possible opportunity, like one of the little birds that perches on a mighty rhinoceros.

It was characteristic of the case that the witnesses produced by the prosecution were so much less colourful or inspiring than those speaking on behalf of the defence, who paraded a cavalcade of famous faces before the court. 'Big Ron' Atkinson, for example, wafted into the chamber in a cloud of aftershave, his skin glowing like a radioactive tikka masala. Trevor Burke, who had called him on behalf of John Fashanu, listed the clubs he had managed: Kettering Town, Cambridge United, West Bromwich Albion, Manchester United, Athletico Madrid, Aston Villa, Coventry. 'Have I missed any out?' he asked.

'I don't know,' said Atkinson. 'There've been that many. You might have left out Sheffield United.'

He confirmed that he had long been an admirer of John Fashanu, because he had always caused trouble to any team Atkinson had sent out against him. When Fashanu had played for Aston Villa they had been unbeaten. 'Did he give 100 per cent?' asked Burke.

'Only when he wasn't trying,' came the answer. 'When he was trying, he gave a lot more than that.'

Desmond De Silva, for Hans Segers, asked him if goalkeepers were a breed apart. The manager's response was, 'That's the legend. They're supposed to be crackers.'

Up got Rodney Klevan. There had been some discussion earlier of teams who had long winning or losing streaks. 'Why is it, then, that my team always lose?'

'Because you're a Brighton fan, I would guess,' retorted Atkinson, quick as a flash.

As the laughter subsided – Brighton, at the time, were at the foot of the Third Division, struggling to avoid relegation from the Football League – Klevan adopted a mock-mournful voice. 'Are you expecting those comments to be reported in the Brighton papers?'

'What about the sanctity of court?' asked Atkinson.

'Ohh,' murmured Klevan. 'There's little sanctity here, I'm afraid.'

Atkinson went on to confirm that he had as good an opinion of Grobbelaar as he had of Fashanu. But Fashanu himself would not be joining him in the witness box. He had chosen to exercise his right to silence. Explaining his decision, Trevor Burke told the court, 'He has uttered two words to the prosecuting authorities since this sorry saga so disrupted his life: "Not guilty." These words convey one message: prove it if you can. That's what John Fashanu invites them to do. You are obliged to judge the case on the evidence and you will hear none from him. Silence cannot be misquoted. Silence cannot be misunderstood. Silence cannot be twisted in the hands of an expert prosecutor. Silence never embarrasses anyone. He is perfectly entitled to stay in the dock. It is his absolute right, as it would be yours if you were ever unfortunate enough to be implicated in a case and charged.'

Even if Fashanu did not give evidence, others did on his behalf. His wife Melissa – who came from an African family of enormous wealth and political influence and carried herself with the elegant, haughty air of one of Nature's princesses –

described how she had looked after his Far Eastern money, which had to be kept separate from his normal funds because it consisted of loans. She had never, she said, enquired about John's business affairs.

Her father, too, spoke on Fashanu's behalf, as did his agent Ian Wilson, a senior representative of Unicef and David Littlechild, a businessman whose company BusinessMart UK was developing a duty-free shop in Lagos, Nigeria, in which Fashanu had invested £243,000. Littlechild could testify to Fashanu's ongoing business connections with Johannes Joseph because he had travelled to Jakarta in September 1995 to meet him and collect 100,000 dollars in travellers' cheques, which he claimed Joseph was investing for Fashanu.

Fashanu sat impassively in the dock as all these details were described. The other three men, however, all took the stand. Heng Suan Lim explained the story of his friendship with Johannes Joseph, a benefactor whom he regarded as a father-figure and for whom he had provided forecasts of English and Dutch football matches. Bruce Grobbelaar and Hans Segers had helped him with those forecasts. That was all. He had paid Hans Segers a total of £45,000 over two years. Grobbelaar had received around £8,000–9,000, paid to him on various occasions, including two meetings at the Royal Lancaster Hotel in London and one at a hotel in Liverpool. There was no corruption whatsoever. Any calls between the men had been concerned with forecasting. His meeting with Grobbelaar in Manchester had been to discuss Mondoro, not match-fixing. He had not met him at Heathrow airport on 6 October 1993. The meeting at the Hilton, on the night before the Norwich game, had merely been to pass on information he had gleaned while in the Far East about Bruce Grobbelaar's chances of pursuing his career out there when his Liverpool days were over. He had taken the opportunity to pass on £1,500 he owed Grobbelaar for his forecasts and information. His relationship with Johannes Joseph had ended in 1994, because Joseph was angry with him for losing £170,000 in the ten casinos of which he was a member.

In the cross-examination, he told David Calvert-Smith, 'Mr Joseph does not bet with syndicates or bookies, he bets with friends and associates on a friendly basis. It's very hurtful to suggest that I'm a representative of an illegal syndicate from the Far East – it's absolutely not true.'

Mr Calvert-Smith was clearly sceptical of such protestations, and attempted to show that Lim's actions and his income – virtually all of it from the Far East – could only be explained by his involvement in corruption. He had been in Malaysia at about the time, in the summer of 1994, when an enormous match-fixing scandal had been made public. Lim agreed that he might have read about that in the papers. 'From what I recall, they arrested 120 players, seven or eight from each team, and one or two coaches.' But he knew no more than what he had seen in the press.

His friendship with Fashanu arose because they had plenty in common. 'We liked clubbing, business, we both came from the same background. When you know someone is like yourself, bonding is closer than with other people.'

'It wasn't just that you were the source of large sums of money from generous people in Indonesia?' queried Calvert-Smith.

Lim looked puzzled. 'I don't quite get your question.'

If there was continual contact between himself, Fashanu, Grobbelaar and Segers (though none between Segers and Grobbelaar) that was because 'Mr Joseph was a very good and dear friend for Fash, and if I needed a second consultation I would ask Fash to speak to Segers or even Bruce just to check.'

It emerged that he had owned two Rolex watches, similar to that described by Grobbelaar in his conversations with Vincent, and he had given one of these watches to John Fashanu in settlement of a debt. He might have been wearing such a watch at the Hilton, but he could see no reason why he would offer it to Bruce Grobbelaar. In general, he found it impossible to recall what any individual telephone conversations with Grobbelaar or Segers could have been about and he was outraged at the suggestion that he might have attempted to corrupt either man.

'This is a catalogue of impossibilities,' he exclaimed. 'Imagine me standing in front of Bruce, asking him to fix matches.'

'Since you ask me to imagine, I will,' said Calvert-Smith.

'He is a football legend for many years, and I ask him to fix games – it is totally out of the question.'

'You say you will pay small sums of money for information,' suggested Calvert-Smith.

'Let me finish!'

'When you suggested he could make a great deal more money, he was probably at your mercy.'

Lim was appalled. 'If I suggested that nonsense, I'd be flying down from the window of the penthouse! Mr Segers would faint and not get up again!'

'I didn't suggest it,' said Calvert-Smith, who was beginning to reveal a steely mind beneath that moth-eaten wig. 'Mr Grobbelaar did . . . at some length.'

When Segers gave evidence he began by describing his involvement with Ties International, a company founded by a Mr Thuys (pronounced 'ties') who came from a family of tie manufacturers and had, said Segers, been born with a tie on. The company had made souvenir ties for football clubs, including Wimbledon, and had sold around twenty-five or thirty thousand in 1993–4. He had a share of the profits. He had first spoken to Richard Lim in 1992, because Lim had been trying to sell a car and Fashanu had advised him to call Segers, who regularly bought and sold cars.

They later met at Fashanu's office, where Lim proposed that he act as a tipster on Dutch football matches (he had a satellite decoder which enabled him to receive Dutch TV channels and Teletext, and regularly bought Dutch football magazines). Fashanu had helped negotiate the deal with Lim. Shortly before the Grobbelaar story broke, he had been called by a *Daily Mirror* sports writer who told him there was about to be a football scandal in the *Sun*, in which his name would be mentioned.

He had spoken to fellow players at Wimbledon and the club's owner, Sam Hammam. Then he read the FA rules and realized that he was assisting people with their betting activities, which was against those rules. Knowing what had happened to Lou Macari after his involvement in a betting scandal at Swindon Town, he had been terrified about what would happen to his career. That was why he had lied to the police. He had also been worried about paying tax on his undeclared income. 'I thought, if I make a story up about money coming from Holland, I've got no problems with the taxman and no problems with the FA.'

Both institutions had sent representatives to the trial. 'The gentleman over there with the big smile, that's Mr Taxman,' said Segers.

'Why do you abuse him?' asked De Silva.

'I don't want to abuse him. I want to keep him as a friend.'

Segers said he had not told the truth about Fashanu because he and John had used one another as excuses for their various sexual adventures, and he did not want to reveal that to the police for fear of the effect on his family. Fashanu, he said, had been having an affair with 'a well-known pop singer'. He would call Segers up and ask him to cover for him if necessary.

'I want to ask about your domestic life,' said De Silva. 'Did you always play at home?'

'I played a few away matches,' said Segers.

'What was the consequence of playing non-footballing away matches?'

'I had a really bad period in my marriage. Things went from bad to worse. I had an affair and asked John quite a few times to cover for me.'

Desmond De Silva took Segers through a number of payments, totalling £59,000, which he had made to his RNB account in the autumn of 1994. Of that, Segers said, £50,000 had been lent to him by John Fashanu for investment in a joint property venture – they planned to buy houses, repossessed during the early-nineties slump, at below market rates, then sell them on at a profit. De Silva then played Segers a number of videotapes, covering nineteen games mentioned in Calvert-Smith's opening speech as ones which might have been thrown. Segers absolutely denied any wrongdoing on his part. Of the controversial third Everton goal on 7 May 1994 he said, 'I'm not sure who scored. He hit a shot and I dived. I had it covered all the way, but it hit a divot, popped up and changed direction.'

David Calvert-Smith had a rather different view of that goal. He asked Segers, 'After the Everton game, did [the Wimbledon manager, Joe Kinnear] suggest he could have saved the last goal, that it went straight through your hands, and that he didn't realize you had a favourite uncle up there on Merseyside?'

'I can't remember,' said Segers.

Over two days Calvert-Smith attacked Segers' account, repeatedly asking him what calls had been about, why they were clustered around certain games, what specific payments represented. Segers was equally repetitive. He could not remember what calls had been about all that time ago, but he was just as likely to be sorting out tickets or discussing team tactics as making forecasts. And he was certainly not fixing games. Besides, the calls were not just clustered around games Wimbledon lost: 'I don't know what you're trying to get at,' he protested. 'It's been phone calls, win, lose or draw.'

'Sometimes the bets don't come off,' said Calvert-Smith.

'Sir, that's not true. I was doing forecasting for Richard and calling Richard and John on numerous occasions. It's got nothing to do with betting, or anything you accuse me of.'

As the questions continued, the strain faced by any witness subjected to prolonged cross-examination began to tell. Segers took long pauses before answering questions. At times his voice seemed about to crack. At the very end of his cross-examination, Calvert-Smith put it to him that, far from panicking when arrested by the police, he had told a number of carefully planned lies. When asked if he knew Richard Lim he at first denied it, but then suggested that he might be a reporter who called him on match days. He did know one Oriental, he had said, 'But he owns a Chinese restaurant in Wimbledon.'

'That's not panic, it's deliberate deceit,' said David Calvert-Smith. 'The lies came about because you had received money for trying at least to influence the results of Wimbledon's matches so that [the people in the Far East] could win money. That's the reason you told all those convoluted lies.'

'No, I didn't,' replied Hans Segers.

And so we came to Bruce Grobbelaar. He described how, as a soldier fighting in the Rhodesian civil war, he had told his mates that one day he would play for Liverpool. That dream had come true, and though there had been some hard times – he spoke of the terrible tragedies of Heysel and Hillsborough – the Liverpool years had been a fantastic period of his life. 'There were fourteen or fifteen magic moments,' he said. 'When I signed, every time I won a medal, and when the Queen arrived at Anfield.'

He spoke about his charity work, his desire to give something back to the people of Liverpool and the constant requests he received for help at charitable events. Speaking of his involvement with the Special Olympics movement, which provided sport for the handicapped, he said, 'I'm blessed. I can play sport and I've got all my faculties. If you see children struggling you want to help them out, and the best way to do that is to bond with them. That's the best way I could show my appreciation for being normal.'

He described how he had met Chris Vincent – their two accounts tallied exactly – and immediately put down £5,000 as an investment in his safari park project. 'The proposal he put to me was very good. Even today, it's still one of the best ideas I've seen,' he said. The two men became friends. 'We were very close – embarrassingly so. He was taking my time away from my family.'

'Were you seeing him to the exclusion of others?' asked Klevan.

'Yes, more or less all the time. I don't know why,' replied Grobbelaar.

His involvement with Fashanu had begun when Fash suggested he worked for his company Blue Orchid, which was hoping to bring African footballers to play in Europe. They met in November 1992, and at the meeting Grobbelaar mentioned

Mondoro. Richard Lim had been present. A short while later he got a call from Fashanu saying that Lim might call him to talk about match-forecasting, which he had been doing in the late eighties for a Norwegian newspaper called *Dagbladet*. Lim did call, and offered £250 for every correct forecast. Lim would name a match and Grobbelaar would tell him what he thought. He certainly did not think he was doing anything improper, because he never forecast Liverpool games. There was no point: he always thought they would win. There was no question at all of match-fixing. He had told Vincent about the arrangement, but had never discussed how much money he was getting.

Grobbelaar said that he had met Richard Lim at the Manchester Hilton to discuss Mondoro. He had promised to show Lim a business plan for the project, so that he could pass on the information to his associates, but Vincent failed to provide a plan. 'I was very upset and disappointed.' He told Vincent he was meeting Richard, but went alone to the meeting so that he could apologize for himself, without the embarrassment of Vincent's presence.

He had never discussed match-fixing on the telephone in Vincent's presence (or anywhere else), nor had there been – as Vincent had claimed – a code: Wimbledon for a win, Dundee for a draw, Leeds for a loss, and so on. He never talked about 'doing the business with the Short Man'. He had never thrown a football match in his life. He absolutely denied collecting £40,000 from John Fashanu. He had given Chris Vincent £20,000, but it was money Vincent was supposed to use as a deposit on a property at Prince's Grant, outside Durban. 'I had £25,000 at my house. It had been growing for two years. I kept it in a sock-drawer. I'd been going round South Africa after-dinner speaking, and got money from coaching in Norway and Sweden, all cash. There could have been a little bit of forecasting money, but not much.'

Rodney Klevan, conducting the examination-in-chief, asked Grobbelaar to watch the whole of the classic 3–3 draw with Manchester United. The tape they used was from Sky Sports. It came complete with commentary, including Andy Gray's spontaneous exclamation: 'Four magnificent goals – and you couldn't fault either goalkeeper for any of them.'

Grobbelaar's business partnership with Vincent had ended in Zimbabwe in the summer of 1994. He had not had any desire to hurt Vincent – 'Why should I want to hurt a business partner?' – but he had wanted to know where all Mondoro's money had gone. The bank accounts in Victoria Falls had been cleaned out and all the money in them had disappeared. The whole matter had come to a head in a meeting with Mr Hewlett. Vincent would not tell him where the money had gone. He had never had a straight answer from Vincent and had lost 'around £60,000'.

In September he had met Vincent at the Swallow Hotel, Waltham Abbey. They began by talking about Mondoro, then, 'He came out with a blinder, as I say. He said he had met some people at Chester races that liked to bet on sure-fire runners, and he wanted to know if I was interested in throwing games for them. It was the first time I'd ever heard it mentioned. I said, "You must be daft. Nobody could throw a game. No one person."'

Vincent had then told Grobbelaar he was skint and that his family had rejected him. He asked Grobbelaar to lend him some money. Grobbelaar had refused.

They met again in Southampton. In the snooker room at the De Vere Grand Harbour Hotel, Vincent had come up with the same story. 'I can get your money back if you're interested in throwing games.' Grobbelaar said, 'I thought I'd go along with it and see what his reaction would be, let him talk, let me find out what I can. He said, "Aah, I'm sure you must have tried to throw games." I thought, why not agree? He mentioned the Newcastle game. I said I might have.'

Vincent had gone on to mention the Manchester United game and a recent game between Coventry and Southampton. Up in his hotel room, the conversation continued. They had talked about Mondoro, and Grobbelaar had said that he had been upset about Vincent telling his brother that he,

Grobbelaar, would pay the bills for the Jungleman Classic.

The only money he had lost against Manchester United was his win bonus – he was telling Vincent lies to gain his confidence. He had not dived the wrong way. He never intended to throw any games. All the stuff about 'JF' and his Merc, his Rolex and so on was mentioned because, 'I thought I'd throw it in for a little spice.' All the questions he asked about Vincent's supposed associates were because he wanted to know who he was working for: 'I had an ultimate plan in the end.'

When he found himself confronted by the *Sun* reporters at Gatwick, 'I knew exactly what [Vincent] had done. Unfortunately for me, my plan didn't work. His did.' He had told the reporters that his £40,000 came from his testimonial because, 'When your back is against the wall, you'll say anything.'

When David Calvert-Smith got up to cross-examine Grobbelaar on the afternoon of Friday 14 February he was rather subdued, as if feeling the fatigue of a long week more than a month into an exhausting trial. Grobbelaar for his part dealt with his questions with absolute ease and confidence. Nothing seemed to be going right for Calvert-Smith. At one point he stopped his questions and played a brief videotape of Grobbelaar leaving the pitch after the game against Manchester United, looking somewhat glum. 'Is that the face of a man who has just lost a lot of money, Mr Grobbelaar?' asked Calvert-Smith.

A groan echoed across the room, whether from the jury-box or the public gallery one could not be certain. But the tone of the groan was all too apparent: contempt, as if saying, 'Come off it.'

'That's the face of a man who has let in three goals against one of our biggest rivals,' said Grobbelaar.

'I just wondered,' was Calvert-Smith's feeble retort.

One moment of the cross-examination, though, had an electric effect upon me, if not upon anyone else. Calvert-Smith was discussing with Grobbelaar why Lim had come to meet him in Manchester on 30 September 1993. 'The main reason was to pick up the business plan for John Fashanu,' said Grobbelaar.

'But there was nothing in writing, nothing said, nothing given?' asked Calvert-Smith.

'There's nothing in writing to this day,' replied Grobbelaar.

I was in the annexe, copying this exchange down in one of the heavyweight A4 notepads in which I was transcribing the proceedings, when it hit me. There *had* been something in writing. In fact, there had been a business plan. And I had seen it. Better than that, I had had it in my house for several months until I gave it back to Chris Vincent.

In the next tea-break I informed the police that I knew of the existence of a Mondoro business plan and advised them to ask Chris Vincent about it, because he might know where it was. If the plan could be presented in court on Monday morning, it would not only be a stunning coup but would also blow a hole in a crucial defence alibi.

The next morning I got a call from Detective Inspector Brian Mitchell – the man who had conducted the Segers interview – informing me that Vincent had given the plan to another would-be investor in the summer of 1996. Did I have any other leads? I scrabbled through my notes and called back. How about Stuart Dyer? My original interviews with Vincent suggested that the plan might have been put together at around the time he was negotiating with National Mutual in the spring of 1993. The police called Dyer, who did not have a copy but could testify to the existence of Mondoro paperwork. That was not good enough. They needed the actual business plan. Sadly, it was not found. Not then, at any rate.

As frustrating as this was for the prosecution, it did not seem to have mattered. When the court reassembled on Monday morning, we began to see why Calvert-Smith had acted as he had on the Friday. He had been saving his fire so that all his best shots could come after the weekend.

His main aim was to demonstrate that the *Sun* tapes, far from being filled with nonsense made up by Grobbelaar to string Vincent along, were actually a long and detailed confession of crimes that had actually been committed. To this end, he pointed out the continual similarities between what Grobbelaar said on the tapes and what the charts showed to have happened.

For example, Grobbelaar had said that Vincent was the one who first raised the subject of the Liverpool–Manchester United game in the snooker room at the De Vere Hotel. 'Who suggested £120,000 – you or him?' asked Calvert-Smith.

'I'm not sure,' replied Grobbelaar.

'You never said anything to Vincent about throwing the Manchester United game?'

'No.'

'So he's lying when he said you did. He had nothing to go on. He just made it up and you agreed?'

'I agreed, yes.'

Calvert-Smith moved in: 'But what he cannot have known is that on the Monday [the day before the game] you tried to speak to Lim four times and on the day of the game three times. That's pretty bad luck for you.'

'Why is that bad luck for me?' asked Grobbelaar.

'Vincent invents it, and you go along with him, and by pure coincidence you've been on the phone to the Short Man seven times in two days.'

'The calls could have been about anything.'

'Yes, but it could also be that if you had lost, you'd have made a great deal of money.'

'That's your assumption.'

'That's the reality.'

Grobbelaar shook his head. 'Not at all.'

Later, talking about the same game, Calvert-Smith reminded Grobbelaar that he had said, 'I'm my own worst enemy because I don't like to lose. It's instinct . . .'

'When it comes down to it,' said Calvert-Smith, 'you have a competitive instinct which takes over.'

'That's what you say,' replied Grobbelaar. 'I don't know what I was saying – it came off the top of my head.'

Calvert-Smith made it simple for him: 'Out went your hand. Bang went £125,000.'

'I went the right way . . . I went the way the ball went. You always keep your eye on the ball.'

'It was your instinct, rather than what you intended.'

'That's what it looks like,' said Grobbelaar.

'But that's just the drink talking . . .'

'Probably.'

All through Monday, Calvert-Smith continued hammering away doggedly at the tape, the phone calls, Vincent's evidence and Grobbelaar's denials. ('He's the Mike Atherton of QCs,' the BBC's Neil Bennett remarked as we listened in the press annexe.) Grobbelaar had said on tape that the Short Man had called him on the Thursday before the Coventry game . . . and Lim had done. He said that he had pushed the ball into the back of the net . . . and (according to Calvert-Smith) he had. He said that the Short Man had been at the game . . . and Lim had been. But again and again Grobbelaar dismissed what was on the tape as 'coincidence' or 'spice'.

There was another fascinating piece of information, quite unrelated to football, hidden away in the cross-examination. On two separate occasions Grobbelaar asked for records of all the calls he had made on specific dates, apart from the ones to his co-defendants. On the first occasion he asked for the calls for 3 and 4 January 1994. The records revealed that on both days he had twice called a name which I knew to be that of the Wild Thing. Calvert-Smith mentioned *en passant* that he had called that number on the journey down from Norwich, too. Grobbelaar also asked for the records for 22 September 1994. Again there were two calls to the Wild Thing.

That, though, was a matter only for those of us who had a trainspotter's familiarity with the case. The key point was the battle of wills between Calvert-Smith and Grobbelaar on the question of the tapes. And yet it was a battle that was, to some extent, futile. For just a few hours after Grobbelaar had finally left the box, Klevan played his trump cards: Bob Wilson, Alan Hansen, Alan Ball and Gordon Banks. Two football stars who had become instantly recognizable TV pundits; two members of the 1966 World Cup-winning team . . . and they were all equally certain in their assessment that Bruce Grobbelaar was a fierce competitor who not only would not betray but had not betrayed his team or his fellow players.

Bob Wilson was the most powerful, if only because he was the most boring. Who could doubt the patent honesty of this vastly experienced goalkeeper, who had not only played in Arsenal's double-winning team of 1971, but now coached the great David Seaman, England's world-class goalkeeper? With punctilious, pedantic care he went through every single game in which Bruce Grobbelaar had played, noting the exact times and details of every save he had made, analysing every goal, and explaining how it was that slack defending or brilliant forward-play had repeatedly left Grobbelaar with no chance of making a save.

He discussed Grobbelaar's positional sense, the way he pre-pared himself in the instant before a save, flexing his body to generate maximum agility and spring, spreading himself to put the biggest possible barrier between an opposing forward and the goal he was trying to defend. When Calvert-Smith attempted to question and undermine Wilson's analyses, he was met with a magisterial, 'I think you're nit-picking.' Picking the ball out of the back of the net, more like.

And yet a couple of days later, when Calvert-Smith put his entire case together he used his analytical skills to draw together all the disparate strands of the case – which seemed to have become more, rather than less, tangled the longer it went on – to present a compelling argument. But there was only one of him and four defence counsel, each of whom was equally persuasive on their client's behalf. It fell to Mr Justice Tuckey to pull the various facts and arguments together and sum them up for the jury. I shall not reproduce his speech, except for one brief element: his comments about Chris Vincent.

'In opening the case, Mr Calvert-Smith made it clear that there was every reason to scrutinize Vincent's evidence. I repeat that warning. Although he was not concerned with fixing matches, he did nothing to stop it and was happy to benefit from it. He is not an accomplice, but you should treat his evidence with caution. His desire to expose Mr Grobbelaar arose out of his desire to destroy Mr Grobbelaar and not to expose corruption. He stands to make substantial sums if the prosecution is successful.

'But there is nothing illegal in kissing and telling. Just because he has done that, it doesn't follow that he is lying . . . He sat here for the best part of three days answering questions from five different counsel. Almost every uncomplimentary adjective under the sun' – there was laughter in court at the unintended pun – 'has been used to describe him. Your task is to look at his evidence and decide whether or not it is safe to convict upon it.'

So they looked. The jury were sent out to consider their verdict shortly after 11 a.m. on Monday 28 February. As soon as they had disappeared, the press and the bar got down to the serious business of organizing the sweepstake for the time at which they would return. Jerome Lynch, acting perhaps on expert forecasts, chose 4.07 on Monday afternoon and 11.09 on Wednesday morning. For a while it looked as though he might clean up, because at 3.50 on Monday afternoon we were summoned back to the courtroom. But no verdict had been reached. The jury simply wanted more time to study the tape of the £2,000 handover between Vincent and Grobbelaar.

The defendants prowled the corridors, talking to their lawyers, families and well-wishers. 'Let's play golf when it's all over,' said one man, shaking Grobbelaar's hand in the wide corridor outside Court No. 3.

'If I get the result I need, I'll have a round with you,' said Bruce. 'Otherwise I'll be playing on a computer game.'

'There's one prison that has a course,' said the man.

'Thanks for the moral support,' laughed Grob.

He had a cool nerve all right. On Tuesday afternoon, at 2.15, the call came that the jury were coming back into court. Everyone rushed to their appointed places. Surely this was it.

The defendants were gathered in the dock. Grobbelaar, as was his habit, was standing to attention, army-style. I was slouched in a chair a few feet away from him, wearing a very old, very lurid, but very, very comfortable suede jacket . . . a green suede jacket to be precise. Suddenly I heard a voice echoing across the courtroom. It was Adam Mynott, the BBC's tall, slender, laid-back sports correspondent. 'Jerome wants to know . . . where did you get that jacket?' he shouted.

The entire chamber seemed to fall instantly silent as an appalling beetroot blush spread across my face. Grobbelaar looked down from the dock, raised one eyebrow and drawled, 'If you think that's bad, you should have seen the trousers.'

Here was a man who was minutes away from the possible ruination of his entire life's work, and he could crack a gag like that. You had to be impressed.

In fact, there was no verdict then. The jury were deadlocked and wanted more time. Everyone trooped back out of the courtroom and got on with the serious business of exchanging gossip. One of the barristers had been spotted chatting up a Norwegian student at one in the morning. 'I must have been rat-arsed,' the legal eagle told a reporter who quizzed him on the subject, adding, 'If there was anything to kiss and tell, I'd tell you. But there isn't.'

Another member of the bar – never more appropriately named – had been running through the corridors of his hotel at 3 a.m. calling for more bottles of brandy. 'But my staff need to sleep,' protested an exhausted hotelier. 'Nonsense!' countered the brief. 'If I can stand the pace, so can they!'

He, though, knew that he did not have too many more laps to last out before he could collapse across the finishing line. At 4.04 p.m., after ten hours and fifty-nine minutes of deliberation, the jury reached their verdict . . . which was no verdict at all. They were deadlocked and, said the foreman, there was no chance of agreement. After all those weeks, all those witnesses, all those speeches . . . we were going to have to come back in a few months' time and start all over again.

# 24

## Groundhog Day!

In the film *Groundhog Day* Bill Murray, playing a grouchy TV weather-forecaster sent upstate to cover a small-town celebration of the annual emergence of a much-loved ground-hog, finds himself trapped in time. Every night he goes to bed, and every day he wakes up to hear the same words on the radio: 'It's Groundhog Day!' To his horror, he has been condemned to relive the same day – 2 February – again and again, with only minor variations.

Well, the second trial was a bit like that. In the summer, that traditional season for repeats, the same people were tried in the same place for the same charges, with many of the same witnesses giving much the same evidence.

The same metaphors, too: the veterans of the classroom-like press annexe all reassembled in Winchester on 4 June like schoolchildren (the press) and their masters (the bar) beginning a new term after a prolonged holiday. The veterans of Trial No. 1 caught up with one another's news, re-established contact with the defendants and their lawyers and speculated what the new judge – our incoming headmaster, as it were – would be like.

As the first cups of coffee were being bought in the canteen, the *Sun*'s Paul Thompson came up to the table where I was sitting with a bunch of reporters and said, 'Fashanu's back to his old self. He was saying, "Hello, my love," to the [female] security guard, big handshakes, putting his arm around my shoulder.'

He'd noticed something else, too: 'Segers has gone grey.'

'Debbie Grobbelaar's gone blonder,' I added.

'And,' concluded Thommo, 'Astrid Segers is prettier than ever!'

'Aah,' sighed the *Guardian*'s Nick Varley, 'That summer dress . . .'

We were, it was immediately apparent, part of a greatly reduced press corps. The feature-writers and atmosphere-grabbers had all gone off in search of fresher stories. Only the news hacks were left behind, and even these were many fewer in numbers. The Press Association, which had frequently had three reporters covering the winter's proceedings, cut their staff to one. The *Sun* was virtually the only tabloid paper to send any representatives (though the *Mirror*'s Harry Arnold would re-appear, majestically, as the proceedings neared their final conclusion). And for long stretches of the early summer the only people in the courtroom press box would be PA's Paul Edwards, the *Sun*'s Paul Thompson and Simon Hughes, Guy Toyn of the *Southern Daily Echo*, Sue Greenfield of Meridian, the BBC's Daniela Relph and me.

So the whole proceedings became more intimate: less a showbiz spectacular than a sort of private ritual, with which all the participants, save the judge and jury, were deeply familiar. We all became used to the sight of Guy Toyn, his expression unfailingly hangdog, grabbing a final fag outside the courtroom once the announcement had gone over the tannoy that pro-ceedings were about to recommence; or to Jerome Lynch, never failing to leave the courtroom without first leaning on the press box, directing a twinkling eye at one or both of the female reporters and fixing them with his devilishly handsome grin, while a few feet away David Calvert-Smith went into his regular conclaves with Brian Mitchell and his fellow police officers.

Minor distractions took on enormous significance – Sue Greenfield's toes, for example. A blue-eyed blonde, she knew that her looks, which qualified her for one of those eyelash-batting sofa-jobs towards which pretty young TV women frequently gravitate, were almost a disadvantage to anyone wishing to be taken seriously as a reporter. So she dressed with sober restraint, usually sticking to a plain black trouser-suit. She did, however, make one concession to girldom. On hot days she wore sandals, through which peeked nails painted to match her blouse, be it pale green, pale blue, pink or cream (she had violet varnish, too, she said, but not the blouse to match). As the trial dragged on through June, July and into August, the thought of Sue Greenfield's toes, and a burning urge to discover what colour they would be, was sometimes the only thing that got me into the car for the hour-long journey to Winchester.

At least proceedings began with a bang. As everyone was milling outside the courtroom waiting to go in to watch the jury selection, the BBC's Adam Mynott – a semi-detached member of the press pack this time around: he would grace us with his presence on an occasional basis, just to keep himself up to speed – rushed up to the gaggle of hacks milling around the broad corridor. His normally languid manner had temporarily deserted him. 'You'll never believe this!' he exclaimed. 'Mrs Doubtfire is sitting with the Segers outside the canteen.'

There were gasps of astonishment. Mrs Doubtfire was the nickname we had given to the eldest-looking of the female jurors from the first trial. Sure enough, when I went downstairs there she was chatting to Hans and Astrid. A little while later she appeared upstairs and – doubtless unaware that she was breaking the law – revealed many of the first jury's opinions about the evidence they had seen during the first trial. It would constitute a criminal offence to repeat what she said. But I can say that she disclosed that several members of the jury had kept in touch after the end of the first trial and some had written to the defence teams. She had come to the reopening of the case to show her support for the defendants, because, as she said, 'I feel very strongly and so do the others. All eight are coming during the trial.'

The police were informed of her presence, and her

descriptions of the reasoning behind the first jury's decision – or lack of it – and Mrs Doubtfire was asked to leave. A short while later, she was visited at home by the police and warned that she had been breaking the law. She was, we later discovered, bitterly upset by her nickname: 'But Mrs Doubtfire's a man!' she complained. The law's message struck home, however, for she did not return to the trial. Several weeks later, another member of the first jury made an appearance. He too was swiftly warned off.

The new jury – by and large a younger bunch – were sworn in after much the same process of questions as to sporting loyalties and excuses for non-attendance, and we all settled down for our first look at the new judge. Mr Justice McCullough was a very different man from Tuckey. He was older, for a start – sixty-six to Tuckey's fifty-five – but the age-gap was exaggerated by the difference in manner. If Tuckey was energetic and relatively informal, McCullough was much more like one's imaginary notion of a judge: venerable in appearance, slightly crusty, extremely concerned with precision and detail. Right from the off, for example, this case was referred to as that of 'Lim and Others', as it was formally listed, rather than 'Grobbelaar and Others' as it had informally been known. McCullough had a slight air of unworldliness, which would slip from time to time to reveal rather more awareness of the world outside than he might initially let on. He had a wonderful range of grandfatherly expressions, too, conveying disbelief, dis-approval, irritation or bafflement exactly as required.

From their first exchanges it was obvious that he knew and liked Rodney Klevan – their conversations as to the best route between Winchester and the North of England would become a regular feature of Friday afternoons – but that did not mean that he was disposed to agree with everything Klevan said.

When, for example, Klevan attempted to have the entire trial called off before the jury were even selected, because media coverage had made it impossible for a jury to consider with unbiased eyes, McCullough assured him, 'Lots of people don't read the sports pages, or the arts pages, or the business pages

. . . I won't ask you to recall what you saw on the TV news last night. Even the most vivid reporting is pretty transitory.'

Nor was he interested when Klevan asked that he instruct the jury to ignore Vincent's evidence, arguing that, 'He is probably an accomplice in the second count [the charge of corruption against Grobbelaar, Fashanu and Lim] and certainly an agent provocateur. He has written a book. He is not the sort of witness one would ever want in a criminal trial.' McCullough, though, was not going to be rushed into any hasty decisions. He had already told Klevan that, 'I know nothing more than what I read in part of Mr Calvert-Smith's opening, and after a while I got lost . . . There were references to so many documents I gave up and decided it was best to come fresh to the trial.' One point, though, he had remembered. 'The Crown say that important things Vincent has to say are supported in many respects by independent evidence.'

The differences in McCullough's approach to the case became even more evident in his handling of the accused. Aware that there had been close proximity between jurors and defendants in the first case, when both groups had taken lunch in the canteen, he laid down strict instructions. Jurors were not to enter the canteen. Defendants had to arrive early every day and be segregated away from jurors. Rather than making their own way into the courtroom, as they had done before, they would be taken into custody before each of the day's four sessions. They would enter the dock, escorted by an officer, only after the judge had entered and bowed to the court. They would then bow to the judge. He would not bow back.

The same strictness applied to prosecution as well as defence. It was no good the Crown simply putting forward admissions. McCullough needed to know that every individual admission had been agreed by each of the defendants who might be affected by it. One began to understand why, according to courtroom gossip, he had never had a single one of his convictions overturned on appeal: he simply left no margin for error.

He knew how to treat the jury, too. Having urged them to try the defendants 'exactly as you would someone you'd never heard of before', he went on: 'If you know nothing at all about football, please don't feel in the least embarrassed. If there is anything you don't understand, there's a high chance I won't either . . . Some of the evidence – I hate to use the word turgid – but some may be a little indigestible.'

Speaking of which, David Calvert-Smith now rose to give his opening speech. As before, he introduced his fellow members of the bar; outlined the various charts and document bundles (McCullough interrupted a couple of times with queries about these); went through the counts on which the men were charged; explained why a potential match-fixer would approach the goalkeeper rather than any other member of the team; and gave the now familiar warnings about Chris Vincent.

This time around, he was able to outline some of the defence's arguments, too, noting as he did so that, 'No evidence the Crown brings will attempt to prove that Mr Grobbelaar was deliberately trying to let a goal in.'

The judge seemed puzzled by this: 'You allege that he accepted money to throw matches, but you are not alleging that he actually threw a match. If one makes a corrupt agreement, how can one do that unless one intends to throw a match? Where is your evidence that he intended to throw matches? It needs to be made clear whether you are saying that he never threw a match, or whether he intended to throw a game but [you] cannot prove that he did.'

There was another point that worried McCullough. 'Mr Fashanu told nothing to the police and said nothing to the court, yet you told the jury about his defence.'

'That was based on the evidence given by him in the last trial,' explained Calvert-Smith.

'Putting something on behalf of a defendant is not establishing a defence,' said the judge. 'I shall tell the jury that all counsel can do is deny the Crown's charges or say they are not proven. You cannot say nothing to the police and nothing to the court and advance a positive defence.'

Exchanges such as these seemed to litter Calvert-Smith's

opening speech. There were times when he hardly seemed able to talk for five minutes without interruption from the bench. As the first two days of the case wore on, the intense frustration being felt by this outwardly mild and gentlemanly figure was evident from the colour of his ears, which progressed from pink, through magenta, through scarlet to puce. Only occasionally was there any verbal evidence of his inner mood.

Once, for example, McCullough queried whether it was really necessary to see a section of the Grobbelaar/Vincent video. 'I can't see what's to gain. But it's your opening case. I'm just sitting here making the odd comment.'

'I'd noticed!' snapped Calvert-Smith.

'I'm just being the thirteenth juror, making comments.'

'I was rather hoping that the imaginary juror would want to see the video,' said Calvert-Smith, with a tone of wistful desperation in his voice.

McCullough was bothered, too, by the 200-page transcript of the police interviews with Hans Segers: 'These days the police go on and on, round and round about the same topic, instead of simply asking a man, "What have you got to say for yourself?" and leaving it at that.'

After a while, the pressure imposed from the bench began to have its effects on Calvert-Smith's coherence. At one stage, describing the case against Grobbelaar, he kept confusing Manchester United and Newcastle United. 'Oh, did I?' he sighed, when the mistake was pointed out to him at the end of the day. 'I was out on my feet.'

A sympathetic court official suggested that, 'Maybe we should just get a ball for [the judge] and start from there.'

John Fashanu, for one, was delighted by the way things were going. 'Calvert-Smith has lost all his authority. The judge can see it's all circumstantial,' he said, leaving court on the first Friday. His counsel, Trevor Burke, was less ready to jump to conclusions, saying, 'He'll be just as nit-picking with us.'

Despite the handicaps, Calvert-Smith did a simpler, better job of explaining facts in the second trial than he had in the first. Although he took the jury through the key phone calls, matches and cash deposits, along with the salient facts and arguments of the case, he seemed to do so more quickly than before and with clearer signposts as to where he was going.

The prosecution had come up with some new evidence, too. The court was told that Mr Thuys, Hans Segers' partner in Ties International, would give evidence not only to the effect that he had never paid Segers anything like the amounts of cash that had been claimed, but also that Segers had asked him to make a statement saying that he had, thus providing an alibi for at least some of his cash payments into his RNB 'Gloves' account.

One other noticeable factor was the far greater involvement of the jury, who began asking questions on a regular basis via the judge. These were often extremely acute. For example, Lim had called the Far East during a game between Wimbledon and Leeds: was there any correlation between the time of the call and time of a goal? Sure enough, there was: a goal eighteen minutes after a 3 p.m. kick-off, the call at 3.21.

The judge, however, still seemed to have fundamental worries about the very nature of the case itself. What if Grobbelaar, for example, had accepted Lim's offer of money without ever intending to do anything himself? 'Grobbelaar could say, "The result was inevitable, we were going to lose anyway. I was just pretending." "Doing the business" may mean going through the motions with the people from the Far East and not meaning it, which may not be a crime.'

And what, exactly, was the Crown's main case? What did Calvert-Smith mean when he said that Lim, having made friends with two goalkeepers, 'judged the time was right to move into full-scale corruption'?

'What is your allegation?' asked Mr Justice McCullough.

'That at some time in 1993, a financial relationship developed into corruption.'

'But what are you saying about the relationship?'

'That there was one.'

The judge looked frustrated. 'It's the nature of the relationship I want to get at, and I can see that the defendants' lawyers are just as puzzled: what is your case?'

Calvert-Smith was not best pleased. 'At some point in 1993, or earlier, the scheme began,' he said, attempting to disguise his irritation. 'If it began with forecasting, we cannot dispute it. But by [September] 1993, whatever the relationship was before then, it became corrupt ... Mr Lim came to Manchester to pay Mr Grobbelaar money and to introduce him to the possibility of "big bucks". He persuaded Mr Grobbelaar to join the scheme.'

'The scheme being to throw matches,' said the judge.

Calvert-Smith concurred. 'On 21 November Newcastle beat Liverpool. When Grobbelaar went to London on 25 November, he did so to collect the proceeds of the scheme.'

Well, that was clear enough. And perhaps that was the judge's intention: to force Calvert-Smith – as he would later force others, on both sides of the case – to state his position in unmistakable terms, so that the jury would know exactly what they were expected to believe and what evidence was being brought before them.

Enter, then, Chris Vincent, who had been released from Winchester jail some three months previously and so arrived at court from the hotel where he was being kept by the CPS a free man, rather than a prisoner. Looking much healthier and more confident than he had done in January, he told his story once again. The only sign of any nerves he may have been feeling was a slight but perceptible tic in his left cheek.

Essentially, he covered the same ground as he had done so many times before. But there were new emphases. Knowing what Grobbelaar had said during the first trial about the lack of any business plan, Calvert-Smith asked, 'Did you have anything on paper?'

'We had, in conjunction with National Mutual, produced an investment proposal ...' He hesitated for a moment, as if looking for the right word ... 'Produced all the financial figures – a professionally prepared document.'

'Do we really need this?' asked the judge.

'M'lud, yes,' replied Calvert-Smith.

Vincent also made another significant point. When asked who took the lead in any negotiations with potential investors, he replied, 'Basically, anything to do with presentation was done by me, and possibly Stephen Wundke.'

When the time came for Rodney Klevan to begin his cross-examination – appropriately, perhaps, on Friday 13 June – he concentrated on the fact that Vincent stood to gain from a guilty verdict and that he was thus not wholly objective. He went into the original contract for this book (not, incidentally, the one under which it has actually been published), once again stressing the clause that appeared to demand delivery of the manuscript within twenty-four hours of sentence, before going into the payment schedule in line-by-line detail. 'You had pre-pared the text before the first trial commenced. Between March and now you have been updating . . . You have a book ready for the printers.'

'Since the beginning of committal proceedings I have not updated the book,' said Vincent, before explaining that he had a ghost-writer who had been attending court on his behalf, taking notes of what went on.

The judge, who had been asking Vincent a series of questions relating to the degree to which his book anticipated a con-viction, interjected: 'Is he in this room now?'

As Vincent answered yes, and the rest of the press box struggled to suppress their giggles, I bent my head – my ears burning, this time – over my notepad and pretended to scribble furiously away. I was longing to march up to the witness stand, shout out that I was not a ghost-writer, that Chris Vincent had not written one word of 'his' book, and his outstanding debts meant that he would receive little more that £1,000, if that, from the remaining portion of his publishing contract, and that I fully intended to publish, irrespective of the final verdict in the case.

But I had to keep my silence. A short while later, while the court was adjourned, I passed Bruce Grobbelaar in the corridor. He started humming the theme from *Ghostbusters*. Then he sang, 'Who you gonna call? Ghost-writers!' and went chuckling on his way. I smiled ruefully . . . that made two good jokes by him at my expense.

Vincent's business conduct came under severe scrutiny from both Klevan and McCullough. It was made clear that he had not had any money at all, bar that which was in his pockets, when he first met Grobbelaar. Klevan asked Vincent whether he had used the £5,000 he had initially received from Grobbelaar, not to invest in Mondoro, but to pay off private bills: his rent, electricity and so on. 'The moment you got the money, you were sitting pretty,' he concluded.

The judge intervened, 'You said, "Anything I do for Mondoro, I can take the money and pay for bills."'

'All my expenses in the UK were related to that venture,' replied Vincent.

'Domestic rent? Domestic bills?' asked McCullough.

'I wasn't drawing a formal salary,' protested Vincent.

'What about the butcher and the tailor?' interjected Klevan.

'I doubt "the tailor",' observed McCullough.

'Did you buy a new suit – any clothing?' asked the QC.

'No, sir,' said Vincent.

'You're quite right, m'lud,' oozed the accommodating Mr Klevan.

A picture had successfully been painted of Vincent as a man whose sole intention, right from the off, was to milk Bruce Grobbelaar for all he was worth. As the other one of the two men in the room who had actually given money to Vincent and done business with him, I knew better than anyone how frustrating, infuriating and downright impossible working with him could be, and I had no illusions whatever as to the purity of his motives. But no one seemed prepared to point out the facts of the matter, which were that Vincent had sold Grobbelaar shares in his company, and he was entitled to spend the proceeds of that sale in any way he chose.

Still, the fact that Rodney Klevan had created an unfavourable impression was not the key issue. The real question was why the Crown did so little to protect their own chief witness. For all the personal attacks distracted attention from the most significant aspect of Christopher Vincent's evidence. Here was a man who had allegedly offered to disappear; who was only in court at all to make money; who was denounced as a pariah; despised even by his own family. And yet, for the second time, and despite the most searching cross-examination, he scarcely wavered at all from his evidence about the case and the allegations it contained.

There were, however, a few occasions on which his claims were not just flatly contradicted by the defence but either undermined by force of argument or made to seem ridiculous. Jerome Lynch, for example, set about the whole business of the code of which Grobbelaar and the Short Man allegedly communicated. We had long been used to Wimbledon, Dundee and Leeds for Win, Lose or Draw. During Vincent's evidence-in-chief he had said that Grobbelaar used code words for football teams. The point he tried to make was that he could not just say, 'this week' or 'next week', because Liverpool often played two matches a week, so he and the Short Man needed to know which of those games he was referring to.

In cross-examination Vincent said, 'When he was trying to indicate which game he was playing, he might say Amsterdam when he was walking about Arsenal, so that they would both be talking about the same game.'

Lynch mentioned that Vincent had cited 'Holland' for 'Home' (as opposed to Away).

'What Premier club begins with H?' asked McCullough.

'I was just using that as an example,' flailed Vincent.

'There is no team beginning with H,' insisted the judge, who had just checked.

The increasingly *Alice in Wonderland* interrogation continued. 'If Liverpool were playing Leeds to lose – what would he say then?' enquired Lynch, emphasizing all the Ls.

'He would say, "Next week, London," or some other word for lose,' said Vincent. 'One word he did use was Lisbon.'

The jury burst out laughing. Vincent's evidence, potentially so damaging, had now been rendered absurd.

A similar fate befell the mysterious Mr Thuys. His arrival had been keenly awaited by the now depleted press corps. Here, it was felt, was a witness who would not only blow apart one of the defendants' alibis, but who could – far more importantly from their point of view – supply a hot story for news editors bored with the Grobbelaar trial. When Alphonsus Franciscus Maria Thuys appeared in the witness box, looking tall, burly and blond (slightly thinning on top), ears were pricked and pens poised. But anticipation soon gave way to anti-climax.

Thuys could speak passable English, but had asked for an interpreter, a nervous-looking man of about sixty. He was informed by the judge that he should repeat precisely what Thuys had said in answer to any question. The clerk of the court then began the oath, 'I swear by Almighty God . . .'

'I swear by Almighty God . . .' began Thuys, in English.

No, no, the judge interrupted, this wouldn't do. The clerk must read the oath, line by line. It should then be translated into Dutch, line by line, by the interpreter. Mr Thuys should then answer in Dutch, and have his oath reinterpreted back into English, line by line.

The clerk, interpreter and witness did their best to assimilate their instruction. 'I swear by Almighty God . . .' began the clerk, whereupon the interpreter said something that sounded – to the untrained ear – like '*Ach swaar by aalmachty Gott . . .*'

The judge interrupted again, exasperated. 'You must translate it!' he said.

The interpreter tried to explain. He *had* translated the oath. It was just that the first line sounded almost exactly the same in Dutch as in English. The judge harrumphed, clearly unimpressed by this pathetic excuse.

And so Thuys got under way, with constant pauses for translation, the dramatic effect of his evidence quite undermined by the absurdity of its delivery. He explained that he had met Hans Segers in December 1993 and gone into business with him. He had written a letter setting out the details of their partnership, but had not paid any money up-front. Such money as he had paid to Segers – beginning on 11 August 1994, nine months after the November 1993 payment claimed by Segers – had been banked in Holland, not the UK, and the only cash Thuys ever paid Segers was a few hundred pounds to cover travelling expenses.

He then came to the nub of his evidence. On 28 January 1997 Thuys, wanting to end his association with Segers because of bad publicity created by the trial in the Dutch press, had come to England with a letter from his lawyer. Segers, however, had other plans. Via the interpreter, Thuys said, 'He required me to work together with him on an alibi for him to declare that 50,000 guilders would be earned very rapidly for ties in Spain.'

'Can you say what Mr Segers said to you about the 50,000 guilders?' asked Calvert-Smith.

'If you declare this, then I'll walk straight out of the case.'

'Declare what?'

'That 50,000 guilders were earned on the black market.'

Once again, Mr Justice McCullough interrupted. Was the point that the money *would* be earned, or actually had been earned?

The question was put, via the interpreter, to Thuys and a number of replies, each greeted with increasing dissatisfaction, emerged. The money should be earned, should have been earned, shall have been earned . . . It sounded to me as though the interpreter, sticking to his duty to translate precisely what he had heard, was giving a literal translation of a Dutch construction that had no English equivalent. Or not one that made sense, anyway. But this was not the judge's view. 'I find this quite unsatisfactory.'

Calvert-Smith agreed. The two men discussed the fact that the interpreter could obviously not speak proper English, while the poor man – who could certainly understand exactly what was being said about him – listened to their words in ever-deepening humiliation. Finally Calvert-Smith returned to the cross-examination, this time in English. At the end of it, McCullough summed up: 'I think it comes to this. Mr Segers said to you, "Will you please declare that I earned 50,000 guilders from black-market sales of ties in Spain, and that you are unable to come to England to give evidence?" Have you understood?'

Yes, said Thuys, he had understood and that was what Segers had said. 'I told him, "No hair on my head will I think about this! How dare you say this?"'

Thuys went on to describe another meeting the following day. Segers had said he was disappointed that Thuys had dropped him. A week after that, Segers had telephoned him and told him not to tell the police anything. 'I said, "Hans, we are friends."'

As Thuys said this, John Fashanu was staring blankly at the press box, holding his head in his hands.

It looked as though Calvert-Smith had rescued the evidence from the teeth of destruction. But that was to reckon without Desmond De Silva who, over the rest of that afternoon and the following morning, demonstrated that Thuys still owed Segers considerable sums of money which he wished to avoid paying. He thus had an obvious financial motive for doing down his old partner. Thuys responded with increasing irritation, thereby helping to create precisely the effect that De Silva intended. It did not matter that Mrs Thuys, who had been at the 28 January meeting with Segers, confirmed her husband's story, nor that McCullough reminded the jury that both Mr and Mrs Thuys had come of their own accord to court: the impact of the evidence had been dissipated.

There was one final poignant moment for the Thuys family, caught on videotape by an ITV cameraman. The couple were standing outside on the courthouse steps with their lawyer, talking to the *Sun*'s Simon Hughes. He then left and, as he did so, Astrid Segers came through the main doors, saw the couple who had once been her friends and went over to them. Mr Thuys backed away a step at her approach. 'I'm so sorry,' she seemed to be saying. Thuys started talking to her, emphasizing his points with his hand, pointing it at Astrid who was by now in tears. She kissed Thuys twice, then his wife three times and walked away, distraught.

Astrid need not have worried. When her husband came to give evidence, Calvert-Smith managed to cast doubt on his account of his dealings with Ties International, but was never able to crack his defence. Apologizing to the jury for the stupidity of his lies to the police, Segers repeated, again and again, that he had acted out of fear for his career and family. He was, if anything, stronger than he had been in February. 'He played a fine night-watchman's innings,' a contented Desmond De Silva declared. It was an innings assisted somewhat by the umpire. Mr Justice McCullough repeatedly interrupted David Calvert-Smith's questions, asking if they were really necessary, correcting him and making points on Segers' behalf. When, for example, Calvert-Smith suggested it was absurd that both Segers and Fashanu could deposit cash into the same bank at the same time without each knowing the quantity and origin of the other's money, McCullough mused, 'I'm just wondering how many barristers wander up Middle Temple Lane, each putting money into a bank, neither dreaming of telling the other how much money they are going to put in.'

But that is to get ahead of ourselves. Segers followed Lim and Fashanu. As he had done in the first trial, Trevor Burke attempted to have John Fashanu's case dismissed – an application made while the jury were out of the room. In January, Mr Justice Tuckey had rejected his motion, and now, in June, Mr Justice McCullough did the same.

Having now studied the telephone and financial records in detail, he felt that Fashanu had a case to answer. There then followed an extraordinary exchange. Burke argued that the money could have a number of sources, 'some of them criminal'.

'Give me one,' said the judge.

'It could be money-laundering.'

'I don't think so.'

'It could be stolen cars,' argued Burke. 'It could be drugs.'

'It's the other way round with drugs,' said the judge. The money in other words, was paid from Britain to the Far East, where the narcotics came from. McCullough pulled together the financial evidence as he saw it, relating it to the charge and asking, 'All these large sums of money . . . what else could it be?'

The barrister admitted defeat. 'I think it's Trevor Burke 0, David Calvert-Smith 2,' he said.

He had more luck later in the trial. I was talking to David Calvert-Smith outside the courtroom one day when Trevor Burke approached him to discuss an admission the two men were trying to hammer out about John Fashanu's financial affairs. Calvert-Smith had drafted a text that was, of necessity, vague about the possibility of additional bank accounts as yet unknown to the Crown. Burke did not think that McCullough, a man who insisted on cut and dried evidence, would approve: 'He'll go Polaris.'

'Well,' said Calvert-Smith, 'You could let me see the other bank accounts.'

Burke grinned. Then he leaned forward, exposing a strip of sunburned neck between his wig and his gown. He pointed at his flesh. 'Do I look green?' he asked. 'Do I?'

Once again, he told the jury that Fashanu would not go into the box. But with McCullough's merciless attention to detail it was less easy to create the impression of Fashanu as a super-successful businessman conducting global trade with Johannes Joseph. McCullough wanted documents and proof: assertions were not enough.

This proved particularly troublesome in respect of Mr Littlechild, Fashanu's partner in the Lagos duty-free shop who had gone to pick up 100,000 dollars from Joseph. A substantial proportion of the money appeared to have been lent, or given, to Mace. But there were no records, apart from a scribbled note on a piece of Filofax paper, to account for any of it. Nor was Littlechild in any mood to provide any records, particularly any bank statements.

'Why not?' asked the judge.

Littlechild responded like a man who had no particular fear of the judiciary. 'At the end of the day, I have an amount of money from John Fashanu. How it was used is my business.'

'What's the problem in seeing statements?' asked the judge.

'Because they're private to me.'

The 100,000 dollars would be dealt with in full in his

company's next accounts. Sadly, these were not available as yet. Nor, it later transpired, were the records of Imran Khan, the estate agent (no relation to the cricketer of the same name) who had acted for Hans Segers and John Fashanu in their claimed attempt to purchase property. Owing to an unfortunate computer malfunction he had no details of any appointments to view properties with either of the two men which could give some indication of their activities.

Khan was one of the case's most splendid minor figures. As smooth as a mink-lined jockstrap, as shy and retiring as a fairground barker, he seemed like the Platonic essence of estate-agenting as he explained how he had repeatedly hammered home to his good friends Fashanu and Segers how important it was in the property game to be able to deal in cash, so that one could snap up cheap, repossessed properties with maximum speed and efficiency. He explained his operating principles to McCullough in a three-word sentence that was a motto for the entire trial. 'Hard cash talks,' he said.

'Indeed it does,' I thought.

But what of Lim and Grobbelaar? How did their case proceed?

Calvert-Smith set about Heng Suan Lim in a manner which seemed to arouse the judge's interest far more than his examination of Hans Segers. When, for example, the subject of Hans Segers' Dutch forecasts came up, it was the judge who pointed out to Lim that, 'When the police came, there was nothing about Dutch football in your house.'

'Apart from *World Soccer Magazine*, which has a Dutch section,' said Lim.

Calvert-Smith piled in. 'I invite you to point to any document with anything to do with Dutch football.'

'There are no documents for Dutch matches,' agreed Lim.

'That's because the Dutch forecasting is a complete lie,' said Calvert-Smith.

The question of how any such evidence might have been disposed of was also covered. Lim agreed that a shredder had been found at his house. This was a subject that later aroused

Mr Justice McCullough's interest when he conducted an extensive examination of Lim at the end of Mr Calvert-Smith's questions. 'How much did you pay for your shredder?' he asked.

Lim could not remember.

'When did you buy it?'

'About 1993 or '94.'

'What business required you to have a shredder?'

'When I wanted to shred documents . . . My office was in my home . . . I just got a shredder for completeness.'

As always with McCullough, the devil was in the details. Lim had described the business his benefactor Joseph had transacted with Fashanu. McCullough wanted to know exactly how much Lim had known about this business: had he seen documents, witnessed meetings, and, if so, on what subjects? He wondered why it was that no letters or cards from Joseph to Lim had ever been found 'as one might send to a nephew'. And he also wondered what Lim and Grobbelaar had talked about in their various discussions about Mondoro in November 1992 or September 1993. Lim had been interested in the project as an investment opportunity for Fashanu or Joseph. So . . . was the area of land it would cover discussed?

'I did ask,' said Lim. 'He said he was going to lease a big piece of land in a very strategic location. I remember him mentioning Victoria Falls.'

'What does "strategic location" mean?' asked McCullough.

'Where you can get game as well.'

'Was the migration of animals discussed? Was there mention of any specific animals?'

'I only mentioned something about lions.'

'What about lions?'

'That there have to be lions in the park that tourists could see.'

'So the land had been earmarked . . . how big was it?'

'All I know was it was a big piece of land.'

'Did it contain a river?'

'I don't remember. I heard about Victoria Falls.'

'There was nothing about the importance of having a river – otherwise the tourists can't see hippos or crocodiles?'

Lim said there had been no such mention. Nor, as the judge continued his enquiries, could he remember anything about the number of employees the safari park would need, the number of vehicles, the presence of rival parks or the dangers of poachers. None of these had been subjects covered in his attempts to discover the value of Mondoro. One got the impression, as Lim attempted to answer his questions, that Mr Justice McCullough might have been a bit of a demon in his younger life as a barrister.

There was one other interesting point which arose – or to be more specific, failed to arise – out of Lim's evidence. He said that he was a keen football fan who travelled all over the country to watch matches: something over a hundred games in all. I wondered, listening to the evidence, whether he had called Johannes Joseph or Lo Bon Swe from any of these games – as he had done from matches in which Segers and Grobbelaar were involved – to keep them up to date with developments. So I asked the police: were there any calls recorded from cell-sites indicating that Lim had (a) been at any such football matches, and (b) called the Far East? No they said, there were not. So far as they knew, the only calls were made from matches featuring Segers or Grobbelaar. It was, I think, something of an oversight that this fact was not communicated to the jury.

As Bruce Grobbelaar took the stand, David Calvert-Smith revealed why he had been regarded as the best man to prosecute this case. He conducted his cross-examination with an aggression that had not previously been present in his conduct of either trial, and Grobbelaar found it much harder than before to cope with his time in the witness box. I have a note in my transcript, taken on the afternoon of Thursday 17 July, the second full day of Grobbelaar's cross-examination. It reads, 'Grob is clenching jaw, blinking, almost in tears.' I was sitting at the end of the press box nearest to the witness box, with an unimpeded view, no more than twelve feet from Grobbelaar, when that note was written.

The pressure had come from the same relentless examination of the similarities between the material on the *Sun* tapes and the known facts in the case. 'You were saying Fashanu had a lot of money from the syndicate and got a Mercedes, and the fact of the matter is he did have a Mercedes, paid for with money from the Far East . . . You said [the Short Man] sits on the phone, "He talks to me and he talks to overseas and that's all he does." And, as we can see, he does talk to you, and he does talk to overseas.'

Again, Calvert-Smith went into the competitive instinct which Grobbelaar had described on the tapes as his biggest problem, because he liked to win. 'You're saying that, unfortunately for you and your bank balance, if the ball comes towards you, you can't help sticking out your hand.'

'This has got nothing to with my bank balance,' said Grobbelaar. 'These tapes are a load of rubbish from one end to the other.'

A tone of menace entered Calvert-Smith's voice. 'If we are not careful, we will have to listen to it all, and I don't think you want that,' he said.

At the end of the day, that same possibility arose for a second time. Calvert-Smith had been noting how, during the third taped meeting of 3 November 1994, Grobbelaar had told Vincent that the Short Man had been in touch again, and that he was going to throw the game on the following Saturday against Manchester City: 'By how many, I don't know. I've got to speak to him later.' As it happened, the telephone records revealed that Lim had indeed been in touch with him in the days leading up to the Manchester City game. 'Yet another case of the facts happening to coincide with what you were saying,' remarked Calvert-Smith.

'Inferences could be drawn from it, yes,' replied Grobbelaar.

'That's no coincidence, is it?' retorted the prosecutor.

There was a long, long pause as Grobbelaar looked through the schedule of calls. An atmosphere of palpable tension filled the courtroom. Grobbelaar said nothing.

'Is it?' Calvert-Smith pressed him.

'Sorry?'

'It's not just a coincidence.'

'It goes with these charts,' agreed Grobbelaar. 'But it's not what you're saying. I was ringing Richard Lim because he had left so many messages. I really couldn't tell you what we spoke about.'

'So what you told Vincent was all made up?'

'For Mr Vincent and my purposes, yes.'

Mr Justice McCullough intervened. 'You referred to earlier conversations which were not transcribed. The jury want a transcript of any further conversations you think are relevant.'

In a subdued voice, Grobbelaar replied, 'With respect, I would rather the jury didn't see those. It's got nothing to do with the case and would put me in a worse light than I am.'

The judge was sympathetic. 'They're asking if there's anything that could influence your case . . . it's only fair.'

Mr Klevan got to his feet. 'There's no other material that would help the jury, m'lud.'

There was, however, material that would help the defence. Calvert-Smith ended his cross-examination of Grobbelaar looking like a forward who has rounded the keeper and only has to put the ball into an empty net. Except that there was a second keeper. No sooner had Bruce Grobbelaar sat down than Bob Wilson came striding towards the witness box. Once again, he was the soul of honest decency, describing his positive analysis of the games in which Grobbelaar and Segers had played, the saves they had made and the goals they had conceded with a certainty in their sportsmanship that reflected his own personal integrity and his faith in the integrity of others.

We were moving towards the endgame and, so far as canteen gossip among lawyers and media was concerned, the result was too close to call. But amidst the ever-increasing tension one man at least was maintaining his usual ebullient air. 'This is so weird,' said Simon Hughes of the *Sun*, approaching the hacks' table in the canteen one day towards the end of the trial. 'Fash comes up to me, slaps me on the shoulder, says, "Smiley!"'

'And you're going to stitch him up,' mused the Beeb's Adam Mynott.

'Big time!' agreed Hughes.

I, too, had enjoyed a canteen chat with Fash. 'How's the book going?' he asked one lunchtime as I passed him, tray in hand. I said it was going fine and would continue to do so, irrespective of the verdict. I was not, I insisted, Vincent's ghost. The defence case would be properly represented. We started talking about Vincent. Fash, like so many others, was fascinated by Vincent's motivation for betraying Bruce Grobbelaar. He had, however, come up with an entirely new explanation. 'It's a bitch thing,' he said. I was puzzled. So Fashanu explained his theory: Chris Vincent was gay. He wanted to be Bruce's bitch. Since Bruce was clearly not interested, he felt hurt and, like a bitch, lashed out.

With the excitement of someone lighting the blue touch-paper and retiring, I passed the theory on to Vincent the next time we spoke. As, well . . . bitchy as that gesture was, I felt a certain sympathy for the Zimbabwean. It is not often you come across a man who is accused, to your face, of being both a heterosexual rapist and a frustrated homosexual. But Fashanu's idea contained a germ of psychological truth. Chris Vincent was certainly obsessed by his relationship with Grobbelaar. In the weeks he spent at my house, his determination to win his personal battle with Grobbelaar was equalled only by the evident pride he still took in their friendship. It was, quite obviously, one of the high points of his life. He was still thrilled by their adventures in Britain and Zimbabwe – the drinking, the sex (with women, I should add), the manic drives from one wild jape to another. Did Chris Vincent want a sexual relationship with Bruce Grobbelaar? Categorically not. But was he just a tiny bit in love with him? Almost certainly.

But enough of an author's opinions. What did the judge think of it all?

# 25

## Summing It Up

Mr Justice McCullough spoke for more than three days. He covered every important incident in the case, every significant cash transaction, a large number of telephone calls, every match – including every goal and save – in which the result (or the influences upon it) was controversial and, of course, the various arguments that had been placed before the jury by the Crown or the defence. But before he considered the evidence, he took care to put the relative importance of the case – and, by extension, of football itself – into its proper perspective. 'No one has been killed, no one injured, no one raped or assaulted. No child has been violated and no one has been robbed. Nevertheless the charges are serious, both for the defendants and for the honour and reputation of English football.'

Having defined the legal issues at stake, he came to Christopher Vincent. McCullough took a rather dimmer view of the prosecution's star witness than Mr Justice Tuckey had done. 'You must be very careful indeed with Vincent . . . If ever there was a man to distrust, you may think it was him. You should think long and hard before accepting a word he says unless it is supported by someone else. You should consider the case without placing any reliance at all on anything Vincent has said, where that stands alone. People like that have only themselves to blame if their evidence is disregarded.'

He moved on to the defendants, taking scrupulous care to describe their characters and achievements in the fairest possible way, while pointing out, too, those agreed facts which the prosecution felt were important. So, for example, 'Mr Lim, you may think, is the most intelligent of the defendants to have given evidence. He came to the UK in 1986, aged twenty-one, as a student . . . From March 1989, he began to receive money from Mr Joseph . . . By May 1994 he had received more than £580,000, of which £480,000 was sent by, or on behalf of, Mr Joseph. Other than small sums Mr Lim earned, he accepts that his only source of money was from the Far East.'

He was, said McCullough, in regular contact with Joseph and his associates Lo Bon Swe, Benny Santoso and a Mr Sutanto. Joseph and his friends liked to bet large sums on football matches, which was illegal in their own countries. None of the men had ever been arrested, charged or convicted of a crime, 'although whether that makes them distinguished members of the community is perhaps another matter.'

Fashanu was an influence for good in Africa as a Unicef special representative. He was held in high regard by many national leaders. According to the testimony of his PA, Miss Mackintosh, he owned three companies. But, 'There is no evidence that any of his companies provided Mr Fashanu with any income, or any connection with Indonesia, and Miss Mackintosh said she had no memory of doing any business with the Far East. Mr Joseph [a former Wimbledon footballer who had testified on Fashanu's behalf] never saw any business with the Far East.'

He had, however, received hundreds of thousands of pounds from the Far East, either directly or via Melissa Kassa-Mapsi. 'There was no evidence from Mr Fashanu, but his counsel asks you to say that it doesn't follow that the money was for corruption. The Crown say this is the only realistic inference.'

The judge went on to describe the careers of Hans Segers and Bruce Grobbelaar, noting their incomes as footballers, their connections with Fashanu and Lim, their banking arrangements, and the quantities of money they had received in cash. That done, we broke for lunch. Just as we were re-assembling in court for the afternoon session, news of another trial – that of Tracie Andrews, a young woman accused of killing her boyfriend and faking a road-rage story – came in. Trevor Burke announced the result to the world at large: 'Did you hear? Tracie Andrews has been convicted of murder. She was cleared of the football-fixing charge, but—' The rest of his sentence was drowned in laughter.

After the recess, McCullough began by considering the importance of the expert witnesses such as Bob Wilson, Alan Ball and Gordon Banks, going through their testimony in detail and noting that none of them had seen evidence of impropriety in any of the games played by Grobbelaar connected with the case. But the judge told the jury, 'That can't be the complete answer. None of these men had heard the evidence, seen the videotapes or read the transcripts. The case cannot be deter-mined by the evidence of experts.'

For all McCullough's absolute even-handedness so far as his presentation of evidence was concerned, his questions to the jury increasingly suggested the particular aspects of the case that had made an impression upon him. There were, he noted, limitations to what any player could do in the world of tele-vision and action replays. 'Opportunities would be few. What would be needed would be a judicious mixture of doing one's best and doing the opposite if the opportunity presented itself. Any experienced goalkeeper would have another difficulty. Their reactions would be automatic – just as your reactions driving a car – after years of training, years of doing their utmost to win. The Crown suggests they would be their own worst enemy. There are twenty-two men trying to influence a result. If twenty-one are honest and one is corrupted, inevitably there will be games where the corrupt one is frustrated.'

Mr McCullough then moved into one of the most fascinating passages of his speech. He posed a hypothetical situation. 'If the men in the Far East want to bet on English football matches and it occurs to them it might help to pay a player, how would

they set about persuading a player to cooperate? The Crown
suggest they would need an agent, who would have to start to
get to know one or two suitable players. What sort of player
would be most suitable? A goalkeeper. Preferably, suggest the
Crown, a goalkeeper old enough to be facing a substantial drop
in earnings. You would start by asking for forecasts – the goalkeeper would be paid generously. You would progress, perhaps,
to telling him that information on his own team would be useful, and he might be paid for this. After you've gained his
friendship, you might raise the possibility that temptingly large
sums could be available if, from time to time, he could agree to
do what he had to [to lose]. That sort of approach is what you
would expect to be adopted. And the Crown suggest that is
precisely the technique adopted by Mr Lim at the behest of his
paymasters. Once the player had agreed to take part, he's
vulnerable to the next suggestion.'

The syndicate, suggested Mr McCullough, would need an
agent to swim into their net. 'You would tell Mr Lim that, out
of respect for his poor mother, you would support him in his
studies. You would need to support him all year, and his wife if
he had one. Then, after an interval . . .'

That, he suggested, was how the operation might have
started. But, 'Mr Grobbelaar, Mr Segers and Mr Lim have told
you that was not what happened. They were paid for forecasts,
that's all, so that Mr Lim could assist Mr Joseph to lay bets. Mr
Lim says everything he received from Mr Joseph was the result
of generosity. Mr Burke has been confined to suggesting that
the evidence of what Mr Fashanu received from the Far East is
consistent with the decision by Johannes Joseph to invest in
Africa. The Crown have not proved that was not the reason,
therefore his client is entitled to be acquitted.'

As McCullough went on to look at the precise financial
transactions involved in the case, he continued to make
pertinent observations about the implications of that evidence.
Between 1989 and 1991 Lim received £120,000 from Joseph.
'An average of £10,000 per month, paid to a twenty-six-year-
old accountancy student, coming from a friend of his mother's

whom he never even met until 1990,' the judge observed.

He noted the four simultaneous payments from Joseph to Lim and Fashanu. Why, he wondered, was £18,500 given by Lim to Fashanu – apparently in repayment of gambling debts – placed in accounts with false names? And why, in 1994, did the relationship between Lim and Joseph alter so much? At the start of the 1994–5 season, the judge said, Joseph had visited London. 'Fifty-seven attempts were made to call one or other of Mr Fashanu's numbers from Mr Joseph's room. There was not a single call to Lim. Something had happened to cause Mr Lim to fall out of favour. Was it because [Joseph] disapproved of his gambling? Or was it because he had not produced results on the field to give the men in the Far East the results they wanted?'

And what of the £170,000 which Mr Lim had claimed to have lost in casinos, as a result of which Mr Joseph disowned him. 'Was the £170,000 lost on the tables? Or did some go to other people as inducements or rewards?'

Questions like those put a smile on the faces of the prosecution team. But the unsolved mysteries to which McCullough kept pointing revealed the limitations of the Crown's case, too. He noted that there had never been any direct contact between Segers or Grobbelaar and the Far East. So money paid to the goalkeepers must have come from Lim or Fashanu. But there was no correlation at all between withdrawals from Lim's accounts and the known payments into Segers' RNB account. Furthermore, 'There are simply no withdrawals from any Lim account that could have funded £40,000 to Mr Grobbelaar, or account for the sums Mr Segers deposited.'

Far from Lim withdrawing cash on 25 November 1993, he was depositing £22,000. 'Mr Lim paid in some other big sums,' noted the judge: '£25,000 on 20 April, £10,000 on 17 June – whether from gambling or some other source, no one has asked him.'

Equally, Fashanu was not withdrawing cash on the days of Segers' first deposits. He was depositing cash as well. The only correlation between Fashanu's and Segers' accounts was in October 1994, when Kassa-Mapsi received £23,000 from Joseph; of this, £21,350 was paid to Fashanu five days before Segers paid in £19,000, which might well have come from that source.

Apart from that, there was nothing to show that Fashanu could have funded Segers or paid Grobbelaar £40,000. And yet, by his own admission, much of the money Segers deposited had come from Fashanu and Lim: how? The judge offered some suggestions.

'You will remember evidence that it was the habit of Mr and Mrs Fashanu to keep large sums of money at home. When police searched the penthouse, they found £10,000 in a wardrobe. In support of the allegation that Mr Grobbelaar was given £40,000 that must have come from Lim or Fashanu, the Crown suggest there must have been a further source of cash which the police have not discovered. They remind you of the ease with which Mr Littlechild imported 100,000 dollars from Indonesia and turned it into cash – that did not pass through any bank account.

'Quite apart from that, the question is raised of how Lim had £22,000 to deposit in the bank on 25 November. Where did Fashanu's £31,500 [deposited at RNB in October 1993] come from? Where did his £30,000 [deposited that November] come from? It's all cash. You don't know what the source is. Have you seen all the relevant documents? Have the police discovered all the sources of money available to Mr Lim and Mr Fashanu?'

Something was clearly going on, the judge seemed to be saying. But could anyone be sure, beyond reasonable doubt, exactly what that something was?

The same limitation applied to the telephone evidence. Even if one knew that one telephone had been used to call another, it was impossible to say who had called, who had answered or what was said. There were gaps in the charts, too, where bills had not been available. 'Most significantly, every call from the Far East is missing.' McCullough ended the first day of his speech with a person-by-person breakdown of telephone activity – just the sort of statistical recital to which we had all become painfully accustomed and which was apt to induce a mid-afternoon snooze. The following morning, however, the court received its wake-up call.

The subject addressed by McCullough as he began his second day's summing-up was the financial relationship between Johannes Joseph and John Fashanu. It was the defence's case that the two men had been business partners, and that money paid to Fashanu represented investments in joint commercial projects, or personal loans.

Yet, of the money paid to Fashanu before Segers or Grobbelaar became involved in the case, some £43,000 had been spent on the two Mercedes cars, not on business ventures. When the payments began again, 'We have evidence for £69,500. It wasn't kept separate. It was treated like any other money – given to Mr Fashanu [by Kassa-Mapsi] and used to pay bills.

'Entries [in Kassa-Mapsi's notebook] suggest £20,000 went to Mr Segers. He says it was so he could buy property. I draw your attention to the fact that he did not say that he understood Mr Fashanu to be investing it for someone else, nor did Mrs Fashanu say it was being invested on behalf of anyone. Her evidence was that he described it as loans.'

The judge then noted that Mr Fashanu's business associate Mr Littlechild had flown to Jakarta to pick up 100,000 dollars in travellers' cheques from Mr Joseph and had given Mace £20,000 from that money in cash, allegedly as a loan. Littlechild had produced a note to that effect, but, 'The words on the note are not "lent to Mace", but "paid to Mace". If the money was returned, he made no note.'

Littlechild claimed that the 100,000 dollars had been an investment in his duty-free store, via his company BusinessMart, but he would not produce any bank statements. 'You may be left wondering how much of that 100,000 dollars went to BusinessMart.'

Mr McCullough then looked at Lim's evidence, which

described Mr Joseph's interest in projects in Africa, including cocoa, mining, logging and the duty-free store. 'None of this amounts to any first-hand evidence that Joseph invested anything in Africa,' said McCullough. 'There are no documents evidencing Fashanu's investment. There are no receipts. There are no documents setting out terms of investments. There are no faxes, no letters indicating that Mr Joseph was even thinking of investing directly in Africa, or through Mr Fashanu.'

Was Mr Joseph lending Fashanu money? Once again, 'There is no evidence that any of what Mr Joseph sent was a loan. There is no copy of any receipt; no document setting out terms, interest, at what rate; no document saying the loan was interest-free; no document saying when it was to be repaid; no correspondence about Mr Fashanu borrowing money . . . The police found no evidence of any business dealings between Joseph and Fashanu.'

It was not for the defence to prove that the money was either an investment or a loan. But, asked the judge, 'Is there any indication that Mr Fashanu ever treated the money as anything other than his own? If you can safely rule out a loan, and if you can safely rule out the possibility that Mr Joseph was sending money to him to invest, what's left? If you come to the conclusion that it can only have been payment for a service, what was the service?'

And on that note, he sent the jury out to lunch.

In the afternoon, McCullough looked at dates of money transfers to Fashanu, noting the gaps that tended to occur in the summer months. 'When football stops, the money stops,' noted the judge. 'Is that an indication that football was the reason for payments?'

Mr Justice McCullough now moved on to the evidence concerning Bruce Grobbelaar. He went into every significant event in considerable depth, comparing the evidence of Grobbelaar and other defence witnesses with Vincent's evidence, which he repeated in detail, frequently prefacing his account with the words, 'for what it's worth'.

Looking at the alleged meeting at Heathrow on 6 October, for example, the judge asked, 'Did Vincent see the men meet, see the money, or did he work in false details, realizing that that was how the Short Man and Grobbelaar would have behaved? There is always a chance that a man like Vincent will add dramatic extra bits to make a better story. There is also a danger that he will make up a story, not in part but wholesale. The defence say this account is pure invention.'

The judge then ran through the events surrounding the Newcastle match on 21 November, and the debate over the significance of the meeting at Byron Drive. He drew the jury's attention to the way in which Vincent had spent £20,000 in the weeks after 25 November 1993: 'Note when the payments began: 26 November – the day after the flight to London.' He then referred to the note found in Fashanu's diary, which referred to 'Commission 10%' next to £50,000 (written over £40,000). 'Is Mr Fashanu calculating commission?' he asked. 'Whose commission? For what service? No explanation was given in evidence.'

Looking at events surrounding the drive down from Norwich to the Hilton Hotel, McCullough noted that Lim had travelled to Malaysia on 16 January, returning on the morning of 4 February. The meeting with Grobbelaar was held, the men said, to discuss footballing opportunities in the Far East. Lim had told Grobbelaar that there were leagues in Singapore and Malaysia, but that the Japanese league was the best bet.

'Would Mr Lim not have known all that before he departed for the Far East?' asked the judge. 'Mr Grobbelaar says Lim gave him £1,500 for forecasts and information provided before Lim went abroad. It was the first time he had been to London before a game in which Liverpool were playing away from home . . . Why did this happen? It was the only time Vincent went to the team hotel. The only time Grobbelaar went away from the hotel. Something highly unusual caused this trip of over 200 miles. The information Lim is said to have given Grobbelaar could have been given on the phone.'

After the match between Liverpool and Norwich, attended by Lim, contact between the two men tailed away before resuming again in August 1994. The judge drew the jury's attention to the concentration of calls around the game between Southampton and Coventry. 'On the evening of 23 September there are linked calls involving all the defendants in the space of eight minutes. Then the match is played. In the morning Mr Fashanu calls Mr Santoso [an associate of Joseph's], then Mr Lim calls Lo Bon Swe in Indonesia for nine minutes. He says that call could be about the Coventry game and others that weekend. Southampton win, despite conceding a goal in the first minute. Mr Lim is there. The next day he calls Indonesia.'

Grobbelaar and Vincent now renewed contact, which led McCullough to consider the evidence of the *Sun*'s videotapes, including Grobbelaar's apparently self-incriminating remarks about the game against Manchester United. The judge emphasized that none of the expert witnesses had anything but the highest praise for Grobbelaar's performance. Yet on the tape he had said, 'I dived the wrong way and it hit my hand . . . I'm my own worst enemy because I don't like to lose. It's instinct.'

'These saves must be from Giggs and Keane,' said the judge. 'Mr Grobbelaar says that all of this is a pretence and that the saves were intentional. Mr Banks says, "If Grobbelaar was diving the wrong way, I've been keeping goal the wrong way all my life."'

McCullough then made a fascinating observation: 'Had Mr Banks read the transcripts, he might have realized that the way [Grobbelaar] dived was wrong because he saved the goals. The right way would have been the way the ball wasn't going.'

Soon afterwards, McCullough blew the whistle on his day's work. On the morning of Thursday 31 July he continued with his examination of the *Sun* tapes, beginning with the conversation recorded on the morning of 25 October 1994. He went into the betting system, noting that the code about which Vincent had been so brilliantly teased by Jerome Lynch had actually been mentioned by Grobbelaar. 'Mr Grobbelaar denies, when speaking about team information, that he used the

Wimbledon, Leeds and Dundee code. But here he is doing it on tape. He says he's only doing so as an invention, pretending to Mr Vincent.'

On 3 November Grobbelaar and Vincent had met again, and Grobbelaar had taken Vincent's £2,000. McCullough observed that, 'Between forming his plan, before 6 October and then, he had met Vincent three times and spoke with him twice on the telephone. Mr Grobbelaar accepts that he did not tell his wife (which may be understandable because of her disapproval of Vincent), he told no colleague at Southampton, or his management. He did not go to his solicitor, didn't go to the police. He didn't tell anyone. He took no steps to record the conversations and made no notes. When asked what evidence he would have, he said, "The money."'

'All he could do was go the police, say Vincent had put a proposal in the name of "Richard and Guy", and it would be his word against Vincent's. Grobbelaar would have expected that Vincent would simply deny the accusations. What hope was there, you may ask, that Grobbelaar would have been able to bring anyone to justice?

'What do the Vincent tapes tell you about what was going on in Mr Grobbelaar's mind? Is this the plainest admission of involvement in a corrupt scheme? Is this the plainest willingness to go along with Vincent's scheme? Or may it be, as Grobbelaar tells you, that he was leading Vincent along?'

McCullough was equally pointed when examining the meeting between Bruce Grobbelaar and the *Sun* reporters, John Troup and Guy Patrick, at Gatwick airport on 8 November. Grobbelaar's first response to their allegation that they had evidence against him had been, 'You're going to have to prove it first.'

'Is that response significant?' the judge asked the jury. 'Use your common sense about a guilty man's response. Use your common sense about an innocent man's response. Look at that response.'

Equally, when Grobbelaar denied taking the £2,000, the *Sun* men told him they had video evidence of him doing so. Grobbelaar had then twice sought confirmation: 'Have you got a video?' The judge remarked that, 'You may ask yourself why it matters to Mr Grobbelaar whether there was a video or not.'

The *Sun* reporters had asked Grobbelaar why, given his distrust of Vincent, he had not simply told him to go away. Grobbelaar responded by saying, 'I've never thrown a game in my life.'

McCullough asked, 'Was he given the opportunity to tell the *Sun* that he was making false admissions to lead Vincent on? Mr Grobbelaar says that, "I didn't know if these were the two who Vincent said were behind him." In other words, he didn't want to tell them he would report them to the police.'

But the *Sun* had asked him again, 'Why not say, "I don't want any more dealings. I don't want to get involved"?'

'Mr Grobbelaar's answer,' said McCullough, 'was not, "Because I'm stringing him along so that I can report him to the police, the FA and the PFA."'

'The *Sun* then asked why he said to Vincent, "I'm doing a Short Man on Saturday." The reply is not, "Because I'm stringing him along." The reply is, "You can run that story, you'll probably destroy me, destroy my marriage, what you'll get out of it, I don't know."'

McCullough carried on through the transcript of the interview, until Grobbelaar got to the point where he mentioned 'evidence against Vincent'. He then said, 'We're several pages into the tape before [the phrase] "evidence against Vincent" and even then you haven't had a clear admission that he was gathering evidence against Vincent.'

When considering the case against Segers, McCullough was equally fastidious in the detail with which he considered both the Crown's allegations and the defence's counter-arguments. He went through all the games which the Crown alleged had been connected with payments by Segers into his 'Gloves' account, detailing all the calls, meetings and financial transactions involved. Considering the defence claims that Segers was only ever paid for forecasting the results of Dutch football matches, the judge said, 'There is nothing to show that Mr Lim had any interest in Dutch football, or was passing on forecasts:

nothing to show that Mr Segers was doing forecasts. His magazines were unmarked. Mr Segers had struck out his note of Mr Lim's telephone number.

'There are two explanations. One: Segers had done forecasts, but fear of the FA caused him to remove the evidence. Two: He never forecasted. The Dutch matches were an invention to account for the £104,000 and hide his true relationship with Lim.'

A long account of the business dealings between Hans Segers and Ties International, and of the evidence given by Mr Thuys, then followed. Up to now, Segers had heard nothing to fear from McCullough's summing-up. But the judge's sharp eye for detail, and his insistence on proper evidence, began to tell when he turned to Segers' claims that he had planned a joint venture buying property with John Fashanu.

Segers had said his contribution to the project would be provided by money from Ties International, the sale of investment bonds and a small mortgage. The property would be in Segers' name, although Fashanu's company, Hanler Construction, would do the maintenance. As Fashanu was often out of the country, he gave Segers his share and Segers dealt with the estate agent Imran Khan.

One property in Cunningham Place – worth around £130,000 – was surveyed, and a solicitor was paid around £300, but the deal fell through. There was no documentary evidence that Segers or Fashanu had looked at any other properties. 'On that evidence, was there a joint venture to buy property between Mr Segers and Mr Fashanu?' asked McCullough. 'Or was that simply Mr Segers getting an idea from Mr Fashanu? The house was in Mr Segers' name alone. The solicitor was employed by Mr Segers. To what extent was Imran Khan involved with Mr Segers? You may think Mr Segers must have consulted Imran Khan on the advice of Mr Fashanu, but did he have any real interest in property apart from the one surveyed?

'How would he have paid for any property? ... The solicitor's bill was dated 14 June 1994. By then he had paid

£66,000 into his RNB account, of which £19,000 came from Mr Fashanu. How does that square with Imran Khan being told that £130,000 was immediately available in cash? Where was the rest to come from?

'For how long after June 1994 did Mr Segers' interest in property last? Imran Khan says four to six months, which takes you to October–December. No further house was surveyed. And what money was available? £30,000 had gone into the retirement fund. Of the Swiss money £70,000 had been spent on bonds. What was left in the Swiss account?

'The bank closed the account in March 1995. There was then £80,000–£90,000 in the account, which was transferred directly to Mr Fashanu. Up to that point, Mr Segers had withdrawn £12,500 from his account in cash.'

McCullough then began a series of calculations. It seemed as though we were in for yet another mind-numbing recitation of figures. But, as we would soon discover, the judge had a surprise in store. McCullough totted up all the money known to have gone in to Segers' RNB 'Gloves' account. It came to £130,500. He also calculated the amount that had either been withdrawn from the account or was still in it when the account was closed. That came to £167,500. 'Mr Segers told you he paid in no more than he says,' McCullough observed. 'So the extra £37,000 must have been earned by the bank. If you look at the balance of his account through the period, you may decide that the sooner everyone opens an account in the bank, the better for them.'

A sound halfway between a gasp and a giggle echoed round the court as the judge's audience reacted to what he had just said. Then he added another line: 'Or is there something wrong with the figures?

'The prosecution say that the property story is ridiculous. The reality is that since the £19,000 deposited in October 1994 had come from Indonesia, via Miss Kassa-Mapsi and Mr Fashanu, some plausible story had to be invented for giving the money to Mr Segers. They don't dispute that Mr Segers considered buying property, but the Crown point out that it came to nothing. So, say the Crown, he decided to construct an elaborate story that Mr Fashanu was an equal partner in a long-term venture, who had given Mr Segers three sums of money as a contribution. Not a single document evidences any such venture: no receipt for cash, no letter, nothing. All you have seen is a single cheque, written by Mr Segers to a solicitor. You haven't heard from Mr Fashanu. You haven't seen any documents from Mr Fashanu. It is not for Mr Segers to prove that he got what he says he got from Mr Fashanu. It is not for Mr Segers to prove that he got what he says he got from Mr Thuys. It is not for Mr Segers to prove that he got what he says he got from Mr Lim. It is for the Crown to prove. You've got to be sure that Dutch forecasting, Mr Thuys and property were not the source of the money that went into Mr Segers' account.'

With that, Mr Justice McCullough concluded the third day of his speech. It was, as it happened, Jerome Lynch's birthday, and the prosecution team had sent him a card. On the front was a Victorian engraving of a woman who had fallen over being helped to her feet by a kindly gentleman. 'Ice?' read the bubble coming from his mouth. 'No,' she was saying. 'It was the Scotch.' On the inside, hand-written in capital letters, were the words, 'HAPPY BIRTHDAY, BIG BOY', and the signatures of David Calvert-Smith and his juniors. No matter how serious matters became in the case of Lim and others, there was always jollity to be had somewhere about the place.

On the morning of Friday 1 August Mr Justice McCullough ran through the sequence of seven cash payments made by Hans Segers into his RNB 'Gloves' account, via the bank's Berkeley Square branch. The final payment was on 7 November, just a day before Bruce Grobbelaar was confronted at Gatwick airport, when Hans Segers paid £20,000 into his RNB account.

'There are indications that Mr Segers was not just paying in what had accumulated at home, or payments for his house,' said McCullough. 'Can you draw the conclusion he was paying in money recently given to him by Mr Lim or Mr Fashanu?'

He then went through the various interviews or statements

given to the police. Segers, he said, had lied with 'increasing elaboration and improbability', devising a story about stealing cars, he didn't know how, with a cousin who had died, who was the son of an aunt and uncle whose whereabouts were not known. 'Doubtless it was only the charm of the story which saved you from the tedium of being taken through 200 pages of transcript. I don't think I need say more.'

He drew attention to the lack of any contact between Grobbelaar and Segers. 'They didn't know either had a relationship with Mr Lim. They didn't know either was doing forecasts. Mr Lim didn't tell them. Obviously Mr Fashanu did not tell them either.'

He ran through the schedule of arrests, mentioned the various pieces of evidence found at the defendants' homes. 'Mr Lim agrees he has a shredder,' he reminded the jury. 'He got it for the sake of completeness. He didn't get rid of anything incriminating. Mrs Lim says there was no purge of documents. Why did he need a shredder?'

He then went on to highlight some of the major arguments put by both defence and prosecution. Since I have not reproduced the defence barristers' speeches, it is only fair to note the judge's distillations of the arguments that they put.

Lim, he said, would have run a huge risk of being caught in a corrupt scheme. The money from the Far East was not so great, seen through the eyes of phenomenally wealthy men. Cell-site evidence was not conclusive, so there was – to take one example – no evidence that Lim had been at Byron Drive on 25 November 1993. Lim had a very good memory: he didn't need to write down telephone numbers. Vincent only gave one piece of evidence against him – the meeting at the Manchester Hilton.

For his part, Fashanu was a humanitarian and stressed his links with Unicef and charity work. He was Wimbledon's most prolific goal scorer. If he was corrupt and being paid by Wimbledon, why did he retire from the club? It would be unlikely that Wimbledon would achieve their highest-ever place in the league if their goalkeeper and striker were corrupt. Fashanu was taking a huge risk to his status as a hero and role-model. His business with Joseph continued after the *Sun* allegations and their interest in African projects was real, even if it was not in writing.

Segers' defence was that Thuys was evasive and unbelievable. The telephone calls might seem suspicious, but not when one saw Dutch fixtures. Segers too stood to risk his family, income and hero status. He had consistently been picked by Wimbledon throughout his time at the club, and had been given an improved contract in 1994. Would Wimbledon have reached sixth in the league with a corrupt keeper? When they played without him for fourteen matches, they didn't win a single one: the first game he came back, they won. His lies to the police were caused by fear he had broken FA rules. The Swiss payments followed wins and draws, as well as losses.

In Grobbelaar's case, the defence pointed to his charitable work in Britain and Africa and the enormous respect in which he was held in Zimbabwe and on Merseyside. Again, if he was caught, he would risk everything. They emphasized that the jury should not rely on Vincent. Grobbelaar was stringing him along, intending to report him and his associates to the authorities. The stories he told were all made up.

In general, McCullough then remarked upon the enormous amounts of money received by Lim and Fashanu before Lim met Grobbelaar or Segers. 'Though you may have your suspicions, the Crown can point to no specific reason why the money was paid, nor to any other players in the frame before Mr Grobbelaar or Mr Segers. The Crown cannot explain why the earlier money arrived.'

About Mondoro, McCullough observed, 'There is no documentary evidence to indicate Mr Fashanu was ever interested in Mondoro, or that Lim was ever interested in Mondoro. You just have their assertion. Mondoro was simply used as an excuse for meetings. Even if Mr Lim was interested, he would never have gone up to Manchester simply to see a business plan. When Mr Grobbelaar and Mr Lim spoke on 30 September 1993, Vincent wasn't taken to the meeting. Mr Lim wasn't at Byron Drive on 25 November, but Mondoro was said to be one of the topics discussed – Vincent was left outside in the car. The Crown invite you to say it wasn't about Mondoro at all.'

The jury were then briefly sent out of the courtroom in order to give the bar a chance to make any observations concerning the judge's summing-up, before being formally asked to consider their verdict. Jerome Lynch was insistent that not enough had been made of the absence of any evidence showing withdrawals from Lim's and Fashanu's accounts that corresponded with payments to Grobbelaar or Segers. 'That has another side to it,' mused McCullough, but he agreed to remind the jury of the issue.

So the last words they heard before retiring were as follows. 'There is a general defence point that, on the evidence of his accounts, Mr Lim cannot be shown to have been able to fund £40,000 on 25 November 1993. There is no indication that Mr Lim withdrew or had £40,000. Equally, there is no evidence that Mr Fashanu had withdrawn enough to fund £40,000.

'But, say the prosecution, there must have been some other source of funds you haven't heard about. When Mr Fashanu paid in £31,500 to the RNB on 19 October 1993, there was no corresponding withdrawal to show how he got that. When he paid in £30,000, there was no corresponding withdrawal to show how he got that. So here's £60,000 in a fortnight, and no indication of where it came from.

'Mr Lim was in his bank or building society in Kilburn High Road on 25 November 1993 and he paid in £22,000 cash. There is no entry to show where that came from. There must have been a source of money.

'[Look at] the ease with which Mr Littlechild brought 100,000 dollars in travellers' cheques into the UK, cashed them at the Bank of East Asia and turned them into sterling cash. He gave £20,000 cash to Mace.

'[Look at] Admission 95, Mr Littlechild's evidence that Mr Fashanu paid a whole lot of money into BusinessMart: £155,123, add on a further £26,000. If Mr Fashanu paid those sums to Mr Littlechild, there's no indication of where they came from, no corresponding withdrawals.'

And with that analysis of the defendants' financial affairs, Mr Justice McCullough invited the jury to retire to consider their verdicts.

# 26

## 'Mr Foreman, Have You Reached Your Verdict?'

The jury were not expected to take long to reach their verdicts. It would not, most people agreed, be reasonable to expect anything in the few hours that remained of Friday – not unless we were to have another OJ on our hands – but given the frequency and detail with which the evidence had been rehearsed in court, David Calvert-Smith, for one, seemed confident that there would be an answer by Monday. It would not, however, be an answer he would hear. As we would discover on re-assembling after the weekend, he had a prior engagement: a grandstand seat at the World Athletics Championships in Athens, where he would spend the following week.

By these last days of the trial, Winchester Crown Court had filled up again with all the media representatives who felt – or, more accurately, whose editors and producers felt – that even if the proceedings themselves had been of little interest, the verdict certainly would be. The massed banks of TV crews and photographers reassembled at the foot of the courtyard outside, looking damp and bedraggled in the rain which now began to fall and continued throughout the jury's deliberations. The press box itself was suddenly filled with telly people, barging the regulars out of their usual spots, but bringing an undoubted glamour to the place. It might take an astonishing gaggle of directors, researchers, cameramen and presenters to get a thirty-second item on the air, but a remarkable proportion of them were young, female and dressed to kill.

The defendants spent most of their time huddled in canteen conclaves with their wives, while their lawyers held court surrounded by happily fawning hacks. The general mood at the start of the long wait was mixed. The defence counsel – well aware that McCullough's summing-up had contained some extremely pointed questions for the jury to consider – verged on the pessimistic. David Calvert-Smith was equally wary. He had good reason to feel that he had come very close to gaining a conviction on Count Three (Grobbelaar's £2,000 bribe), first time around. But he also believed that the jury could be split, both between themselves and between the defendants. Segers, in particular, had done well and had, he thought, impressed the judge.

The media-people, meanwhile, busied themselves for the final result. All the broadcast journalists had prepared background pieces, covering every possible verdict. This was a phenomenon I had encountered at the first trial, too. As a supposed expert on the case, I was interviewed by a number of news teams. They would set up a camera in a suitably photogenic location and ask: 'So, what does this guilty verdict say about the state of British football?' I would give an answer, whereupon the camera would be turned through a few degrees, a new backdrop found, and another question asked: 'Bruce Grobbelaar has been found not guilty: How do you think Chris Vincent will be feeling tonight?'

The *Sun* team had long since completed a sixteen-page supplement on the case, to be printed in the event of a guilty verdict. They had, they claimed, been researching with particular zeal into the life and business of John Fashanu. 'He won't be able to get a job as a shoe-shine boy by the time we've finished with him,' said the normally affable Paul Thompson.

Others, meanwhile, were trying to organize their real lives. At lunchtime on Monday 4 August, Trevor Burke could be found pacing up and down the mezzanine outside the court canteen, an anguished look on his face and a mobile phone clamped to his ear. He was trying to book a holiday. The plane tickets were fixed, the car hired, the places on the golf course reserved . . . but there seemed to be a problem trying to find a hotel room. 'If Jesus comes back to earth, he'd better not pick Spain in mid-August. He'll never get in!' Burke exclaimed. I didn't have the heart to point out that there hadn't been any room at the inn the first time around, either.

The jury, meanwhile, were having technical difficulties. On Tuesday they wanted to watch the football matches and the Grobbelaar/Vincent tapes, and their jury room was not fully equipped. They also wondered if they could start every day at 10.30, instead of 10 a.m. 'Except for Friday,' said the judge, reading the foreman's note, 'which they are content to do if we're still here.' Oh, how we laughed.

McCullough was in no mood to hurry the jury up. 'This has gone on for forty-two days. It's insulting to suppose that they could decide in a day and a half. They listened to the summing-up for three days, speeches for five days, many days of evidence. There's no sign at all that they're locked.'

Wednesday . . . still it rained. TV presenters who had booked into local hotels on Monday morning were rapidly running out of clean clothes to wear on screen whenever the big moment came. By now the judge and the bar were beginning to debate when, if at all, to ask for a majority verdict. 'They've been out sixteen hours,' observed McCullough. 'If you divide that by seven [the amount of judgements that would have to be made] that only leaves a little over two hours per verdict.'

Everyone had their own theory about what was going on in the jury room. When word got out that the jury were looking at the final Vincent–Grobbelaar meeting, Sue Greenfield remarked that they could be reaching their decisions in reverse order. Trevor Burke raised a sceptical eyebrow. 'Sue,' he said, 'this is not *Miss World*.'

From time to time, we would all be called into court. Each time the tannoy burst into life one felt a brief surge of adrenaline, a pounding of the heart. Hans Segers, in particular, seemed to be feeling the stress, hugging Astrid before going back into the box. I passed the BBC man, Adam Mynott, heading into court on one of these occasions. He grinned. 'There's no theatre, no sport, nothing quite like the atmosphere when a jury reaches its verdict.'

By the third or fourth time we were called, some finer points of courtroom fieldcraft were becoming obvious. The *Daily Mail*'s Bill Mouland, for example, well aware of his paper's interest in the female angle, had managed to find the one seat in the press gallery from which one could see both the defendants and their wives, sitting in the front row of the public gallery upstairs.

The swelling numbers of reporters had done wonders for the local restaurant trade. Green's Wine Bar, just a couple of hundred yards downhill from the court, was said to have installed a new floor, paid for by the proceeds of lunching hacks during the Rosemary West case. Local gossip maintained that the bar had made an extra £12,000 during the first Grobbelaar trial, and had built new toilets in expectation of the second. Some of the regular trial folk virtually lived at Green's in the off-duty hours. Astrid Segers, for example, only ever saw the *Sun*'s Nigel Cairns taking photographs, or supping in Green's: 'Do you own this place and take photographs part-time?' she asked him in all innocence.

By Thursday the weather had turned hot and steamy – a little reminder that this was a case whose heart was in the tropics. Some keen telly-watchers claimed to have spotted David Calvert-Smith among the crowd at the Olympic Stadium – although whether he was, as they claimed, wearing a white hat and waving a Union Jack, I rather doubted. His team, though, were becoming less optimistic by the minute: 'The longer they stay out, the worse it is for us,' one of them told me.

Then, out of the blue, came an extraordinary development. The jury had spotted a mistake in the transcript of the Grobbelaar tapes. A conversation at the very end of the final meeting had been misattributed. It appeared that virtually the last words between the two men, as they left Vincent's flat, with

Vincent passing the envelope containing the £2,000 to Grobbelaar, went like this:

Vincent: 'Do you want to carry this?'

Grobbelaar: 'No, no, no . . . that's yours.'

Vincent: 'I don't have a jacket, you carry it.'

A deputation of lawyers was sent away to see if they agreed with this new interpretation. They returned with the news that the jury was 'very probably' correct. Mr Justice McCullough, a man who took enormous pains to ensure the precision of evidence, was not best pleased: 'Very probably? Am I to say it is very probable? So this is agreed as the best that can be said . . . ?'

The fact that the jury had uncovered evidence which appeared to show Grobbelaar's unwillingness to take a bribe immediately altered the entire mood of the court building. This was the part of the case in which the prosecution seemed to be strongest – they thought they had caught their man red-handed on tape – but the jury were clearly sceptical. It now was all but certain how they would react to the rest of the charges, where the evidence was far more open to debate. 'Who says the jury system doesn't work?' asked an exultant Trevor Burke. 'The forty-sixth day of the second trial, and it takes a juror to spot something.'

Desmond De Silva felt sure he had seen a flicker of irritation cross the judge's face when he read the jury foreman's note: had it contained some other piece of information, he wondered? In De Silva's opinion the defence speeches had been crucial, since they had been the first opportunity for the defence to put its case together. He thought the Crown had made a major mistake by ignoring the games completely: 'If they'd had to go through the match tapes, there was bound to have been someone on the jury who'd think they'd noticed something.'

Finally, on Friday afternoon, after twenty-six hours and twenty minutes of deliberation, the jury returned their verdicts. The atmosphere in the court was strangely subdued – a bit like a film when someone has told you what the ending is going to be. The foreman rose and was asked if the jury had reached a verdict on Count One of the charge, in the case of Heng Suan Lim. They had, and it was unanimous: not guilty.

Next came John Fashanu, on the same charge: not guilty. Up in the visitors' gallery a sob echoed through the air as Melissa heard the verdict. Down beneath her Fashanu bit his lip, trying to fight back his emotions.

Hans Segers: not guilty. Now it was Astrid's turn to gasp.

Count Two, Heng Suan Lim: not guilty. Now the barristers began to shake one another's hands, offering mutual congratulations. When Fashanu was found not guilty, he shook hands with Lim. But when the first not guilty verdict was delivered on Bruce Grobbelaar he remained impassive in the box. He still had one more to go.

The jury foreman came to Count Three, against Grobbelaar alone . . . no decision yet.

The judge told the other three that they were discharged. As their names were called out, Fashanu and Segers bowed to the jury and left. Finally Bruce Grobbelaar was left alone in the box, standing rigidly to attention as always.

In the immediate aftermath of the verdicts, reporters scurried to and fro like flocks of anxious starlings, trying to find defendants to interview. Henri Brandman, John Fashanu's solicitor, read a statement on his client's behalf. John, he said, was greatly relieved. It had been a terrible strain over several years. Now he looked forward to spending the rest of his life with his family, without the burden of this hanging over him. He had always maintained his innocence. He had said 'Not guilty' several years ago and now the jury had come back and confirmed that view.

In the brilliant sunshine that had broken through, bathing the courtyard in light, Hans Segers said it had been a nightmare but this was a great result. 'It's an absolutely brilliant day, and I just want to get home to my children and tell them the good news.' Heng Suan Lim was 'very, very happy and very relieved'.

'John, give us a high-five, mate!' shouted the *Sun*'s irrepressible Nigel Cairns, as Fashanu prepared to get into his

Mercedes to drive away. Fash grinned, kissed the lovely Melissa and stepped into the car.

Amidst the general revelry there were some long faces, notably among the *Sun* reporters – who had hoped, above all, that the verdict would vindicate what they saw as a legitimate piece of investigative reporting – and the police officers who had worked on the case. Detective Inspector Brian Mitchell, a few of his officers, Simon Hughes, Paul Thompson and I repaired to the Bell Inn, on the road out of town, to sink a few pints of mutual commiseration. The beers were just being ordered when Bruce Grobbelaar's solicitor, David Hewitt, walked in with a couple of other members of the defence team. One of the coppers, displaying good sportsmanship above and beyond the call of duty, offered to buy them a drink. 'To show there's no hard feelings.'

'I'll have a half,' said Hewitt. Then he changed his mind. 'Actually, to show there's no hard feelings make it a pint!'

Outside in the beer garden there were long faces all round. Simon Hughes's lugubrious, oyster-eyed features were perfect for the occasion. Even Brian Mitchell – a tall, solidly handsome thirty-three-year-old who looked like the sort of man every mother would wish her daughter brought home – was visibly depressed. He had spent two years and nine months on the case. A man whose career had previous had 'fast-track' written all over it now found himself unexpectedly derailed. 'Oh well,' said Hughesy. 'One day you'll look back on this and laugh.'

'Not in this fucking century,' muttered Mitchell.

Oddly enough, the police felt no resentment at all for the defendants who had frustrated them. They all liked the quartet as men, and – like every other man in the neighbourhood – loved Astrid Segers. Their next job was returning all the possessions seized from the defendants. It would be no problem, they thought, except that John Fashanu might crow a bit.

Like passionate football supporters whose side had just lost a big game the disconsolate crew of policemen and reporters went through all the what-ifs and might-have-beens of the trial. Was there anything anyone could have done? Any different course of action that might have produced a different result?

The police were irked, to put it mildly, by the feeling that the prosecution had not used all the ammunition available to them. They had wanted the jury to see all of the Grobbelaar tapes, to get some picture – not, as Grobbelaar himself had admitted in court, a particularly flattering one – of the man beyond the bare bones of evidence. But the prosecution had refused, apparently saying that they didn't mind ruining the men's careers, but they would not ruin their marriages. Since any marriage would have been severely stressed by a guilty verdict, and since two of the four had admitted to infidelities during the course of the first trial, these seemed like unnecessary scruples. But David Calvert-Smith was always a man who played fair, even if nobody else did.

The police thought, too, that they had footballing evidence against John Fashanu, in particular a 1991 game against Sheffield United in which he was twice seen apparently handling the ball in his own penalty area. But would that really have made any difference? Their belief was that the tape helped to explain the money that had been paid out to Lim and Fashanu before Segers and Grobbelaar became involved. But there may have been perfectly good explanations for those incidents, if they had taken place, which could have been advanced in Fashanu's defence. Any ordinary football match contains a host of disputed decisions that provoke heated, unresolvable arguments. And the case had clearly demonstrated that disputes which may divide fans, players or TV pundits can never be settled with the standard of proof required in a criminal court.

The *Sun* men were equally frustrated. None of their additional material on the defendants would now run. It was not the first time work had been wasted. The *Sun* had made two expeditions to the Far East in search of information. On the second of these they had found an Australian footballer who had played in the Malaysian league and who had told a local reporter that he had regularly taken the field knowing what the final score of the match would be, so great had been the extent of corruption in the local game. When the *Sun* tracked him down, however, he had clammed up, terrified that he would never work again if he spoke to them.

They were angry, too, that information they had gleaned about the Selangor team had never been brought before the court or used in cross-examination. Two Selangor players, they had discovered, had been convicted of match-fixing within a year of the tournament in which Bruce Grobbelaar had played. And Bruce, they claimed, had been the only British-based player invited to play as a guest in that tournament.

That was fascinating, but what did it prove? Grobbelaar was not accused of corruption in Malaysia, and no one at any stage had suggested that he had been corrupt out there. If it served to underline that there were a number of remarkable coincidences between what he had said to Chris Vincent on the *Sun* tapes and what had actually happened, well there were more than enough of those coincidences already and they clearly had not served to convince either jury.

For myself, I was drained, frustrated and hopelessly torn between my gut feelings about the charges that had been brought against Lim and others, and my rational analysis of the case that had twice been played out in court. Having spent the best part of a week going through the *Sun* tapes frame by frame with Chris Vincent, having watched extracts from them again and again in court, and having twice seen David Calvert-Smith cross-examine Bruce Grobbelaar with steely, forensic intensity, I still believed that they were exactly what they purported to be – a series of discussions about events that had actually taken place.

Then again, having repeatedly watched the games upon which the case against Bruce Grobbelaar was based, and having listened to the expert analysis of those games, I could not say that Grobbelaar had done anything nefarious to influence the outcome of those games, nor that he had conceded one single goal that would otherwise not have been scored. Not beyond a reasonable doubt.

What, then, of the financial and telephone evidence against

Fashanu, Lim and Segers? Their explanations of why they had been paid so much money from known gamblers in the Far East – or not been paid that money, in Segers' case – lacked any documentary proof whatsoever. Huge amounts of cash had been handed out without a single contract, invoice or receipt. Something odd had been going on, that seemed certain. But 'something odd' was not enough. Had the Crown been able to prove, beyond a reasonable doubt, that the money had been paid as part of a scheme to corruptly influence the outcomes of specific football matches? No, they had not . . . not beyond a reasonable doubt.

The two glaring weaknesses in the Crown's case were the games themselves and the Far Eastern connection. Prior to the first trial, a *Sun* team consisting of reporters, a photographer and a lawyer had made their first journey to Indonesia to try to track down Johannes Joseph and his associates. It proved impossible. The men could not be found.

When the *Sun* returned from that first trip to the Far East without any solid leads, the police had known that there was no point in going out there themselves. They had no legal authority overseas, no power to detail or interrogate suspects. The only circumstances in which it would have been worth pursuing enquiries in Indonesia, Malaysia or Singapore would have been if they had known exactly whom they were going to speak to, what questions they would ask and what answers they would receive.

Fair enough, but there were still arguments that could have been put more fully and more clearly in court by the prosecution. For example, one of the remarks that one heard time and time again when discussing the case was, 'They can't be guilty, because it's not possible for one player to fix a football match.' Everyone agrees that it is very difficult to do so. Even by the prosecution's own account Bruce Grobbelaar had only managed to lose one out of five games. But whatever people in England may think, there are people in the Far East who believe that games can be fixed, and who have successfully managed to fix them.

Even as the second trial was proceeding, an international under-21 tournament was being staged in Malaysia. So concerned were the authorities about the possibility that players would be corrupted that every team had to stay in specific FIFA-approved hotels, under constant guard, lest anyone try to bribe them. If you belonged to a Malaysian or Indonesian syndicate, and if you had pulled off successful scams at home, you might very well think it would be possible to do the same thing in other countries, too.

Which leads to another question that was never fully explored: what was the true status of Johannes Joseph, Lo Bon Swe, Benny Santoso, Sutanto, Lukito and all the rest? Were they, as the defence put it, enormously wealthy men who liked an innocent (if, strictly speaking, illegal) flutter amongst themselves? Or were they on the other side of the deal – were they running the book?

During the examination-in-chief in the second trial, Lim told Jerome Lynch, 'Mr Joseph has never been a bookie.' He said that he was one of a number of friends who simply bet against each other – although on a scale that dwarfed any normal, friendly punt. Joseph, he told David Calvert-Smith, 'Bet week in, week out at an average of £15,000 per game, for three or four games.'

But the court was also told by Lim – even if the charts had not made it self-evident – that he passed on information to Lo Bon Swe and Joseph more or less interchangeably. So those two at least cannot have been betting against each other. It was agreed, too, that money from Lukito was effectively money from Joseph: again a sign that they were in concert, not in competition. So here were a group of individuals all engaged in the same enterprise. What was it?

'Of course I think they're bookmakers,' said David Calvert-Smith when I put the question to him one day.

I was puzzled. Was there some reason why he could not put this idea before the court, or develop it in cross-examination? I had discovered in the past that what seemed like fascinating information did not qualify as legal evidence.

'But I have!' protested Calvert-Smith. 'I continually refer to them as a "syndicate".'

It was, I'm afraid, a subtlety that had been lost on me, and, I suspect, the jury. But the bookmaking argument might have had some power, in several respects. Jerome Lynch had argued, tellingly, that the system of betting in the Far East appeared to offer no better than even odds. That being the case, what was the point in these mysterious Far Eastern gamblers splashing out vast sums on bribes to players if the very best they could hope to do was double their money?

It was a fair comment. But it is also fair to say that someone in the Far East thinks that games are financially worth fixing, even if that someone is not Johannes Joseph. And if you are the bookie, rather than the punter, you do not have to win every time to make the business worthwhile. Casinos make their profits from tiny margins in their favour. To a bent bookie, one successfully corrupted game in a hundred is like the white space on a roulette wheel – it is all the edge they need to keep ahead of the punters.

None of those hypothetical observations, though, did anything to prove that Joseph and Co. were bookmakers, still less that they had attempted to corrupt English football via Lim and others. The defence's argument that they were merely supplying forecasts of matches would apply equally well, whatever the status of their Far Eastern associates.

What might have happened if I had not given Chris Vincent his papers back? What if I had kept the Mondoro business plan and handed it to the police on the Saturday morning, hours after Bruce Grobbelaar had denied its existence? Would that have demolished his alibi for the Manchester airport meeting with Lim? Vincent could still have forgotten to bring it to the meeting, thereby embarrassing Bruce Grobbelaar and forcing him to meet Lim alone.

What if Lim had been asked why he only seemed to call the Far East from games in which Segers or Grobbelaar were involved and never from any other games, between any other teams, anywhere? Would it have made any difference if that interesting omission had been pointed out?

And would it have helped the jury if their attention had been drawn to the inconsistencies in the various accounts of the first meeting between Fashanu, Grobbelaar and Lim on 3 November 1992? In his evidence to the first trial, Grobbelaar said that forecasting had not been mentioned at that meeting. Instead, Fashanu had called him afterwards to say that Lim would be getting in touch to discuss the subject, which he then did.

In the second trial, however, Lim told Jerome Lynch that Fashanu had suggested at the meeting that Grobbelaar could do forecasts for him. 'It was a great pleasure for me to meet a legend like Bruce,' he said. 'I wasn't very keen [about his doing forecasts]. I did not feel I needed to have another English forecaster because I knew the English game very well. But since the suggestion came from John and Bruce was a legend, I had no choice but to say yes and give it a try.'

Was that discrepancy merely the natural and entirely innocent result of attempting to recall events that were now almost five years old? Or was it two men not quite getting their stories right?

On the subject of Bruce Grobbelaar, a similar question arose about a telephonic dog that stubbornly refused to bark. Grobbelaar said that Chris Vincent had mentioned the Newcastle, Manchester United, Norwich and Coventry games to him in the snooker room of the De Vere Hotel, suggesting that they might have been ones he had tried to throw, even though only one of them had actually been lost. The jury were shown, in extreme detail, the series of coincidences between these games and calls between Lim and Grobbelaar; calls between Lim and the Far East; at least one meeting between Lim and Grobbelaar; and Lim's presence at two games.

But the jury were not shown a single example of a game which involved Grobbelaar and had been attended by Lim, or surrounded by the sort of 'back-to-back calls' described by David Calvert-Smith but which had *not* been mentioned during the *Sun* tapes. To judge by the evidence presented in court, the only Grobbelaar games which demonstrated the pattern of behaviour the Crown saw as evidence of attempted corruption were, by complete coincidence, the ones that Chris Vincent plucked from thin air in the snooker room at the De Vere Grand Harbour Hotel and which Grobbelaar then described on videotape. Had there been evidence of innocent calls and meetings around entirely non-controversial games, would the defence not have been at pains to present it?

There was another piece of evidence never explored by the Crown, perhaps because it was, at best, circumstantial. Vincent claimed to have told Stephen Wundke that the payments made into Mondoro via Ace Gold and Leisure after 25 November 1993 would be the first of many. More would follow over the New Year period. Wundke was due to be away in Africa for the holiday period, so he passed the message on to his partner at Ace Golf and Leisure, Ian Chilton. Sure enough, Chilton made a statement, read out to the first trial, to the effect that he had been told by Wundke to expect large sums of cash to be paid into Mondoro. He was never told what the source would be.

There is no independent evidence whatever to connect these hypothetical cash payments to Bruce Grobbelaar. Still less is there any evidence – other than Vincent's own allegations – that the money was to have been earned by corrupt means. Neither Wundke nor Chilton was given any indication whatsoever of any match-fixing scheme. But there is, at least, a coincidence of circumstances. At Christmas 1993, more than nine months before his showdown with Grobbelaar in Southampton, Vincent was discussing a cash-instalment scheme that roughly coincided with two of the games which – in the defence's account – he would pluck out of thin air during that mysterious conversation in the hotel snooker room.

Two last post-trial observations: Bruce Grobbelaar's claim to the *Sun* reporters at Gatwick airport that he had lost '£50,000–60,000' on Mondoro, and his evidence in court that he had lost 'around £60,000', only made sense if you included the money paid into the company by Chris Vincent after 25 November 1993. But his defence relied upon the assertions that he knew nothing about those payments and that he had given the 'sock-drawer' money to Vincent to invest in a real estate deal in South Africa. Without that cash, his losses were closer to £40,000 than £60,000. If this apparent inconsistency had been pointed out, would it have challenged the jury's evident and unanimous faith in his innocence?

Similarly, Grobbelaar told the court that he was intending to keep the £2,000 given to him by Vincent at the end of their third taped meeting, to be used as evidence against Vincent. Yet during the course of the videotape of that meeting – in a section not played to the jury – he could be heard offering to let Vincent keep the money in order to pay off Mondoro's outstanding debts in Victoria Falls. Was that offer consistent with his need for hard evidence against Vincent? Or was it consistent with a relationship in which Grobbelaar's extra-curricular earnings were the source of Mondoro's funds?

I spent Thursday evening, and much of the night, asking myself questions like that. And in the end, I concluded that none of it would have made any difference. The Crown's case, though packed with circumstantial detail, lacked vital answers. It had always felt oddly insubstantial: smoke and mirrors, rather than a smoking gun. And there was not one unbiased, entirely reputable witness who could stand before the jury and give them evidence against the defendants which they could entirely trust – enough, that is, to use as the basis for sending four likeable, celebrated men to prison. Chatting to Brian Mitchell one day, about halfway through the second case, I had said, 'You've got the garlic. And you've got the cross. But you don't have the stake through the heart.' Nothing had happened to make me change my mind.

But all was not quite what it seemed that Thursday night. Trials, like games of football, can be packed with incident right up to the final whistle. On the morning of Friday 8 August the jury were sent out to consider their final verdict. They were reminded by the judge that it had not been part of Mr Grobbelaar's defence that he had taken the money just because Vincent did not have a jacket. He had said that he had the money on him, but was going to hand it to the authorities as evidence against Vincent. (In other words, one might think, don't get carried away with your own detective work.)

While the jury were out, the defendants' lawyers made their application for costs. This was a crucial issue for John Fashanu in particular, who had not received legal aid and whose costs were said to be in excess of £650,000.

Trevor Burke pointed out to Mr Justice McCullough that when a person had been tried and acquitted there was always a cost order granted in his favour 'unless there were positive reasons for not doing so'. Specifically, a defendant had to have brought proceedings upon himself and acted in such a way as to lead the authorities to believe that the case against him was stronger than it actually was. In Mr Fashanu's case, 'A conscientious and industrious jury have considered their verdicts over many days and unanimously acquitted him.'

'That's not the point,' replied the judge. 'The point is, did his own conduct bring suspicion upon himself? He chose to receive very considerable sums from the Far East in the names of other people, and that can only have led the prosecution to believe the sums were obtained nefariously, coupled with the total absence of any indication of business activities that could account for the proper use of those monies.'

McCullough also drew attention to the role of Melissa Kassa-Mapsi. Burke objected: she had not been charged, and had never been less than cooperative with the Crown. The argument pounded back and forth, with both men showing equal determination to fight their corner. 'In such cases, where because of their own conduct defendants bring suspicion on themselves, it is proper that the public should not bear the costs of the defence,' insisted McCullough.

'That is an indirect punishment,' retorted Burke. 'Mr Fashanu is having to pay an indirect fine of several hundred thousand pounds to establish his innocence. All he has done is to maintain his absolute right to say, "Prove it, if you can."' The Crown, he said, had brought nothing new to the second case. 'Even their speech was virtually identical. They persisted with their allegations, despite the fact that they had not been able to persuade a jury.'

'There were no documents,' insisted McCullough. 'Either there never were any, or there were documents and they have been destroyed or removed before the police arrived.'

'One thing is certain,' Burke fired back, 'the money coming from Joseph was certainly not for corrupt football payments. The Crown have never been able to prove their case. To stay silent is not to provoke the Crown into thinking that they have a stronger case.'

Burke argued that if defendants felt that their silence would be taken as grounds for refusing costs, they would effectively be forced to abandon that right. 'Mr Fashanu may conduct his business affairs in a way some people might think curious, but he has lost his *Gladiators* contract, lost his *Sun* contract, he has not been able to earn a living, has had to sell properties to pay his legal fees. This is a proper case for tax costs.'

McCullough remained entirely unmoved. He formally denied costs, citing the reasons he had given to Burke and saying that, 'In these circumstances it seems clear that Mr Fashanu's own conduct brought suspicion on himself and led the prosecution into thinking that the case against Mr Fashanu was stronger than it was.'

When Desmond De Silva made a costs application on behalf of Hans Segers – who had received legal aid, but was still liable for some £40,000 – that, too, was rejected. McCullough ruled that, 'His introduction to the police was that he had paid in £100,000, all in cash, none of it declared for tax purposes. There were no documents. Either there never were, or they had been destroyed. When given the chance to explain the money, he told lie upon lie. He clearly brought suspicion on himself and misled the prosecution into thinking that the case against him was stronger than it was.'

After twenty-seven hours and forty-nine minutes of deliberation, the jury announced that they had still been unable to reach a verdict on Count Three against Bruce Grobbelaar. They were told that the judge would accept a majority verdict with which ten jurors agreed.

At 2.25 p.m. the jury returned again. Grobbelaar, bolt upright in the dock, gulped – the only sign of emotion on an otherwise impassive face. After thirty hours and thirty-three minutes of deliberation, the foreman revealed that the jury were deadlocked. For the second time, the case had been hung. The jury were discharged. The Crown then formally announced that they would not be bringing a third trial against Grobbelaar alone. A verdict of not guilty was therefore entered and Bruce Grobbelaar was discharged. In the public gallery, John Fashanu rose to his feet and gave a thumbs-up.

The judge then addressed the police who had worked on the case. 'I commend Mr Mitchell and all who worked with him. The compilation of the charts must have been very, very time-consuming. Quite regardless of the result, you are commended for the industry you have shown.'

He then said something which came as a surprise to those who had heard the remarks he had made at the very start of the trial about Mitchell's interview with Hans Segers. 'I particularly commend Detective Inspector Mitchell on the manner and conduct of his two interviews with Mr Segers. If only that manner of conducting interviews was adopted by more detectives, a lot of time would be saved. The way the Inspector exposed [Segers'] lies without any pressure on him was exemplary.'

While Mitchell, his career prospects restored to glowing health, beamed in his seat, McCullough thanked the jury for the application they had shown throughout the case that had gone on far longer than expected. 'If you have holidays coming, I hope you have happy holidays,' he said.

And so it was in a festive mood that we all trooped outside for the last time to see Bruce Grobbelaar and Debbie Grobbelaar emerge from the court, arm-in-arm, to greet the waiting media before disappearing to the town hall for a full-scale press-conference. As Grobbelaar was talking Desmond De Silva drove off in an open-topped Mercedes 280. On the edge of the scrum stood a man in tight Armani jeans, with a matching Armani belt, a white T-shirt and cool Persol shades. This was Jerome Lynch, who had speedily changed into mufti. His junior arrived to pick him up in a surprisingly modest Vauxhall. 'It's only rented for the day!' he exclaimed, as if to reassure those of us who had created an altogether more stylish picture of a modern media barrister.

It was over – for the time being. The FA and the Inland Revenue still had investigations to carry out, and none of the defendants had emerged entirely unscathed. John Fashanu was facing £650,000 in costs, plus possible back-taxes (plus interest and any fines that might be levied) on the £260,000-odd which he had received from the Far East, plus the £61,500 deposited in cash in his bank from sources unknown. The Inland Revenue might well have an interest, too, in the origins of the £243,000 apparently invested by him in BusinessMart's duty free store at Lagos airport. Allowing for the income he had forgone as a direct result of the trial, he was looking at a total loss of around £1 million.

Richard Lim's costs, which he had not attempted to claim, were said to approach £30,000. He had admitted receiving close to £600,000 during his time in the UK, none of it taxed as yet. If the Inland Revenue felt inclined to pursue a claim against him, complete with interest payments dating back to the beginning of the decade, the bill would be mighty indeed.

Hans Segers owed an estimated £40,000 in costs and had admitted to depositing £104,000 in cash in a Swiss bank account, specifically to avoid the Inland Revenue. The judge's calculations had also indicated that his Swiss account might well have contained monies as yet unaccounted for and, presumably, untaxed.

Bruce Grobbelaar, who also made no application for costs, was said to be facing legal bills of around £50,000, plus a potential tax liability on the £8,000–10,000 he had admitted receiving from Lim, and the £35,000 'sock-drawer' stash. Including the money he had lost on Mondoro, the events that had unfolded since he met Vincent had cost him the best part of £120,000. Even had he been found guilty as charged, the monies he was alleged to have received from Lim amounted to less than £45,000 and his defence that he had been passing information and forecasts to Lim led to an FA fine of £10,000. By any reckoning, he had had the worst of the deal.

The lawyers, on the other hand, were far better off. Informed estimates put the average fees for the four leading defence barristers, taken over both trials, at somewhere in excess of £200,000 a man. Some refreshers are clearly very refreshing indeed.

But what of the reason they had all assembled in Winchester in the first place? What of Christopher Vincent? Far from making himself rich from his revelations, he had given a substantial proportion of his original *Sun* payment to Bernice Bala'c in the form of cash, jewellery and holidays. He had pocketed around £20,000 from further sales of his story and unrepaid loans from people, including this author. His money from this book totalled £25,500, of which a considerable proportion was retained by his bankruptcy receivers.

At the end of it all, having been the only person in the entire saga to have done any time in jail, he was still facing his own trial for attempting to pervert the course of justice. And so it was, after more than five years of ducking, diving, scrabbling to make a living, selling his best mate to a tabloid newspaper, telling and retelling his story to journalists, policemen, authors and lawyers, spending long months of poverty and imprisonment, facing hours of public humiliation and contempt in the witness box, seeing all his hopes of profit come to nought . . . after all that, Christopher James Edward Vincent was the only person involved in the whole sorry saga who stood any chance at all of being found guilty.

# 27

# A Bad Man in Africa

For six months or so after the case had ended Chris Vincent remained in England, living in and around Windsor, earning his keep by doing a series of odd-jobs for friends in the area. Twice a day, he had to report to the local police station. Despite the fact that he had twice given evidence against Bruce Grobbelaar, John Fashanu and Richard Lim, he was still facing a charge of attempting to pervert the course of justice by offering not to give evidence. And, just as he was the only person involved in this entire saga to be jailed on remand, so his bail conditions were more severe than those imposed on any of the four defendants in the main case.

We met from time to time to touch base. One such encounter, just before Christmas, took place at the Groucho Club in Soho. Chris arrived with a ravishingly pretty nineteen-year-old girl, who wanted to be an actress or TV presenter. When Chris went to the men's room, I asked her how they had met. She said it had been in Windsor, a couple of days beforehand. Chris had told her that he was looking for someone to present a promotional video for a safari business he was intending to set up in southern Africa – she was really looking forward to going out there with him. It was all I could do to stop myself giving her twenty quid for a cab and a train fare and yelling,

'Leave now, while you still have a chance!'

Meanwhile, his case kept being delayed. Despite attempts by his solicitor to speed up proceedings and force the Crown Prosecution Service either to bring the case to court or drop it entirely, months went by and still no date had been set. As 1997 gave way to 1998, Chris was longing to go back to Africa and get on with the rest of his life. It had now been three and a half years since he first went to the *Sun*, and the repercussions of that action were still going on.

Not that he was entirely downhearted. Convinced of his own innocence, Chris saw his trial as yet another opportunity for vindication. His first defence witness, he bragged, would be a policeman, DI Mitchell. The whole story of the first alleged approach by Shaa Wasmund – acting he claimed, on Fashanu's behalf – would be examined in detail. His defence would be that the same thing had happened in September 1996: it was he who had been approached, not he who had done the approaching.

Paradoxically, he held more power as a defendant than he had as a witness. The police had been obliged to hand over a great mass of documents to his solicitors, among them a number of transcripts of taped telephone conversations and other documents relating to the financial transactions between John Fashanu and Aston Villa before and after his departure from that club. There was also a full breakdown of everything that had been found at the time of Fashanu and Melissa Kassa-Mapsi's arrest. Much of this material, I later discovered, had formed the basis for the *Sun*'s unpublished sixteen-page pull-out, abandoned after the not guilty verdict in Winchester. Vincent claimed it would provide powerful ammunition when Fashanu stepped into the witness box. For Vincent was longing to see Fash receive the same sort of grilling that had been meted out to him. Now the tables would be turned. Now it would be Fashanu upon whom the Crown would be relying and Vincent's barrister who would – over a period of several days, Vincent said – be giving him the third degree. It would be impossible to consider the case against Vincent without considering the 'match-fixing' trial: that, after all, was the particular course of justice he was accused of trying to pervert. Chris believed that Fashanu would have to do what he had thus far steadfastly avoided – give evidence under oath about his relationships with Lim, Grobbelaar, Segers and Johannes Joseph.

The prospect of that fascinating event was considerably dampened for me by the thought of having to go over the whole sorry business for a third time in court. But in the end, all our expectations were dashed. In March 1998, the Crown told a court hearing that they no longer wished to proceed with the case against Christopher Vincent. He was a free and innocent man.

He departed at once for Africa, ending up in Kenya, where he seemed to be living – so far as I could tell – at some sort of hotel or holiday development. From time to time he would call me with news. Most of it seemed good. He said he had made a deal to act as marketing representative in the UK for a number of Kenyan hotels. He delighted in telling me about the chaos and inefficiency of life in Kenya, which he said made Zimbabwe look like paradise by comparison. 'Do you know how the Americans won the war?' he asked one day. 'I'll tell you. They just dropped two Kenyans over Hiroshima and told them not to touch anything.'

On the personal front he had, he said, renewed contact with old friends like Stephen Wundke. Most importantly of all, he was mending fences with his brother Keith, whose business ventures with Colin Bell, boss of Wilderness Safaris, had become immensely successful. Some of them were based on projects originally conceived during the Mondoro days, projects which Chris would have co-owned had Mondoro not fallen apart. Chris was furious that he had missed out, and knew exactly whom to blame: 'If I ever see Hewlett or Grobbelaar, and I have a rifle in my hand, they had better fucking watch out. Because I am going to shoot them. Believe me, Grobbelaar is going to be seeing his arse in technicolour if I ever catch up with him.'

He kept telling me that he would be back in England soon. But he never arrived.

Then, in May, the pace of calls increased. Now he was saying that he had a new deal. Keith Vincent and Colin Bell had, he said, bought an island in the Seychelles and were preparing a magnificent luxury development. He had an option to go in with them, running a charter boat for their tourists. Later, he would be able to invest in a hotel development of his own. Trouble was, he needed to raise £2.5 million as his price of admission to the deal. He still had a number of Arab investors with whom he had been in touch two years earlier, but before he received their money he needed operating cash to tide him over. He was planning to come back to England to generate that cash by selling shares in a new company.

I could not believe it. This was the Mondoro scheme – or even 'scam', some might say – all over again. Had he not learned anything?

Then came another call, on 20 May. Chris said he needed to get back to England to get his short-term investors, but he did not want Keith and Colin to know what he had in mind. So here was the deal: if I would fax him a letter, informing him that he had to return to England to work on this book, and thus be paid for his part in it, he would renounce all the rights given to him by our original contract. Everything would be entirely mine.

Since he still owed me £4,000-plus, and since the book I had written was no longer the book we had originally contracted to write, nor did it have the same publishers, I was not sure that he was really giving me anything. On the other hand, the thought of being definitively free of contractual ties with Christopher Vincent was an attractive one. So I wrote and faxed a letter emphasizing the truth, which was that his presence in Britain would be of great assistance in checking the final manuscript and that it would be essential for sorting out our various business issues. That, I thought, would give him reasonable grounds for getting back to the UK.

A few days later he called again in considerable agitation. My fax had not mentioned money. It was vital that I write another one, specifically saying that he had to come back here to get his money for the book. But, I countered, the whole point was that he was not getting any money. He had given up his rights to the book, even assuming that they still existed; and in any case he was in debt to me. Vincent accepted all that, but insisted that he needed the fax. That day.

I did not send the second fax.

On the morning of Thursday 28 May, he called again. Twelve hours earlier, my wife Clare had given birth to our third child, a boy. Oddly enough, I had other things on my mind apart from the troubles of Christopher Vincent. Still, I apologized for not sending the second fax. Chris said it was too late. His brother and Colin Bell were going with someone else (he later amended this, maintaining that he had another two weeks to get his money together). But he said our deal would still stand. All I had to do was send a dozen red roses to a girl in Rome, along with a message saying that he would see her soon. Amazingly, I did. It cost about £45. I had not, at that point, bought any flowers for Clare.

There was one other thing: Chris said that the company he had been working for in Kenya had gone bust. That was one of the reasons he needed me to help.

On Friday the 29th, Chris called again. He was booked on two flights from Malindi, north-east of Mombasa on the Indian Ocean coast of Kenya, to Nairobi. He then had a flight from Nairobi to London, on Sabena. Could I fix the tickets? He would pay me back. He said he had asked Peter Staunton, an ITN reporter who had helped him in the past, but Staunton hadn't been able to fix it up before he left for a week in Spain. Chris had checked with a local travel agent, and the tickets would cost about 620 US dollars.

You might wonder at this point why I didn't just tell him to fuck off. There were two reasons. In the first place, Chris is an Olympic-standard cadger. He has spent years living off loans and favours and is thus entirely immune to the normal sense of embarrassment or consideration that would prevent most people from asking someone to whom they already owed money and whose wife had just had a baby to spend time and more money organizing their travel arrangements. It would be less trouble just to do it, I thought, than to spend the next few days being pestered. Plus I had something to gain. The sooner I could get Chris to Britain, the sooner I could get his signature on an agreement cancelling our initial contract.

I called Sabena. They said that the cheapest fare available in the UK was over £700. Since I was not the person flying, I could not just pay for the tickets over the phone with a credit card. I would have to go to their offices in person. I called Kenya to let Chris know. He was insistent: he had to have the ticket.

I called the American Express travel service. They could do nothing for under £1,000, but they gave me the name of their travel agency in Kenya. I called Nairobi. The company there could not issue tickets unless I appeared in person with my card. I called Chris again, suggesting I simply wire him 620 dollars so that he could buy the tickets himself. No, he said, that would not work. A money transfer would take four days. He needed the ticket now.

After making another half-dozen calls to various companies in England, I found that I could get £500 to Malindi more or less instantly for a fee of about £40. This would enable Chris to pay for his air fare, with a bit left over. So I sent the money. That was at about four o'clock on Friday afternoon.

On Sunday morning I received a call from a woman at the Foreign Office in London. She said she had been given my name by the British Consulate in Nairobi, who had in turn been given it by Chris Vincent . . . who was currently in jail in Nairobi. He had been arrested trying to leave the country and charged with attempting to defraud the hotel at which he had been staying of some 10,000 dollars, which – it was alleged – he owed in unpaid bills. The hotel had offered to drop all charges if he paid the money. He had suggested two people who might be able to help him do this: his brother Keith, and me.

Somewhat to the surprise of the Foreign Office official, I laughed. Even by Chris's standards, the idea that I would bung him ten grand was pushing it. Now I began to understand why he needed the mention of money so desperately in my fax: not to persuade his brother or Colin Bell, but to persuade the hotel that he had a means of paying their bill. He had cast me as his unwitting accomplice.

His trial was set for 9 July 1998, but adjourned because the owner of the hotel, who was pressing charges, was not in the country. A few days later, I tracked Chris down in the very last place I expected to find him. He was staying with the manager of the same hotel whose owner was trying to get him jailed. I sent him a number of messages, but he did not return my calls.

Eventually we spoke again. He had, he said, spent the £500 I had sent him on bribing his way out of jail. Now he needed another £600. Once again, I sent it. I was by this stage trapped by Chris Vincent's demands, just as Bruce Grobbelaar had been. Like Grob, I was lying to my wife, pretending that I was not giving Vincent money when in fact I was. Like Grob, I was being dragged ever deeper into the mire of Vincent's affairs.

The events of the following few weeks and months are too tedious and too painful to relate. On the positive side of the ledger, I obtained Vincent's written agreement to hand over all his rights in this book to me. Chris gave me a large box-file containing vital evidence about the various charges of perverting the course of justice with which he had been involved. I also received a copy of the missing Mondoro business plan. This was the one Bruce Grobbelaar repeatedly claimed had never existed; the one he repeatedly lied about when under oath in court; the one that proved that the account he gave of his meeting with Heng Suan Lim at the Manchester airport Hilton was as false as so many of his other alibis (and the one, incidentally, that I still have in my possession). I was then able to call Keith Vincent and confirm that he had another copy of the plan and had done so before September 1993. Vincent also confirmed that he had spoken to Bruce Grobbelaar about his brother's accusations of match-fixing before Grob left Zimbabwe in August 1994, thereby establishing that Grobbelaar had not simply made it all up on the spot when speaking to Chris Vincent in those Southampton hotel rooms two months later.

So the good news was that I had Bruce Grobbelaar bang to rights.

The bad news was that Chris Vincent stiffed me again. He needed some help with a hotel bill. I gave – and I can scarcely believe it as I write these words – I gave his Windsor hotel my American Express number. I specifically stated I was only meeting one particular payment for approximately £1,000. It was not until I received my statement some weeks later that I discovered that Chris was using it to rack up enormous bills, phoning his business associates in Africa. Between 26 and 30 September 1998, he ran up bills amounting to £2,663.75 – and this at a place where his room was costing just £45 a night. By the middle of October, he had spent another £2,000-plus.

When I called American Express, desperate to stop this unrelenting drain on my resources, I was told that there was nothing I could do. My card was the guarantor of Chris Vincent's bills. As far as 'Fernando', the operative to whom I spoke at Amex, was concerned, he could stay there for as long as he liked, quaffing champagne, eating *filet mignon* and calling Antarctica until he got bored or I went bankrupt. I argued that Fernando was wrong. Vincent had not booked or checked in using my card (he'd prevailed on Peter Staunton's Barclaycard for that). Amex began to budge. Then I pointed out that I was a journalist and asked whether they would care to comment on the record for an article I was preparing about credit card fraud. We came to an agreement. A substantial portion of the bill that had been run up against my card was refunded.

Chris Vincent, meanwhile, had disappeared. He had sworn blind that he was going to repay every penny that he owed me. He had listed the businessmen who were supposedly lining up to support his charter-boat operation. He had even asked me to draft on his behalf a letter to the Royal Bank of Scotland's Offshore Banking Centre, Box 678, 57/63 Bath Street, St Helier (sort code: 16-58-93), where he had opened an account no. 60126327, requesting a cheque for £7,000 to be sent to my home address.

The cheque never arrived. Chris Vincent left his hotel and did not return. The next I heard of him was just before the *Sun*'s libel case was finally heard in July 1999. The paper had tracked Vincent down to a hostel in the Earl's Court area of London. Simon Hughes had been appointed his minder. Summoning up his old, cocky ebullience, Vincent told Hughes: 'It'll be a very different gorilla going into court this time.' What he did not realize was that Hughes had been given the task of ensuring that he never came within a mile of the High Court. The very last thing that George Carman wanted to see was Chris Vincent striding towards the witness box.

# 28

## Their Lordships Decide

And so in July 1999 the case was heard all over again. Suffice to say that the groundhogs were once more out in force. The tapes were played again, Grobbelaar gave his usual explanations, Carman hit him with all his famous verbal artillery, Bob Wilson testified that Grob's performances showed 'no evidence whatsoever of anything other than good goalkeeping' and the jury reached their verdict. There were, as always, some moments of levity – I will long treasure the memory of George Carman cross-examining Bruce Grobbelaar on the vast wads of money supposedly hidden away in his sock drawer. Who, Carman enquired, washed the socks in the Grobbelaar household?

Grobbelaar replied that this was the housekeeper's job.

Carman was intrigued: what did the housekeeper do when she had washed the socks? Did she put them away . . . in the sock drawer?

A barely suppressed titter rippled round the public gallery as the spectators conjured up the image of the Grobbelaars' Mrs Mop desperately trying to find room for her master's socks amid the piles of contraband cash.

No, said Grobbelaar. She left all the washing on the bed. He put it away. He was very particular about that sort of thing.

It was, of course, a lot less funny when Grobbelaar got away yet again. But by then I had long since become resigned to his victories. I could even give a wry smile when Ong Chee Kew was sentenced to four years in jail for his part in a plan to pull off a £30 million betting scam by fixing the floodlights at Premier League matches. Ong, the man who had written to the young Heng Suan Lim in 1987, shortly after he arrived in Britain, telling him to mix with footballers: 'Try to tackle Wimbledon . . . Wimbledon is a good team.'

'I think we can make some pounds and ringits here,' Ong had written. Later he had warned, 'Don't make any promises to the players. Just make friends and talk about football – and you must be careful.' Well, Lim had been careful enough. Ong had not. He had been caught and now he was a guest of Her Majesty.

And then, out of the blue, came the Appeal Court verdict on 18 January 2001. Lord Justice Brown's ruling went through Grobbelaar's account of his relationship with Lim and Fashanu, his reasons for possessing tens of thousands of pounds in cash, his apparent confessions on videotape and his reaction to the *Sun*'s approach at Gatwick airport. In every case, he dismissed Grobbelaar's version of events.

'His whole account of his relationship and dealings with Mr Lim beggars belief at every turn,' Brown declared. It simply did not make sense that he would, for example, drive through the night from Norwich to London, hours before a match, simply to talk about his career. 'I come to consider the probabilities of the case and it is at this point that to my mind Grobbelaar's story falls apart. He had, as it seems to me, just too much to explain away – his entire dealings with Mr Lim. It is not credible to suggest he was anxious to discuss with Mr Lim his prospects for playing out in the Far East, the evidence being that Mr Lim was merely a football enthusiast with no connections whatever in the professional game.'

He was equally dismissive of the explanation that Grobbelaar visited John Fashanu just to talk about business, adding, 'His explanations for having very large sums of cash seem to me equally implausible.'

The judge then turned to Grobbelaar's relationship with Vincent and their taped conversations. Grobbelaar had claimed that he had invented all his claims about match-fixing in order to gain Vincent's confidence and expose him as a crook. But, said Lord Justice Brown, 'It is too difficult to suppose Mr Grobbelaar capable of such spontaneous and sustained invention. Even if it made sense to fabricate previous corruption, it would be absurd to invent in it a role for John Fashanu. That could cause problems for both of them. Perhaps more striking than any of these points, however, is that absurdity of supposing that Mr Grobbelaar would ever have gone to the authorities when such a step would inevitably have brought to light all his murky past dealings with Mr Lim which, even on his own account of the matter, must irreparably have damaged his reputation in the game.'

Lord Justice Parker agreed. There was, he said, no need for Grobbelaar to lie in order to win Vincent's confidence. 'It is absolutely clear from the tapes that he already enjoyed Mr Vincent's full confidence.' Grobbelaar did not tell anyone about his plan to trap Vincent. Nor did he report Vincent when he gave him a £2,000 bribe. 'I would have no hesitation in rejecting Mr Grobbelaar's explanation of his taped admissions relating to his corrupt arrangements . . . In my judgement, Mr Grobbelaar's explanation of those admissions is so utterly implausible that no jury, acting reasonably, could have accepted it as true.'

The judges' verdict meant that Bruce Grobbelaar was a ruined man. He had lost his £85,000 damages award and now faced legal costs, for both sides in the case, amounting to £1.5 million. When contacted in South Africa where he was working as a football coach for the Supersport team in Pretoria, the nation's capital, he insisted that he was innocent. 'I find it astounding that the Appeal Court can overthrow the decision of twelve jurors. It's devastating. I have always said I'm innocent. I have proved it three times – twice in a criminal court and once in a civil court. My mother always told me it was not the disappointment from setbacks in life but how you cope with them [that matters]. I'm strong and my family are strong. We will manage.'

He had a message for British soccer fans: 'I have done nothing to blemish football, despite what has happened today.'

By this point, Grobbelaar was in deep trouble. He could not possibly pay his vast legal bills, and was facing bankruptcy. Nor was the *Sun* in any mood to be merciful. So far as its executives were concerned, they had done a good job, unearthed a true and important story, and Grobbelaar had done nothing but lie and discredit them ever since. Daniel Taylor, the paper's in-house lawyer, is normally the most affable of men, but even he had been angered by Grobbelaar's relentless deceit. I asked him once, at about this time, whether Grobbelaar still owned any property in the UK. 'Yes,' said Taylor. 'I believe he's got two houses. And I'm going to sell both of them.'

When not working in South Africa, Grobbelaar had been living with his family in Tisman's Common, near Horsham in West Sussex. Now he decided to roll the dice one more time, double or quits, and appeal to the House of Lords. As we know, he won a Pyrrhic victory, establishing that he had in principle been libelled, since he had not actually thrown any matches. But his corruption was underlined, his actions and character described in savage terms, and the value of his tattered reputation set at a measly £1. Above all, he was still liable for the costs of the proceedings.

In the months since the Lords' judgement, those costs have not been paid and Grobbelaar's property remains unsold. As I write these words, he is believed to be in Zimbabwe – possibly the only white man in living memory who has chosen to leave the United Kingdom and seek refuge under Mugabe's tyranny. Grobbelaar's wife and daughters are believed to have remained here. But should he ever return to the UK to see them, he can expect an immediate writ from the *Sun*. And what of the other players in the drama?

John Fashanu is as ebullient, energetic and ambitious as ever. Now the official sports ambassador of Nigeria, he was recently voted the most influential black African in Britain. In December 2002 he became chairman of the League of Wales side Barry Town. He was soon announcing ambitious plans to use his African connections to bring over young Nigerian players, showcase their talents and sell them on to top English and European clubs at a healthy profit. He also hoped to use the interest in Barry Town that would be generated in Africa to get their games shown on the TV-Africa network.

'It's quite fortunate because I'm the vice-president of that television network,' said Fashanu. 'It's now being shown in forty-four different African countries, so I'm in a position to make sure Barry Town are given the right exposure.' He was also, he added, hoping to become chairman of the Nigerian premier league. In May 2003, Fashanu entertained millions as one of the contestants on *I'm a Celebrity, Get Me Out of Here!* He began his fortnight in the jungle as the victim of the British public's apparent dislike, being voted onto four Bushtucker Trials, specifically tailored to exploit his fears of snakes, bugs and heights. But his unique combination of ebullient charm and obsessive fitness routines won the viewers over. He finished as the programme's runner-up.

Hans Segers is the goalkeeping coach at Tottenham Hotspur. In his spare time, he frequently preaches at churches and schools.

Heng Suan Lim is believed to be pursuing his business activities in London.

As for the lawyers, Rodney Klevan, whose presence had done so much to enliven proceedings at Winchester Crown Court, received a knighthood in 1998. Sadly, he died in December 2001, aged just sixty-one. In his obituaries it was noted that he had been the model for Kavanagh QC, the barrister played by John Thaw in the series of the same name.

The remaining defence counsels have found themselves involved in some of the most high-profile cases of recent years. Desmond de Silva successfully defended both Lee Bowyer, then of Leeds, and the Chelsea defender John Terry, against accusations of assault. Trevor Burke QC, as he now is, defended Gary Glitter, when the singer was accused of rape and child internet pornography. And Jerome Lynch QC has combined a successful sideline as a Channel 4 TV presenter with a continuing legal career. In March 2003, he defended Sheik Abdullah el-Faisal, the Muslim cleric sentenced to a nine-year jail term for preaching hate and urging his followers to kill non-believers, Americans, Hindus and Jews.

David Calvert-Smith, meanwhile, has been appointed Director of Public Prosecutions. In 2002, he faced considerable criticism for his handling of the trial of Paul Burrell, the royal butler accused of stealing the possessions of his dead employer, Princess Diana.

Which leaves us with just one final member of the cast: Chris Vincent. He made a brief return to the limelight, appearing in a Channel 4 documentary about people who had lost fortunes, though it has to be said that the only fortune he lost (apart from Bruce Grobbelaar's, of course) was the imaginary one in his head.

Just a few days before these words were written, I received a call from Daniel Taylor at the *Sun*. He told me he had spotted Chris Vincent walking down a street near King's Cross station. Taylor said he looked unkempt, as if he was down on his luck. I must confess, I have yet to go looking for Chris Vincent, to see if I can help.

# Index